Withstanding Hitler

The jacket illustration comes from a film
made of trials before the People's Court.
There is nothing to show the prisoner's
name, his supposed offence, or his
punishment.

Withstanding Hitler
in Germany 1933–45

Michael Balfour

R

Routledge
London and New York

First published in 1988 by
Routledge
11 New Fetter Lane, London EC4P 4EE
29 West 35th Street, New York, NY 10001

Set in 10 on 12pt Sabon
by Input Typesetting Ltd, London
and printed in Great Britain
by Richard Clay Ltd
Bungay, Suffolk

Library of Congress Cataloging in Publication Data
Balfour, Michael Leonard Graham, 1908–
    Withstanding Hitler in Germany, 1933–45 / Michael Balfour.
    p. cm.
    Includes index.
    1. Anti-Nazi movement.   2. National socialism—Psychological
    aspects.   3. Germany—Biography.   I. Title.
    DD256.3.B27 1988
    943.086—dc19

British Library Cataloguing in Publication Data also available
ISBN 0–415–00617–1

Contents

Preface

Friends who knew of my long-standing interest in the subject have often urged me to write this book. But at first I felt that any attempt to pass judgment would be premature. By the time that had ceased to be the case (if it has ceased to be the case) so much material had accumulated that I doubted whether a single individual (and a foreigner into the bargain) could ever write an adequate chronological account of all that had happened. A full history would be long and expensive; Scholder's admirable account of the German Church Struggle takes 1370 pages to reach October 1934. Any attempt at abbreviation would mean omitting or underplaying some aspects which some people regard as important. Or the book would become one of those skilled pieces of précis-writing which mean little to anyone not already familiar with the subject.

Yet there is at present no satisfactory book in English to offer as an introduction to anyone coming new to the subject. Rothfel's *The German Opposition to Hitler* (2nd edn 1963) was only 160 pages long and concerned primarily to establish the thesis that the opposition deserved more help from the English and the Americans than it received. Wheeler Bennett's *The Nemesis of Power* (2nd edn 1963) was primarily concerned to establish the reverse. The four essays in *The German Resistance to Hitler* edited by Schmitthenner and Buchheim (English edn 1970) were primarily concerned with the aims of that resistance rather than with its origins, difficulties or course. Peter Hoffmann's invaluable (but misdescribed) *History of the German Resistance* (English edn 1977) was primarily concerned with the military aspects. The Adam von Trott lectures *The Challenge of the Third Reich* (1986), which were published after the first draft of this book had been written, asked most of the right questions but had only space for limited answers. Many good biographies or studies of individual aspects have appeared in English but these are by their nature limited in range.

I have therefore yielded to the temptation of writing a book which concentrates on explaining why more Germans did not stand up to Hitler and why those who did failed to get rid of him. I realise that the combination of a bare analysis with a number of personal case-histories involves some repetition, but I feel that the first part by itself would lack life and think there is some advantage in showing how different people reacted differently to the same basic problem.

I have read many relevant books since 1930. I had the privilege of knowing one of the leading figures, Helmuth James von Moltke, closely from 1936 to 1939. During the later years of the war I had access to virtually all the information reaching Britain about German civilian conditions and attitudes. Recently I have tried to fill the gaps in my reading but there are still many volumes which I have left unopened. Yet the book is already a third longer than I intended and is therefore in danger of failing to fulfil its purpose of an introduction. Moreover I shall be in my eightieth year when it comes out so that to have postponed writing any longer would have been tempting providence.

If I have said little or nothing about anti-Nazi activity by Germans outside Germany or in the prison camps it is not because of any lack of interest but because of concern about the length of the book.

I should explain at the start that I have used the German noun *Widerstand* or derivatives of it rather than 'resistance' or 'opposition' because one of the first steps to understanding what did or did not happen is to realise that the activities associated with those English nouns in many countries were not practicable in Germany after 1933.

I am grateful to the Anglo-German Group of Historians for having allowed me to join in a Conference on the subject at Düsseldorf in 1974 and to the Anglo-French Committee for the History of the Second World War for having done the same over a Conference at Leeds in 1986. I have received much help from library staffs and in particular St Antony's College, Oxford, the German Historical Institute, London, the Institut für Zeitgeschichte, Munich, and the Bavarian State Library. Quotations from material under British Crown Copyright appear by permission of the Controller of HM Stationery Office.

I am much indebted to Mary Hannah and my wife who between them typed the manuscript and helped to remove from it some of the many solecisms and obscurities which it contained.

M.L.G.B.
Burford, November 1987

Notes on terms used

AA *Auswärtiges Amt* = Foreign Office.

Abitur Leaving certificate awarded at end of secondary education, qualifies for entrance to a university.

Abwehr Literally 'Warding off'. Department of Reichswehr Ministry (later OKW) responsible for collecting and evaluating military and foreign intelligence and counter-intelligence, also for sabotage and subversion.

Beamte Established civil servant. Could include jobs like engine-driver. Officials who were not *Beamte* were *Angestellte* = employees.

Bendlerstrasse Street in central Berlin in which was situated building containing headquarters of the Replacement Army. Headquarters of Abwehr were in the same building with entrance round the corner in *Tirpitzufer*.

DAF *Deutsche Arbeitsfront*. German Labour Front = organisation set up by the Nazis in May 1933 as a substitute for trade unions.

DNVP *Deutsche Nationale Volkspartei*. German National People's Party, main conservative party 1919–33.

Einsatzgruppe Unit of SS, including various specialist units, used as a task force, primarily in occupied territory.

Freikorps Unofficial military gangs formed from demobilised soldiers in 1919–20 in defiance of Armistice terms to protect Germany against Communism.

Gestapo *GEheime STAats POlizei* = Secret State Police. One of the two main elements in Security Police.

Gleichschaltung Co-ordination, term applied to process by which most German organisations were brought under Nazi control in 1933–4.

Gymnasium Grammar or high school.

HJ *Hitler Jugend* = Hitler Youth.

Hochschulen Institutes of higher education, including universities, technical high schools, etc. Does *not* mean secondary high school.

KPD *Kommunistische Partei Deutschlands*. Communist Party of Germany.

Kripo *Kriminalpolizei*, other main element with Gestapo of Security Police.

Kristallnacht Name given to attacks on Jews and Jewish shops on 9 November 1938, characterised by smashing of *Kristall* = plate-glass windows.

Land Name given to each of the *Länder* or states into which Weimar Germany was divided.

Landrat Official, primarily in Prussia, who was chief administrative officer of a *Kreis* (district) council and also local representative of central government. Post often held by local *Kreisleiter* of Nazi Party.

Landtag Lower house of parliament of a *Land*.

Machtergreifung Seizure of power, name given (misleadingly) to what the Nazis did on 30 January 1933.

Mittelstand German term used for middle classes.

NKFD *Nationalkomitee Freies Deutschland* = National Committee of Free Germany. Organisation of German prisoners-of-war set up under Soviet auspices in July 1943.

NSBO *Nationalsozialistische Betriebszellenorganisation* = National Factory Cell Organisation. Body originally intended to replace trade unions but made insignificant by DAF.

NSDAP *Nationalsozialistische Deutsche Arbeiterpartei* = National Socialist German Workers Party, full title of Nazi Party.

NSDStB *Nationalsozialistischer Deutscher Studentenbund* = National Socialist German Student Association.

OKH *Oberkommando des Heeres* = High Command of the Army.

OKW *Oberkommando der Wehrmacht* = High Command of the Armed Forces, set up in February 1938.

OSS US Office of Strategic Services (predecessor of Central Intelligence Agency).

Putsch German word for a coup d'état. Most celebrated was right-wing putsch attempted by Kapp in March 1920.

RSHA *Reichssicherheitshauptamt* = Head Office for Reich Security. Department set up on 29 September 1939 to formalise de facto combination of state Sicherheitspolizei with party Sicherheitsdienst. Chief of Office was Heydrich till his death in May 1942, then after an interregnum Kaltenbrunner from January 1943.

Reichswehr Title of Defence Forces in Weimar Republic, superseded by 'Wehrmacht' in 1934.

SD *Sicherheitsdienst* = security service of SS.

SHAEF Supreme Headquarters, Allied Expeditionary Force 1944–5.

SPD *Sozialdemokratische Partei Deutschlands* = Social Democratic Party of Germany.

SOE Special Operations Executive. British organisation responsible for sabotage and subversion in Germany and German-held Europe 1940–5.

Staatssekretär State Secretary. Highest official in a government department, allegedly non-political.

Stahlhelm Steel helmet, paramilitary organisation of German conservatives 1920–33.

Stammtisch Table in an inn at which seats are reserved for regular customers.

Volksgemeinschaft Popular community, integrated national community which it was the professed aim of the Nazis to establish.

Wannsee Lake (really enlarged river) on west side of Berlin.

Wilhelmstrasse Street in Berlin containing Reich Chancery and Foreign Office.

Wolfschanze 'Wolf's Lair', code name for headquarters of Hitler and OKW near Rastenburg in East Prussia, January 1941 – November 1944.

Zossen Camp south of Berlin which contained rear headquarters of OKW and OKH.

Chronology

This book is not a history of Germany between 1930 and 1945, but readers whose knowledge or memory of that period is inadequate may find the following list of dates useful for reference.

1930

27 March   Great Coalition Cabinet, under Müller (SPD), splits over unemployment insurance and resigns. Brüning (Centre) appointed Chancellor instead.

30 June   French troops of occupation evacuate Rhineland.

16 July   Brüning uses emergency clause in constitution to pass two laws rejected by Reichstag. SPD carry a motion demanding their withdrawal. Reichstag dissolved.

14 September   At ensuing election, National Socialists win 107 seats, to become second strongest party. Brüning continues governing by decree.

1931

19 March   Brüning and Austrian Vice-Chancellor sign pact for Austro-German Customs Union.

20 June   President Hoover proposes 12-month moratorium on reparations payments. French postpone consent.

13 July   Darmstädter-Nationalbank suspends payments. Fear of general economic collapse.

5 September   Hague Court declares Customs Union incompatible with treaties.

October   NSDAP join with DNVP and other right-wing parties to form Harzburger Front. Demand Brüning's resignation. Brüning wins vote in Reichstag.

1932

March   Number of unemployed reaches 6.1 million.

April   Britain, Italy and the USA agree to give Germany parity of rights in a system of armaments providing security for all. French delay agreement.

13 March–10 April   Von Hindenburg re-elected President with 53 per cent of votes. Hitler receives 37 per cent, Thälmann (Communist) 10 per cent.
29 May   Hindenburg refuses to sign emergency decrees for Brüning, who resigns and is succeeded by von Papen.
30 May   French withdraw their objection to German parity of armament rights.
9 July   Conference at Lausanne agrees to end reparations.
20 July   Papen takes over Prussian Government as Reich Commissioner.
31 July   Election for Reichstag gives NSDAP 230 seats as strongest party.
13 August   Hindenburg refuses to make Hitler Chancellor. Hitler refuses to serve under Papen.
12 September   Papen Government, on being defeated in Reichstag, dissolves it.
6 November   Fresh elections reduce NSDAP strength in Reichstag to 196.
3 December   General von Schleicher replaces Papen as Chancellor.

1933

30 January   Hitler becomes Chancellor of a Coalition Cabinet.
27 February   Reichstag Fire.
28 February   Presidential Decree for the protection of the nation and state authorises the Government to override a number of personal rights. Communist Party proscribed.
5 March   NSDAP win 43.9 per cent of votes (and 288 seats) in Reichstag election.
21 March   Day of National Rebirth. Ceremony at Garrison Church at Potsdam.
23 March   Enabling Act, giving Government power to rule by decree for four years. Opposed only by SPD.
31 March   First law co-ordinating *Länder*.
1 April   Organised boycott of Jewish shops.
7 April   Law for restoration of professional civil service.
2 May   Dissolution of trade unions.
June–July   All parties other than NSDAP made to disband.
20 July   Concordat with Vatican.
23 July   Elections of Evangelical Churches won by German Christians.
21 September   Niemöller invites all pastors to join Emergency League.
22 September   *Reichskulturkammergesetz.*
27 September   Müller chosen as Reich Bishop by Synod.
29 September   Law on hereditary farms.
14 October   Germany withdraws from Disarmament Conference, League of Nations and International Labour Office.
12 November   Plebiscite gives overwhelming approval to withdrawal.
13 November   German Christian meeting at Berlin Sportpalast.

1934

26 January   Hitler receives 12 Evangelical Church leaders, accuses Niemöller of disloyalty. Non-aggression Pact with Poland.

20 April   Himmler made head of Prussian Gestapo.

22 April   First general meeting of 'Confessing' Church at Ulm.

31 May   First Synod of Confessing Church at Barmen approves Declaration.

14 June   Hitler and Mussolini meet for the first time, at Venice.

17 June   Papen, in a speech at Marburg, criticises Nazi policy and performance.

30 June   'Night of the Long Knives'. Röhm and other SA leaders murdered along with right-wing opponents of Party and persons against whom leaders had grudges.

13 July   Hitler justifies himself to Reichstag.

25 July   Unsuccessful Nazi attempt at a coup in Austria.

2 August   Death of Hindenburg. Hitler combines office of President with that of Chancellor. Reichswehr required to swear an oath of personal allegiance immediately.

19 August   96 per cent of voters approve in plebiscite arrangements made on 2 August.

1 November   Anglo-German trade and payments agreement signed.

1935

13 January   Plebiscite in Saar under League of Nations supervision results in 91 per cent vote for return to Reich.

16 March   Hitler announces plan to reintroduce conscription and expand army to 36 divisions.

18 June   Anglo-German Naval Agreement.

16 July   Hanns Kerrl made Minister for Ecclesiastical Affairs, replacing Müller.

15 September   Anti-Jewish laws passed by Reichstag during Nuremberg Party Rally.

3 October   Italy invades Abyssinia.

October   Central Committee of German Communist Party meets in Moscow ('Brussels Conference').

8 December   Hoare–Laval Plan for Abyssinia.

1936

January   Pamphlet 'The State Church is here' by Dibelius issued under Niemöller's name.

7 March   German troops occupy area in Rhineland demilitarised by Treaty of Versailles, thus violating Locarno Treaties.

29 March   99 per cent of German voters approve remilitarisation of Rhineland.

May Letter listing evangelical grievances sent to Hitler, later leaked to press.
18 July Civil War breaks out in Spain. A fortnight later, Hitler decides to aid Franco.
1–16 August Olympic Games in Berlin.
9 September Hitler at Nuremburg Party Rally announces Four-Year Plan to make Germany ready for war by 1940.
25 October German–Italian Axis Treaty.
25 November Anti-Comintern Pact (Germany–Japan).
1 December Membership of Hitler Youth made compulsory.

1937

4 March Encyclical of Pope Pius XI, 'With Burning Anxiety' (*brennender Sorge*), over treatment of Catholic Church, read in all Catholic churches.
1 July Niemöller detained.
5 November Hitler meets with Foreign Minister von Neurath and heads of three services to discuss his long-term plans ('Hossbach memorandum').
18 November Lord Halifax, in a visit to Berlin, fails to reach a long-term settlement with Germany.
26 November Schacht resigns as Economics Minister.

1938

4 February Retirement of War Minister von Blomberg after shady reputation of his second wife comes to light. False accusation of homosexuality concocted by the Gestapo prevents his natural successor (General von Fritsch, Army Commander-in-Chief) from taking over. Hitler assumes post himself and sets up Supreme Command of Wehrmacht (OKW) under Keitel to do routine work. Von Brauchitsch assumes command of army. Sixteen other generals retired. Ribbentrop replaces Neurath as Foreign Minister.
12 February Austrian Chancellor Schuschnigg visits Hitler at Berchtesgaden.
2 March Niemöller acquitted on major charges but sent to concentration camp.
12 March German troops enter Austria.
18 March Court of Enquiry declares case against von Fritsch groundless.
10 April 99 per cent of voters approve attachment of Austria to Germany.
20 May Czech army mobilises after rumours of impending German attack: British and French governments warn Hitler against such an act.
30 May Hitler signs directive announcing his intention to smash Czechoslovakia by military action in the near future.
5 May, 29 May, 3 June, 16 July Beck submits memoranda to von Brauchitsch opposing Hitler's plans.
4 August Conference of senior generals supports Beck but takes no further action.
18 August Beck offers his resignation.
15 September Chamberlain meets Hitler at Berchtesgaden.
22–24 September Chamberlain meets Hitler at Bad Godesberg.

29 September   Munich Conference.

9 November   *Kristallnacht*: organised actions against Jews in retaliation for murder of a junior German diplomat by a Jew in Paris.

1939

20 January   Schacht dismissed as President of Reichsbank.

15 March   German troops invade rump of Czechoslovakia.

23 March   Germany annexes Memel.

31 March   Britain and France guarantee independence of Poland.

23 August   German–Soviet Non-aggression Pact.

1 September   Germany invades Poland.

3 September   Britain and France declare war on Germany.

27 September   Surrender of Warsaw. Reich Central Security Office (RHSA) set up.

6 October   Hitler's 'Peace Appeal' to the Western Powers.

9 October   Hitler's first directive for the western campaign.

end October   Dr Josef Müller in Rome.

5 November   Brauchitsch intimidated by Hitler: collapse of attempt to prevent western campaign.

8 November   Elser's attempt to kill Hitler in Bürgerbräu cellar.

9 November   Two British agents kidnapped by SS at Venlo.

30 November   USSR invades Finland.

1940

17 February   Halifax, Foreign Secretary, writes to Rome, for onward transmission via Pope, about likely attitude of British Government to a new régime in Germany.

1 March   Sumner Welles in Berlin.

9 April   Occupation of Denmark. Norway invaded.

10 May   Invasion of Holland, Belgium and Luxembourg. Churchill becomes Prime Minister.

15 May   Dutch Army surrenders.

27 May   Belgian Army surrenders.

28 May   Dunkirk evacuation begins.

10 June   Italy declares war.

22 June   France signs armistice.

20 July–31 October   Battle of Britain.

22 July   Hitler's Peace Offer rejected by Britain.

31 July   Hitler decides to attack Russia in May 1941.

1 August   Protest by Catholic Bishops against euthanasia programme.

12 October   German preparations for invading Britain suspended.

12 November   Molotov in Berlin.

1941

8 March   Lend-Lease Act signed by President Roosevelt of USA.

6 April   German attack on Yugoslavia and Greece.
17 April   Yugoslavia surrenders.
23 April   Greece surrenders.
10 May   Hess flies to Scotland.
27 May   *Bismarck* sunk.
22 June   Germany invades Soviet Union.
July   Bishop von Galen attacks euthanasia programme.
14 August   Atlantic Charter.
August   Euthanasia programme modified.
19 September   Jews required to wear star of David.
9 October   Dietrich announces Russian campaign has been decided.
1 December   German advance halted before Moscow.
7 December   Japanese attack at Pearl Harbor.
11 December   Germany declares war on USA.
19 December   Hitler takes over command of army from Brauchitsch.

1942

20 January   Wannsee Conference decides on 'Final Solution' of Jewish Question.
11–12 February   *Scharnhorst, Gneisenau* and *Prinz Eugen* escape from Brest through English Channel.
15 February   Fall of Singapore.
24 February   Norwegian Bishops resign as protest against German interference.
10–18 April   Moltke and Bonhoeffer in Norway.
8 May   Speech by Eden in Edinburgh on attitude of British Government to Germany.
22–25 May   First gathering at Kreisau.
26 May   Heydrich assassinated near Prague. Village of Lidice destroyed in retaliation. Anglo-Soviet Treaty signed.
30 May   First British raid using 1000 bombers (on Cologne).
26 May–1 June   Schönfeld and Bonhoeffer meet Bishop Bell in Sweden.
4 June   Americans defeat Japanese in Battle of Midway.
3 July   German-Italian advance in North Africa halted at El Alamein.
2 August   Germans reach Caucasus and Black Sea.
19 August   Dieppe Raid.
31 August   Arrest of Schulze-Boysen group.
15 September   Germans announce that struggle for Stalingrad is nearing a successful end.
16–18 October   Second gathering at Kreisau.
23 October   Battle of Alamein opens.
7 November   Anglo-American landings in north-west Africa.
11 November   Germans enter unoccupied zone in France. Allen Dulles reaches Berne.
23 November   Germans encircled at Stalingrad.

late autumn   Goerdeler visits Central Army Group and talks to Kluge.

Advent   Pastoral letter on Recht read in all Catholic churches.

1943

8 January   Meeting between Beck and Moltke groups.

24 January   Anglo-American decision to demand Unconditional Surrender announced at Casablanca Conference.

27 January   All German men between 16 and 65 and women between 18 and 45 required to register for war work.

2 February   Surrender of Sixth Army at Stalingrad.

18 February   Goebbels calls for total war. Hans and Sophie Scholl arrested in Munich.

10 March   Debate in House of Lords, initiated by Bell, on British attitude towards Germany. Simon states Government's position.

13 March   Attempt by Tresckow and Schlabrendorff to explode a bomb in Hitler's aircraft fails.

21 March   Attempt by Gersdorff to throw himself with a bomb on Hitler fails.

5 April   Dohnanyi, Bonhoeffer and J. Müller arrested by Gestapo. Oster sent home.

13 April   Discovery of graves at Katyn announced.

12 May   All German resistance in North Africa ceases.

12–14 June   Third gathering at Kreisau.

5 July   German offensive begins at Kursk.

10 July   Allied landing in Sicily.

13 July   Failure of Kursk offensive.

19 July   National Committee for Free Germany issues first manifesto.

24 July–6 August   Heavy air raids on Hamburg.

25 July   Fall of Mussolini.

24 August   Himmler becomes Minister of the Interior.

August   Kreisau Fundamental Principles for the New Order.

8 September   Italian Armistice announced. German troops occupy Rome.

9 September   Allied landing at Salerno.

12 September   Mussolini rescued by SS.

1 October   Stauffenberg takes up post as Chief of Staff to Olbricht in Berlin.

18 October–1 November   Conference of Foreign Ministers in Moscow.

28 November–7 December   Conference at Tehran.

11–16 December   Moltke in Istanbul.

Christmas   Roosevelt in broadcast denies intention to enslave Germans.

1944

19 January   Solf group and Moltke arrested.

22 February   Churchill in parliament says unconditional surrender means victors have a free hand.

4 June   Allies enter Rome.

6 June Allies land in Normandy.
13 June First flying bomb (V1).
22 June Leber and Reichwein meet Saefkow and Jacob.
23 June Russian offensive against central front.
1 July Stauffenberg takes up post as Chief of Staff to Fromm.
2 July Kluge replaces Rundstedt as C-in-C West.
3 July Collapse of Central Army Group in Russia.
4–5 July Leber, Reichwein, Saefkow and Jacob arrested.
17 July Rommel seriously injured in air attack.
20 July Failure of attempt to kill Hitler and stage putsch.
31 July American breakthrough at Avranches.
7–8 August First trial (of 8 conspirators) by People's Court.
12 August Goerdeler arrested.
15 August Americans land in south of France.
17 August Kluge replaced by Model. Commits suicide on way back to Germany.
23 August Paris liberated.
8 September First V2.
11–17 September Allied Conference at Quebec – Morgenthau Plan.
17–26 September Battle of Arnhem.
16–24 December Ardennes Offensive.

1945

14 January Russian troops enter East Prussia.
4–11 February Yalta Conference.
13 February Allied bombing of Dresden.
7 March American troops cross Rhine at Remagen.
24 March British troops cross lower Rhine.
9 April Canaris, Oster, Bonhoeffer and three others executed at Flossenburg.
12 April Death of Roosevelt.
25 April Russian and American troops meet at Torgau on Elbe.
30 April Hitler and Goebbels commit suicide.
7–9 May Documents of unconditional surrender signed at Rheims and Berlin. Fighting ends in Europe.

PART ONE
Analysis

CHAPTER I
Why was Hitler allowed to gain power?

(a) The historical background

Getting rid of Hitler and his henchmen proved so difficult as to make many Germans regret that they had ever been allowed to gain power. Dr Schacht, whose intelligence few would dispute, said shortly after his resignation from the Ministry of Economics in 1937, 'We have fallen into the hands of criminals. How could I foresee that?'[1]

To account for National Socialism in a single paragraph is a foolhardy venture. But one explanation which goes deeper than most is to say that the German people had been induced by their political and intellectual leaders to entertain for their country a higher position in world power relationships than the resource-endowment of that country justified, even if the population made the high level of self-sacrifice which was repeatedly called for. Progress up the lower rungs of the international power-ladder went successfully and encouraged the assumption that attempts to rise higher would be equally successful. When between 1914 and 1918 this hope proved fallacious – by a narrow margin – many Germans refused to accept the verdict. Having believed uncritically what they had been told about their strength, they could not see that the Allies had won because of being stronger and concluded that weakness on their own part must have been to blame. Instead therefore of resting content with the status quo or with non-violent methods of changing it, they accepted and in many cases welcomed a ruler who promised to eliminate the weakness. He had the added attraction of seeming to be the man most likely to solve an economic crisis which was putting everybody's livelihood and possessions at risk.

To put flesh on this skeletal overview convincingly would take up many pages. What follows is merely intended to show on which parts of a familiar story the emphasis should for present purposes be put.[2]

(*i*) During the Middle Ages administrative centralisation went far enough in today's Germany to create the ingredients (notably a distinctive language and a more-or-less distinctive territory) which any group needs in order to recognise itself as a distinctive nation. This explains why unification was later sought on a German rather than a Prussian, Saxon or Bavarian basis. But, chiefly owing to distractions outside Germany, the central imperial government failed to establish its authority and act as a coherent political unit so that the area emerged at the end of the fifteenth century as an association of semi-independent lands. By the nineteenth century this had become recognised as a weakness in international relations, thus creating a favourable disposition towards any government strong enough to secure common action from all its constituent parts. If Germany was to count in the world, she needed to be integrated both administratively and ideologically.

(*ii*) The function of the Teutonic Knights and others in defending the medieval Eastern Frontier against the Slavs encouraged emphasis on the heroic virtues – discipline, endurance, sacrifice, courage, strength. The military came first in social precedence.[3] At a later date, the desire of Prussia's Hohenzollern rulers to make their lands into a European Power called, in view of limited material resources, for much the same qualities, including industry, patience and thrift. These virtues are essential to civilisation since without them it is impossible to establish security and order. But their exercise does not in itself constitute civilisation which requires in addition compassion, imagination and respect for truth.

(*iii*) The medieval failure to consolidate meant that the Reformation had a divisive effect instead of, as in England, an integrating one. Protestantism survived because some princes protected it against others who were supporting the Catholic counter-attack. One result was that the churches became unusually subservient to the temporal rulers. The religious wars wasted the material resources of the area and delayed its economic development.

(*iv*) The process known as 'modernisation', pioneered by eighteenth-century Britain,[4] starts with a rise in population and hence pressure on resources. The pressure is met by raising capital investment, i.e. applying increased savings to improving techniques, installing new machines and developing new forms of energy with the result that production grows at an accelerating rate. The proportion of the population engaged in agriculture falls and the surplus moves into cities. The accompanying rise in real wealth permits, and indeed requires, higher standards of education and sophistication. Customary behaviour is replaced by rational initiatives. The resulting changes in status, outlook and values threaten to undermine the privileged position of the pre-industrial ruling class unless they can find a way of capturing control over the new classes seeking to move upwards at their expense.

In Germany the modernisation process started later than in Western Europe but, once begun, moved forward faster. The national respect for industriousness, discipline and knowledge provided a highly suitable work force. But the initial beneficiaries, the middle classes, did not become numerous or powerful enough to grasp a share of political power until the workers were beginning to have similar ambitions. They therefore shrank from challenging the position of the pre-industrial élite by revolution for fear that they would thereby help the lower classes to power. In return, the administrative techniques essential to a modern state (such as a uniform code of laws and a sound financial system) were introduced from above, primarily in Prussia. Industrial power was concentrated into a small number of hands with the state playing a larger part than in Britain.

(*v*) Germany's development was complicated by the fact that modernisation and socio-political adaptation to it were taking place at the same time as the process of consolidating the various German states into a single and more powerful Reich. As every undergraduate essayist knows, this was not achieved by liberal means but by 'blood and iron'. What was equally significant however was the alliance of 'rye and iron' symbolising the coalition between land-owners and industrialists. The bulk of the middle classes were induced, chiefly by Bismarck, to give national unity priority over popular government and accept the values of the previous ruling classes instead of, as in the French and Russian Revolutions, repudiating them. The Chancellor, as the chief executive, continued to be appointed by the head of state and his tenure of office did not depend on his maintaining a majority in the Reichstag. The armed forces and bureaucracy (which included the Protestant Church, judiciary and the teaching profession) similarly looked to the monarch rather than to parliament, an institution which they antedated. Prussia, with five-eighths of the area and population, acquired a dominant influence. Elsewhere industrialisation had gone hand in hand with liberalism; now it was shown to be compatible with a modified feudalism.[5]

(*vi*) This solution allowed little power to the workers and thus provided the ingredients for a proletarian revolution. But at Bismarck's instigation the new form of authoritarian state accepted a degree of responsibility for its subjects' welfare which liberal individualism had repudiated. Several decades were however needed before the various schemes of social insurance (coupled with steadily increasing prosperity) began to reconcile the proletariat to its masters. In an attempt to distract attention from internal strains, the heroic virtues were invoked on behalf of the national state. The claim was made that Germany, having achieved the status of a European Power, was entitled to that of a World Power. It was also argued that, surrounded as she was with neighbours who viewed her growing strength with alarm, she could not afford the debilitating luxury of government by the people at large.

(*vii*) The hostilities between 1914 and 1918 amounted to two wars fought simultaneously. The first resulted from the challenge which modernisation presented to the Habsburg Empire. The demand by its non-German inhabitants for its reorganisation on a basis of self-governing national states threatened to break it up. Its leaders decided that this threat must sooner or later be met with force and that the murder of its Emperor's heir provided the best opportunity ever likely to arise of doing this with success. The German Government encouraged them to act because an Austrian collapse would have left Germany to face France and Russia unaided. The prospects of facing them with success would not have been bad if the German Government had not simultaneously driven Britain into their arms by making a bid to take over her position as a World Power with the world's biggest navy. (This ambition was always denied but, now that the records are open, its existence is deniable no longer.⁶) The German generals decided that their only hope of defeating three combined opponents lay in attacking and eliminating France before Britain and Russia could give her effective help. They considered that the need to preserve Austria made that attack a defensive operation. The gathering together of the three states likely to lose by German expansion was presented inside Germany as a hostile act of 'encirclement'. As a result there was a fundamental misunderstanding between the belligerents as to the extent to which the actions taken by each side were justifiable. The outbreak of war evoked from the German workers such a wave of loyalty that the country achieved for a moment the level of integration which had been the dream of the ruling classes.

(*viii*) The German public were never clearly told in 1914 that the Army's initial plans for winning had failed, while in 1918 they were led till July to expect victory. To hear at the end of September, before the enemy had even crossed the frontier, that they were defeated came as a shock for which it was widely felt that there must be some sinister reason. If the Germans had always been the kind of people their leaders had always told them they were, they should have been incapable of losing. Many refused to accept that their leaders had overestimated the country's relative international strength (and aggravated that mistake by a number of other misjudgments). They insisted that defeat was due to inner weakness, that the civil population in general and the Socialists in particular, had 'stabbed the armed forces in the back' by mutinies and demonstrations. The implication was that Germany did not need to change her character or course but only pursue it more whole-heartedly. The war had been expected to enhance respect for the heroic virtues. Instead it was widely considered to have caused a decline in morality – particularly by black-marketing to supplement the totally inadequate rations.

(*ix*) Although the Treaty of Versailles did not depart from the terms on which the Germans had surrendered by nearly as much as their propagandists led them to believe, it was harsher in respect of annexations, disarmament and reparations than they had been led to expect (although less harsh than the treaty which the Germans had imposed on the Russians at Brest-Litovsk). It was also alleged to pin on Germany the sole 'guilt' for the war, whereas all it in fact said was that she was 'responsible' for the damage caused by the war (and should therefore pay reparations⁷). The Germans were allowed almost no opportunity of negotiating about the terms but were left to choose between accepting them and taking up arms again. Nearly all Hitler's opponents put the main blame for his rise to power on the injustice of the treaty. But since the real thing that the Germans resented was having been defeated, it is unlikely that milder terms would have much altered their later behaviour.

(*x*) The US Senate refused to ratify the treaty, thus indicating that the degree of armed force without which the Allies could never have won an outright victory would not be available to maintain the settlement which that victory was used to impose. The British and French soon disagreed as to whether it should be revised or enforced. The Russians were absorbed in the aftermath of their revolution. Germans had good reasons for hoping that before long the treaty could be defied without incurring serious penalties.

(*xi*) The Allies had only granted an armistice on the understanding that the Germans would change their political system so as to make their executive responsible through the Reichstag to the people at large. Many upper- and middle-class Germans had refused to accept such a change before the war on the ground, first propounded by Ranke, that it was unsuitable to their national circumstances. They now regarded its establishment as an unwise piece of outside interference of which they would get rid as soon as they dared. They further rejected (in spite of Kant and von Humboldt) the claim of 1776 and 1789 that the individual, as a pre-requisite to self-realisation, has a right to a say in how he is governed. Social cohesion was not to be obtained by discussion in a plural society but by the imposition of order from above. Parties were not seen as a means of fostering agreement by channelling discussion but as sources of disagreement by fostering argument.[8] In any case the constitutional reform was not accompanied by a social one. Far too many of the posts which were vital to the character and conduct of public affairs remained in the hands of people who were out of sympathy with the document which was drawn up by a National Assembly at Weimar, and were prepared only to tolerate it until a chance to change it arose. Others sought actively to bring that chance about.

(*xii*) The war had everywhere dislocated the international economy of the nineteenth century, causing widespread poverty and unemployment. Naturally these results were worse for the vanquished than for the victors. Germany's attempts to postpone devaluation and escape from reparations aggravated the situation by precipitating runaway inflation in 1923. The conditions were interpreted as suggesting that industry, thrift and honesty did not bring their due reward. A misplaced desire for accurate representation had led to a voting system which encouraged parties to multiply, leading to weak coalition governments and constant manoeuvring. Many felt outraged by the disorder which they saw around them. When after a transient improvement between 1925 and 1929 American obtuseness brought about a world slump, resentment and fear combined to make many Germans sympathetic to drastic remedies incompatible with Germany's obligations under Versailles. The Catholic politician Heinrich Brüning was appointed Chancellor in March 1930 on the implicit understanding that he would move towards ruling by emergency decree rather than by parliamentary majority – which was in effect a return to the pre-1914 system. In elections in the following September, the number of seats won by Hitler's party rose from 12 to 107, making it the second strongest after the Social Democrats. But what unnerved many German property-owners more was that the seats won by the Communists rose from

54 to 77. Rightly or wrongly, apprehension grew that, if conditions got much worse, Germany would go the way of Russia in 1917.

(b) The psychological background

The idea of 'national character' is often dismissed as an illusion. Yet the incidence of types of personal character does vary from society to society. How far this is a physiological matter and how far due to the values and norms held up for admiration in each society is open to argument which is conveniently resolved in the formula 'Character moulds institutions; institutions perpetuate character'.[9] The prevalence of a particular type is assisted by the number of individuals with fairly weak characters which lead them to go along with whatever trends are dominant. It is a thesis of this book that the type of character now known as 'authoritarian' (which is not necessarily the same as 'strong') played a larger part in German society than in British, American or French.[10]

The ideal male was seen as strong and courageous but at the same time as disciplined, obedient to his superiors while expecting obedience from those beneath him, ready to sacrifice himself for the common good without insisting on having a say in how that good was defined. Family relationships were expected to correspond. The father was assigned the role of patriarch, the wife should do as her husband told her and concentrate on meeting his needs, holding up in front of the children an uncritical picture of him as an example to be followed. The sons should be dutiful and manly, repressing the tender feelings which they felt towards their mother, since sentiment was thought to breed weakness. But, since tenderness is natural, the attempt to repress it resulted in stress, which also arose where a male doubted his ability to fulfil the role expected of him. He tended to overact his part so as to dispel the doubt. He showed an insensitivity to the use of force which opened the door to sadism and exaggerated estimates of what force could achieve. He buttressed his personal sense of inadequacy by identifying himself with something stronger, be it individual leader or group or nation. He expected this substitute source of strength to exert itself in relation to its peers, i.e. impose its will on others. He tended to regard with unreasoning hate any person or institutions which frustrated this aim, making 'the other side' wrong or guilty.

Of course these phenomena can be found in most societies and one in which they were entirely absent would have difficulty in achieving the internal cohesion needed to maintain itself in a competitive world. The inculcation of rules by parents and teachers is an essential part of growing up. It involves the socialisation of the infant's essentially selfish interests; without it, orderly communal life is impossible. Every society has a different 'mix' of encouragement, emphasis, prohibition and taboo. But in some societies these rules of conduct are gradually internalised by the individual and imposed on him or herself as much voluntarily as by the external threat of sanctions. The extent of this internalisation will be higher where the society in question seeks to provide rational justification for the rules. In proportion as this happens in families and societies, individuals can be expected to emerge with integrated personalities, relatively free from internal stress and bias. Such attitudes are easier to achieve in prosperous and stable times, while the prevalence of them in turn contributes to stability and to effective common action in face of the challenges presented by current events. Individuals and families of this kind were of course to be found in Germany and the picture of the authoritarian German family was on occasion ridiculed. But her history and environment militated against their predominance, impeding the achievement of mutual consent in internal government and externally constituting a threat to the security of other states.

The aim of both the authoritarian and of the liberal approach is to produce a society with a high degree of integration. What else was the Nazi ideal of *Volksgemeinschaft*? The problem for the authoritarian society is that the methods it uses may well frustrate that aim as much as they forward it. Yet if the preconditions for spontaneous internalised integration do not exist, the need for effective action by the society may become so urgent as to produce an irresistible pressure for violent compulsion.

CHAPTER II
How the various sections of society reacted to Hitler's rise

By 1932 almost every section of German society had its own reasons for finding fault with the Weimar Republic, although opinions differed as to what was wrong with it and how it should be reformed. Hitler is said to have succeeded by 'mobilising disaffection',[1] i.e. persuading each dissatisfied group that, if allowed power, he would put right what each thought most wrong. In July 1932 he induced 37 per cent of the electorate, or 13.7 million people, to vote for him. This protest vote thus included a wide variety of backgrounds and a review of the main components will help to make intelligible the situation which had come about. The first four of the categories which follow constitute the classes which had hitherto been running the country.

(a) Aristocrats and landowners

The kings and ruling princes followed the example of the Kaiser in 1918 and abdicated, but continued for the most part to live in the country; when they died, their heirs used their second title, e.g. *Markgraf* of Baden rather than *Grossherzog*. The Weimar Constitution required the lower orders of nobility to treat their titles as part of their names as commoners. No fresh titles were bestowed. Although the Prussian aristocracy had at one time had their differences with the monarchy, those days were long past and for over a century personal allegiance to the king was expected of and obtained from them. When on one occasion before 1914 a nobleman and aide-de-camp to the Kaiser voted with the Progressives, he was deprived of his right to wear uniform. The aristocracy felt politically homeless in the Republic and longed for a restoration. They regarded Field-Marshal von Hindenburg, after his election as President in 1925, as a sort of Regent, although some of them looked at him askance for having anything to do with the new system.

One of the criticisms later made of the Republic was that it had failed to carry through an extensive redistribution of land in 1919 but, although the aristocracy retained their estates, these were economically as much of a liability as an asset. To stave off bankruptcy, the Government made them grants which were increased when the bottom dropped out of the rye market in 1930.

Scandals occurred about the distribution and use of this money and when in 1932 Brüning proposed to foreclose on some of the more heavily indebted lands and use them to settle peasant proprietors, the owners reacted to what they called 'agrarian bolshevism' by conniving to bring about his fall.[2] They were neurotically anti-Communist and traditionally anti-Slav although forced to use Polish labourers to replace the Germans who were moving from agriculture to the towns.

The aristocrats and landowners mostly voted for the right-wing German National People's Party (DNVP) and supported the move of that party in 1928 from reluctant co-operation with the Republic to active work for its overthrow, personified by the election of the publishing and film magnate, Hugenberg, as its chairman. The Nazi Party's inclusion in its title of the words 'Socialist' and 'Workers' led to an accusation that it was 'Bolshevism in nationalist wrappings';[3] the ultra-conservative Ewald von Kleist-Schmenzin published in 1932 a leaflet describing it as a version of Socialism hostile to property and religion.[4] It was justifiably suspected of preferring small men to big ones, which might lead it to dally with resettlement. The great and good turned up their noses at the social background of some of its leaders and von Hindenburg took a personal dislike to Hitler. But every year that passed made the position of the aristocrats more of an anachronism and they could see no chance of obtaining the two-thirds majority needed for the changes which they wished to make in the constitution. There was therefore considerable attraction in joining forces with the lower-middle-class Nazis much as their predecessors had done fifty years earlier with the upper-middle classes in the rye-and-iron alliance, trusting that with their own political experience they could use the newcomers as tools. Hitler might not be a gentleman (*Herr*) but he had character (*war ein Kerl*).[5]

The nobility of the south and west was more inclined to totalitarianism than the Prussian while the urbanised nobility, who often held official posts, were really part of the upper-middle classes.[6]

(b) The armed forces

The connection between the aristocracy and the Prussian Army had always been close and the Republic not surprisingly shrank from the confrontation which would have been precipitated by any attempt to democratise the officer corps; such a conflict was expected to benefit only the extremes, whether of right or left. As a result 21 per cent of the lieutenants newly commissioned in 1922–3 were aristocrats, while in 1931–2 the figure was 36 per cent;[7] in 1925 52 per cent of the senior officers were themselves the sons of officers.[8] The abdication of the Kaiser deprived the Army of its basic personal foundation; someone said it was like 'burying a dear friend'.[9] The attempt to find a substitute in the institutional idea of the state was seen as distinctly a second-best. Some of the troops returning after the Armistice had been met by hostile crowds who tore off their insignia. This was not easily forgotten, while the markedly unmilitary sentiments of the parties of the left were not easily overlooked. Few Socialists had, like Julius Leber, the sense to see that, as the Republic had to have an army, steps ought to be taken to win its loyalty. In 1928 a new Defence Minister was appointed in the person of General Gröner whose career between 1914 and 1919 had given him exceptional opportunities to see how in modern war the military and civilian spheres were interdependent. He sought to bring them closer together and obtain in return a relaxation of the Reichstag's control over the Defence Budget. But his policy found little understanding or support among his subordinates.[10]

Although some of the officers knew better than to accept the legend that the Army had never been beaten in the field, the defeat was a lasting source of shame which they longed to redress. The Treaty of Versailles had deliberately cut the Reichswehr down to a size – seven divisions – at which its only functions could be maintaining internal order and policing the frontier. It was incapable of winning a war even against Poland so that Germany was not *bundnisfähig*, i.e. of any value to anyone as an ally. The Army moreover distrusted the theory embodied in the League of Nations that inter-state relationships could be based on something besides force. The Republican Armed Forces Law of 1926 forbade soldiers to engage in political activities, including membership of political parties and voting in elections.[11] If there had been no such bar, many members of the forces would have given active support to parties of the right.

By the end of the 1920s the officer corps were impatient to sweep away the Versailles restrictions and create a new modernised army which would enable Germany to resume her place among the Great Powers. The personal advantages which rearmament would bring (42 per cent of the officers discharged in 1919 were still unemployed in 1930 and living on their pensions[12]) were not the only motive, although they were not overlooked. After a reshuffle in 1928–30 the officer corps was remarkably young, increasingly urban in background and socially ambitious. As a trial of three lieutenants from Ulm in 1930 showed, the younger members wanted freedom to take sides for the national cause. Their seniors, although sympathetic, suspected the Nazis as social upstarts and military amateurs. A body which was better educated than is normally recognised (49 per cent of the officers had their abiturs, 12 per cent had spent at least three years at universities[13]) was put off by the anti-intellectual atmosphere of the Party. They knew of the Storm Troops' ambition to replace them by becoming a 'People's Army' and were not prepared to yield to it. But they saw that, to win a modern war, the fighting forces had to have behind them the whole-hearted support of the entire population. They began to think that the NSDAP might be the best available instrument for mobilising such support. At the same time they feared that any attempt to suppress the Party would split the community;[14] they worried about the possibility of being called on to support the police against Nazis and Communists simultaneously. Whether they would stand in the way of a Nazi accession to power would therefore largely depend on their being satisfied that they would remain the basis of the nation's organised strength and retain monopoly control of heavy weapons.

(c) The upper-middle classes (or, as the Germans call them, *der obere Mittelstand*)

These had three main elements: (*i*) the urbanised nobility, already mentioned, who mostly also belonged to one of the other elements, helped towards this by the fact that all the children of most noblemen carry their father's title; (*ii*) 'established' officials (*Beamte*, as distinguished from 'employees', *Ange-stellte*); and (*iii*) the professional classes. At their lower ends (*ii*) and (*iii*) merge into the lower-middle classes, *untere Mittelstand*, although it was the aspiration of many in those lower ends to use their positions to win a rise on the social ladder, if not for themselves then for their children.

The civil servants who formed a large proportion of this category (especially if the Protestant clergy and teaching profession are counted as such) had had much the same attitude to the monarchy as the landowners and officers; some of them had been reserve officers or regular soldiers dismissed in 1919. They regarded themselves as servants of the state rather than as subordinates to ministers, who indeed until 1919 had been officials rather than politicians. Fifty per cent of all senior civil servants were lawyers and 50 per cent of lawyers civil servants.[15] Being the kind of people who invested their savings in government bonds, they had been particularly hard-hit by the inflation and considered that the level of revalorisation provided by the Emergency Tax Decree of February 1924 was unreasonably low. They would perhaps have come to accept the Republic (as some of them like Ernst von Harnack and Erwin Planck did) if it had been successful but as things were they saw its continuation as a threat to their social position and standard of living; Brüning's deflationary cuts reduced their incomes by some 23 per cent.[16] Many of those less well-off were afraid of sinking into the *untere Mittelstand*.

National Socialism has rightly been seen as predominantly a movement supported by the lower-middle classes. But samples of Party membership have shown more members of the upper classes than their proportion of about 3 per cent in the population would lead one to expect. In the election of 1932, upper-middle-class districts in Berlin and Hamburg returned a considerably higher vote for the Nazis than was given in those two cities overall.[17] From the days of the romantic rejection of the Enlightenment there has always been a strong anti-rational element in German thought. Professors and headmasters (who had a higher status in Germany than in many other countries) took a prominent part in the Pan-German League at the turn of the century. It is an unfortunate fact that by no means all who earn their living by applying reason to some specific subject extend the practice to life as a whole. *Wissenschaft* is not automatically linked to *Menschlichkeit*; the fallacy that it should be apolitical was widespread.[18] No natural scientists were prominent in the *Widerstand*. Opportunists guessed that Party membership was going to be the quickest route to power. By 1938 there were 3000 lawyers and 3000 doctors in the SS. The staff of the Propaganda Ministry was later said to be largely composed of 'alienated intellectuals'.[19] The importance which the upper classes attached in general to the rule of law did not prevent some of them from showing impatience with Hitler for his obstinate adherence (after the experience of 1923–4) to constitutional methods in gaining power. Hence the jibe of '*Adolf Légalité*'.

The proportion of them who were Party Members by 1932 has been put at 4 per cent.[20] More would have joined if membership had not been forbidden or discouraged by employers (as in *Länder* where Socialists had a share in the government). In some cases they were actually asked to stay outside by the local Nazi leaders who felt that it would be advantageous for them to appear non-partisan. On the other hand agitators in the Hanover area spread the rumour at the end of 1931 that when Hitler came to power all civil servants who were not by then Party Members would be dismissed.[21]

This is an appropriate place to mention the Jewish question. In 1933 Germany's 503,000 professing Jews[22] only made up about 0.75 per cent of the population, a proportion which had fallen from 1.09 per cent in 1880 and would have fallen further if it had not been sustained by immigrants from Russia's western provinces and Poland ('The Pale'), distinctive, at any rate on arrival, in dress and manners. Having been for long forbidden to own land or ply a craft, Jews had gravitated to the cities, where they formed a disproportionate section of the population – 3.8 per cent in Berlin, 4.7 per cent in Frankfurt – and earned livelihoods by exercising their wits in such occupations as trade and transport, the law, medicine, journalism and finance, providing 16 per cent of Germany's lawyers and 11 per cent of her doctors.[23] To qualify themselves for such ways of life they pressed into higher education, taking up about a third of the places in Berlin's Gymnasia; in 1910 0.1 per cent of all Germans but 0.4 per cent of Jews went to *Hochschulen*. They inclined to the left in politics, partly because their sharpness of intellect made them susceptible to new ideas, partly because it was people on the left who had advocated their emancipation in 1869; much of the Liberal and Socialist press was written by Jews. Not surprisingly this disproportionate competition inflamed among their Gentile rivals throughout the middle classes an anti-semitism which had long existed in Germany. They came to symbolise to all who disliked Liberal, rational, industrial, urban society all the things which were dislikable about it, especially as unsuccessful people are often in debt and creditors were not infrequently Jewish. This is not to excuse or palliate the barbarities which the Nazi radicals were to inflict on the Jews. But it does help to explain why more civilised Germans, who might have been expected to protest against such behaviour, were mostly slow to do so.

There were of course among the upper classes and intellectuals a considerable number to whom National Socialism and all the ideas associated with it were from the start so abhorrent and nonsensical that they often could not understand how it could have so wide an appeal. Many of them had experience of and links with the world outside Germany. Their tragedy however was that they were not numerous or persuasive enough to save their country from shame and disaster, possibly because it was that very outside world which German nationalists resented for its refusal to take them at their own valuation. In the early days of the Third Reich considerable moral stature was required to discern the full extent of the Nazi challenge to civilised values and the perils of compromise. By the time that the need to stand firm had become evident, the obstacles to doing so had significantly increased.

(d) Finance, trade and industry

The popular Communist doctrine that Nazism was instigated and paid for by large-scale capital is a gross oversimplification. Certainly the Republic was widely disliked in German trade and industry. The contributions required from employers under various schemes of social welfare (and notably that for insurance against unemployment introduced in 1927), combined with the state's power to make binding awards in management–labour disputes, raised costs substantially. Not only were the prices of German exports made uncompetitive but the reduction in profits led to inadequate capital formation, which reinforced the effect of the lost war and of reparations in preventing adequate investment. This lack was seen as a major cause of Germany's economic difficulties. Any political development which offered hope of a remedy was sympathetically regarded. But most remedies involved changes in the constitution for which a two-thirds majority in the Reichstag was required and, even when the democratic parties began to lose ground after 1930, this looked unattainable. A line of escape was seen in a régime which would govern by emergency decree without detailed Reichstag approval. But even when Brüning adopted this course, he was thought by some businessmen to be unduly cautious about alienating workers and foreigners. Von Papen's May 1932 Cabinet came much closer to the ideal and received as a result massive financial support. But it suffered the palpable defect of having virtually no representatives in the Reichstag so that it could not obtain the periodic vote of confidence needed to authorise resort to decrees.

National Socialists by contrast and Hitler in particular were thought suspiciously evasive about their economic intentions. In the autumn of 1930 the general manager of the organisation of iron and steel producers described them as 'half-socialist and fog-shrouded'.[24] The Party was known to be split into a number of factions and there was no knowing which would come out on top. Its need to gain popular votes in order to reach power peacefully deterred it from making clear commitments to the economic leaders. Their suspicions were intensified when Hitler lurched to the left in August 1932 in order to discredit Papen for his lack of popular support. Most senior industrialists (with the notable exception of Thyssen) viewed the Nazis with misgiving right down to January 1933 and would have preferred that they did not come to power. They were more a 'last hope' than a 'first choice'. This did not prevent some businesses taking out a sort of insurance policy by including the NSDAP among the parties to which they gave money (although even then less than has been popularly supposed) as well as making payments to individuals like Göring and Funk in the hope of strengthening such supposed 'moderates'. There was considerably more support from smaller firms manufacturing such things as lace, pianos, gelatine, plywood and hair-bleach, who saw their position becoming more and more desperate as the economic crisis deepened in 1931–2.[25] They were particularly attracted by Nazi promises of protection against big impersonal firms.

(e) The Evangelical (i.e. Protestant) Churches

In post-Reformation Germany each non-Catholic state had had its own Church, to which all inhabitants were usually expected to belong. When one state (notably Prussia) absorbed another, the Churches were sometimes but not always included in the process. In 1919 there were 38 Lutheran, Reformed (i.e. Calvinist) and United Churches, with the Old Prussian Union outnumbering all the others. A move to amalgamate them merely resulted three years later in a reduction to 28 and the establishment of an Evangelical Federation which left the individual bodies independent but helped them to act in concert on matters of common interest. There were those who wished to go further; some of them hoped that the greater unity which the Nazis promised to introduce might be extended to religion. The Protestants outnumbered the Catholics by about three to two.

Evangelical political thought was dominated by the emphasis which Luther had given to St Paul's edict in the Epistle to the Romans (Chapter 13) that each soul must be in subjection to the higher powers, since they had been ordained by God. This view was reinforced by the doctrine of the Two Realms. The kingdom of man ruled by the sword may not at first sight appear Christian but it fulfils an essential function by maintaining order and thus enabling the word of God to be preached. It is however rooted in sin, so that it cannot be expected to develop into the kingdom of God. The Christian should concentrate on things above and judge political systems by their ability to let him do so.[26] To free the Church for performing its essential functions of expounding the Gospel and administering the sacraments, the state assumed responsibility for its business management. Instead of individual members being left free to decide for themselves how much they would contribute, the state fixed the rate of tax, and collected and distributed the proceeds. The training colleges and qualifying examinations for pastors were supervised by the Ministries of Culture. It is hardly surprising that in 1928 one German churchman could tell another, 'The Protestant Church corresponds roughly with the mentality and sociological status of the German National People's Party.'[27] Over 100 Bavarian pastors had served in a *Freikorps* after 1918. Having virtually no Nonconformists, Germany lacked socially radical Protestants; her left-wingers, as Marxists, were atheists. Luther's teaching had included other more liberal attitudes towards life in the world but significantly they had become lost to sight.

Relations between the Churches and the Republic had got off to a bad start. In November 1918 a Ministry had been set up in Prussia for Knowledge, Art and Popular Education, under the joint control of a Majority Socialist and an Independent Socialist. For two months the second dominated events, during which time he separated Church from State, stopped the payment of all state subsidies, ended religious teaching in schools and simplified the procedures by which individuals could opt out of church membership (and of paying church taxes).[28] In January 1919 he resigned, in common with the other Independents, and his laws were suspended. The Weimar Constitution confirmed church privileges while reducing state control.[29] But the damage had been done. Many church officials and pastors remained convinced that what Socialists had tried once, they would try again. Before long the Republic was being accused of failing to maintain social and moral order and thus, under the Two Realms Theory, justifying Christians in transferring their allegiance to any alternative system which looked likely to do better. In 1919 and 1929 the Churches ordained 'Sundays of Mourning' over the Treaty of Versailles and 'the lie of war guilt'.[30]

Nineteenth-century German Protestantism had led the world in applying the principles of historical and literary criticism to Christianity. The result had been to bring out the reservations with which the Bible had to be accepted. The message was susceptible of many varying interpretations; the revelation of God contained in it needed supplementing by conclusions drawn from science and history. But if they were to be invoked to provide evidence of God at work, what was the answer to those who claimed that the (so-called) Aryan principle and the 'Volk' constituted such evidence? If the study of comparative religion suggested that all faiths represented variant approaches to an underlying secret, what was the answer to those who claimed validity for Teutonic myths? Thus Liberal theology unintentionally played into the hands of those who wanted to argue that National Socialism, instead of being incompatible with Christianity, was its fulfilment. The 24th Article of the 1920 Nazi Programme, which said that the Party represented the standpoint of 'positive Christianity', was nicely calculated to reassure those who feared that it would prove anti-Christian while at the same time attracting those who could not accept traditional interpretations of the Gospel.

But from 1919 onwards an answer to Liberalism had been in process of formulation in the shape of the Dialectical Theology or Theology of Crisis propounded by the Swiss Calvinist Karl Barth who from 1921 to 1935 taught at Göttingen and then at Bonn. Barth moved the discussion away from arguments as to the existence of God and historical justification of the Christian message towards a consideration of the meaning of that message for Christians today:

The Bible was rediscovered, not simply as the greatest devotional classic, not as a miscellaneous collection of documents, to be dissected and analysed by the critic, nor yet as the Fundamentalists' storehouse of texts to be applied in a rigid mechanical fashion. The Bible was rediscovered as the Voice of God speaking to those who seek his revelation and are ready to hear it.[31]

This was an act of faith for which in the last resort no rational justification could be demonstrated. The Barthians thus reaffirmed the traditional Lutheran belief in justification by faith.

(f) The Roman Catholic Church

One of the handicaps of German Protestantism in confronting Nazism was the absence of any single generally-accepted source of authority. The same could not be said of Catholicism. The Vatican was no friend to Liberalism, whether in politics, society or theology. But it disapproved just as strongly of such neo-pagan works as Rosenberg's *Myth of the Twentieth Century* published in 1930. In several dioceses Catholics were forbidden to become Party Members and the ban was made country-wide by the Bishops' Council in August 1932.[32] Cardinal Bertram, the elderly Archbishop of Breslau who was chairman of that Council, explicitly condemned the idea of a German Aryan Church, combining both Catholics and Protestants and independent of Rome.

Yet although the ultimate dependence of German Catholicism on an authority outside the country was to prove a source of strength in the long run, in the years immediately before 1933 a personal factor gave it an opposite effect. In 1930 Eugenio Pacelli, who since 1917 had been Papal Nuncio first in Munich and then in Berlin, became Cardinal Secretary of State; his previous experience made him the natural arbiter of Vatican policy towards Germany. He was dominated by two considerations. The events of 1918–19, and in particular the attempt of the Independent Socialists to separate Church from State and close church schools, left him an inveterate anti-Communist. Secondly he had as a young man worked on the revised Codex of Civil Law which was promulgated in 1917. The purpose of this was to lay down consistent rules for regulating Catholic church life in all countries. But a main ambition of its authors was to secure secular approval of those rules by means of Concordats with governments. When Pacelli arrived in Germany, he had seen it as his main task to reach such agreements not merely with as many of the *Länder* as possible but with the Reich as a whole. It took him until 1925 to reach one with the most Catholic of them all, Bavaria. He would have liked to proceed immediately to negotiate with the Reich. But the Prussian Government, where Social Democrats had a decisive say, not merely put a halt to any such negotiation until it had itself received similar treatment to Bavaria but made difficulties over accepting similar terms, especially as regards schools. In the end Pacelli had to agree to the whole question of education being omitted from the agreement signed in 1929. The Prussian authorities made clear that they would ban any Concordat with the Reich unless it was similarly limited and, as Pacelli refused to consider such a restriction, the road to a Reich Concordat was blocked.[33] To reopen it seemed more important to the Vatican than to most Germans.

Politically the Republic rested on co-operation between the Catholic Centre Party and the Social Democrats. But ever since the days of Bismarck's *Kulturkampf* the Centre's leaders had been anxious to avoid the charge that they lacked patriotism. In proportion as the Republic's difficulties grew, their association with it became irksome. In 1928 the Party's deputies in the Reichstag elected as their leader a priest called Kaas who was more to the right than his predecessors. In May 1932 they did nothing to impede the dismissal of Brüning.

(g) The lower-middle classes (*untere Mittelstand*)

The Nazi movement has been commonly explained as a *petit bourgeois* affair. This has been challenged. Further research has certainly established that it was by no means exclusively so, particularly in the higher ranks. The fact remains however that over thirty different sets of figures giving Party Members and Party joiners between 1925 and 1932 show an average of over 50 per cent coming from the lower-middle classes, although that category only amounted to 43 per cent of the gainfully employed population in 1933.[34] Included in this grouping were master craftsmen, professionals without academic qualifications, lower and intermediate employees, lower and intermediate officials (including elementary school teachers) and owners of small businesses. The important thing about these people is that, taken together, they were about fifteen times as numerous as the upper classes. By the end of the 1920s it was becoming clear that the efforts of the Strassers, Goebbels and others to make the Party attractive to workers were only going to have limited success. If Hitler was to win enough votes to make himself an attractive ally to the ruling classes and come to power constitutionally, it was from the *untere Mittelstand* that the votes would have to come. The success achieved in winning them is shown by the fact that between 1928 and 1933 the share of votes won by the traditional parties of the middle (*Deutsche Volkspartei, Deutsche Demokratische Partei, Wirtschaftspartei*, etc.) dropped from 25 per cent to 5 per cent while that of the NSDAP rose from 2.69 per cent to 43.9 per cent.[35]

The tide of economic advance was moving against small men, even in times of prosperity; recession naturally made things worse. They were either losing their jobs or frightened of doing so; they often earned less than skilled workers. Even before 1930 the struggle for profit had led firms to cut costs by improving methods or enlarging their size. As things got worse those who could not or would not do either found it increasingly difficult to compete. Brüning's policy of fighting unemployment by deflation hit the weak more severely than the strong. High interest rates, tight credit, higher taxes, falling profits, cuts in pay combined to complicate life. The call for radical remedies grew stronger;

the NSDAP seemed the party most likely to adopt them. It claimed to be Socialist without being egalitarian and Nationalist without being plutocratic.[36] It gave the impression of being opposed to big, impersonal companies (rather than to the successful individual) and of being ready to spend its way out of depression. Whereas unemployed blue-collar workers tended to vote Communist, unemployed white-collar ones took to voting Nazi.

The place to hear the *untere Mittelstand* express itself was, in Germany as elsewhere, the pub. (*Die Stammtisch Mentalität war das eigentlichen Terrain des 'gesunden Volksempfindens'*.)[37] There one would hear exemplified the hostility to anything unfamiliar, whether in persons, styles or ideas; the capacity to begin a train of thought without seeing the objections to it; the uncritical acceptance of statements which help to justify established attitudes; hostility to opposition; over-emphasis on the heroic virtues. To most Nazi leaders adoption of the same attitudes came naturally. In the course of time they learnt that, to succeed in the modern world, a good deal which was out-of-date had to be discarded. But the need to maintain the loyalty of the rank-and-file compelled them to go on paying lip service to many of the notions which they had adopted to gain power. This was to prove a distinct liability.

(h) Peasants (i.e. self-employed small-scale farmers)

In 1925 96 per cent of agricultural undertakings in Germany covered less than 50 acres. The peasants' demands were simple and persistent – higher and guaranteed prices for their produce, especially fats; lower prices for their needs, such as fertilisers; relief from their mounting debts. These demands could only be satisfied at the expense of other sections of the population. Higher prices for food meant higher costs, both for consumers and manufacturers, handicapping exports (including grain exports by the big estates). If higher prices were obtained by keeping out cheaper imports, this might provoke retaliation against Germany and reduce the chances of the Allies being ready to scale down reparations. Hence, although Republican governments had gone some way to meet the demands, they had refused to go as far as the peasants wanted. The NSDAP, particularly after the failure to win urban votes in the 1928 elections, had no such inhibitions and managed to reduce bucolic suspicions of those two double-edged adjectives 'Socialist' and 'Workers'.[38] It was relevant that, in many country districts, the wholesale meat trade was in the hands of Jews. The swing of the north German Protestant peasant vote was part of the explanation of the dramatically improved results in the 1930 and later elections. In Lower Saxony the Nazi share of the vote went up from 4.5 per cent in 1928 to 23 per cent in 1930 and to 45 per cent in July 1932.[39] In south Germany peasants in Baden and Württemburg were more inclined to stay faithful to the Catholic Centre and in Bavaria to its counterpart the *Volkspartei* (except in Protestant Franconia where the Catholic challenge fostered radicalism).

(i) Workers

It has long been an article of faith among left-wing historians that German workers proved more immune to Hitler's appeal than any other section of the population. Certainly the available figures suggest that, whereas workers formed nearly 55 per cent of the population, they only produced between 30 and 40 per cent of Party Members.[40] But (assuming that they provided the same proportion among Nazi voters) 5.2 million of them would have voted NSDAP in July 1932, which is a considerable figure. A closer analysis of worker attitudes is therefore necessary.

From the foundation of the Social Democratic Party in 1875, the hostility of the upper and middle classes had left the workers with little choice but to live in a self-contained, self-reliant world, with exclusive organisations in most walks of life. In spite of some relaxation after 1919, the habit had persisted:

> The Social Democratic skilled worker was not only a member of his party and his union but his cultural interests were catered for by the Social Democratic Book Club 'Gutenberg Guild'. Once a week he met his comrades in the man's voice choir 'Forwards'. The women used the rehearsal for a chit-chat and the eldest boy was in the cycling club 'Solidarity'. Shopping was done at the cooperative to which one belonged and where again one met one's friends.[41]

The bigger the city, the more likely was this to be the case and where it was, the NSDAP had difficulty in making headway. Their prospects improved in proportion as workers were less organised, living on their own in small towns, working on their own or in small firms, commuting from country districts or proving social misfits. For obvious reasons, those out of work were more vulnerable. When one is down and out, it is not easy to be sure from one week to the next which radical party is going to give most help. Even if the working-class unemployed were more likely to turn Communist than Nazi between 1930 and 1933, over half the Storm Troopers were drawn from unskilled or semi-skilled workers who thereby obtained food, shelter and clothing. From 70 to 80 per cent had been unemployed.[42]

But the working classes were split between Social Democrats and Communists. The latter accused the former of having betrayed the proletarian cause by supporting the war effort, helping to prevent defeat from leading to revolution and joining with non-Marxist parties in coalition governments (as the only way of gaining power). Each side bitterly attacked the other; the Communists tended to be younger and poorer. They sought to establish a 'United Front From Below' by poaching the SPD rank-and-file. Under orders from Moscow (which too often judged German by Russian conditions), they regarded 'Fascism' as the last stage of 'Capitalism' and were even anxious to see it established in the conviction that it would hasten their own arrival in power. A typical leaflet spent four-fifths of its space in attacking the SPD and only one-fifth the NSDAP. On occasion they were prepared to co-operate with the Nazis, as in the Berlin tram-strike of November 1932.

The Communists were much readier to fight. The failure of the Republic to solve its problems had demoralised the Social Democrats: there was nothing glamorous about defending the status quo. In 1930 only 10 per cent of their

Table II.1.   *Results of elections 1930–3*

Date	SPD	KPD	NSDAP	Turn-out%
September 1930	24.5% (8.6m)	13.1% (4.6m)	18.3% (6.4m)	82
July 1932	21.6% (7.9m)	14.3% (5.25m)	37.3% (13.75m)	84
November 1932	20.4% (7.3m)	16.9% (5.9m)	33.1% (11.7m)	81
March 1933	18.3% (7.18m)	12.1% (4.84m)	43.9% (17.28m)	90

Reichstag representatives were under 40 compared with 60 per cent among the Nazis:

> The assumption of top-level political responsibility after 1918 and the position of a secure and legally-recognised democratic mass-movement in the Republic had brought to prominence hard-working experienced Parliamentarians and proficient bureaucrats. Such men were absorbed in routine activites for their Party or Trade Union, associated almost exclusively with people of their own type and seldom looked beyond the horizon of their own sphere of work. Their political judgments were apt to be influenced by a short-sighted and illusory over-estimate of the power of their organisation. There was an almost complete lack of charismatic leaders and people ready to engage, when need arose, in revolutionary conspiracies.[43]

A crucial moment came in July 1932 when Papen replaced the SPD-led Government of Prussia (which was denied a stable majority by the refusal of the KPD to give it regular support) by a Reich Commissioner. Many of the rank-and-file, including the million organised in the *Reichsbanner* (the democratic counterpart of the Storm Troops), wanted to match force by force and urged a general strike. But the SPD and Trade Unions refused to act illegally and merely lodged a futile appeal with the Supreme Court. They doubted whether a call to strike would have been followed when unemployment was so high. They were afraid of finding themselves face-to-face with the Reichswehr (although the Prussian police would probably have been on their side). The failure to act was repeated in January and February 1933 because the leaders were too conscious of their weakness. After that, it was too late. Two ill-founded beliefs encourage inaction. One was that since Socialism had survived Bismarck's persecution, it could survive Hitler's; the ruthlessness of the Nazis and the development of new repressive techniques were not taken into account. The second was that the Nazis, if given a chance to govern, would soon show their incompetence and become as discredited as many other politicians had been. This was to prove true as regards many of the older Party Members and Storm Troopers, who rapidly became unpopular as a result. But it did not apply to Hitler or to many of the hard-faced executives who found places in his realm.

(j) Women

After women received votes in 1919, they outnumbered men in the electorate by some 2 million (largely as a result of war casualties). But a lower proportion of them went to the poll and the percentage of them voting NSDAP was for long small – Hitler would have fared better quicker if women had lacked votes. The percentage of women in the Party membership was lower than in any other party except the Communist. In view of the anti-feminist bias which pervaded the Party – a sign of anti-modernism – one begins to wonder why women voted for it at all, until one remembers that many German women accepted the view of their menfolk about their proper sphere being children, church and kitchen, politics being something which the sexes hardly discussed together. Forty per cent of all wage-earning women were employed in agriculture.

The dominant position of the husband/father in the stereotype of a German family has been mentioned (p. 8). It naturally led many women to vote as the head of the household did. It also created an emotional urge to rally to the *Volk* when he identified himself with it. Husband and *Volk* admittedly had a rival in Church, especially in Catholic areas. Women went on voting for the Centre or its Bavarian variant when the men had already switched to voting Nazi or Communist. But women began to take more trouble about going to the poll as the economic crisis deepened and the notion spread that the Nazis were the people most likely to do something about it. The leadership reacted to the trend by toning down their anti-feminism and pretending to support traditional religious and cultural values. Hitler would never have achieved his electoral successes without a substantial number of female voters. Indeed by 1932 they had come to outnumber male ones in Protestant, although not in Catholic, areas.[44]

(k) Youth

German university education was based on the assumption that students would be well-to-do. The absence of compulsion and supervision was a matter of pride. Courses took a number of years, even if they were only carried as far as the examinations for admission to state service instead of to a doctorate. There was not and never had been any adequate system of scholarships. As a result most students had to depend on their parents until they were well on in their twenties. Those who were hard up took jobs in the vacations or combined work with study, thereby prolonging the time needed for getting degrees.

The war and inflation invalidated the assumption without causing it to be abandoned. Many parents could no longer afford to help; only a third of the student body remained able to finance themselves.[45] But with recession and deflation, part-time work became hard to get. The living standards of undergraduates tended to be lower than those of skilled workers. Yet the numbers in the universities went up, partly because study postponed the need to find a regular job, partly because many children from the *untere Mittelstand* looked on academic qualifications as passports to social advancement. And while only 9.5 per cent had been women in 1918–19, in 1932–3 the figure was 18.5 per cent.[46] But the number of posts requiring a degree or diploma was not rising to correspond. In 1929 1147 qualified jurists were said to be competing in Prussia for 351 vacancies; in the 1930s there were 1500 surplus doctors a year. By the time the Republic ended, there were 40,000 superfluous graduates and the Nazis were forecasting that by 1935 there would be 325,000.[47]

In the late 1920s Helmuth von Moltke told Dorothy Thompson that 'the students were the worst class in Germany'.[48] The largest fraternity association, the *Deutsche Bursenschaft*, had been aggressively nationalistic since its foundation in 1817. In 1921 the *Deutscher Hochschulring*, a right-wing racist organisation, included in its membership two-thirds of those in the *Deutsche Studentenschaft*, the main umbrella organisation.[49] In 1931 the Union of German Democratic Students had only 500 members in the entire Reich.[50] The Union of German National Socialist Students, founded in 1926, was the first subsidiary NS organisation to base its membership on the criterion of occupation; it also proved in June 1931 to be the first one to capture control of the Reich association in its field. A year later it reckoned to have 70 per cent of students behind it. As a 1930 recruit, who was later to hold a prominent post in the SD, explained, 'For four years I lived as a student in Heidelberg on twenty marks a month, until I asked myself whether a society which allowed such a thing was at all healthy. I answered my question by enrolling in the Party.'[51] When Baldur von Schirach, the ambitious socialite who became leader of the NSDStB in 1928, told Hitler that it had obtained a majority on the Council of the *Studentenschaft*, the Führer replied 'You have no idea how much this means to me. Now I am able to say that the majority of the young intelligentsia stands behind me.'[52] But while the Party encouraged the students to demand such things as lower fees and a limit (or even a ban) on Jewish admissions and thereby created the impression that their concern for student welfare was more active than that of the democratic parties, which had allowed themselves to be hamstrung by shortage of cash, the harmony was superficial. The aristocratic fraternities, jealously watched by their old members, still set the tone of university life and, although the Enlightenment might be out of fashion, *Wissenschaft* was still respected. The Nazis, in their hearts, hated both intellects and class distinctions.

Prior to 1933 there were over 100 youth organisations in Germany with a total membership of between 5 and 6 million. In 1932 the Hitler Youth had only 20,000 members, although by January 1933 this figure was to reach 100,000.[53] Until the take-over of power it was primarily a junior branch of the Storm Troops, supporting their paramilitary activities, so that there was little co-operation with other youth organisations. Those most sympathetic to Nazi ideas were the *Bündische Jugend* (from whom in fact many of the ideas came) and the Evangelical Church Youth. By contrast, the Catholic Church groups, to which the Church attached great importance, were firmly anti-Nazi.

(l) Conclusion

Enough has been said to explain why many people in Germany had some fault to find with the Republic; even the Social Democrats felt apologetic about Brüning's deflation. Those who did consistently oppose Hitler often underestimated his political skills. But whereas one group, the Communists, wanted to bring about a completely new system by revolution, the others wanted to see some feature or features of pre-1914 society restored. They did not necessarily accept all the Nazi doctrines, which helps to explain why, after surrender in 1945, so many Germans could say, without total hypocrisy, 'I was never a Nazi.' There were issues (particularly involving the Churches and respect for law) over which clashes might develop. But they thought on balance that a Nazi accession to power would further some cause or interest which they considered important, and they were therefore prepared at least to acquiesce in its happening. But what was it about National Socialism which attracted them?

The first answer must seem a paradox because a number of Nazi attitudes (e.g. to women, bureaucrats and chain-stores) have been dismissed as 'anti-modern', i.e. out of keeping with the kind of society which economic growth was bringing into existence. But this applied to ways of thought rather than to hardware. The Nazis seized on and made skilful use of a number of techniques, such as those associated with Madison Avenue – Hitler was the first politician to do his campaigning by air. Later they were to pioneer the *Autobahnen*, the *Volksempfänger* (cheap wireless set) and the *Volkswagen*. But they also claimed to be bringing in a new type of society, more egalitarian and mobile. When Goebbels was asked, before 1933, for an advance text of a speech he was about to give, he replied, 'No need for a text. The message is simple. Under National Socialism everything will be different.'[54] Whereas the Republic had given priority to the individual and the Socialists to class, they would give priority to the nation. Dr Ley was later to boast that Germany had been the first country to overcome the class struggle.[55] The 1918 Revolution has been criticised, with some justice, for failing to sweep away enough outdated privileges and traditions; the 1933 Counter-revolution did it instead but with a different purpose. Liberal democracy was disparaged as the creed which had been rendered obsolete by the new concepts of *Volk* and *Führer*. What the Communists insist on calling 'Fascism' (a bad label because it suggests that the Italian variety was typical of all the others) is essentially a post-Liberal phenomenon.

Secondly the Nazis could, at any rate in these early years, be very efficient. They had an organisation to deal with every branch of life which could be of use to them and controlled the activities of each closely from the centre, reducing overlapping.[56] Much of the secret of successful propaganda consists in having the right material at the right place at the right moment and while the material calls for a certain type of imagination, the time and place can be planned for ahead. Diligent thoroughness is, after all, a prominent German quality.

Thirdly they had mobilised enthusiasm by promising action. Not for nothing was Nazism called a 'movement' (*Bewegung*). They kept the public in a state of eager anticipation as to what the next excitement would be. The Germans were tired of being told that something which they wanted to see done could not be done because of possible repercussions. They felt that the Nazis would not be held up by such inhibitions. This energy and enthusiasm was not confined to the leadership. Many of the rank-and-file were prepared to spend time proselytising and agitating – and collecting. For long it has been thought that the Party's ample funds (even if not always as ample as appearances suggested) could only have come out of the pockets of rich men; they are now seen to have resulted from small but widespread subscriptions and persistent begging.[57] The energy was sufficiently welcome for the violence which accompanied it to be condoned, if not positively applauded.

Lastly but most important of all came Hitler himself. Some form of personal magnetism he undoubtedly possessed and personal magnetism had not been a notable quality among the dutiful and level-headed men who had come to the top during the Republic. A society which had lost its way was looking for a leader. Hitler does not seem to have thought of himself at the outset as Germany's predestined leader but only as a forerunner or drummer-up; his articulate claim to the post developed gradually as he found his listeners willing and even eager to accept him in that role. The phrase 'Our Führer Adolf Hitler' was used in the *Volkischer Beobachter* from 1923 while the habit of addressing him as 'My Führer' was developed (not by him) about 1931.[58] He had an ability to divine what the audience wanted to hear and a carefully-developed technique of presenting it. His talent lay in communicating to a mass audience the impression of intense conviction which he himself acquired from their presence (he was ineffective in a studio by himself).[59] He could allow himself to be carried away and at the same time calculate coolly how to get the effect he desired. His capacity for sensing what those around him were thinking made him into a shrewd political tactician and stopped him from acting on some of the wilder ideas which flourished among his supporters. He avoided alienating the Church by refusing to take Rosenberg seriously; he avoided alienating the Reichswehr by refusing to let the Storm Troopers riot their way to power; he avoided alienating Prussia by toning down his associations with south Germany.[60] He refrained from talking in public about his long-range plans for Germany's expansion outside her frontiers and made most Germans think that his object was the generally accepted one of escaping from the fetters of Versailles.

It was as Führer of the German *Volk* that Hitler chose to be addressed, rather than of the Party, or as *Volkskanzler*. For a major concern of the movement, and one which commended it to the conservatives, was to create a *Volksgemeinschaft* or People's Community. This can be seen as a desperate longing for unity among a people who felt that their national aims had too often been frustrated by insistence on sectional interests or as an attempt by the ruling classes in a capitalist society to overcome the effects of competition without parting with any of their essential advantages. The former is apt to become a more-or-less sincere and more-or-less conscious justification for the latter. A higher degree of integration was seen as vital both by those who doubted whether German international competitiveness could be restored without a reallocation of the national product to the benefit of investment and by those who doubted whether Germany could become a Great Power again without a war which could only be won if the public were ready to endure greater hardships than they had faced in 1914–18.

Here lay one side of the foundation for the understanding which was worked out in Berlin in the closing days of January 1933. President von Hindenburg was induced by his entourage to appoint Hitler Chancellor. The post was one to which the leader of the largest party in the Reichstag had a good constitutional claim. No scandal was caused by the fact that the decision resulted from a backstairs intrigue rather than from a vote of the Reichstag, since this had been the regular practice in Germany since 1871. Rule by decree under Article 48 of the Constitution had been going on for over two years. The Enabling Bill freeing the Government from parliamentary control got the two-thirds majority which it required. The many Germans who attached importance to keeping the law could not object on legal grounds to what had happened.

Hitler in return was taken to have promised that he would share his power with the old upper classes who provided the other component of the coalition Government. Not only were the two constituent elements in that Government agreed on the three basic aims of restoring unity, prosperity and external power. Not only were the newcomers expected to allow their seniors an equal say in deciding how these aims were to be pursued. Not only did the greater experience of the seniors make such deference appear common sense. What seemed to be the key posts of economics, defence and foreign policy were in senior hands, with Papen as Vice-Chancellor to provide reinforcement. In the Cabinet the Nazis were outnumbered by three to nine. The unholy alliance was dedicated by a 'sentimental comedy' staged on 21 March 1933 at the grave of Frederick the Great in the Potsdam Garrison Church. Hitler shook hands with Hindenburg, ministers and generals mixed with Storm Troopers and the sermon was preached by Otto Dibelius, General Superintendent of the Prussian Protestant Church.

Yet the history of the next twelve years can be seen as the story of how this understanding, always more tacit than explicit, went unfulfilled. The three Cabinet posts which the Nazis were allowed to hold carried with them the control of the police. Von Blomberg at the Ministry of War bore out his nickname of 'Rubber Lion'. By no means all decisions were taken in the

Cabinet; during the next twelve years only seven laws were passed by the Reichstag, as compared with 218 decrees issued under the Enabling Act in 1933 alone.[61] The real *Machtergreifung* did not occur on 30 January 1933 but in the following eighteen months. The whole shape of Germany was changed by *Gleichschaltung*, Goebbels was quite right when he reminded his subordinates that a revolution was in progress. Late in 1933 François-Poncet the French Ambassador wrote that 'the astounding thing in this revolution is the speed with which it was carried out but also the facility with which it was everywhere completed.'[62] A German historian said later that 'the mass of the German people lost their freedom without fully noticing what was going on.'[63] Concern did however grow, particularly among the experts who are essential to modern society, that Nazi methods, besides being immoral, were going to bring disaster. For about a year in 1940–1 these doubts were stilled, only to revive with increasing force. As hopes dwindled and disillusion grew, increasing numbers of Germans who had been inclined to give Hitler the benefit of the doubt began to consider how he could be induced to change his courses and then, when that seemed hopeless, removed.

It is to this gradual development of the *Widerstand* that we must now turn, once again examining the various sectors of the population separately.

CHAPTER III
The development of the *Widerstand*

(a) Aristocrats and landowners

Whereas the Republic had acquired 602,000 hectares of land and settled on them 57,457 peasants, the Third Reich in the period 1933–8 acquired 328,000 hectares and settled 20,000.[1] There was therefore no need for big landowners to fear wholesale expropriation. The Potsdam ceremony had its intended effect and the beating-up of Communists was popular. The dissolution of the DNVP in July 1933 (along with all the other parties) was regretted and the 1934 Treaty with Poland viewed with suspicion (although it could be explained away as a tactical expedient). The other external and defence measures of the regime gave satisfaction and counteracted the underlying (and correct!) suspicion that the Nazi leadership despised inherited rank and wealth. But quite a few noblemen took positions inside the regime; by 1938 18.7 per cent of the *Obergruppenführer*, 9.8 per cent of *Gruppenführer* and 8.8 per cent of *Oberführer* in the SS belonged to the nobility.[2]

Set against these positive developments was the apprehension caused by high-handed Nazi methods and the growing realisation that the traditional ruling classes were allowing themselves to be used as tools. By no means all aristocrats put law on a pedestal but respect for it and for regular procedure was deeply engrained in the Prussian tradition. There was a gradual increase in the numbers of those who regarded National Socialism as incompatible with the moral standards on which they had been brought up. Fifty of the 165 persons on the latest list of those who died as a result of the 20 July plot bore titles.[3] Of the 4000 members of the Order of St John of Jerusalem, 14 were executed but only 411 had left when given an alternative between resigning from it and from the Party.[4] One particular set of friends which was labelled by the SD as 'The Counts Group' included Fritz Dietlof, Graf von der Schulenburg; Peter, Graf Yorck von Wartenburg; Caesar von Hofacker; Ulrich Graf von Schwerin-Schwanenburg; and Albrecht von Kessel; all of these held jobs as officials or diplomats.

(b) The armed forces

One of the first things which Hitler did as Chancellor was pledge himself to a rearmament programme even more extensive than the one for which the Reichswehr had obtained the secret approval of the Socialist-led Cabinet in 1929.[5] A second such was due to start taking effect in April 1933; it was immediately accelerated and completed in the following year. But there was a choice of ways for carrying the process forward. The Disarmament Conference had in 1932 agreed to permit Germany equality of armaments in a system giving security for all. What this would mean in practice had still to be negotiated. But if any sort of agreement could have been reached, it might have enabled Germany to rearm without inciting her neighbours to consider whether they ought not to rearm as well. Hitler was not averse to starting off on this path, since he realised that, once Germany began to rebuild her strength, she would pass through a period of risk, as the Kaiser and Tirpitz had done before 1914, during which she would be unable to resist any country which chose to apply military or other sanctions against her. He would therefore have been willing to negotiate a Land Agreement, parallel to the Naval Agreement reached with Britain in 1935, with the firm intention of repudiating it immediately it ceased to serve his purposes.

This course however was opposed by the War Minister von Blomberg, the Commander-in-Chief von Fritsch and the Chief of Staff Beck who refused to have their hands tied by promises given to other countries. They insisted that Germany must stop negotiations about arms control and leave the League of Nations without further delay. Hitler fell in with their wishes but accelerated the speed and scale of the proposed rearmament in the hope of shortening the period of risk. By this .time the current programme was approaching fulfilment and its successor, providing for 36 divisions by 1938, was too big to be achieved by voluntary enlistment. Internally this precipitated a show-down with the SA whose dream of becoming a People's Army could not be realised if all the eligible young men were taken by the regular forces. In the 'Night of the Long Knives' on 30 June 1934 the Army appeared to receive the assurance they sought that they and not the Party constituted the basis of the nation's organised armed strength. The SS squads which executed the brown-shirt leaders were provided with Reichswehr transport for the purpose.[6] Just over a month later on Hindenburg's death Hitler presented the army with the bill for his support in the shape of a demand that they should immediately swear a new oath of loyalty to him personally and not, as previously, to the constitution (p. 81).

But conscription could not be introduced clandestinely (although 280,000 men had been recruited by the spring of 1935). The generals wanted it announced in the autumn of 1934. When the AA objected that after the various excitements of the previous summer this would be unwise provocation of French and British susceptibilities, they reluctantly agreed to wait until the following spring. The same story was repeated in 1936. The Rhineland demilitarised zone which had been set up at Versailles and was an integral feature of the 1925 Locarno Treaties made the Ruhr vulnerable to a French attack. Consequently the heavy arms needed by the latest programme could not be safely manufactured there until the Reichswehr had reoccupied the area, which it accordingly proceeded to do.

In all these three cases the timetable was set by the generals rather than by Hitler. What they failed to appreciate adequately was that their insistence on achieving their immediate aims by unilateral action without any attempt at negotiation was self-defeating. It alarmed those countries which thought that the new arms might be turned against them and set off an accelerating race. This lengthened the period during which Germany was at risk; the more she attempted to hurry, the further did the safety-line recede. To provide the money for the new weapons without precipitating either inflation or civilian shortages was in any case something of a miracle, owing much to Dr Schacht. In 1936 when demand threatened to outrun supply, Hitler instituted the Four Year Plan to increase output. But modern arms grow obsolete quickly. The fact that France and Britain started on the race after Germany gave them an advantage (important in the case of the Spitfire). Before long she might have to choose between using her weapons even though she had still not gained an adequate margin of advantage and finding the finance for a further programme.

Not surprisingly in these circumstances, priorities for the allocation of armaments between the three services had by the autumn of 1937 become keenly contested and on 5 November a meeting was held at Blomberg's request under Hitler's chairmanship to sort the tangle out.[7] It was also attended by Göring (head both of the Air Force and of the Four Year Plan), by Fritsch, Admiral Raeder and Foreign Minister von Neurath. Unexpectedly, it turned into a two-hour disquisition by Hitler on his future plans. He made it clear that he intended to act, if opportunity arose, without waiting for Germany to get a margin of advantage which would assure victory. He also spoke for the first recorded time as though counting Britain among Germany's enemies and as though the prospect did not unduly alarm him.

Such a scenario was wholly out of keeping with the thinking of his hearers, who were aghast at the risks which they considered it to involve. They criticised a number of his assumptions both at the meeting and afterwards. He drew the conclusion that they must be replaced by more compliant characters. Within three months he was given an opportunity to achieve this when it came to light that Blomberg had married an ex-prostitute and the SD produced evidence which they knew related to a Captain von Frisch in order to discredit General von Fritsch as a homosexual. Before the latter villainy could be exposed, Hitler had taken over Blomberg's post as War Minister himself, converting parts of the Ministry into an *Oberkommando der Wehrmacht*, OKW (a sort of Ministry of Defence) under Keitel (p. 143), while Fritsch was succeeded not by Beck but by the more pliable von Brauchitsch. The changing of the guard was completed with the replacement of von Neurath by von

Ribbentrop. The services and the AA thus received heads who could be counted on not to withstand Hitler. Any challenge from those quarters would henceforward have to come from people in subordinate positions. How far such challenges developed will be described in the case-histories of Stauffenberg, Beck and Weizsäcker.

Most officers knew little about the conflict described in the last six paragraphs. They were on the whole well-satisfied with the trend of events. The hated Versailles restrictions were being removed, apparently without incurring damaging repercussions. They were getting promotion; the 44 general of 1932 had become 261 by the end of 1938.[8] The Army had recovered its honoured position on the national stage, symbolised by the reappearance of pre-1914 flags and badges. They were also extremely busy organising a rapid and extensive expansion which was handled with characteristic German technical efficiency. Doubts had begun to form in the minds of a very few when Hitler included in the victims of 30 June one or two people whom he thought capable of leading a right-wing move against him, including Generals von Schleicher and von Bredow. A rather larger number felt indignant at the treatment of Fritsch in 1938 and would have pressed for some sort of open recantation by Hitler if attention had not been distracted at the crucial moment by the absorption of Austria. More will be said later about the misgivings aroused by the plans to attack Czechoslovakia and Western Europe; they constituted the first crisis of confidence between Hitler and the Army. But doubts were temporarily stilled by the successes at Munich, in Poland, in Scandinavia and in France. Recovery of the Corridor had been for so long a deep German desire that nobody objected to an operation designed to achieve it (especially after the Russo-German pact). By 1941 confidence was so high and belief in Soviet Army weakness so strong that nobody sought to stop Hitler from attacking Russia. In talking to senior generals four days after coming to power, he had mentioned as a desirable aim after rearmament the conquest of living-space in the east and its ruthless Germanisation.[9] In a paper of August 1936 on the Four Year Plan he ordered the *Wehrmacht* to be ready for an offensive war in 1940.[10] On neither occasion was any dissent expressed.

After the outbreak of war a certain number of officers were outraged by the action taken by the SS to eliminate the upper classes and Jews in Poland. General Blaskowitz, the Commander of the Army of Occupation, protested to Brauchitsch but was told that 'the necessary performance of *volkpolitisch* tasks in accordance with the Führer's orders must inevitably lead to unusually harsh measures against the Polish population'.[11] Similar cruelties in Russia called forth similar protests from von Tresckow and others (p. 126) but received similar answers; other German commanders, including people like Hoepner and von Stülpnagel who were to die for their share in the conspiracy, acquiesced in face of the argument that this was no ordinary war but a struggle between two creeds. Mass executions by Army units were explained away by the need for security against Russian partisans and the excuse that the alternative to death by shooting could only be death by starvation and disease. A few other officers failed to gain any hearing for the argument that Germany should be trying to win the support of the Russian masses against their Communist overlords and that the measures were mistaken because they were doing the opposite. From 1942 onwards an increasing number of officers were criticising among themselves Hitler's general conduct of the war. But the extent of Army disaffection should not be overestimated. There were some 2000 generals in 1944;[12] only twenty-two of them lost their lives for their part in the conspiracy, although a number more were involved to less incriminating extents.[13] The officer corps, limited to 4000 by the Treaty of Versailles, reached a peak of nearly 250,000 in September 1943.[14] Many of the newcomers had been Party Members, Storm Troopers or Hitler Youth; by no means all had lost their enthusiasm. In the early summer of 1943 Manstein rebuffed an appeal to join in the conspiracy by saying that it would split the Army as the young officers were as loyal to Hitler as ever.[15] (See also Chapter V.)

Hitler once said that he had a Prussian Army, an imperial Navy, and a national-socialist Air Force. The only sailor to be seriously involved in the conspiracy besides Canaris and Berthold von Stauffenberg was Lieutenant Commander Kranzfelder of Naval Headquarters Berlin. General of the Air Force Udet was said to have died in an air crash in November 1941 and Colonel Molders actually did so when on the way to Udet's funeral but the stories that they were eliminated because they had lost faith in Hitler derive from the fertile brains of the emigré playwright Carl Zuckmayer (*Der Teufels General*) and the staff of the British propaganda radio station *Gustav Siegfried Eins*.[16]

(c) The *obere Mittelstand*

The Prussian civil service, which set the pattern for the rest of the Reich, had always allowed officials to take sides more openly in politics than is the case in Britain; in this respect it more resembled the United States. Hence no particular surprise was caused by 400 of the 1600 comprising the upper ranks being removed on political or racial grounds between 1933 and 1937. A law, misleadingly described as providing for the 're-establishment of a career civil service', promulgated in April 1933, regularised a process where the SA had been intervening arbitrarily. The Party, represented by the Office of the Führer's Deputy (in effect, Bormann) thereafter made persistent efforts to infiltrate convinced Nazis into administrative posts and give them priority in promotion.[17] On the whole their efforts succeeded, creating bitterness and disillusion among the non-Nazis. By 1939 20 per cent of *Beamte* were Party Members; four-fifths of them had joined since January 1933 but later on admission to the Party was barred. At the end of the war 40 per cent of *Beamte* in Bavaria were Party Members.

To judge by a sample of 5250, about 40 per cent of senior SS officers belonged to professions which placed them in the *obere Mittelstand*. Jurists were over-represented, although what many of them joined was the *Allegemeine* SS where they could continue to hold their normal jobs. Of 7758 university teachers in 1932, 1145 had been dismissed by 1934. At Hamburg 136 out of 212 professors were Party Members, the percentage in the various faculties being: Philosophy 41, Mathematics and Natural Science 57, Law 66 and Medicine 80. (Many were however said to wear their Party badges as 'safety pins'.) At Tübingen only 20 per cent of the professors are known to have been non-members. All professional associations outside the government service were Nazified; nobody could work in the relevant field unless he or she belonged to the appropriate body, and could not hope for advancement if they tried to remain mere passengers. Even intellectuals have to live and for many it was a question of earning an income in the least objectionable way; people whose records were otherwise good were to be found writing for *Das Reich*, Goebbels's highbrow weekly, or scripting films anonymously.

Hitler justified his behaviour in June 1934 by emphasising the threat to order and morality which had been constituted by an 'unruly, degenerate element' and openly admitted that he had by-passed the ordinary processes of law. 'In this hour I was responsible for the fate of the German people and thereby became the supreme judge of the German people.' The majority of the population seem to have hailed this action with relief, as the re-imposition of law, order and morality, or in other words as the end of the period of arbitrary violence.[18] A stop was also thereby put to the talk which had been current of a second and socially radical revolution. But some more thoughtful officials and soldiers were concerned at the departure which was involved from the rule of law. Experience was however to show how easy it was by the use of decrees to codify oppression and throw a cloak of legality over conduct which would normally be regarded as a violation of human rights. 'The Nazi Party's obsession with giving all internal measures the semblance of legality can be interpreted not as propaganda but as a touchy gesture of self-justification towards an opposition which allegedly did not exist.'[19] Gradually the lesson was borne in on a few perceptive spirits that more was required than the rule of law.

All bureaucratic organisations are prone to regard outdoing rivals as more important than serving the common good. But the Third Reich was unusually susceptible to this weakness. To begin with, Hitler had a liking for disposing of a problem by setting up a new body to deal with it, yet leaving in existence any which were supposed to be doing so already. Before long he had 42 separate executive bodies responsible directly to him and completely failed to co-ordinate them. Secondly totalitarianism led to many measures of centralisation at the expense of *Land* and local governments but once again these governments were neither wound up nor rationalised. It was calculated in 1942 that there were approximately 45 official bodies active at the bottom level of administration, while 22 had to be consulted to build a block of workers' flats.[20] Finally, although the Party never fulfilled its original dream of taking over the government of the country, it retained its own organisations for dealing with almost every aspect of life. Thus on every hand there were liable to be two or more bodies claiming a voice and a rivalry between central and local, official and Party, old Government or new creation. It is hardly surprising that administrators got frustrated or resorted to irregular and even corrupt procedures for getting their way. To avoid criticising other parts of the machine was impossible and to avoid criticising the system as a whole became difficult.

But in high Party circles it was fashionable to speak deprecatingly of administrators. On 26 April 1942 Goebbels wrote in his Diary that 'just as one cannot expect a cow to lay eggs, so one cannot expect a bureaucrat to look after the interests of the state properly.' On the same day Hitler convened the Reichstag for one of its rare meetings in order to demand unlimited power to dismiss or punish as he thought fit any German who was found lacking in ardour or honesty. His impatience was particularly directed against the scruples and methodical procedures of officials, especially judges. He thereby offended – and meant to offend – many members of the *obere Mittelstand* who were beginning to have serious doubts as to the wisdom of his leadership.[21] He had once before dilated on them, in talking to journalists in November 1938.[22] 'If I look at the intellectual elements of our society, I think what a pity it is that they are needed. Otherwise one day one might, well I don't know, exterminate them or something like that' (at this point the record interpolates 'commotion'!) 'But unfortunately they are needed.' The National Socialist movement never succeeded in producing from its own ranks all the experts necessary to a modern society; the deficiencies had to be made good by believers with reservations or by opportunists. The winter of 1942–3 has been convincingly seen as the date at which many of these half-hearts turned against the régime.[23]

(d) Finance, trade and industry

After the NSDAP's accession to power, the attitude of businessmen towards it naturally grew less reserved; the owners and managers of money are always reluctant to quarrel with the holders of political power for fear of being expropriated. Their hankering after a secure and predictable future causes them to welcome any régime which looks likely to keep order and remain in office. Those in Germany had plenty to do in obtaining and fulfilling the government contracts which soon began to multiply.

Hitler's ideas about economics were based on common sense rather than theory.[24] He came to power without any clear-cut plans for restoring confidence and employment. But his Government gave the impression of being resourceful and what was needed at that juncture was unorthodoxy, especially after a three-year dose of the orthodox remedy of deflation. The one solution which Hitler did propound was the gaining of living-space. It is in fact doubtful whether the realisation of that dream would not have done more harm than good.[25] But the rearmament which was seen as an essential preliminary was exactly what the situation required, a large-scale programme of government-initiated investment, supplemented as it was by expenditure on things like roads and housing.

There was of course a danger that the large volume of extra money would result in the great German bugbear of inflation. The experts insisted that, to prevent this, the public must be made to tighten its belt. But Hitler was also obsessed by what has been called 'the 1918 syndrome' – the belief that too much had been asked of the ordinary man in that year and that a comparable demand must never be repeated. The German people should not be confronted again by the choice which Göring professed to offer them – they should have *both* guns *and* butter. One way of achieving this might have been to stretch the time taken in rearming. But this was precluded by the need for Germany to gain a lead over potential enemies before they had time to take counter-measures. It was only when the attack on Russia failed to produce a lightning victory that this scheme to get the best of both worlds broke down. But until its practicability had been demonstrated between 1939 and 1941, German business circles were loud in their forecasts of doom. The British Government have been criticised for expecting a German economic collapse which did not happen. But in doing so they were only going by what their economic intelligence staff were told by alarmed German tycoons. In fact Germany went to war with her stocks of raw materials so low that the British Ministry of Economic Warfare could not believe the figures which they obtained and doubled them![26]

One thing which Hitler did insist on was that economics must be subordinate to politics. In his memorandum of August 1936 on the Four Year Plan he wrote that

> it is for the Economics Ministry to state the requirements of the national economy and for private enterprise to meet them. If private enterprise finds itself unable to do so, the NS State will be able to accomplish the task by its own efforts.[27]

This was a concealed way of saying that the goods needed to make possible the achievement of NS political ends must be forthcoming, regardless of short-term calculations of profit-and-loss. It overlooked the fact that behind monetary restraints lie material ones, which are not so easily surmounted. But provided industrialists were prepared to accept this basic principle, Hitler was quite prepared to let them run their own shows in a system of organised capitalism. The chemical industry, by grasping the opportunity, prospered greatly; the Four Year Plan was managed by men from IG Farben rather than by Göring, its nominal head.[28] Iron and steel tried to make conditions and found themselves side-tracked in favour of the state-run Salzgitter complex. The management of the coal mines, remembering the years of surplus output before 1934, were reluctant to invest in an industry which was working at a loss and sought to avoid increasing capacity, instead of devising ways of overcoming obstacles. The non-expert commissioners put in over their heads could not see how to do what they did see needed to be done. As German coal was the primary source of German and West European energy, the failure to increase output significantly after 1937 reduced the ability to wage war.

Smaller firms were bullied into compliance and gained considerably less than they had expected.[29] By 1938–9 the official Trustee of Labour had been empowered to fix wage rates and conditions of work, while hiring and firing could only be done through the Labour Exchanges. The manpower shortage which developed after 1936 gave skilled workers plenty of scope for bargaining about fringe benefits. Employers were provided with raw materials, told what to use them for and given fixed prices for purchases and sales. The need to make the most of Germany's resources meant that the waste involved in small-scale competition could not be afforded.

The most prominent dissenter in the business world was Dr Schacht who, having helped to undermine the Republic by resigning as President of the Reichsbank in 1930 and having helped Hitler to finance rearmament by resuming the post in 1933 and becoming Minister of Economics in 1934, resigned again from the latter post in 1937 rather than support any longer what he described (after the war) as a policy of 'reckless expenditure, predatory exploitation of the national resources, uneconomic production, excessive rearmament and disregard of the interests and feelings of Germany's neighbours'.[30] He took a considerable part in the plans for a coup in 1938 and was rewarded by being dismissed from the Reichsbank in 1939. But his previous record made him suspect to most other conspirators and his name did not occur on the list of contemplated Cabinet appointments in 1944. He was however arrested and included in the party of distinguished prisoners which ended up in the south Tyrol in April 1945.

The most consistent industrial dissenter was Robert Bosch of the Stuttgart electrical firm, who financed Goerdeler from 1936 to 1939 and, with his right-hand man Hans Walz, provided employment for a number of people dismissed from other firms on account of their race or political opinions, besides helping many Jews to leave Germany.[31] Similar help was given by Hermann Abs of the Deutsche Bank who took under his wing a number of Jewish finance houses which would otherwise have been confiscated or forced out of business. Both Abs and Karl Blessing of the Reichsbank, who were to be prominent in the Federal Republic, maintained a discreet contact with Helmuth von Moltke. Paul Reusch, manager of the Gutehoffnungshütte steel concern and a leader of Ruhr opinion, 'gravitated to the fringe of Goerdeler's movement' in the closing years of the war. None of these men suffered any serious inconvenience as a result of their activities. (See also case-history of Goerdeler.)

(e) The Evangelical Churches

Many German Protestants regarded Hitler's arrival in power as a heaven-sent opportunity to apply to their Churches that consolidation of authority (*Gleichschaltung*) which was being introduced into other walks of life, and thus realise the long-held dream of a single united German Church, headed by a Reich Bishop. Others however wanted not merely to unite the Churches but to revise their creeds so as to bring them into line with National Socialism. A 'German Faith Movement' was founded in June 1932 by a Berlin pastor, Joachim Hossenfelder, who described its members as 'The Storm Troops of Christ'[32] and demanded the application of the Aryan principle to the Churches as a whole. It held its first nation-wide conference on 3–4 April 1933, where it called for the application of the leadership principle to church government, symbolised by the appointment of a Reich Bishop. In reply a group of middle-aged pastors, including Niemöller and Bonhoeffer, formed themselves into a 'Young Reformers' Movement'. While they agreed that the Churches needed reform and greater unity, they insisted that change must come from within and not be imposed from without. While describing National Socialism as 'God's gift to the German people', they wanted the Churches to remain self-governing. Under the influence of Barth, they insisted that the only evidence of God was to be found in scripture and not also in creation or such concepts as 'race', 'nation' and 'honour'.

The controversy was first fought out over the choice of a Reich Bishop. The German Christian candidate, supported by Hitler, was an ex-army chaplain called Ludwig Müller, who had attracted attention by converting General von Blomberg to National Socialism. By a narrow margin the opposition succeeded in getting a more praiseworthy character appointed who however proved too gentle to hold the job down. At elections in July 1933 the German Christians received the full support of the Party and, in an eve-of-the-poll broadcast, Hitler called for votes to go to them with the result that they won easily. Müller was duly elected head of the Old Prussian Church and confirmed as Reich Bishop by a synod held at Wittenberg in September. But almost simultaneously a Pastors' Emergency League was inaugurated with the object of helping anyone persecuted in contravention of the Christian faith, as set out in the scriptures and in the Reformation Confessions which interpreted them.

A prime purpose of the League was to oppose the exclusion from the Churches of all non-Aryan pastors and all Aryan ones with non-Aryan wives. By mid-January 1934 over 7000 pastors (out of a total of over 18,000) had joined the League.[33] Yet within a month of its formation Niemöller and four other Berlin pastors who had played a large part in initiating it sent Hitler a telegram congratulating him on his 'manly act to preserve Germany's honour by leaving the League of Nations'. They wanted to make clear that they accepted his leadership in other walks of life provided he did not try to lead the Churches in what they considered to be a wrong direction.

Immediately after a plebiscite had given Hitler overwhelming support for his defiance of the international order, the Gau Headman of the Berlin German Christians, at a mass meeting in the Sportpalast, called for the creation of a *Volkskirche* which would eliminate all Jewish elements in its faith. His contention that Christianity must be based on what Jesus himself said would not have been much out of line with the Barthian theology had he not added that this coincided exactly with National Socialism. He went on to demand 'liberation from the Old Testament with its Jewish money morality and the elimination of the Rabbi Paul with his inferiority complex.' Such outspokenness scandalised not only the Pastors' League but the members of the South German Churches (Hanover, Bavaria and Württemberg) who had accepted their Bishops' advice not to join it and who were therefore known as the 'intact' churches. So much pressure was brought to bear on Müller that he found it expedient to disown what had been said and make Hossenfelder resign. The episode seemed to show that the Evangelical Churches could get their way when, but only when, they stood together.

Unfortunately this newly-found harmony was shattered again in January 1934 at a meeting between Hitler and Church leaders when Niemöller allowed himself to be outwitted by Göring and was accused by his companions of having strengthened Müller's position (p. 213). He was suspended from office and in February the Westphalian Provincial Synod was dissolved by the Gestapo. Two thousand pastors left the League. But as was to happen more than once, the official Church leaders overplayed their hands by issuing orders absorbing the Württemberg Church into the National one. The result was a meeting at Ulm on 22 April attended by 5000 representatives of almost all the Protestant Churches (Calvinist as well as Lutheran) at which they claimed to be in the eyes of Christendom the lawful Church in Germany. It was from this meeting that the Confessing Church (a body containing both pastors and laymen) may be said to have originated. It owed its name to the role it attributed to the Reformation Confessions in interpreting scripture and one of the first acts of the Council of Brethren (*Brüderrat*) set up to run it was to call a Synod to Barmen in May at which the project of a 'modern' Confession was finally realised.

The essence of the Barmen Declaration[34] (for which Barth was principally responsible) was that Jesus, as attested in scripture, is the ultimate source of authority and alone reveals the nature of God. This principle cut right across all claims that God revealed himself anywhere else, in creation, in history, in nation or race, not to mention Adolf Hitler. The Declaration went on to assert 'God's mighty claim upon the whole life of Christians', while at the same time denying the right of any state authority to direct them in matters of faith. It thus implicitly rejected the claims of the Party to total control and those of the Führer to overall leadership.

The Barmen Declaration was a resounding affirmation of principle. But its practical effect on the Church's struggle with Nazism is hard to measure. Some German churchmen who were not German Christians challenged the right of the Synod to promulgate it; some eminent German theologians disputed its contents. In this they could find support outside Germany where plenty of people, while ready to agree that Hitler did not reveal the nature of God, were not ready to say that such revelation could be found only in the Bible. In a book published in the year of Barmen, Archbishop Temple, in spite of his sympathy with those opposed to Hitler, indirectly referred to the

Barthian theology as 'heresy'.[35] The Declaration did nothing to unite the Evangelical Churches inside Germany or to unite the 'hard core' of the Confessing Church with Protestants outside Germany. Moreover it did nothing to prevent the German Government from disregarding its ban and continuing to intervene in Church affairs.

The government machinery for dealing with the Churches took a succession of forms, as each proved unable to resolve the dispute. The tendency was for churchmen to be replaced by officials. In 1935 Müller gave way to a new Department of Church Affairs under Hanns Kerrl whose previous field had been Town and Country Planning. He was handicapped by the jealousy of the Party which thought that his job should have been theirs and by the time he died in 1941 had little authority left. The power of initiative passed to Dr Werner, a German Christian lawyer who sought to enforce the state's will by a variety of unobtrusive legal measures, such as requiring a Dortmund pastor who supported the Confessing Church to live in east Germany.[36] Recalcitrant pastors were deprived of position, pay and access to the laity. The colleges which had been improvised to train new blood were closed down. Barth was forced in 1935 to retreat from his Bonn chair to the security of Basel. As Germany's armed strength grew and Hitler's hope of an English alliance was replaced by contempt (p. 31), he became less worried about alienating foreign opinion. Niemöller's arrest in 1937 was a direct challenge to his oecumenical supporters. The prospect for the Confessing Church was one of continual uphill struggle. The practical help which the Pastors' League continued to give became more important than questions of doctrine. By 1937 700 pastors were in custody, one of whom died after eighteen months. Many decided reluctantly to conform rather than join in action to overthrow the régime. By 1938 membership of the League had sunk to 3933.[37]

The intense concern of the Barthians with man's duty to God had been apt to distract attention from man's duty to his neighbours. Their insistence on making the Bible the sole source of authority impeded them from invoking ideas which were not specifically Christian but came from the main stream of European liberal thought such as the rights of man, the brotherhood of men and the freedom of the individual. Accepting the Bible as the voice of God left open the question whether the God speaking in it was he of the Sermon on the Mount or the angry God implied in the Pauline doctrine of the Atonement – and it was the German Christians, not the Barthians, who wanted to get rid of Paul. To some of those abroad who were otherwise inclined to sympathise, the Confessing Church seemed unduly preoccupied with the treatment of Jewish converts to Christianity, instead of with the whole Nazi challenge to humanity and justice. Only gradually as the Third Reich progressed did the view spread in Germany that the role of the Churches as guardians of morality could not be confined to ecclesiastical affairs, that fulfilment of duty towards God could not be complete unless it also found expression in concern for the common man.

Bishop Wurm of Württemberg had sought as early as March 1933 to protest against the Jewish policy but had got no support from his fellow churchmen.[38] In May 1936 the Provisional Administration of the Confessing Church drew up a paper which said that incitement to hate Jews was contrary to the Christian commandment to love one another, while concentration camps and the extra-legal activities of the Gestapo were an affront to the Christian conscience. The document was sent to Hitler privately in the hope that he would pay more attention if he had not been criticised openly. When he paid no attention at all, certain restive spirits leaked it to the foreign press. One was executed as a result, the remainder were arrested and the leadership was forced to disown what had been said.

In 1941 Wurm, while admitting that Luther's anger was justified against Jews who rejected the Gospel, reminded the Church Chancellery that in the teaching of the Church 'there is neither Greek nor Jew' (Colossians III 11). He sent a series of messages to the authorities emphasising the desire of the Churches to support the war effort but asking in return that the measures against them (often taken under the pretext of wartime needs) be suspended.[39] In July 1943 he wrote to Hitler, in a letter obtained and broadcast by the BBC Norwegian Service, appealing for an end to the persecution and destruction being carried on, without judicial verdict and against the commandment of God, in the camps and subjugated nations. His efforts to maintain a conciliatory attitude without disowning essentials gradually won him wide respect, especially when the growing prospect of defeat suggested that German Protestants might soon badly need someone who was skilled in reconciling.

In October 1943 the Prussian Confessional Synod said, in a pastoral letter, that 'to annihilate people, simply because they are old or mentally sick . . . or belong to an alien race is not a use of coercive power granted to authority. All men's lives are God's alone.'[40] This and the paper of 1936 were virtually the only formal condemnations of the practical consequences flowing from the Aryan doctrine which were issued by the Evangelical Churches during the Third Reich. The resistance of those Churches has been described as 'reluctant'.[41] The moving spirits among them denied any claim to be an opposition at all. Not only did they accept the policy of the state in most respects and feel no call to overthrow it. All they were seeking to do was in the first place to make their own beliefs plain and then persuade the government to bring about changes in such parts of its policy as were inconsistent with those beliefs. They did not consider themselves blameworthy if the leadership chose to take offence. Such an attitude was naive. National Socialism and Christianity were only compatible if both were watered down. But not only was practical experience necessary before this became clear. The whole tradition of German Protestantism made it hard for Church members to conceive that a head-on collision with the state was possible. And there was understandable concern about the consequences for personal religious life and for the buildings and funds facilitating that life if such a collision were provoked. (See also case-histories of Niemöller and Bonhoeffer.)

(f) The Roman Catholic Church

Hitler's accession to power provided the opportunity for which Cardinal Pacelli had been waiting. The subordination of the state governments (and particularly Prussia's) to the Reich removed the obstacle which had been preventing the negotiation of a satisfactory Concordat at national level. The new leader for his part realised that he could never achieve his aim of uniting the German people behind him as long as the Catholic hierarchy maintained its ban on Catholics becoming Party Members (p. 18). He could not achieve his parallel aim of abolishing the parliamentary and party system without getting the Catholic Centre Party to vote in the Reichstag for the law enabling him to disregard that system, since such a law required a two-thirds majority whereas the NSDAP by themselves never even achieved an ordinary one. His somewhat insecure standing in the world would be considerably improved if he could induce the Vatican to treat his Government as trustworthy enough to negotiate with. He sought to obtain for Germany a ban similar to the one which the 1929 Lateran Treaty had placed on political activity in Italy by the clergy and church organisations. It did not escape the notice of the Pope and of his Secretary of State that Hitler was the only European head of state who had openly described Bolshevism as a menace. They saw considerable advantage in getting the rights of the Church in Germany set down in a black-and-white agreement with the Reich. The Nazis for their part seemed ready to promise the Church a reasonable degree of freedom, including the maintenance of Catholic schools in places where enough parents showed a desire for them.

When Hitler pressed for action by sending his Vice-Chancellor von Papen to Rome, along with the Centre leader Kaas, Pacelli showed such readiness to co-operate that even Holy Week did not hold up the negotiations. The German bishops were not consulted until a late stage but when they were, only Cardinal Schulte of Cologne and von Preysing of Eichstadt suggested that the Vatican might be misjudging the situation. The Chairman of the Bishops' Conference, Cardinal Bertram of Breslau, had grown up during Bismarck's *Kulturkampf* and wanted to avoid repeating that experience; Hitler professed an identical desire to Bishop Berning of Osnabruck.[42] The Concordat was not merely signed on 20 July, a week after the Centre and Bavarian People's Parties, along with the other German Parties, had been abolished. It was signed before a number of details, notably the rights of the various Catholic organisations, had been properly defined. While there were good, although not necessarily decisive, arguments for making a comprehensive agreement, there was little to be said for leaving details to chance.[43] Kaas never went back to Germany.

It soon became evident that, when the Nazis spoke of allowing freedom to the Church, they meant allowing it to go on conducting services and administering the sacraments; any attempt by it to influence the character of German society was obstructed in innumerable ways. The imprecisions in the Concordat were exploited to close down all Catholic organisations whose activities were not strictly religious. The instruments by which the régime controlled the press (the Chamber of Culture and the Editors' Law) were soon used to wind up all Catholic daily papers and make periodicals confine themselves to purely religious topics. (After war began, even these were constricted by paper rationing.) Processions were banned or limited (with the result that such as did occur acquired political significance). Schools attached to convents were closed and nuns teaching in state schools were dismissed. In 1935 denominational schools began to be closed down in Munich and else-where on the pretext that (intimidated) parents had ceased to desire them; comprehensive schools were opened instead. Catholic youth organisations were harassed by various means; membership of them was made incompatible with that of the Hitler Youth. Although they fought back at all levels, and although the Pope assured them at Easter 1934 that 'your cause is our cause',[44] they gradually lost ground and between 1936 and 1939 were closed down on a variety of pretexts. In 1940 able-bodied men were forbidden to enter monasteries.[45]

The Church was punctilious in calling attention to each violation of the Concordat and in the earlier years the régime more than once climbed down. In Advent 1933 a series of sermons by Cardinal Faulhaber of Munich attracted much attention; they were devoted to defending the Old Testament against its German Christian critics and to contradicting Party views on race. When in January 1934 Rosenberg was made the Führer's Delegate for supervising the entire spiritual and ideological schooling and education of the NSDAP (a pretentious title which carried little power), the Vatican replied by putting his *Myth of the Twentieth Century* on the Index. Hitler was in no position to complain because in order to avoid trouble he had always denied that the book had any official status. In March 1937 the Papal Encyclical 'With burning anxiety' (*Mit brennender Sorge*) was smuggled into and read from all the Catholic pulpits of Germany. It listed the points on which the Concordat had been violated and the teachings of the Church which were incompatible with the Party's ideology, ending with an appeal to Church members to remain faithful.[46] The government fought shy of abrogating the Concordat as the Catholic leaders half expected and as Nazi radicals advocated, but instead brought a series of much-publicised prosecutions against priests for currency and sexual offences. A counter-attack by the Cardinal Archbishop of Chicago precipitated an inflammatory speech by Goebbels. The situation was however defused by reminders from the Church that similar charges could be brought against many Party Members.

In 1941 came Bishop von Galen's attack on the euthanasia policy, which contrary to the general belief had little or no effect on its scale but merely led to it being carried out in places or by methods (such as undernourishment, hypothermia or excessive doses of permitted drugs) where it was less easily detected.[47] In the same year Gauleiter Wagner of Upper Bavaria, who was also Education Minister, raised a hornet's nest single-handed by decreeing that crucifixes were to be removed from schools and Nazi slogans substituted for prayers. Ordinary churchgoers hardly needed the encouragement which they got from their priests to create a situation in which hasty retreat became imperative. How could such a thing be allowed to happen, it was asked, in a country which had just gone to war with 'godless Russia'?

Undoubtedly the disposition to withstand the Third Reich was stronger among Catholics than Protestants in Germany.[48] There was no Catholic equivalent to the German Christians. Between 1939 and 1943 693 priests were condemned for 'oppositional activity' as compared with 175 pastors. Of 5500 clergy in Bavaria, only 25 had to undergo denazification after the war.[49] The only bishop in Germany to be expelled from his see was Michael Rackl of Eichstadt. In April 1940 Diego Orsenigo, the Papal Nuncio in Berlin, reported to the Vatican that

> some of the clergy have adopted an almost openly hostile attitude towards
> Germany at war to the extent of wanting a complete defeat. This attitude arouses
> not only the displeasure of the Government but gradually also that of the whole
> people . . . which makes me afraid that a painful reaction will one day follow.[50]

Three months later he reported disapprovingly that scarcely any Catholic priests, in contrast to Protestant pastors, had held a thanksgiving service for German victories.[51] On the other hand the Catholic Church at the end of the war produced nothing comparable to the Protestant Declaration of Guilt (p. 249).

Once the Vatican, with the concurrence of the Bishops, had decided to place relations with the régime on a legal basis, it felt constrained to honour the undertaking implicit in the Concordat that it would not seek to frustrate the political and social aims of the other signatory. It could merely defend itself against attempts by that signatory to frustrate its own aims. In such circumstances there could be no official Catholic *Widerstand* and those Catholics who did join in active *Widerstand* did not do so on the orders of their Bishops. The episcopate may never have deserted priests who got into trouble but it did not give them much active help.

Hitler and his henchmen were probably more frightened of the Catholic Church than its leaders realised, primarily because it was an international body with headquarters outside their control (although Hitler considered occupying the Vatican in July 1943)[52] and possessed time-honoured ways of exerting pressure such as interdict and excommunication. But a decision by the Pope to denounce the Concordat and exercise these weapons would have brought ruthless reprisals rather than a reversal of Nazi policy. A major consideration restraining the Pope and bishops was doubt as to how far their flock would stand up to the penalties of supporting them, just as the régime was alive to the danger of creating situations in which such support would be forthcoming. Many priests gave priority to enabling church members to carry on the exercise, and in particular the reception of the sacraments, by which alone they believed that souls could be saved. Moreover the Papacy had in the course of its long story outlasted many tyrannies. As a sympathetic observer wrote, 'They reckon in centuries and plan for eternity and this inevitably renders their policy inscrutable, confusing and on occasion reprehensible to practical and time-conditioned minds.'[53] Not much knowledge of history was needed to generate the conviction that people who behaved like the Nazis would last for a good deal less than a thousand years.

In the meantime however two things might happen which could not be dismissed as of merely short-term importance. One was that leaving the task of overthrowing Hitler to others might in the context of 1941–5 mean abandoning Eastern Europe to Communism, a creed little better in Catholic eyes than Nazism and more likely to endure. But that need not happen if the Western Allies would make a compromise peace with a regenerated Germany and that for the rest of the war was a major Vatican objective. They hoped to get a chance of acting as mediators between Germany and the West, as the Pope had, to the SD's knowledge, shown himself willing to do in 1939–40. The other development was that a number of people would die on battlefields or in murder camps whose lives might be saved if the Church put all its resources into rescuing them. If in the process some Catholics might have been deprived for a time of the consolations of their religion, would that have been an unreasonable sacrifice to ask of them in the name of their fellow human beings? Even if rescue had proved impossible, would not the Church's reputation at the bar of history have been enhanced if the effort had been made? Responsibility here may ultimately have rested with the Vatican, but it received little encouragement to speak out unmistakably from the German Bishops. This was an outstanding instance of the perennial question as to how far Christians, whether as individuals or Churches, can be expected to live up to their founder's gospel of self-sacrifice and how far practical prudence is bound to combine with human frailty in inducing them to come to terms with the world. (See also the case-histories of von Preysing and Lichtenberg.)

(g) The *untere Mittelstand*

On arrival in power the Party gave the lower-middle classes, as represented by the Storm Troops, a free run of three to six months. Exploiting the position which Göring created by using them as auxiliary police in Prussia, they polished off a number of scores. This was the period of the first attempt to boycott Jewish shops and chain-stores. It was also the time when books were burnt.

Thereafter however, until the closing months of the war, discipline was more or less re-established. The 'Night of the Long Knives' was a grim warning against attempts by the tail to wag the dog. In compensation, jobs were found for a number of the boys. By 1935 over 3000 low-ranking civil service posts had been taken over by Party Members under the regulations for preferential appointment (p. 33); only 369 of these had been unemployed, the rest merely changed jobs. At this time, only 711 'old fighters' were still unemployed. Between 1933 and 1942 the total number of *Beamte* rose from 750,000 to

1,290,000 and of employees from 200,000 to 725,000. Most of these posts were in communes and therefore at a fairly low level.[54] The sample already mentioned (p. 33) suggested that 52 per cent of the SS leadership came from the *untere Mittelstand*.[55]

A steady barrage of propaganda was kept up about the importance of the small man. But the reality was less satisfactory to him. Minor officials and the lower grades of teacher felt their position slipping; their real income is said to have fallen by 15 per cent between 1933 and 1937 and nothing was done until the latter year to restore the cuts made by Brüning.[56] Small manufacturers, retailers and dealers got few favours because the need for speedy rearmament and for providing butter as well as guns put a premium on efficiency and small uneconomic units could not be encouraged. Once war began they came under a growing threat of being closed down so as to provide directly or indirectly more manpower for the forces (although even then they would have been able to get alternative, if more subordinate, employment quite easily).

Nor did high prestige make up for hard work and low pay. On the contrary, the Party became increasingly unpopular while the jobs which it was called on to do were humdrum, if not thankless. In the war Bormann and Ley made the mistake of insisting that local Party leaders should take over from the pastors the task of breaking the news to families who lost relatives at the front. This led to the comment that all the Party did was take money and bring bad news.[57] Corruption was widespread; as has been said, the jungle of Nazi administration made it hard to avoid. The people who had done so much to help Hitler to power felt that they were overworked and underappreciated. Small wonder if some of them began looking for ways of escape; the story went round of an advertisement offering a Gold Party Badge in exchange for a pair of seven-league boots![58] But on the whole the grumblers, instead of deciding that Germany was on the wrong track, took the line that the Nazi track was not being followed energetically enough. Between November 1945 and January 1948 the proportion of those in the US Zone who still thought Nazism 'a good thing badly carried out' was never to fall below 42 per cent.[59]

(h) Peasants

Two of the main peasant demands were quickly granted by the Nazis, who did not allow themselves to be inhibited by fears that actions might have repercussions. In September 1933 the Reich Food Estate (*Reichsnährstand*) was set up to control all food production and distribution, with power to regulate output, marketing and prices. The farmer was offered fixed prices for specified amounts; all imports were brought under control. In May 1933 a Law of Hereditary Entailment (*Erbhofgesetz*) had been published, which applied to all farms large enough to support a family without any need for further revenue (between 7.5 and 150 hectares). No such holding was to be sold without permission or sequestered for debt (which meant that it could not be mortgaged). The owner had to name one sole heir. The farm could not be partitioned nor could money be paid to anyone other than the heir. These requirements acted as deterrents to the contracting of debts. Over the next three years the farmers' share of the national income rose from 8.2 per cent to 9.7 per cent.[60]

In February 1933 Countess von Moltke wrote to her mother in South Africa that 'the whole village [of Kreisau] is for the Nazis because the price of pigs has risen.'[61] But in general peasant enthusiasm was limited. Interference with ancestral ways is seldom popular. Even in areas where primogeniture had been the rule, the introduction of legal restrictions on inheritance was resented as an infringement of private liberty, while the guaranteed prices tended to be accompanied by increasingly precise instructions as to what was to be grown where. The Party regarded agriculture as essential to the nation and were therefore prepared to foster it. But they also considered that the peasant had a national function which he must be made to fulfil. Relations were not improved when Hitler, in his determination to prevent inflation, refused to allow prices to rise, with the result that the farmers' share had by 1938 dropped back to 7.8 per cent. A variety of factors operated to withdraw labour from the land, a process intensified by war, so that the burden on the proprietor, and still more on his wife, grew (in 1933 half the agricultural work-force was female). There was a good deal of grumbling, particularly in Catholic areas. But farmers are notorious grumblers and Catholics were particularly afraid of Communism. The dissatisfaction did not prevent the 1942 harvest from being a record in some areas and the 1943 one from improving on it. The *Erbhofgesetz* regulations were less resented when it turned out that they were being applied elastically. From 1937 onwards, more and more foreign workers were brought in to help, despite 'racial dangers'.[62] The countryside was not in a state of suppressed mutiny, even if output was not as high as whole-hearted enthusiasm for the cause might have made it. One obstacle to stimulating keenness was that many peasants did not read, owned no radio and kept away from Party meetings, thus rendering themselves almost impervious to propaganda.[63] A frustrated Party official in Hesse wrote in 1943

> The peasant population knows precious little of what this war is about. It is quite likely – and this is even worse – that they do not *want* to know. Despite the efforts of the Party and its agencies, a large number of them just will not come out of their state of indifference.[64]

(See also case-history of Jägerstätter pp. 231–3.)

(i) Workers

At first sight the conditions of the working classes were getting worse between 1933 and 1939. National Socialism's success in solving the unemployment problem was only possible by maintaining a high rate of investment. To prevent the economy from overheating, wage levels had to be kept down. But the growing demand for labour made this increasingly difficult. In February 1938 a Brunswick firm complained that although they were paying 88 pfennig an hour when the legal minimum was 59, they were losing 5 to 7 workers a day to the Volkswagen works.[65] In June 1938 the 'Trustees of Labour' were empowered to fix maximum rates (so as to eliminate bonuses for overtime) and apply partial direction of labour. This was extended in February 1939 and in the following September made to cover conditions of work (so as to counteract fringe benefits). But restrictions on overtime and on bonuses proved unenforceable; in November 1939 they were virtually abandoned. Although Trade Unions had been replaced by the Labour Front which was supposed to be impartial between employers and employed, it found in practice that it could exert no influence unless on occasion it sided with the latter;[66] in any case its branches were often run by former trade unionists. By 1938 the standard of life, although not lavish, was as high as it had ever been. There was a minor boom in sales of consumer goods. It is better to be overworked than unemployed. Skilled workers could earn quite high incomes (and increasing numbers of unskilled workers were in the forces). With the economy expanding, chances of advancement for the individual were good. The 'Strength Through Joy' organisation pioneered new ways of enjoying leisure; in 1938 every third worker went on one of their trips.[67]

The result is that we are presented with two pictures of the working classes under Nazi rule. According to one, the régime never won the workers' hearts. They had borne the brunt of the SA oppression and memories of what had been done to the trade unions and left-wing parties were too vivid to fade. Only 40 per cent of the workers took part in the 1934 Works Council elections and though the figure rose in 1935, the numbers voting for the official candidates were so low that the results had to be faked. The event was never repeated. There is evidence of a certain amount of going slow and malingering and more probably occurred than is recorded because to be successful it had to be concealed.[68] Strikes are known to have taken place at the Blöhm and Voss shipyard in Hamburg and the Opel Factory near Frankfurt, but it is not clear what they achieved.

The alternative picture is one of working classes which were becoming reconciled to the régime, above all because it had removed the spectre of unemployment. Workers joined the Party in increasing numbers[69] and, in spite of enemy bombing, brought the production of arms to a peak in July 1944.[70] While much of the credit must go to Speer's management, he himself said that 'the Armament Miracle is mainly, and one can almost say entirely, due to the German worker.'[71] Absenteeism and go-slow are likely to have been caused as much by fatigue and deteriorating equipment as by ill-will; the figures for absenteeism due to sickness were much the same in 1938 as in 1929.[72] Good and skilled workers became too valuable for employers to acquiesce in their being persecuted by the police.

There is some truth in both pictures, with variations caused by date, area, type of factory and age.[73] Workers enjoyed the benefits which came to them but with misgiving out of fear that before long the progress would be obliterated by a second war. When that war arrived, fear of the Gestapo and (later) of the Russians combined with inherent patriotism and a tradition of discipline to keep most workers at their machines. Propaganda sustained a belief in Hitler, even if in nobody else. Fatigue is likely to make most people take the line of least resistance which, in the Germany of 1942–5, was to get through one's daily round as best one could, obeying rules so as to avoid trouble. The worse the strain got, the less likely a revolution became, especially since the coercive authorities grew tougher as the military situation grew worse. Loyalty to one's comrades on the production line, or to the foreigners and prisoners who were under one's supervision, or to the men at the front who were the people most likely to suffer the effects if weapons were lacking or defective, all helped to sustain effort. Trott spoke of 'the passivity of the workers'.[74] But there was a hard core who remained unreconciled and who did as much to put sand in the machine as they judged, not always correctly, to be safe. Among them Communists predominated.

Not that the Socialists were wholly passive. In the early years they formed between 10 and 20 per cent of those in concentration camps.[75] But they were quicker to realise the futility of traditional methods of resistance against the new Nazi ruthlessness, once the initial months of 1933 had been allowed, wisely or unwisely, to pass without mass protest:

> In the course of time and in the face of the consolidation of the régime, there was increasing realisation of the futility of traditional methods of anti-Nazi propaganda, in which in any case only a few could engage, and the disproportion between what could be achieved on the one hand and the dangers and sacrifices on the other. Even supposing that there had ever been a real prospect of overthrowing the régime by one's own efforts, which influential groups of the socialist emigration for a time tended to foster, this disappeared by 1936/7. Thereafter Socialists in Dortmund confined themselves to maintaining personal contact between like-minded people and political discussions in rigidly limited circles.[76]

It took the Communists rather longer to reach the same conclusions. At the outset their hostility to the Socialists made immediate common action out of the question, while their 300,000 members and 4.5–6 million voters were insufficient for mass action on their own. They had long been under police surveillance so that their leaders were quickly picked up; the entire central leadership in Berlin was arrested on 27 March 1933.[77] The close control which they had exercised over outlying branches made it easy for these to be tracked down: 100,000 of the Party members were calculated to have been rounded up at once.[78] Strategy was laid down by a body outside the country which had an imperfect idea of conditions inside it.

For two years the conviction lasted that Nazism was a transient phenomenon which would quickly provoke a counter-revolution. Successors to the arrested leaders emerged from the 100,000 active members left at liberty, only to be rounded up in turn; the area leadership in Hamburg had to be renewed seven times between spring and autumn 1933.[79] The average life of a cell before discovery was put at three months.[80] Of 383 persons arrested by the Bavarian Political Police in 1934 for attempted High Treason, 325 were Communist and only 31 Socialist.[81] Of the personal files held by the Düsseldorf Gestapo, 64 per cent belonged to the KPD and only 4 per cent to the SPD.[82] The Senior Land Court at Hamm in Westphalia had a rule that Communists were to be more harshly punished than Socialists.[83] The devotion which the Communists showed to their cause was matched by the ferocity with which they were persecuted. Their total loss of life during the Third Reich has been plausibly put at 20,000.[84] On the other hand a group whose number was somewhere between 50,000 and 80,000 joined the NSDAP or NSBO (some intending to carry on the good work from inside').[85]

By 1935 however demands for a change of policy were mounting inside Germany. The heavy losses were not being justified by results; it was not worthwhile incurring imprisonment or death merely to get a few hundred copies of a leaflet distributed. The outcome of the Röhm affair did not bear out the belief in a quick change of régime. But in the nature of Communism, changes in policy had to begin at the top. In 1934–5 the Soviet Union and Comintern gave up trying to achieve revolutions outside Russia in favour of building up as wide an anti-fascist coalition as possible. In October 1935 the Central Committee of the German Party met in Moscow (although, to avoid seeming to be under Russia's thumb, they pretended to have met in Brussels). Ulbricht and Pieck persuaded them to follow suit. They encouraged their members in Germany to infiltrate the Labour Front ('Trojan Horse'). They appealed to the exiled Socialist Committee in Prague to ally with them. They gave priority to survival over quick results. This meant abandoning for the time being any attempt to recruit a big enough membership to overthrow the régime.

These tactics however fell flat. The Socialist leaders could not quickly overcome personal animosities and suspected (rightly) that the ultimate Communist objective remained social revolution, which they were not inclined to assist, especially as they calculated that the more they worked with the left, the harder they would find it to work with the (on the whole more valuable) right. There was a suspicion that Communists might seek to weaken their rivals by betraying them to the police; it was certainly true that Communists, after being let out of prison, were carefully watched and in some cases only got out by promising to act as spies. (This cold-shouldering on principle did not prevent some mutual assistance on a personal level at the roots.) Managements usually knew which workers had Communist backgrounds and were thus enabled to look Trojan horses in the mouth, while the workers themselves preferred to win the respect of their fellows by steady dissent rather than by temporary conformism, which might involve them in charges of collaboration after the Nazis had disappeared.[86]

Communist centres were established in all the countries bordering Germany from which twelve 'instructors' paid monthly visits to exchange information;[87]

some of them were themselves caught in the course of time while after 1940 only tenuous contact with the outside world through Sweden remained possible. The number of trials for political offences in the Rhineland and Ruhr dropped from 126 in 1935 to 60 in 1936, 33 in 1937, 15 in 1938 and 9 in 1939.[88] Whereas 43 cases had been brought against Communist groups in the Munich Special Court in 1933, in 1936 there were none.[89] Whereas 2045 persons had been arrested in 1934 for distributing leaflets, only 540 were caught in 1935 and 267 in 1936.[90] Activity languished after the signing of the Russo-German Pact in 1939 but revived after the attack on Russia in 1941 (when the *Rote Kapelle* had its brief hour of success, see pp. 209–10). When the failure of the winter offensive in 1941 suggested that the turning-point of the war had been reached, the scale of activity rose further. Twelve Communist resistance groups have been identified as at work during the war; most only lasted for a year or so and brought about the execution of perhaps 1100 people.[91] The Communists expected that the Second War would end as the First had done, in disorder and revolution. They saw that their chances of taking charge during that revolution (as they were determined to do) would be much increased if they had an organisation already established. They argued further (as the men of 20 July were to do) that unless resistance had some achievement to show before military defeat arrived, harsh treatment by the victors would be inevitable;[92] 'hesitation meant collapse.'[93] Unfortunately their reading of the situation was too optimistic. How well by contrast the Socialists managed to survive is shown by the fact that within ten days of war ending, 125 SPD groups had emerged.[94]

The most significant of the minor socialist groups was called *Neu Beginnen*.[95] Walter Loewenheim founded it even before the *Machtergreifung* to analyse the reasons for Weimar's failure, with a view to persuading both Communists and Socialists how they should 'do different' next time. In August 1933 he published a manifesto in Prague under the pseudonym of '*Miles*'. In it he attributed the failure to the left's lack of unity, which had prevented the workers from dominating the republic. The first thing to be done in future was therefore to hold together in carrying through a social revolution. Nazism was portrayed as the beginning of an epoch of Fascist rule which might easily last for ten years and could only be overthrown in an economic or military crisis. Members of the group were drawn not merely from left-wing Socialists but also from Communists who were not prepared to follow Moscow blindly. *Neu Beginnen* regarded itself as an élite cadre and did not seek to become a mass movement. It engaged neither in propaganda nor in sabotage but in cautious planning in strict security; as a result it remained undisturbed for a considerable period. Loewenheim emigrated in 1935, despairing of achieving anything in a Nazi-ruled Germany, but the work was carried on for three years by Richard Löwenthal, Fritz Erler and Waldemar von Knoerringen, who in conjunction with two Socialists, Otto Braun and Hermann Brill, sought to establish a German Popular Front. Further arrests in the autumn of 1938 brought activity inside Germany virtually to an end. Löwenthal and von

Knoerringen went into exile where experience reinforced their distaste for Soviet methods already aroused by the Moscow Trials of 1936–7. They drew closer to two similarly-minded groups, the *Internationaler Sozialistischer Kampfbund* and the *Sozialistische Arbeiterpartei Deutschlands*, of which a prominent member was Willy Brandt. All these people were to have a considerable influence on the character of the SPD after 1945.

In 1940 Körner, Göring's Deputy for the Four Year Plan, called for 'clear chains of command, strictest authoritarian direction of the war economy, closest co-operation of all pertinent agencies and, on the part of the people, discipline and self-sacrificing labour.' In the spring of 1945 Wagenfuhr, Speer's deputy head planner, looking back wrote that 'notwithstanding the totalitarian varnish with which economic policy, especially in the field of industry, was coated, we can say that, of all Körner's demands, only the self-sacrificing labour of the people was secured.'[96] A recent historian has written that 'Summing up one can say that, in spite of all the sacrifices which were made, no form of *Widerstand* activity on the part of the workers can be detected which would have caused the system any real embarrassment.'[97] For all the millions of votes which they received in 1930–3, the Communists did not have the masses behind them, while the Socialists – probably wisely – were waiting for Hitler to dig his own grave.

(See also case-histories of Leuschner, Leber, Reichwein, Schulze-Boysen and Saefkow.)

(j) Women

The Nazi attitude to women centred round the birth-rate, which had dropped from 128 per 1000 in 1910 to 59 in 1933. The chief remedial measure introduced was a system of marriage loans supplemented by children's allowances. Divorce was made easier, in the belief that the chances of a childless woman becoming fertile would increase with a new partner. Abortion and contraception were frowned on, to the satisfaction of Catholics. The result was to bring the rate up to 73 in 1934 and 85 in 1939, but this still did not amount to a full reproduction rate, since the average number of children per family was decreasing.[98]

The policy was not primarily intended to reduce unemployment, although the régime maintained at first a republican law requiring married female civil servants to be dismissed. In fact the number of women at work rose slightly between 1933 and 1936 and thereafter, as full employment was reached, more steeply.[99] In 1939 37 per cent of the German labour force was female.

At the start of the war, allowances for the dependents of serving men were fixed unnecessarily high. Some women found that they no longer needed to work, so that between 1939 and 1941 the number in employment fell. In June 1940 a proposal to introduce compulsion was turned down but to meet the preference of the technicians for German women over foreigners (male or female), various attempts were made at persuasion which had little success.

Compulsory registration for war work was introduced in January 1943 but not strictly enforced. This was largely due to Hitler's belief tiat women drafted into industry without previous experience would be bad workers; in May 1943 he told the impatient Goebbels that, even in total war, one must not fight the women.[100] Consequently the number of women employed in Germany only rose by 274,000 during the course of the war.[101] In the end, the need for more labour was met by bringing in prisoners-of-war and foreigners, mostly under compulsion.[102]

Old-fashioned Germans who had expected the Nazis, once in power, to send women back to their children, churches and kitchens suffered a disappointment since this proved another sphere where real needs were found more compelling than inherited prejudices. This did not apply to the menial sphere alone. The requirements of the community for trained social workers meant a growing demand for female doctors and teachers; the Labour Service, the *Bund deutscher Mädel* and welfare services all needed types of professional advice which women were quite as qualified to provide as men. For women to become lawyers was more questionable and in 1936 Hitler laid down that they were not to become judges, while in the following year he ruled out their appointment as senior civil servants. Yet the growing shortage of trained people made a consistent anti-feminist policy impossible and steps had even to be taken to attract more women to study at universities.[103]

The absence or death of men on war-service in due course affected the NSDAP itself. At the end of the war women occasionally had to be put into local posts, such as *Ortsgruppenleiter*, for want of anyone else. Whereas in 1934 they had only formed 5 per cent of total membership, by 1938 they were providing 17 per cent and by 1942–3 33 per cent of the intake.[104] And whereas the female Party comrades had previously tended to be older than their male counterparts, this situation too was reversed. If these trends had continued, the Party would have been rescued from its fear of becoming a collection of grey-beards but at the cost of having its male predominance undermined!

As is so often the case, women tended to get the lower, duller, worse paid jobs in all walks of life; there were no women in really senior posts. Frau Scholtz-Klink, the *Reichsfrauenführerin*, never had a personal discussion with her Führer.[105] How far women resented this is hard to say. Those with higher education, who tended to be the protagonists of emancipation, belonged in any case to that professional élite which it was Hitler's long-term aim to destroy and which had lost faith in him by 1942–3. If it had not been for the loyalty of a preponderance of German women to the *Volksgemeinschaft*, which induced them to shoulder a vast number of chores, particularly on the farms, the war would have been lost long before it was.

(k) **Youth**

The Nazis reduced considerably the number of students in higher education and this has been seen as a sign of their hostility to intellectuals. But it seems also to have been a sensible move to reduce the numbers of unemployed (and therefore discontented) youth by bringing the number of places more into line with the number of jobs available for those who had finished their course. In the summer semester of 1933, 12,966 students matriculated at German universities; six years later the figure was 7305.[106] The number registering in law (the standard qualification for administrative posts) fell from 22,000 in 1928 to 14,373 in 1933, 6237 in 1938 and 2306 in 1941.[107] The proportion of girl students fell from 18.5 per cent in 1932 to 11.2 per cent in 1939.[108] As time went on and the economy expanded, the government realised that they had gone too far and tried to increase the intake again but the growing need of the armed forces and SS for manpower impeded this. A considerable problem was thus created for post-war Germany. Courses in the arts were exploited for indoctrination. Those who wanted to avoid this sought refuge in medicine and the natural sciences (as exemplified by the men of the White Rose, pp. 234–8).

Curiously enough, it was not long before the student leaders began to regard the years before 1933 as a golden age.[109] Once the liberal professors and the dissident students had been thrown out and the offending books burnt, there was no man-size job left to do, so they took to quarrelling among themselves. The main antagonists were the National Students Union under the Minister of Education Rust and the National Socialist Students Association under Hess as Deputy Leader of the Party. Even after the two bodies had been brought under a single head in 1936, the problem of finding interesting or exciting occupation remained. A start was made with organising *Kameradschaft* houses in which all students would pass their first year so as to ensure that they got indoctrinated; the Party intention was that these would replace the old fraternity houses. But Hitler decided that cohabitation might foster homosexuality while Lammers, the Cabinet Secretary, came to the rescue of the fraternities of which he was a leading old boy.

Himmler, as a failed intellectual, wanted the universities to train the leaders of the Nazi future. But the average Nazi had no wish to be led by intellectuals and the average student had no wish to waste time on the verbiage which passed for Nazi theory. What they wanted to acquire was knowledge which might be of practical use in life. 'The real enemy of the NSDStB, and by far its most effective one, was apathy.' This was an opponent with which the leaders did not know how to cope. They could not provide the intellectual stimulus which alone could have won them co-operation. Experience showed that compulsion or punishment were counter-productive.

In January 1933 the Hitler Youth had numbered 100,000; by the end of 1934 it had risen to 3½ million. So rapid an expansion was bound to create problems; it is not surprising that there were complaints about conditions in the camps and other institutions. The Evangelical Youth were absorbed in December 1933 by an agreement with the Reich Bishop but against the wishes of the rank-and-file who remained antagonistic.[110] Much the same thing happened with the various groups of *Bündische Jugend* although it is doubtful whether much more was involved than the *amour propre* of leaders who found themselves ousted from the top jobs; the viewpoints of the two movements were much the same.[111] The Catholic youth organisations remained independent until 1936–9 but were then absorbed against their will. For a time the Hitler Youth had attractions. It gave a certain amount of protection against the authority of family and school; it afforded a certain number of lads between 14 and 17 opportunities of self-projection. Successful membership seemed likely to open a number of doors in life.

But the Hitler Youth never really recovered from the speed of its expansion; any chances it may have had of doing so were set back by the advent of war. Premilitary training quickly assumed a dominant position, to the detriment of sport and travel. Instead of wandering through the woods, they were required to march through the streets. The generations which should have provided the leaders (on the principle that 'youth leads youth') went away to the Labour Service and the forces and often in due course died in action. Many groups became led by teachers, which was the opposite of what had been intended. Where youth was still in control, it often proved incompetent so that the central management took to issuing exact and rigorous rules as to how time should be spent. The cure for inefficiency was found in over-organisation.[112]

Given the innate tendency of some proportion of youth to be 'agin the government', it is not surprising that counter-movements began to appear as early as 1937 and continued spasmodically to the end of the war. The best known of these were the *Edelweisspiraten* who spread out from the Rhineland,[113] and were matched by the *Meute* ('Pack of Hounds') in Saxony.[114] These were essentially working-class affairs. Groups of about twenty gathered in open spaces and particular streets; each had its own beat. They talked, they sang songs, they wore distinctive (but not uniform) clothes, they went on unauthorised expeditions, they helped victims, they passed on news, they created 'no go' areas into which the HJ did not venture for fear of getting beaten up. There was little political motivation except in so far as a totalitarian state gives any deviant behaviour a political aspect. A Communist attempt to enlist recruits among the Oberhausen pirates fell flat, although something of the kind had more success in 1942–3 in Düsseldorf where in December 1942 the police dissolved 24 groups with 740 members.[115] In Cologne in the autumn of 1944 20 groups made up of youths, Communists, foreign workers, escaped prisoners and deserting soldiers created semi-partisan conditions in which 32 people (political leaders, SS, police, HJ, SA and soldiers) were killed. A police order in 1940 had required all under 18 to be off the streets when darkness fell, and to be out of bars, cinemas and cabarets by 9 p.m. Anyone under 16 was forbidden to drink. Resentment of such shepherding led on to a desire to do everything which the Third Reich disliked. Another set of groups, more middle-class, spread out from Hamburg in the early years of the war. They played English records of swing music, wore bowler hats and carried umbrellas.[116] These groups have been seen as a proof that

> Nazi (and even Nationalist) ideals had failed to commend themselves to the younger generation since even the majority of the young, who did not actually engage in such activities, seem to have found them more attractive than the NS alternative. After years of domination National Socialism still did not have German society under control. Parts of it slipped out of their hands in proportion as the formal machinery of oppression was being completed. Both the central concepts of NS society, the suppression of class conflict by the *Volksgemeinschaft* and the destruction of modernity and internationalism, seen as threats to traditional values, by a militarily formed and chauvinistically developed *Volkskörper*, had failed before the Third Reich was brought to an end by military defeat. This was largely because all National Socialism could offer was military drill, anachronistic ideology and stifling bureaucracy. The NS blue-print could not fashion society permanently according to its wishes.[117]

However such a sweeping and optimistic verdict leaves out of account the question how far such a rejection of all that National Socialism stood for may not have been inspired and made practicable by the growing shadow of defeat. Not surprisingly, the young pirates seem to have had no positive political plans of their own.[118] Against them can be set the cadets from an NS school who in April 1945 fought a desperate defensive battle round the Hermann monument in the woods above Detmold and were killed almost to a man.[119] Their readiness to die for a lost cause may have been exceptional. But there were a number of HJ members who went on doing their jobs as army auxiliaries or social workers as long as it remained physically possible.

(l) Conclusion

Extensive interrogation of prisoners towards the end of and after the war, along with other evidence, suggests that by that time the hard core of NS supporters amounted to about 11 per cent of the population, or between 4 and 5 million people.[120] Opposite to them stood a slightly smaller number of hostile activists. Between these extremes there were about 25 per cent 'followers with reservations' and about 15 per cent inactive dissenters. In the middle came a block of perhaps 40 per cent who can aptly be described as the 'don't bother me' vote – people (especially women) who took no active part in politics and only wanted to be left undisturbed to earn their living or look after their families. This latter is of course a frequent phenomenon but one which political analysts tend to forget. A Socialist report from Berlin in 1935 said that

> the average worker is only interested in his work and not in democracy. One needs to recognise that a man is first and foremost the head of a family and a person with a job. Politics take second place and only interest him when they offer him

some advantage. This basic attitude leads many to refuse to take part in illegal activity since they believe it serves no useful purpose and can only land one in prison.[121]

Four years later a police report from Bavaria said that 'the majority of the population are politically indifferent, albeit peace-loving.'[122]

One reason why the Nazis gained power was that they exploited a period of crisis to mobilise and bring to the polls these a-political elements. But keeping them mobilised was no easy matter. Their attention only too easily turned back to their parochial preoccupations and they then grew less keen on promoting Nazi aims:

> Once National Socialism had established itself, traditional anti-modernist influences began to exert an obstructive influence at local level. This was particularly the case in rural Catholic districts with traditionally pious populations. Forces which had had some sympathy with National Socialism while it was still in opposition turned against it once it became the government, and above all the central government (which it strengthened at the expense of the land-governments).
>
> The sum total of the many little *Widerstände* to the measures and demands involved in the NS exercise of power rested much less on principles and political involvement than on the defence of inherited social and cultural forms of life or the undisguised protection of interests. All the same these little *Widerstände* placed many more limits on the ability of the régime to achieve its objectives than many activities of illegal groups and organisations.[123]

Hitler and his Party did not establish a full *Volksgemeinschaft*, although they came closer to doing so in 1940 than many other governments. The former ambassador Ulrich von Hassell, one of Hitler's most persistent opponents, said in June of that year that 'one is driven to despair by one's inability to take pleasure in the victories' (but all the same went on to attribute to the general public 'a dull indifference').[124] The triumph may not have lasted long but the war effort thereafter became one of national defence which made many who did not agree with all that the régime had done reluctant to 'stab their country in the back'.

There has been much discussion as to how the public would have reacted if Hitler had been killed on 20 July or, for that matter, on 13 March 1943.[125] (The conspirators had decided much earlier that what the public might think had nothing to do with the question of whether the murder was desirable.) At first reading, the reports of public opinion supplied by the SD and other sources, even after allowance is made for the bias which their authors had to show, provide a convincing case for saying that only a small minority, to be found among the old élites and unreconciled workers, would have welcomed the event. In ultra-Catholic Freiburg 50,000 people turned out to demonstrate their relief at the Führer's escape; in ultra-Nazi Schaumburg it was 70 per cent of the population. The doubts about the wisdom of killing tyrants, which were widespread among the conspirators themselves, would certainly have been reproduced in the country at large.

But we should not assume that the reactions to a successful assassination would have been the same as they were to a failure. What many felt was relief that Hitler had been spared to continue the war because they still believed that he could win it but that without him total defeat stared them in the face. Secondly none of those who disapproved of either Hitler's morals or his strategy dared voice their views after he had escaped; one of the sequels was a sharp increase in class-feeling, since the *untere Mittelstand* suspected that the old élites were the main focus of disaffection. Church leaders in particular could give no guidance. Had a clear call come from them and the generals, much might have been changed. Even so it is unlikely that the putsch would have been greeted with enthusiasm. For the public to change its mind takes time. A Swedish journalist reported on 22 July, 'The masses are apathetic. They neither hear nor see and remain in consequence unconcerned. They neither weep, nor rejoice nor rage.'[126] Civil war between the two wings which did feel strongly (p. 56) would have been by no means impossible but how long it would have gone on is another matter.

We today may find it surprising that faith in Hitler should have lasted so long when faith in all the other prominent Nazis had vanished. Those who in January 1933 had believed that accession to power would soon show up the hollowness of Nazi pretensions were perfectly right, except where the Führer was concerned. Hitler was regarded as aloof from everyday affairs, absorbed in planning large-scale actions, especially in foreign fields. The sigh in face of something unsatisfactory 'If only the Führer knew' often implied a recognition that he could not be expected to know. Hence the animosity created by Nazi failures was directed against the Party, while the reputation of the man at the top remained untarnished.[127] But there was more to it than that. It has been suggested earlier (p. 26) that, so far from imposing himself on the Germans as their leader, Hitler assumed that role because he sensed that they wanted leadership and saw nobody else better qualified to give it to them. To lose faith in Hitler therefore meant admitting that one had been wrong, wrong about the goals which had been held out for the German *Volk*, wrong about the whole German nationalist interpretation of the world and its history. That could not be acknowledged overnight. Even defeat only proved that Germany was weaker than her adversaries (although the fact that she had twice miscalculated her strength implied that some people had gone wrong somewhere). The process of disillusionment and reorientation was bound to be lengthy. There are still a few Germans who have not completed it.

CHAPTER IV
Modes of *Widerstand*

(a) Terminology

A wide variety of responses was open to those who could not fully accept National Socialism, ranging from complete passivity to active conspiracy or even to what in conventional terms was treason. There has been considerable discussion recently as to how these various forms are best described.[1] As no individual or institution is in a position to lay down the law, the discussion may last indefinitely and little useful purpose would be served by going into the question at length here, especially as labels which are suitable in German are not necessarily so when translated literally into English. A few comments may however be helpful.

(*i*) The people who engaged in these activities did not think of them as '*Widerstand*' and survivors were surprised to find the term being applied to them by foreigners after the war. 'We did not think of ourselves as being part of a *Widerstand*,' said one. 'We merely sought somehow to survive in dignity.'

(*ii*) The exact boundaries between the various forms are hard to define and individuals often passed by stages from one to another – and even back again – without fully realising what they were doing. The most obvious example is a group of friends who started by discussing the situation, perhaps without having met for that specific purpose, and went on to discuss what to do about it.

(*iii*) A distinction can clearly be made between private thoughts, uttered thoughts and action. It is now fairly widely agreed in Germany that only the latter deserves the term *Widerstand*. As has already been suggested (Preface) there is a good deal to be said for using the same word to denote the same thing in English, and thus avoid possibly misleading conceptions associated with 'resistance' and 'opposition' although it is very difficult to avoid using those words occasionally.

(*iv*) The question then arises as to the best term to use for all activity which falls short of *Widerstand*. One term suggested has been *Resistenz* on the medical analogy of the reaction of a human body to infection.[2] But the rather different meaning of the corresponding words in English and French makes this confusing and the suggested alternatives of 'dissent' or 'nonconformity' seem for that reason preferable.

(v) Further questions concern the need for different terms to distinguish between individual activities or attitudes and participation in an organisation, or between on the one hand reading a hostile leaflet which came one's way and on the other passing it or its contents on to other people (where full conformity would have required it to be handed over to the authorities unread). While it is important to realise that these differences existed, there seems little to be gained by trying to put a continuous chain into separate boxes.

(b) Suicide

The most straightforward and final way of removing oneself from NS pressure to conform was suicide. One reason for adopting it was to escape from anticipated ill-treatment. An example was Jochen Klepper, son of a Protestant pastor who took his life in company with his Jewish wife and step-daughter in December 1942; he had been expelled from the Reich Chamber of Writers and was as a result virtually deprived of livelihood; the step-daughter, if not the wife, was liable to be deported to a death camp.[3] A victim for a different reason was the trade union official Anton Reissner who, having emigrated to Amsterdam, took his life along with his wife and daughter as the Germans arrived in 1940.[4] Such acts of desperation did of course mean a reduction in the number of persons whom the Nazis had against them.

Thirteen of the 213 names on the latest list of victims after 20 July committed suicide.[5] While in some cases the motive may have been to escape an unpleasant death, in others it was the desire to deny to the Nazis valuable knowledge (often implicating others) which they possessed and thought they might be unable to avoid communicating under torture.

In the later 1920s about 16,000 people were committing suicide every year. In 1933–5 this figure rose to a yearly rate of 18,600 but in 1942–3 fell to 15,200.[6]

(c) Emigration

This had in the past been the course adopted by such intellectuals as Heine and Marx. Professor Eugen Rosenstock of Breslau University applied for a passport on 31 January 1933 since he foresaw that he could not tolerate or be tolerated by the Nazis (whose rise he had predicted in 1919).[7] About 400,000 people are said to have left Germany between 1933 and 1939 of whom 30–35,000 went for political reasons, the remainder being Jewish.[8] The number of professors in the emigration has been put at 1000, and the same figure has been given for writers. The roll-call was headed by Freud and Einstein and included Hindemith, Schönberg, Klemperer, Gropius, Cassirer, Kockoschk, Beckmann, Weill, two Manns and Brecht.[9] The Central Committee of the SPD moved to Prague in May 1933, went to Paris in May 1938 and finally to England in 1940. The KPD Committee went to Paris in

1933, went back there again in 1936 after a year in Prague and finally to Moscow in 1939.

There has been a tendency to decry emigration as an evasion of responsibility – and suffering. But it is no light matter to maintain a precarious livelihood in a foreign country, especially if one is not fluent in its language. The German qualifications for the professions were not necessarily recognised elsewhere; the difference between the German and Anglo-Saxon systems was a special obstacle for lawyers and civil servants. If progressive artists and writers had remained in Germany, they would probably have been imprisoned and certainly forbidden to exercise their talents. Emigration offered the best way not only to go on doing what they were good at but also to keep the best elements of German culture alive. Nor did those abroad all refrain from withstanding: 5000 Germans fought and 3000 died in the International Brigade in Spain;[10] 30,000 German Jews joined the French Army as well as 8–10,000 non-Jews, while others served in the British Pioneer Corps and its US equivalent. German emigrants to Britain founded some 300 firms and thereby strengthened the British war economy, often by introducing new techniques.[11] Nor was exile altogether safe. A militantly anti-Nazi writer Theodor Lessing was murdered in Marienbad in August 1933 as was the broadcaster Rudolf Formis in January 1935 when he was running an anti-Nazi transmitter from a town south-west of Prague.[12] A pacifist journalist and defence expert called Jacob was kidnapped from Switzerland in March 1935 but the Swiss Government insisted on his being returned.

There were however many like Trott, Bonhoeffer, Reichwein (pp. 181, 221) and Kurt Schumacher who felt that, since all anti-Nazis could not leave Germany, those who did so were deserting their colleagues. It was this feeling which led the Socialist Carlo Mierendorff, who happened to be outside Germany on 30 January 1933, to return, although he knew that he might be put into a concentration camp, as he was.[13] It was the same story with Wilhelm Leuschner (p. 201). Others again, convinced that National Socialism was going to be a transient phenomenon (although failing to realise how long it would last), foresaw that those who had spent the Third Reich outside would be looked at askance afterwards by those who had stuck it out and could only expect to exert a limited influence in a post-Hitler state (a prospect which Willy Brandt's example partly confirms). Those who foresaw that Nazism might well lead to catastrophe also foresaw a need to have the right men available to rebuild after catastrophe. Yet some of those who at first felt like this became worried by the thought that even to remain in Germany was in some sense to aid and abet its rulers. In August 1938 Helmuth von Moltke wrote to his wife:[14]

> Wouldn't it be better to be done with the false values and the pretences here and live extremely humbly in some place where one isn't continually under pressure to conform? I have the feeling that I would far far rather starve in a free land than go on trying to keep up appearances here. For that is what we are doing. We let ourselves be a façade to cover up the atrocities which go on continually and

the only reason for it is that we are left alone for a relatively long time before it's our turn to be got at.

(d) Hibernation

In 1931 Adolf Reichwein wrote that he foresaw a 'period of overwintering'.[15] A number of other people regarded National Socialism as a kind of epidemic, from which one must hold oneself as far as possible aloof in the hope that so flagrant a defiance of human aspirations and social realities could not last. Such a dormouse-like existence involved certain assumptions. One was that someone else would at some stage act to get rid of National Socialism. A second was that one was prepared to renounce for the time being all expectation of exerting influence in the world, except in so far as one could do so in purely human and individual relationships. A third was that the outside world would allow one to exclude it. For some people, whose known views were offensive to the régime, or who were non-Aryans, this was unlikely to happen. Moreover the Nazi *Gleichschaltung* of society involved the creation in each walk of life of one association to which everyone had to belong (p. 34). Whereas an authoritarian government merely expects obedience from its subjects and allows only a privileged few to help in running the state, a totalitarian one expects active agreement and co-operation from all its members. Finally there were a number of trivial occasions on which it was impossible to avoid showing one's attitude, such as giving or not giving the Hitler salute (made obligatory in July 1933), saying '*Grüss Gott*' instead of '*Heil Hitler*' (to say '*Heil Schicklgruber*' was highly dangerous), hoisting or not hoisting flags when told to do so. Count von und zu Lerchenfeld-Köfering, a former Minister-President of Bavaria, refused to give the Nazi salute to an SA officer in uniform and when reminded in a friendly way that this was an obligation, said, 'I can't do it but I'm willing to talk about it,' whereupon he went off, without conforming. He refused to contribute to collections other than that helping the poor in winter. Such nonconformity would not seem to have got him into trouble but in 1936 he was denied an exit visa because he only subscribed to foreign newspapers and maintained a correspondence with Rome and Austria.[16]

For one of the difficulties facing a conscientious hibernator was to maintain non-Nazi channels of information from the outside world, vital to independence of judgment, especially for someone who did not understand a foreign language. Until the war listeners dependent on broadcasts in German had a choice between Moscow, the Vatican, Switzerland, Strasbourg, Luxembourg and Austria; the BBC only began to broadcast in German in the autumn of 1938. Swiss papers like the *Basler Nachrichten* (which Ribbentrop believed to be subsidised by Moscow[17]) had a considerable circulation inside Germany. During the war 'black listening' became a crime on the insistence of Goebbels and against the advice of Gürtner, the non-Nazi Minister of Justice, who said a ban would undermine faith in their own service.[18] Sentences of up to three years' imprisonment were sometimes imposed for it, even when there was no evidence of news so obtained having been passed on.[19]

The poet Gottfried Benn, who, without being a Liberal, was too sensitive to find Nazism congenial, used his medical training to get a post as a Wehrmacht doctor. He was expelled from the Chamber of Writers because he refused to give up contact with his Jewish friends and might have fared worse without the Wehrmacht protection. He it was who described the army as 'the aristocratic form of emigration'.[20] Dr Jakob Stöcker, who had for many years written editorials in a firm but moderately democratic sense for the Dortmund *General Anzeiger*, was warned by a member of the staff in March 1933 of a Nazi plan to beat him up. On the advice of the editor, he at once left the city and spent the next twelve years living in retirement far away.[21] Bernard Göring, who had been an official in the Union of Employees, survived the Third Reich as a cigar-dealer in Berlin. His colleague Hans Gottfurcht worked in an insurance company.[22] It frequently occurred in Bavaria that the local SPD and TU functionaries who had been made to give up political activity in 1933 were the people who took in hand the new organisation in 1945, 'starting to knit the stocking again at the point at which it had been left off'. In some cases they brought along the accumulation of their weekly contributions which they had faithfully put aside throughout the twelve years.[23] Organisations sought the same kind of innocuous concealment. The local SPD branch in Schongau, whose members almost all worked in the same paper-mill, turned themselves into the factory's brass band.[24] Parallel examples in more rarified walks of life were the history professors who took to writing books about Greece, Rome or the Middle Ages ('pure scholarship') and novelists like Ernst Jünger who set their stories in imaginary and distant climes and times. Adam von Trott's edited selection of the political writings of Heinrich von Kleist (p. 181) is another example.

(e) Unobtrusive or minor obstruction

To maintain a purely negative attitude all the time must have been extraordinarily difficult, the occasional temptation to say or do something unacceptable overwhelming. One such opportunity was to attend the funerals of people known to have been against the régime. When the Communist leader Karl Hoffmann was buried in Essen in October 1934, 1500 people turned up although neither the time nor the place had been announced; many carried wreaths of red roses. The police stopped the singing of hymns; next day they arrested the family and deprived them of winter help.[25] Another gesture was to omit references to Hitler in obituary announcements, particularly of war casualties; mentions dropped so much that in September 1944 relatives were deprived of the freedom to choose the form of words.[26] Pieces such as Schiller's *Don Carlos* had to be taken out of the repertory after the line 'give us back our freedom of thought' had been greeted with thunderous applause. Repeating jokes and discreditable stories is of course a universal indulgence which only acquires political significance when public criticism is suppressed. In 1936 fifteen sentences of several months' imprisonment were imposed in Munich for repeating sayings about the régime. In 1944 a baker's wife in Bad Aibling got a year in gaol for passing on a rumour about Goebbels, a waitress in Wagscheid two years for complaining that Hitler wasn't ending the war.[27] Matters were complicated by the Propaganda Ministry's habit of putting out stories as a means of discrediting other Ministers (like Göring) or of giving foreigners a mistaken impression of the progress made in rearmament. In 1942 an old man of 73 was caught writing up in a public lavatory that Hitler must be killed to end the war; it turned out that he and his wife had only RM60 a month to live on after paying their rent and he could not restrain himself from relieving his feelings. He was duly executed after a series of bureaucratic processes occupying 17 pages of documentation.[28] Every society has its gossips and grumblers; they represent a social safety valve, as Goebbels well recognised.[29] But the totalitarian state does not allow for such things, at any rate in theory, especially when its existence is in danger, as after 1942. Such insubordination would only have begun to be dangerous if it had begun to be organised, which it never was.

A regular form of *Widerstand* was the circulation of leaflets and clandestine papers, with which should also be classed stickers and the daubing of slogans on walls. Leuschner was opposed to leaflets because his experience as Minister of the Interior in Hesse had convinced him that they did more harm than good by putting the police on the tracks of the authors and providing evidence for trials.[30] The Communists, by contrast, considered them to be essential, not simply as a means of distributing information but also of showing the public that the struggle against National Socialism had not been given up and of maintaining the morale of those involved by giving them something to do. In 1934 they distributed 12,000 copies of a paper *Die Rote Fahne* every fortnight in the Rhine and Ruhr.[31] The Socialists, after they had decided that distribution to the general public was not worthwhile, went on for some time putting news sheets round among their members; these were not so easily detected. The most famous leaflets were those produced by The White Rose (p. 235).

The impression is sometimes given that the effort put into leaflets by the Communists decreased after their change of policy at the 'Brussels' conference (p. 50) in 1935 and certainly far fewer people were arrested on this charge in 1935 and 1936 than in 1934. But 1.6 million were still being distributed in 1936 and 927,000 in 1937.[32] Some were printed outside the country; those printed inside had smaller circulations. In 1938 the number is said to have sunk to 12,000, in 1939 to 3300 and in 1940 to 1000. In the first half of 1941 the number seized was still only 1450 but the attack on Russia brought a striking rise to 24,500 in the second half of that year.[33] A Communist paper *The Harbinger* (i.e. of a new era) was started in Mannheim in the September and by January 1942 had a circulation of 250 copies.[34] Among the papers left behind by Anton Saefkow were the texts of ten leaflets prepared by him or under his supervision.[35] Even after 20 July, a few stickers were still produced calling for the end of the war.[36] The writing up on walls of F for Freiheit was tried for a time in 1942 but abandoned because it was found to be 'without resonance'. But during the next two years passers-by were sometimes reminded of 1918 by seeing the date painted up, a course which the BBC had been recommending to foreign workers.

Considerable ingenuity went into this work. One left-wing Socialist group mimeographed a leaflet on a motor-boat on the Berlin Wannsee.[37] False covers were often provided; Pieck's address to the 'Brussels' Conference went round as a pamphlet by A. Kosch on 'Mushrooms, Berries and Game', while productions of the Inland Transport Federation appeared under the title 'Do you want to remain healthy?'[38] After 30 June, one leaflet reproduced Low's savage cartoon 'They salute with both hands now'.[39] In addition it has been calculated that during the course of the war the Allies dropped 30 leaflets for every man, woman and child in Western Europe;[40] some at least of these were picked up, read and passed on.

A further important sphere in which the individual could counter NS aims lay in giving help to victims and their families. This help could extend from providing food, money and clothing (not necessarily directly) through offering shelter to forging ration cards and passports. Here one crosses the boundary between acts normally thought praiseworthy and those normally thought criminal; in the Third Reich all were punishable offences. It has been estimated that 5000 Jews were 'rescued' (although it is not clear whether this means 'kept alive in Germany' or 'enabled to escape from Germany'). Both Churches had organisations for this purpose (see biography of Lichtenberg, p. 230). It was a scheme for smuggling Jews into Switzerland which proved the undoing of Oster, Dohnanyi and Bonhoeffer (p. 158). Among private individuals active in this way 15 per cent are estimated to have been persons in senior positions, 10 per cent lawyers, doctors and teachers, 14 per cent writers, artists and musicians, 14 per cent housewives (of whom half belonged to the upper classes).[41]

A good example of what ingenuity and determination could do was provided by Wilhelm Däner, a foreman in a Berlin factory making essential parts for fighter aircraft. He and his wife had always been Social Democrats. He had a sympathetic Works Director who shared his political views, as did the manager of the works canteen and a *Hofmeister* who knew how to lay his hands on provisions. Däner had about 120 Jewesses placed in his charge, many of whom learnt how to do precision work, which enabled him to say that if they were taken away, he would be unable to fulfil his quota for the Luftwaffe. He intimidated the stupid old Party Member who was responsible for handling mobilised workers into getting Jewesses released when they were threatened with deportation. One of them, who had been well-to-do but had had her property confiscated, received a deportation order. Däner advised her to wait until the next heavy air raid, then go to the area worst hit and choose a badly-bombed block in which the Party office had been destroyed. He then gave her a work certificate with a photograph of herself and the number of the block she had chosen but with a false name. She took this to the report centre for the bombed-out who, having no means of checking amid the confusion, accepted it and gave her an Aryan work-permit along with emergency money. She was fed and housed by the NS Welfare Service who evacuated her to Pomerania where in due course she got a job as housekeeper to a senior Party Member! At the end of the war she came back to Berlin.[42] But helping fugitives was a risky business; five of the people who gave shelter to General Lindemann between 22 July and 3 September were executed for doing so.[43] All the same, there were many cases where human-kindness prevailed. One which can symbolise the rest occurred on the Eastern Front where a Wehrmacht NCO called Anton Schmidt helped Jews to escape. Nothing would be known about him or his action if some of them had not recalled his name at the Eichmann trial.[44]

(f) Strikes and sabotage (see also pp. 48 and 276)

Strikes did occur during the Third Reich. Eight were noted in the Rhine–Ruhr area between September 1934 and October 1935. Most of them were however due to disputes about conditions of work and seldom lasted long. A strike in a single factory or area for a political objective would have served no useful purpose.[45] But in October 1941 (the only month for which figures are available) the Gestapo arrested 7729 workers for downing tools. The possibility of organising a general strike, particularly to coincide with an armed move against the régime by generals, was proposed on several occasions. Leuschner is said to have considered that such a strike would only be effective as a defensive weapon, not an offensive one;[46] this does not seem to have prevented him from discussing the possibility with Beck on the initiative of Oster and Dohnanyi in the autumn of 1939 and again in 1941–2, probably during the crisis preceding Brauchitsch's dismissal.[47] Before 20 July preparations are said to have been made for a railway strike in the Mainz area, which might have led on to a general strike.[48] But the failure of the soldiers to act effectively on all these occasions meant that the project never took practical shape.

There is surprisingly little evidence of go-slow and sabotage. Two workers were arrested for sabotage in Nuremburg in 1938 and two more a little later.[49] There are said to have been cases of refusal to work during the earlier months of 1939 and again after the victory in Poland. Yet in the summer of 1940 the Comintern admitted that its agitation was meeting with less and less response among industrial workers.[50] In 1941 fifteen young workers in Oberhausen evaded 1400 hours of work over six months.[51] After air raids in Berlin in February 1944 firemen insisted on waiting for the all-clear to be called before using their hoses with the result that a factory was burnt out; there were two other similar cases.[52] The claim has been made that a third of the V1 and V2 missiles failed to reach their targets because of sabotage but it would be interesting to know how this fact was established.[53] A remarkable case was

provided by the Jewish youth group in Berlin called Baum after its leader which in 1942 set fire to the exhibition called (sarcastically) 'The Soviet Paradise'. There had been much discussion beforehand as to the value of the act but a majority decided it was preferable to do something rather than wait until one was taken away to a camp. The sequel was grisly, including the execution of 250 Jews who had no connection with the group.[54]
In March 1943 Helmuth von Moltke wrote in a letter to England[55]

> The opposition has thrown sand into the machine. It will probably never be known to what extent this has helped your people. But the extent to which it has been done is very considerable, especially in the higher bureaucracy. There is seldom a week where I do not notice something that has been done in order to prevent a command from being executed or at least from becoming fully effective.

Hitler's Chief Adjutant Schmundt wrote to Goebbels in March 1944 that 'the Generals' clique are continually spreading sand in the Wehrmacht machine'.[56] Tresckow and other officers in Russia did their best to arrange that the Commissar and other vicious Orders about killing prisoners were not acted upon; they had some success.[57] In 1943 George Duckwitz, as a Counsellor on the staff of Werner Best, the clever but unscrupulous lawyer who was Ambassador in Copenhagen, was able to give the advance warning which enabled the majority of Danish Jews to escape to Sweden before they could be rounded up for transport to Auschwitz.[58] Hossbach, the Wehrmacht adjutant who took the minutes at the meeting on 5 November, two months later disobeyed Hitler's express order by telling Fritsch of the charge being brought against him. As a result Hossbach was removed from his post and sent to command a regiment.

On a smaller scale, SD agents in Hamburg called in 1937 on the University rector Adolf Rein, who was pro-Nazi but not a Party member, to provide information about staff or students who had been enemies of the NSDAP before January 1933. Rein successively argued that (a) ministerial permission was necessary before the SD could see any files, (b) only the head of the SD sub-district could see them, and (c) they could not be removed from the university. After a year of correspondence, the SD gave up. It is relevant that Rein was on excellent terms with the Gauleiter. At about the same time, the Reich Student Leader called for a separate file to be kept on each student. The Education Ministry objected that this was incompatible with the efforts of the Four Year Plan Office to reduce paper work to a minimum.[59]

(g) Undermining from within

We have by now passed in our consideration of modes of *Widerstand* beyond the stage of what could be achieved by the isolated individual (although we should never forget that it was such an individual, Georg Elser, who came as close as anyone to killing the Führer, see p. 122). The next class of persons to be considered are therefore those who, holding posts of relative responsibility within the administration, judged it better to stay in office, in view of the likelihood that, if they resigned, they would be replaced by a more faithful supporter of Hitler. The first thing to remember however is that the choice was by no means always available. Resignations were not necessarily accepted (any more than they had been in the Second Reich[60]). In 1938, after the *Kristallnacht*, the conservative but anti-Nazi Popitz offered his resignation as Finance Minister of Prussia, only to have it refused.[61] After 1941 resigning was explicitly forbidden. Hitler once said, 'I can't tell my immediate superior God that I can't go on because I can no longer carry the responsibility.'[62] Officers could hardly leave the forces, although they could behave as General Zeitzler did when Chief of Staff in 1944 and simply absent themselves on grounds of ill-health.

The justification which recurs in the apologia of those among Hitler's antagonists who continued to hold office is that they did so to avoid worse things happening – *um schlimmeres zu verhüten*, said to have been first used by the Finance Minister Schwerin von Krosigk, who held on to his post till 1945. In Catholic documents one even comes across a Latin version – *ad maiora mala evitanda*.[63] (The phrase of course implies that the present state of affairs is not the worst imaginable.) There has been much controversy, both at the time and since, as to whether the argument was justified and was not merely used as an excuse for weakness. The obvious objection was that any person using it was enabling the régime to be a little less unsatisfactory and inefficient, and therefore to have better prospects of enduring, than it would have been otherwise, as well as conniving at measures of which they did not approve. Ernst von Weizsäcker is an outstanding example of this class of man and the question will be considered again in relation to him (p. 178). An even more difficult case is Arthur Nebe whose anxiety to stay in a position where he could give the conspirators early warning of impending dangers involved him in taking charge of an SS *Einsatzcommando* in Russia (p. 164). Another controversial case is Kurt Gerstein (p. 239). The crucial question is that of the use which the persons concerned made of the positions which they retained. There were four main possibilities.

(h) Arguing for a change of policy

The writing of memoranda discussing the various choices available to an administration and urging the merits of one different to that which the leadership favours is of course standard operating practice in any bureaucracy. Beck was only following the normal routine when he expressed his objections to Hitler's proposed policy towards Austria and Czechoslovakia in a series of papers between November 1937 and August 1938. Goerdeler's belief that in the long term reason would prevail made it natural for him to do the same. Erich Kordt however wrote with justice later that 'naturally the temptation was great to keep to the traditional routines and satisfy our consciences by writing memoranda and warnings for the record, knowing very well that they would remain futile gestures'.[64] For Hitler was notoriously allergic to documents even when he agreed with them, and expected his generals to do what they were told instead of discussing what they should be told.[65] General von Reichenau realised at an early stage that in a dictatorship it is personal contact and confidential information which count.[66] Those who wanted to get the Führer to change his mind had the best chance of success by standing up to him in private conversation (as had been the case with Wilhelm II).[67] His readiness to listen is said to have decreased about 1937. Halder claims to have forecast where Hitler's mistakes would lead: 'When the unpleasant result occurred, he naturally often tried to saddle me with the blame. That led to controversies which often enough did not follow the normal rules of social behaviour but turned into shouting matches.' He was once heard to say to his superior, 'You're so pig-headed you won't listen to what anyone else proposes.'[68] When General Thomas gave a report about declining morale to Keitel for onward transmission, he got the answer:

> The Führer is not interested in such considerations. It is his conviction that, if the German people do not want to understand him and fight, they will have to perish. I hereby forbid such reports being shown to him. They do more harm than good. The standing of the OKW is only adversely affected. The Führer has other sources of information and would rather believe them than his generals.[69]

When Helmuth von Moltke persuaded Canaris to sign a document protesting against the notorious 'Commissar Order' on the ground that, since it violated international law, it would damage the reputation of the German army and endanger Germans who were taken prisoner, Keitel wrote on it that 'these doubts correspond to military ideas about wars of chivalry. Our job is to suppress a way of life. For that reason I sanction the measures proposed.'[70]

(i) Planning for a post-war Germany

The chief practitioners of this form of activity were the Kreisau Group but plans were also made by Goerdeler and Beck, by Popitz, Jessen and von Hassell and by a group in Freiburg. The Socialists and Communists had less need to do such planning since Marx and Lenin had provided them with blue-prints. The very act of drawing up such a plan implied a belief that Hitler might not be going to win the war – and defeatism was punishable by death. The plans (which will be discussed in Chapter VI) began as informal talks among civilian friends. They felt a compulsive urge to speak to people whom they could trust about the theme that was dominating their lives. They did not include precise proposals as to how Hitler should be removed. The persons concerned realised that they were not themselves in a position to start a revolt or commit a murder; the most that they could do, and did, was to seek to persuade those who were better placed in this respect. While some of the groups may have advanced to the stage of having a series of meetings with agendas, sharing out the preparation of papers and even allocating positions in a post-Hitler government, they never became formal organisations with rules, procedures for admission to membership or subscriptions or for the taking of decisions. Kreisau maintained before the People's court that they had done no more than think, although neither they nor the Court really believed this ingenuous defence.

There was at the time and has been since much argument as to the value of such plan-making. People argued (as Roosevelt did on the other side of the hill) that it was not possible to foresee the conditions under which a new system would be established and that it is always a mistake to attempt answers to hypothetical questions. The planners were of course completely wrong when they assumed that they would be left a free hand by the conquerors after the war and, while some have thought that the victors should never have interfered as much as they did, the idea of them not intervening at all is visionary.

There were – and are – three main answers to these criticisms. One is that the conspirators hoped they would be in a stronger position at the end of the war if they had reached some sort of agreement between themselves as to what it was that they wanted and such agreement could not be reached without discussion. The pros and cons of the various possibilities needed further examination. A second answer is that the various participants would by such discussions get to know one another and learn how to work together, which would be a valuable preparation for the tasks facing them after Hitler had been eliminated. Thirdly planning can be thought of as an exercise in maintaining morale. Most of the plans originated about 1940–1 when Hitler was on top of the world and those who wanted to get rid of him were near despair. To plan in such circumstances was an act of faith, an assertion that in spite of appearances, truth and humanity were going to prevail. It was better than sitting around and wringing one's hands – and there was not much else to be done. We should respect the motives of the planners and not belittle them.

(j) Actively helping the enemy

German law drew a distinction between High Treason, *Hochverrat* (planning to overthrow the Government) and treason to the country, *Landesverrat* (helping other countries to defeat the Government). The second was thought by many, including some of Hitler's antagonists, to be more heinous than the first. Yet a number of Germans engaged in it.

Numerous contacts between Germans and citizens of countries hostile to Germany were made before and during the war. Some were established on the initiative of the German leaders themselves. Thus Hitler in July 1938 sent his personal aide Captain Fritz Wiedemann to London to explore the chances of doing a deal over Czechoslovakia. Hess in flying to Britain in May 1941 not merely hoped to change England from a foe to an anti-Russian ally but seems to have believed that Hitler would approve of the mission. Göring used the Swedish business man Dahlerus as a private channel to the British Government for the purpose of heading off war. Ribbentrop in 1943 used

Peter Kleist, a German with Russian connections, to explore the possibility of peace in the east.

But these and similar contacts were made with the intention of keeping Hitler in power. We are here concerned with those which had the aim of removing him. They can be divided into three broad groups.

(*i*) Before war broke out several individuals tried to persuade foreign Governments (and particularly the British) to prevent it by adopting an unmistakably firm attitude towards Hitler and his supporters. In 1938 (the main year in question) the most prominent people concerned were Ewald von Kleist-Schmenzin (pp. 11 and 125) who went to London in August with the encouragement of Beck and the assistance of Ian Colvin, the Berlin correspondent of the *News Chronicle;* Erich Kordt, a career diplomat who had accepted a post as head of Ribbentrop's Ministerial Bureau in the hope of limiting the damage which the Minister could do; his brother Theodor, who was Counsellor at the German Embassy in London; and a retired soldier Böhm-Tettelbach. The Kordts acted at the instigation of von Weizsäcker, the AA State Secretary, although going rather further than he intended; Böhm-Tettelbach at the instigation of Halder just after he had become Chief of Staff. Von Kleist saw Churchill, Lloyd and Vansittart; Theo Kordt saw Halifax the Foreign Secretary and Böhm-Tettelbach saw nobody worth mentioning. The tenor of their messages was that Hitler was actively planning to invade Czechoslovakia but that, if the British and French Governments acted in such a way as to convince him that they would then come to his victim's aid, he would either hold his hand and thus lose his credit with the German people or, if he persevered, be overthrown by an opposition group which had its plans ready. The missions failed, for reasons which will be discussed in Chapter V, but most of those involved were relieved rather than depressed by the Munich settlement. To help in carrying conviction, Kleist-Schmenzin was authorised to give the date for the German attack as 28 September.[71] This was the only precise piece of military information disclosed, although inciting foreign governments to act in a way which will frustrate the aims of one's own hardly falls within the normal limits of loyalty. Theo Kordt later gave the date as 19 or 20 September. The negotiations leading to the Munich Conference rendered all these dates incorrect.

In 1939 the Kordts were again active while Adam von Trott with encouragement from Walter Hewel and others in the AA (but not from Weizsäcker, as has often been said) managed to see both Halifax and Chamberlain (p. 182). Fabian von Schlabrendorff saw Churchill (p. 125). Colonel Gerhard von Schwerin, the head of the British 'desk' in German Military Intelligence, saw several senior officers, including the Director of Naval Intelligence, but his aim was to suggest how Britain could deter Hitler, not to convey information. Weizsäcker approached the British Government through Burckhardt, the Swiss diplomat who was Commissioner for the League of Nations in Danzig. The object of all these approaches was either to intimidate Hitler into holding his hand over Poland by convincing him that Munich could not be repeated or (after the Russo-German Pact had made such an attempt futile) to find a way of repeating it. They did not involve any communication of military secrets. Such communication was however made on 26 occasions[72] by Colonel Oster of the Abwehr who sought in 1939–40 through his friend Sas, the Dutch Military Attaché in Berlin, to warn the Netherlands Government of intended attacks on Holland in the vain hope that that Government would take precautionary steps and thus prevent the attack from being made. In the closing stages when it was clear that the attack could not be prevented, Oster's aim was to bring about its failure and thereby Hitler's overthrow. In Moscow 'Johnny' Herwath the Second Secretary of the German Embassy kept 'Chips' Bohlen of the American one well-informed about the progress of the Russo-German talks throughout the summer of 1939, his object being to prevent their success and thereby reduce the risk of war.

(*ii*) The second group consists of those who at various stages during the war sought to discover the terms on which Allied Governments would be prepared to make peace with a post-Hitler regime and obtain some sort of a promise that, if a putsch was carried through and led to confusion in Germany, they would not take advantage of German weakness by extracting harsher terms than they would have been content with otherwise or, after January 1943, would not continue to insist on unconditional surrender. In some cases suggestions were made that, if a satisfactory political answer were forthcoming, the anti-Nazis would actively assist the arrival of British and American (but not Russian) troops in Germany. A separate book would be needed to list and discuss all these feelers; an idea of their volume can be drawn from the fact that the British Foreign Office file which contains the main papers about the Bell–Bonhoeffer meeting in Sweden in 1942 – and it is only one among several – also includes papers about 20 other separate feelers![73] But few or none of these contacts involved the transmission of military secrets. Indeed when Helmuth von Moltke met the US Military Attaché in Istanbul in December 1942, the American tried to use the interview to extract such information, whereupon the German ended it.[74] The wisdom of the way these approaches were received will be discussed in Chapter VII.

(*iii*) The third group consists of those who before and during the war did provide the enemy with information of political and economic value with the intention of bringing about a military defeat. The most prominent member of this group would seem to have been Canaris (p. 155) but the security sources from which we derive our knowledge stress that what he conveyed were intentions rather than activities. His messages came to the British, as did those of a highly-placed official in the German Air Ministry, of the Junkers representative in Paris, of two junior secretaries in German Embassies and of an unknown individual who in the winter of 1939–40 deposited a parcel of valuable technical information on the doorstep of the British Embassy in Oslo. In the summer of 1939 it was the Americans in Moscow to whom Johnny Herwath spoke (expecting them to pass the information on to the British, which they did not do), while after Allen Dulles reached Geneva in November

1942 he was provided with information by Fritz Kolbe, a clerk in the AA, as well as by Gisevius.[75] From 1936 until his arrest in 1941 important information was passed to the Czechs by Paul Thümmel, a member of the Abwehr staff in Dresden who seems however to have been working independently of Canaris and Oster. The Russians were fed by Schulze-Boysen (p. 209) and Richard Sorge, whose tip, sent shortly before his arrest in Tokyo in 1941, that the Japanese intended to attack the US rather than the USSR, was perhaps the most important piece of espionage in the war, since it encouraged the Red Army to transfer from the Far East the divisions which helped to halt the Wehrmacht before Moscow in December 1941.[76] On at least three occasions before 22 June 1941 German soldiers went over to the Russians to warn them of the intended attack. Another way of obstructing one's rulers was illustrated by Colonel Kirchbach of the Army General Staff who saw to it that a copy of Colonel Hossbach's record of Hitler's meeting on 5 November 1937 was preserved till the end of the war and then handed to the British, thus enabling it to become a key document at the Nuremburg Trials. These cases however were only the tip of an iceberg.

Conventional thought would have condemned most of the people in all three classes as criminals. When Halder in the spring of 1940 showed his chief the report about British terms of peace with a post-Hitler régime which had been obtained through the Vatican, Brauchitsch said that it should never have been brought to him:

> What is happening here is sheer treason. Under no circumstances can we be involved in this. We are at war. In peacetime you can consider contacts with a foreign power but in wartime soldiers cannot do that. Moreover this is not a struggle between governments. We are concerned about a contest of ideologies.[77]

But none of those who made contact with the enemy in the ways described did so in order to gain money or personal advantage (although some of them might have obtained important posts after Hitler had been overthrown). Some would have pleaded that they were trying to prevent a war which would cost many lives and was likely to end disastrously. Weizsäcker's conduct has been described as 'Treason for the sake of peace.' The others would have argued that, in trying to hasten the end of a hopeless war, overthrow a tyranny and thereby save lives, they were acting in and not against the best interests of their fellow-citizens. Much the same arguments would have been used by those German prisoners-of-war who in July 1943 agreed to co-operate with the Russians in the National Committee for Free Germany.

Three separate issues need to be distinguished here. One is how far an individual is entitled to act on a conviction that he knows better than his governors what is for the good of his country. In this regard treason has often in the past proved just a matter of the calendar. The second is how far an individual is entitled to put what he is convinced to be the interests of humanity as a whole above those of that particular part of humanity to which he under international law belongs (usually by the accident of birth). This is a matter on which views have varied through the centuries; many martyrs who died for a supranational cause at the hands of their national rulers have been venerated by posterity. The third question is how far those who seek to bring victory to Communism over what they regard as Fascism are doing more than replacing one tyranny by another.

A further question which needs to be asked in connection with the betrayal of military secrets is whether it now serves any useful purpose. Belligerents today have so many ways of obtaining intelligence that personal leaks seldom do more than confirm what is already known. On the day in 1938 when von Kleist gave to his contacts in London the date of Hitler's intended attack on Czechoslovakia, the British Government obtained virtually the same information from its Military Attaché in Berlin.[78] Moreover the techniques of strategic deception have been so developed that leaks are apt to be evaluated as attempts to mislead. Stalin is said to have received warnings from 83 different sources of the impending German attack in 1941 and to have disregarded them all as attempts to embroil the Soviet Union with the Third Reich.[79] The Dutch had received from Oster so many warnings of German attacks which proved false that when the real one came they did not believe it. Thümmel's warning in 1940 that the German attack would come through the Ardennes went unheeded because of the French conviction that the Ardennes were impassable. Perhaps the most valuable information which a traitor can give concerns the 'moles' already established in the network to which he is leaking.

A case which defies classification is provided by Colonel von Gersdorff, who on 21 March 1943 had been ready to blow himself up for the sake of taking Hitler with him (p. 128). By July 1944 he had been posted to France as Chief of Staff to the 7th Army. After the failure of the putsch he thought that the choice for him lay between suicide, 'crossing the Channel' or going underground in France. But after hearing that the information held against him by the SD was not incriminating, he tried to persuade Kluge to open negotiations with Bradley directly. When that proved vain (p. 151) he returned to his post. He never seems to have considered surrendering and when he was actually taken prisoner by the English, his 'sporting instincts' made him take a chance of escaping from this 'humiliating captivity'. He then led his troops out of the Falaise 'pocket' after they had been nearly surrounded, for which he received the Knight's Cross on the spot from Kluge's successor, Model. He was promoted Major-General and went on fighting until the very end of April 1945.[80]

(k) Organising revolution or assassination

In April 1943 Helmuth von Moltke wrote to Lionel Curtis that

> in discussions before the war, I maintained that belief in God was not essential for coming to the results you arrive at. Today I know I was wrong, completely wrong. You know that I have fought the Nazis from the first day, but the amount

of risk and readiness for sacrifice which is asked from us now and which may
be asked tomorrow requires more than right ethical principles.[81]

In other words an active faith is needed if an individual is to withstand the
pressure which a totalitarian régime (usually inspired by a rival faith) is under
modern conditions capable of exercising. For this reason the people who
withstood Hitler most firmly were Christians or Communists.[82] People whose
principles derived from a non-supernatural humanism were either less firm
(partly because their principles included toleration and disbelief in force) or,
like Moltke, discovered that those principles had, after all, supernatural roots.
At first, as we have seen, there were relatively few of such people, convinced
of the imperative need to change the régime. By themselves they were too few
and unorganised to give a rising any chance of success and, as events proved,
none ever found themselves in a position where they could kill Hitler, an act
to which many were anyhow opposed. Most Germans believed in Nazism or
believed that it would further some cause which they had at heart, or were
prepared to go along with it for the sake of a quiet life or, if they objected
to it, only objected to individual aspects (especially the interventions in Church
affairs) so that reform in these respects (which they for long believed to be
possible) would remove their antagonism. Gradually however the position
changed.

The coalition government set up on 30 January 1933 was based (p. 27) on
a compromise. Hitler would restore German prosperity, remove the danger
from the left, enlist the support of the masses for the national cause, and re-
establish Germany as a Great Power. All this he duly did. But his partners
had also expected that he would buttress the waning influence of the pre-
industrial élite and allow them something approaching an equal say in his
choice of policies, and in these respects they were disappointed. They lost
their influence in the Cabinet and the Cabinet ceased to be of importance in
running the country. Many Nazi measures militated against their interests.
Others were even more amoral than they were prepared to tolerate. And
instead of stopping short when Germany had recovered her position of 1914,
Hitler launched on a campaign of further conquest which he soon looked like
failing to win. The conditions of the coalition, no less important because they
had never been explicitly formulated, were being broken.

Moreover it gradually became clear that the various modes of *Widerstand*
described in this chapter were not going to be effective. Protests would get
little or no hearing, partly because of Hitler's conviction that he knew better
than his critics, partly because some of the ways by which the Nazis were
endangering their chances of victory (such as the treatment of the subjugated
populations in the east) were fundamental to the Nazi faith. The conviction
gradually grew, among many who had begun as supporters or sympathisers,
that, if Germany's vital interests and good name were to be protected from
further damage, the 'brown pest' would have to be evicted from power. But
the inclusion of Hitler among those to be evicted, while essential, would not

by itself be enough to change the character of the régime. Those who undertook to remove him by arrest or assassination would need to impose their will about what happened next. This would require the use of organised force so that preparations for an overthrow had to be in the hands of people who possessed the authority to command force or had the ear of someone who did possess it. The next stage therefore is to look at the difficulties facing anyone who wanted to achieve such authority.

CHAPTER V
The difficulties of the
Widerstand

(a) The apparatus of repression

In March 1943 Helmuth von Moltke wrote to Lionel Curtis:

> Lack of communication. That is the worst. Can you imagine what it is like if you
>
> a. cannot use the telephone
> b. cannot use the post
> c. cannot send a messenger, because you probably have no one to send and, if you have, you cannot give him a written message as the police sometimes search people in trains etc. for documents.
> d. cannot even speak with those with whom you are completely d'accord, because the secret police have methods of questioning where they first break the will but leave the intelligence awake, thereby inducing the victim to speak out all he knows: therefore you must limit information to those who absolutely need it.
> e. cannot even rely on a rumour or a whispering campaign to spread information as there is so effective a ban on communications of all kinds that a whispering campaign started in Munich may never reach Augsburg. There is only one way of communicating news and that is the London wireless, as that is listened to by many people who belong to the opposition proper and by many disaffected Party Members.[1]

It is only fair to add that the writer of these remarks carried on for over four years a correspondence with his wife which was never once interfered with and which forms the basis for much of our knowledge about the activities of his group. But his letters would have been difficult to identify at the Berlin end while at the country end not only were the people in the post office on good terms with the Moltkes but they were simple folk who would have understood little of what Helmuth was writing about. If the interception had been made in the local town or elsewhere en route, the delay would have been noticeable.

Nazi decrees issued on 4 and 28 February 1933 had made drastic inroads on the freedom of the individual. As time went on, and particularly after the outbreak of war, these restrictions were steadily supplemented.

Severe penalties, including death, could be inflicted for offences against the rationing orders. The Law for the Amendment of the Criminal Law Code of June 1935 required judges to decide whether a case deserved to be handled according to the fundamental principles of criminal law or according to the 'healthy instinct of the people'. A further general clause authorised the continual holding in custody of all those who were suspected of deserving punishment and those who were thought likely to use freedom to commit more crimes. Any critical remark about the progress of the war could be treated as a capital breach of the Special War Crimes Order, forbidding the demoralisation of the Armed Forces. The Public Injury Order made offences committed under cover of the black-out liable to the death penalty.[2] The Malice Law (*Heimtückgesetz*) of March 1933 made it obligatory on all patriotic *Volksgenossen* to bring to the notice of the authorities any activities which might be hostile to the Government. The Broadcasting Order made it a capital offence to pass on news obtained by black listening (p. 62). In April 1942 Hitler obtained from the Reichstag unlimited power to dismiss or punish as he thought fit any German lacking in ardour or honesty (p. 35). Thus the authorities had a comprehensive arsenal of repressive regulations.

They also had plenty of people to enforce the measures. The Gestapo had a staff of 40,000 in 1943.[3] In a relatively small place like Aschaffenburg it had 154 correspondents[4]; admittedly most of these were reporting on the state of public opinion and morale but they were equally expected to watch out for and bring to notice any activities which smacked of subversion. One of the great difficulties of the *Widerstand* was precisely the fact that so many Germans approved of Hitler and had little sympathy for those who did not. Opponents were thus deprived of the very thing which Mao described as being as vital to a resistance movement as water to a fish, namely a well-disposed population. This distinguished the German situation fundamentally from that of the 'Resistance' in German-occupied countries. Terror tightened after 1936 as the various branches of the police all gradually became subordinated to the SS. Repression grew ever fiercer as the war situation grew worse; Himmler, in addition to his other posts, was made Minister of the Interior in August 1943 and Commander-in-Chief of the Replacement Army eleven months later. Every worker was required to carry an employment record while a card-index was instituted of those thought to be politically unreliable.[5] A British officer was sent to Germany in May 1945 with a list of 118 agents who had been infiltrated through France; she obtained information about 117, all of whom had been killed.[6] Russian agents sent in by parachute were persistently caught. A certain number of the trials and sentences were published, with derogatory comment, as a means of deterring imitation. But too frequent publication would have suggested an imperfect *Volksgemeinschaft* so that nobody could be certain that what they had done would be disclosed. Martyrs may hope to light such candles as shall never be put out but their ability to do so depends on their martyrdom becoming known. 'The martyr with us is certain to be classed as a common criminal,' wrote von Moltke. 'That makes death useless.'[7]

SD methods of infiltrating spies were as insistent and ingenious as any now used by Communist intelligence services. The story went that when a man started to criticise the régime to a friend, the other replied 'Hush! One of us may belong to the Gestapo' – but that very story may have been invented by the authorities to intimidate conspirators. A Catholic priest from Stettin who had been Vicar-General of Innsbruck, Karl Lamprecht, was imprisoned in Dachau and on his release, required to live near Swinemünde. Here he met an Austrian who professed to be a Catholic anti-Nazi and to have worked in a factory making flying bombs. He suggested to Lamprecht that plans for the bombs should be stolen and sent to England via the Vatican. Lamprecht thought the idea naive and took no action; the Austrian proved to be a spy who told the authorities that Lamprecht had agreed to the proposal which led to his being executed in November 1944.[8]

A doctor called Reckzeh, who had already worked for the Gestapo in Switzerland, called in the summer of 1943 on Bianca Segantini, the daughter of a famous Swiss artist, at the village of Sils Maria in the Engadine, with a woman who professed to be his wife. The latter lamented that she knew nobody in Berlin with whom to confide about her strong anti-Nazi views; her hostess out of sympathy gave her an introduction to a Fräulein von Thadden who (until evicted by the Nazis) had been the headmistress of a progressive girls' boarding school. Dr Reckzeh himself called soon afterwards on Fräulein von Thadden who invited him to a party which she was about to give for Frau Solf, widow of a distinguished Orientalist who had held two ministerial posts under the Kaiser. The party was attended by a number of friends of Frau Solf (labelled later by the Gestapo as the 'Solf Circle'). It was held on the day after Italy had capitulated and not surprisingly the talk turned on the possibility of the same thing happening in Germany. The general view expressed was that the war was irrevocably lost and that Hitler would have to be got rid of. Before leaving Dr Reckzeh said that he would soon be going back to Switzerland and offered to take letters to people living there. Fräulein von Thadden gave him one to Dr Siegmund-Schulze, a prominent member of the World Council of Churches who had emigrated from Germany early in the Third Reich; she later regretted her action and went to the doctor's house to recover the letter but was told it had been destroyed as too dangerous.

A few days later an official who was sympathetic to the *Widerstand* and worked in a unit responsible for phone-tapping told Helmuth von Moltke that a watch had been placed on the telephone of Frau Solf and a number of her friends. They therefore rebuffed all further approaches from Dr Reckzeh and cut down their use of the telephone to a minimum. Siegmund-Schulze, who had reached his own conclusions about the doctor, accused him openly on his next visit of being an agent. The Gestapo realised that the group had been warned and were unlikely as a result to produce any more information. They therefore arrested Frau Solf, Fraülein von Thadden and others of the circle, as well as Helmuth von Moltke and the official who had given him the tip-off. A number of people were executed as a result and Frau Solf only escaped because the Japanese Embassy intervened on her behalf.[9]

The danger that anyone arrested would not be able to withstand interrogation for long led the Communists to base their organisation on cells of three of whom only one had contacts outside the cell and knew who was in other cells. Böhm-Tettelbach, when sent to London by Halder in 1938 (p. 71), knew nothing of the mission of Kleist-Schmenzin or of the activities or the Kordts; the British regarded this as evidence of *Widerstand* incompetence. One advantage of the way in which conspiracy developed out of more or less casual conversation between friends was that practically no one was brought into a group unless someone already in it knew him well enough to vouch for him. It is remarkable that, although many of the generals who were approached refused to join in the conspiracy, none of them reported the approach to the police. Burckhardt (the Swiss League of Nations Commissioner for Danzig) and Weizsäcker, in writing to one another, always said the opposite of what they meant, which led to misconceptions after the war when the US State Department started to publish their captured correspondence.[10] Schlabrendorff was acquitted by the Gestapo of being a defeatist because he ended a letter 'Heil Hitler and Faith in final victory', thereby meaning the victory of the conspiracy.[11] Field-Marshal von Mackensen wrote to Beck in October 1938, 'A letter is not the place nowadays to discuss things like your resignation.'[12] A Socialist remarked that, when he met his former associates, what was not said was more important than what was.

Inevitably mishaps occurred. A member of the *Rote Stosstrupp* group, who was sending leaflets through the post, 'borrowed' his employer's franking machine. But one of his envelopes went to a 'dead' address and was marked 'returned to sender', with the result that it came back to the employer who was an old Party Member.[13] A Mannheim Socialist group was given away in 1934 when a motor-cyclist carrying material had an accident and all the papers were strewn over the road. Later another agent in the same city hid copies of the underground paper *The Harbinger* under a pile of logs in a cellar. Some electricians came to instal lighting for an air-raid shelter, moved the logs, found the papers and told the police.[14] On the other hand the needs of the front for manpower reduced the numbers of people available to maintain security and the confusion in the bombed areas increased the chances of offenders going undetected or unpursued. The Gestapo reaction however was to replace efficiency by savagery.

Undoubtedly the security authorities knew something and suspected more about the hatching of conspiracies. Goerdeler and von Hassell began to be watched soon after they gave up their official posts in 1938. Müller's activities in the Vatican in the winter of 1939–40 did not take long to reach the ears of the SD.[15] An agent was placed in the house next to Beck's until it was hit by a bomb. Ribbentrop, according to Weizsäcker, 'repeatedly expressed misgivings about the Abwehr, about certain generals, about members of our own department like the Kordts, Kessell and Etzdorf and about my relations with them.'[16] Himmler once told Canaris that he knew perfectly well about appreciable groups in the army who played with plans for an overthrow.[17] He even contemplated joining in himself and in August 1943 arranged through his lawyer Carl Langbehn and the SS *Obergruppenführer* Wolff to have a talk with Popitz. But before anything could come of it, Göring's listening service intercepted an Allied message from Switzerland which gave the game away and Himmler had hastily to order Langbehn's arrest so as to cover his own tracks.[18] The peculiar relationships between the Abwehr and SD will be dealt with in the case history on Canaris (pp. 152–60).

There are three theories as to why the Gestapo did not strike sooner. One is that they lacked hard evidence; this is borne out by their readiness to arrest Moltke and Dohnanyi on minor charges in the hope that this would lead on to something bigger. The second is that they were afraid of the damage which might be done to the régime if the number and distinction of the dissenters became known; this certainly led to a clamp-down on publicity about the July plot once they discovered in September how wide its extent had been. The third is that they foresaw the possibility of using the plotters' foreign contacts to save their own skins after defeat.

(b) The military oath

The upshot of the last section is that positive work against the régime could only be carried on effectively from within an organisation sheltered to some extent from the apparatus of repression: the armed forces, the civil service (especially the diplomatic service), and the terror-machine itself (Gestapo, Kripo, Abwehr). The plans for following up Hitler's assassination in 1943–4 (code-named Valkyrie) were worked out under the pretence that they were an officially sanctioned contingency plan for supressing a rising by the SS or foreign workers. Most army officers however took the line adopted by Beck when at the time of the Fritsch affair in February 1938 he was told by Halder that it was his duty to coerce Hitler by a threat of the collective resignation of the top officers in the General Staff; he quoted von Schlieffen's remark that 'mutiny and revolution are words which do not exist in the dictionary of the German soldier'. And when six months later he pressed precisely that course on his fellow-generals, they in turn were unwilling to follow him.[19]

The formal reason for this was the military oath. Until 1918 all recruits to the armed forces had sworn an oath in the face of God to obey the Kaiser. In 1919 a new formula was adopted in which all reference to God was omitted and the Constitution put in the place of the Head of State. On Hindenburg's death in 1934, when Hitler amalgamated the offices of President and Chancellor, all members of the armed forces were called on at short notice to swear a new oath devised by von Blomberg and von Reichenau on Hitler's instructions (which seem to have been issued before the old President was actually dead). The new form ran

I swear this holy oath before God that I will give unconditional obedience to the leader of the German Reich and Volk, Adolf Hitler, the Commander-in-Chief of the Wehrmacht, and will be ready as a brave soldier to give my life at any time for this oath.

The oath thus represented a contract between the Wehrmacht and Hitler. Allegiance was sworn to the leader of the German Volk and Reich, not to the Leader of the National Socialist Party. It was an attempt to commit Hitler to basing himself on the Wehrmacht which had pledged itself to him, and thus to taking its side where necessary against the NS movement. Although it went back to the days of the Monarchy in restoring the reference to God and to the Head of State instead of to the Constitution, it introduced for the first time a commitment to unconditional obedience.[20]

A number of objections have been brought against this oath. One is that the Wehrmacht were rushed into it without any time for consultation and without it receiving the approval of any statutory body — but for that two senior officers must share in the responsibility. Another is that Hitler's amalgamation of the two posts amounted to an amendment to the Constitution and that the Enabling Act of March 1933 did not extend to such amendments so that, to be valid, the change required a two-thirds majority in the Reichstag. But the strength of this argument is blunted by the facts that Hitler could easily have obtained such a majority if he had seen fit and instead called a retrospective plebiscite which he won overwhelmingly. A third objection is that he bolstered up the gravity of the oath by appealing to a God in whom he did not believe.

The fourth and most serious objection is that an oath is a contract which presupposes a future line of conduct on the part of its recipient as well as of the person giving it. No oath, however solemn, can override the moral law, so that an oath-taker is not justified in requiring the oath-giver to do anything which conflicts with that law, such as shooting an unarmed and compliant prisoner. A paragraph in the Prussian Code of Military Law stipulated that orders with a criminal content were not to be obeyed and that a soldier who did obey was liable to punishment.[21] Hitler himself on one occasion said that any member of any nation whose leaders ordered a course of conduct which was going to lead to its downfall had not only a right but a duty to disobey.[22] This could not be altered by calling the obedience 'unconditional', since the addition of such a term did not remove the presupposition that no immoral action would be ordered. For anyone to promise in advance to obey any command, no matter how immoral, is inconsistent with the invocation of God to give extra weight to the promise. In a memorandum to Brauchitsch on 16 July 1938 Beck wrote

Final decisions affecting the existence of the nation are at stake here. History will bring a charge of blood-guilt against these leaders if they do not act in accordance with their technical and political knowledge and conscience. Their obedience as soldiers reaches a limit at the point at which their knowledge, conscience and sense of responsibility forbids the execution of a command.[23]

These considerations, which have naturally received more prominence since 1945 than they did at the time, did not prevent the majority of members of the forces from treating the obligation to loyalty as binding. Often the oath may have been a convenient excuse for those who were anyhow indisposed to run the risks involved in conspiracy. But it is undeniable that an unusually high level of obedience to commands is essential to an army. And it is one thing to disobey an immoral order and another to take steps towards removing the people giving the order. The oath helped to reinforce the Reichswehr tradition of the non-political officer which received its classic formulation at the Nuremburg trial when von Rundstedt was asked why he had made no attempt to dissuade Hitler from issuing the 'Commissar Order'. 'The political aspect,' he replied, 'does not concern the officer. He carries out the military duty assigned to him by his superior.'[24] Such an attitude treats 'moral' as identical with 'political', while the possibility that the matter is not altogether simple even in the sphere of politics is suggested by the approval which history has given to the action of Peter von Yorck's ancestor in signing the Convention of Tauroggen in 1812 against the orders of his King. Certainly scruples about the oath played only a secondary part in bringing about the failure of the various attempts on Hitler's life (although more than one attempt was abandoned for fear it might cause the deaths of a number of innocent officers). It was of importance that senior members of the Churches were ready to condone actions incompatible with the oath.

(c) The stab-in-the-back trauma

There was widespread fear that action against the régime by the army would precipitate civil war. This was a major consideration among senior commanders – and rightly so. The behaviour of a number of SS, Gestapo and Party Members in official posts when defeat stared them in the face, executing anyone who took steps towards surrender, shows that they were desperate men who would stick at nothing rather than give themselves up to what they imagined would be an unpleasant fate.[25] They were organised, they were armed, they were relatively numerous; the SS are said to have had more men in Berlin on 20 July 1944 than the army.[26] This judgment is not affected by the fact that after surrender there was little resistance or sabotage and that the 'Werewolves' never materialised. If these people did not get beyond talking, it was due to the conditions surrounding them and to the precautions which the Allies took. Had they had their chances, they would have been anything but the stunt as which they are sometimes dismissed.

It was the desire to reduce the risk of civil war which led the conspirators to insist at first that a bomb should only be exploded if Göring and Himmler were present as well as Hitler. Their absence was one of the reasons for the attempts on 7, 11 and 16 July being abandoned. The officers wanted an orderly revolution, a managed defeat (*gesteuerte Niederlage*). Seeing what might have happened if there had been sustained fighting between two (or more!) armed groups inside Germany, and if the Allies had felt compelled to join in (perhaps on different sides) who can say that they were wrong?

Nor is it certain that the army would all have been on one side. Manstein has already been quoted (p. 33) as saying early in 1943 that the young officers were still as mad about Hitler as ever: 'It would split the army.' When an officer a little later proposed to Tresckow that Hitler's headquarters should be eliminated en bloc, that inveterate anti-Nazi replied that a Divisional Commander ready to do such an act could probably be found but not a Division of troops to support him because 'the majority still regard themselves as soldiers of the Führer'.[27] Moreover the public reaction to the Stauffenberg attempt (p. 57) does not suggest that readiness to support Hitler would have vanished overnight.

A considerable number of Germans would have been willing, perhaps even glad, to be rid of Hitler if they could have kept his achievements. But they were afraid that any action taken against him, especially if it led to civil war, would result in external defeat and thus to the loss of his achievements. The fear of once again incurring the stab-in-the-back charge was acute – not only on the German side, since the Allies for their part did not want to provide the Germans with any excuse for doubting that rabid nationalism led to catastrophe. The retired General von Hammerstein-Equord said to his son, whom he knew to be contemplating action, 'Don't kill him too early.'[28] But the fundamental dilemma of the *Widerstand* was that, as von Hassell put it, 'there is no way of avoiding criticism . . . if one waits until everyone can see that we have no chance of victory, we shall have lost the chance of a tolerable peace.'[29] For Germany's enemies were clearly unlikely to negotiate a compromise peace once they felt confident of winning an outright victory fairly soon and then being able to impose their own terms. One of the difficulties was that whereas Churchill and Roosevelt believed that they were going to win from December 1941 onwards, few Germans believed that their country might lose until fifteen months later. In July 1944 the worsening military situation in both west and east was a major factor in inducing the conspirators to act forthwith. But this was a problem for those who, while anti-Hitler, thought in the traditional terms of national patriotism. The relatively few who were primarily concerned with putting a stop to Nazi inhumanities saw the matter from a different angle.

The combined fear of bringing about civil war and precipitating defeat was the basic reason why the commanding generals never moved against Hitler. The conspirators, who had originally thought it essential to have the support of the Army Commander-in-Chief, had to dispense with a requirement which was unrealisable. As Captain Kaiser, the peacetime schoolmaster who kept the war diary at the General Army Office in Berlin, put it in February 1943, 'One half are ready to act when they get orders, the other half are ready to give orders when someone else has taken action.'[30] Manstein told Gersdorff that he would always be ready to put himself at the service of the 'legal government'.[31] The closer one got to the top levels of command, the greater the reluctance became. As Stauffenberg said in May 1943, 'Since the generals have achieved nothing so far, it is now for the colonels to take over.'[32] Had it been otherwise the war might have ended in 1943. But the unconditional surrender which the Allies demanded meant putting the fate of Germany into their hands and trusting that they were too civilised to behave like Tartars and too far-sighted (in spite of Morgenthau) to create a destitute Germany as a power vacuum in Central Europe. Commanders who acted before a decision had been reached in the field were bound, as Hassell said, to be accused of betraying the national interest. Their only effective defence would be that the terms which they obtained could plausibly be considered better than those which they would have been likely to obtain by going on to the end. Otherwise they would be wiser to wait for defeat, after which they could always load off the blame onto Hitler. But we know that, even if the Allies had ceased to demand unconditional surrender, the terms which they would have offered instead would not have been such as to meet the requirements of the German commanders.

If Britain and the United States had been Germany's only enemies, not merely would she have stood in less danger of total defeat (which would in itself have increased the chances of those two countries contemplating a compromise peace) but the danger involved in having to accept whatever conditions the victors chose to offer would have been reduced. Neither country was likely to insist on a serious social revolution inside Germany (even if the Labour Party talked of depriving landowners and industrialists of their economic power). Through all the writings and discussions of the conspirators in the years 1942–5 runs the theme that the Western Powers could not be so obtuse as not to see the need for German military power to be maintained as an essential aid to keeping Communism out of Western Europe. During those years, the main aim of German political warfare, Nazi as well as anti-Nazi, was to break up the unnatural alliance which Hitler called into existence in 1941 by attacking the Soviet Union before he had finished the war in the west.

It was the fear of 'the Cossacks on the Elbe', the introduction of a publicly-owned Planned Economy and the establishment of an atheistic working-class dictatorship, along with the prospect of German males being taken as slave labour to rebuild Russia, which, as Churchill told Roosevelt in November 1944, really perturbed the German military leaders.[33] All the long-established horror of Communism welled up, reinforced by the long-established contempt for Slavs. It is true that, after Stalin allowed the National Committee of Free Germany to be set up in July 1943 (p. 97), with its suggestion that Russia might make peace with a Germany which had withdrawn to its 1914 boundaries, allowing it to retain an army and a democratic social system, some of the conspirators began to toy with the idea of an 'Eastern Solution' (*Ostlosung*). But they used it for much the same purpose as the Soviet Government used the National Committee, namely to frighten the West into being more co-operative. And once the Americans and British had given the Russians much of what they wanted at the Tehran Conference in November 1943, and once it became apparent that the National Committee was getting no response from the German political and military leaders, interest began to wane, although as late as the summer of 1944 von Trott was trying to make contact with the Soviet Embassy in Stockholm (p. 186). The existence of the National Committee was never referred to explicitly in Nazi home publicity until October 1944 and it is hard to discover how much the average man knew about it or what his reactions were. Significantly few of those who showed concern during the war about the danger of Communist influence had expressed similar concern when Hitler made his pact with Stalin in August 1939.

(d) Murder as a last resort and an elusive possibility

The killing of Hitler only became a primary aim of the conspirators at a late stage. What was at first contemplated was an overthrow of the Nazi Government (*Putsch, Staatsstreich*), along with the arrest of the Führer and his main assistants, followed by their trial for breaches of international law and morality. It was believed, perhaps naively, that when the German people discovered what crimes had been committed in their name, they would rapidly repudiate the persons principally responsible and accept that action against them had been justified. An alternative was to have Hitler declared insane; Bonhoeffer's psychiatrist father was prepared to testify to this effect. The possibility was allowed for that in the confusion of the arrest Hitler might get shot (no doubt 'while trying to escape') and in 1938 Oster and Gisevius provided for a Commando squad to do this. But assassination was not a part of the original plans and many people objected to it on moral grounds. One of the chief charges made against the Nazis was their scanty regard for legal process and the view was at first widespread that those who claimed the right to overthrow them on moral grounds should not begin by imitating them in a vital respect.

As time went on however two considerations drove Hitler's antagonists to think that murder might after all be the only practicable way of getting rid of him. One was the fear that his fanatical supporters would not stand idly by while he was put on trial but might try to rescue him (as Mussolini was rescued) and thus unleash civil war. The other was the difficulty of finding the officers and men who would start the putsch off. To expect the rank-and-file of any unit to act on their own initiative was obviously hopeless. Some might be prepared to act on the orders of their officers (although, given the enthusiasm for Hitler among the lower ranks, even this was uncertain). The core of the difficulty was to find officers who were not merely convinced of the need to murder their Commander-in-Chief but who commanded enough troops for the desired aim to be attainable. Most of the conspirators were staff officers and the kind of troops whom such officers command are clerks and cooks, who would be no match for the SS guarding Führer Headquarters. The officers who did command troops were nearly all away at the front, some distance from those Headquarters and fully taken up in fighting the enemy. To move them several hundred miles and leave the front line empty was impracticable, at any rate unless orders could be obtained from a very high level and, as has been said, orders at that level were unlikely to be forthcoming. Early in 1943 Captain George von Boeselager was enabled to collect a cavalry troop of about 1100 men (of whom 650 were Cossack prisoners) near the Headquarters of the Middle Army Group in Russia (the focus of conspiracy on the Eastern Front) with the idea that they might be used to surround Hitler if he ever came on a visit. He did come on such a visit on 13 March 1943 (p. 127) but for some unestablished reason the troops were not used.[34]

Attention was gradually switched to the possibility of persuading some high officer who was outside Hitler's Headquarters to raise the standard of revolt. If those at the Headquarters had not then joined in and arrested the Führer, the danger of civil war would have been acute. Not unnaturally the reaction of such officers as were approached was that of Manstein (p. 33). But there do seem to have been three occasions on which hopes were high. In November 1941, after the first failure in Russia, when Hitler and Brauchitsch were at loggerheads as to whether to stand firm or retreat, there seems to have been some prospect that Brauchitsch would defy him and/or that some local commander outside Berlin (probably in the south-east) would do so as well. Instead, Brauchitsch resigned.[35] Later there were hopes that General Fromm, the head of the Replacement Army in Berlin, and the superior of Olbricht and Stauffenberg, could be prevailed on to act. But the most he would say was, 'Well, if you do make your putsch, at least for my sake don't forget Wilhelm Keitel.'[36] Thirdly hopes were for a long time placed on Kluge but he explicitly forbade Tresckow to try anything while Hitler was at his headquarters on that turning-point at which history failed to turn, 13 March 1943 (which may be why Boeselager's troop was not called in). In July 1944 he showed a lack of nerve at the crucial moment (pp. 151). Whether Rommel would have acted more decisively had he not been severely wounded by the British three days before Stauffenberg struck, is by no means as easy to tell as has sometimes been made out; he was unlikely to have approved of the attempt at assassination (but see p. 150).[37]

These practical difficulties and the loyalty of one kind or another which Hitler could still command among generals, troops and the public gradually made it patent that, if the loss of life at the front, in the bombed cities and in the camps was to be stopped and if Germany was to be rescued from the shame of having left the overthrow entirely to foreigners, Hitler would have to be assassinated as a trigger for setting off a revolt which would not happen otherwise. For Hitler to be killed at the outset would also reduce the risk of civil war; many who would have gone on supporting him as long as he lived would not give the same fidelity to his minions. Some objectors still remained, notably Goerdeler and Moltke. But for most of the conspirators the moral objections to murder were outweighed by the moral objections to leaving things to go on as they were.

The practical obstacles to an *Attentat* however were almost as great as those to a *Putsch*. Some ten attempts are known to have been made on Hitler's life between 1937 and 1944 and there may have been more. But only those of Elser, Tresckow-Schlabrendorff and Stauffenberg came close to being successful.[38] Hitler himself once said that it would be quite easy for a man with a rifle and telescopic sight to kill him from a distance. The British Military Attaché in Berlin, Mason-Macfarlane, suggested more or less seriously in 1939 doing precisely this but was forbidden by his superiors.[39] Nicholas von Halem, an industrialist who belonged to the Solf Circle, had decided as early as 1938 that assassination was the only solution and until he was arrested in 1942 tried hard to find a suitable thug. But this was the exception rather than the rule. In many other parts of the world, Nazi methods would have called into existence terrorist groups which set out systematically to kill prominent men in the régime. It is somewhat paradoxical that in Germany anti-government terrorism should only appear after democracy had been reestablished. But a particularly vicious repression was faced by a movement dubious as to the value of meeting force with force.

Hitler wore a bullet-proof vest and a cap lined with metal.[40] He had his own train, aircraft and pilot, while various fleets of specially protected cars were, if necessary, sent in advance to the airfield at which he was to land. His future movements were kept secret until the last possible moment and he often varied the route and timing which had been prescribed so as to avoid regularity. He had his own cook whom he trusted, making it unnecessary for his special food to be tested by someone else before he ate it. After Elser's attempt in November 1939 advance watch was kept on buildings which he was going to visit. Once war began, and particularly after 1941, he spent most of his time in his various headquarters, chiefly the Berghof above Berchtesgaden and Wolf's Lair in East Prussia. These had elaborate defences against both ground and air attack. SS guards were constantly on the prowl and nobody was allowed into the inner areas without a special pass (which did not however keep out a Pole who took a short cut on his way home from work without realising where he was getting!)

The deed had therefore to be done by someone who had the right of access to Hitler in the normal course of duty. The number of people so distinguished was of course large. But there then intervened a new variant of the old difficulty. Those who had access were not prepared to kill, those who were prepared to kill did not have access. When on 3 September 1939 Erich Kordt asked, 'Is there no way to prevent this war?' Weizsäcker replied, 'Do you have a man with a pistol? I regret that there has been nothing in my up-bringing which would fit me to kill a man' (although he had been a naval officer).*[41] Halder told a colleague two months later that for weeks he had been going to see Emil (as he called Hitler) with a pistol in his pocket yet never came near making up his mind to use it.[42]

As time went on however doubts developed over the practicability of using a pistol. There was some uncertainty about being able to get one into a meeting since it became the custom to leave hats and belts outside the door. Although pockets and brief-cases were not controlled until after 20 July, there were usually SS guards on the watch from behind at meetings of any size. Difficulty was foreseen over producing a pistol fast enough to forestall interference and over hitting the fairly small target on Hitler's head in circumstances which would rule out the possibility of taking careful aim. That was why Stauffenberg used a bomb. But getting hold of a bomb was not straightforward since staff officers no more habitually handle explosives than they command troops. Elser solved the difficulty by working in a quarry for some weeks where he easily managed to steal the necessary dynamite. Stauffenberg and Tresckow could hardly have done the same but this is an example of how closer contact with the working classes would have helped them. Fortunately the main conspiracy did extend into the Abwehr equivalent of SOE which was able to provide the necessary explosive and a British delayed-action fuse which, unlike all German fuses, was noiseless. (Unfortunately the section had failed to capture a specimen of the material which SOE had developed to blow up aircraft in flight regardless of the temperature.[43]) Further difficulties arose about hiding the explosive until it was needed.

Some evidence suggests that Hitler had a premonition when danger impended, perhaps by sensing when someone in his entourage was abnormally tense. He said after Elser's attempt that an inner voice had told him to get out of the beer-cellar as quickly as he could – but that may have been affectation. There is nothing to show that it operated on 13 March 1945 or 20 July 1944 but it may have had something to do with his exceptionally fast tour of the exhibition on 21 March 1943 which prevented von Gersdorff from blowing him up.

The various difficulties which have been listed explain why it was that the attempt came to be made by a man who had only one eye, one hand and only three fingers on his remaining one and why it had to be set off in East Prussia by a man whose presence immediately afterwards three hundred miles away in Berlin was essential because he was the only person who could give orders in the name of the Commander of the Replacement Army and because he was the only man who had in his head all the threads of a conspiracy which had had of necessity to be planned in the greatest secrecy. Indeed, if Stauffenberg had not been promoted seven weeks earlier to be Fromm's Chief

---

* 'Unfortunately assassination appears to be a lost art on the Continent of Europe; and just now it is both morally respectable and more politically desirable than ever! Imagine that a respectable Christian Bishop should ever have been brought to the pass of giving bed and board in his ethical scheme to ASSASSINATION' (Letters of Herbert Hensley Henson (1950) 14.ix.41).

of Staff, a post in which he had on occasion to attend Hitler's daily 'situation conference', the attempt would either not have been made or taken a completely different form at a later date.

The progress of events on 20 July confirmed the gravity of the obstacles. Fromm refused to issue the orders which were needed throughout Germany and Occupied Europe to bring about the take-over of power by the Army from the Party organisations. He was overpowered and Stauffenberg issued them on his behalf, but belatedly. Except in Paris and to a lesser extent in Vienna, they were immediately queried and not acted on. Whether things would have been different if they had been issued three hours earlier, before the news of Hitler's survival spread, or if it had been possible to prevent the Government from getting to the microphone are hard questions to answer. Had Hitler been killed and Fromm then taken responsibility, the situation which all the conspirators hoped for would have been brought about. (See also case-histories of Elser, pp. 122–4; Tresckow-Schlabrendorff, pp. 124–32; and Stauffenberg, pp. 132–41.)

(e) Help from outside

This catalogue of the difficulties facing those who wanted to remove Hitler makes it easy to understand why many of them were inclined to conclude that the task was impossible unless they could get help from outside. They therefore turned to hoping that one or more foreign Governments would inflict on him such a diplomatic humiliation or military defeat as to discredit him in the eyes of the German public. Opportunities for firm action occurred at the times of Germany's departure from the League of Nations in October 1933, of the announcement about rearmament in March 1935, of the reoccupation of the Rhineland in March 1936, of the absorption of Austria in March 1938, of the Czech crisis in the summer and autumn of 1938 and finally of the Polish crisis of August–September 1939. Except for the last occasion, these opportunities were not taken, and until 1938 the great majority of the conspirators did not want them to be taken. After 1939 the nature of the problem changed and will be considered in Chapter VII. Here it is appropriate to consider why the British Government, on whose decisions peace or war primarily depended, held its hand between 1933 and 1939 and why the British public on the whole supported it.

(*i*) There was profound disillusionment about the cost of the war of 1914–18 in human and material resources. Few had foreseen how different an industrialised war would be to those of previous centuries. The flower of a whole generation had been decimated. The beneficial changes made by the treaties signed to end the war received much less attention than the grievances which were created for the losers. Britain's internal difficulties in the 1920s and 1930s were largely caused by her disposal of overseas assets to pay for the war and by the dislocation of international trade. There was great moral and rational resistance to taking any risk which might involve incurring similar losses again, along with doubt as to whether a second war would lead to any better settlement. Many of the people who had these feelings most strongly were among those who were most outraged by Nazi methods of rule. No doubt vigorous leadership by the Government could have helped to stiffen the will to resist but the Conservative ministers who were in power for five-sixths of the period 1922–39 were as uncertain about the best thing to do as the man in the street, as well as being afraid that, if they took too firm a line, they would lose the next election to the Labour Party which would be even less firm and less ready to rearm. The price of not fighting had to be demonstrated before the necessary will to fight could be generated.

(*ii*) Many Britons (although fewer French) considered that there was much to be said in favour of the German case as to the unreasonableness of reparations, the failure to keep promises about all-round disarmament, the denial of self-determination to Austrians, Sudeten Germans and the inhabitants of the Polish 'corridor'. Such ideas were of course nurtured by successive German Governments, even under the Republic. The strategic importance of the undefended Rhineland and of the loss to Czechoslovakia of her mountain frontiers went unrecognised. Doubts as to the wisdom of the 1919 settlement created a dilemma for the British Government in 1939 over the definition of its war aims. Was it to insist on the re-establishment of Poland and Czechoslovakia and of an independent Austria? How was it to explain a refusal to do this to the exiled Czech and Polish leaders?

(*iii*) The financial crisis of 1931 had provided a vivid reminder that the pound no longer dominated world finance. Since then, parsimonious budgeting had restored confidence in the British economy but orthodox thought held that any large increase in Government expenditure, and the higher taxation and/or inflation which it brought, would provoke a relapse. There were held to be both financial and material limits to the amount which Britain could afford to spend on defence.

(*iv*) The German problem would have been difficult enough to handle if it had been isolated but Britain faced three enemies, not one. Until 1939 Britain was committed to defending her Dominions and colonies in the Pacific against Japan, yet the despatch of eight or nine capital ships to Singapore which were the minimum thought necessary for this task would leave the Channel and Mediterranean almost undefended. By applying sanctions to Italy in 1935 for her attack on Abyssinia, yet failing to make them effective (because the desire to win the election led the Government to profess support for a policy it did not really believe in), the British drove Mussolini into Hitler's arms without overthrowing him. The Chiefs of Staff were emphatic that Britain could not hope to fight all three enemies simultaneously. But in each case the arguments against giving way were so strong that all three were appeased at once without any of them being won round. For obvious reasons, little was said in public about British weaknesses, with the result that Anglo-French strength was over-estimated by anti-Nazi Germans, although not by Hitler. The German authorities, by contrast, played up skilfully an exaggerated impression of the length to which their rearmament had proceeded. Ironically the belief in German superiority was fanned by those Britons who, like Churchill, were trying to get the speed and scale of British rearmament stepped up.

(*v*) William Strang, the Foreign Office Under-Secretary responsible for policy towards Germany, wrote in November 1939, 'Without Hitler, Germany might be less evil but not necessarily less dangerous. Unless German military power were first broken, peace would be a brief and uneasy respite.'[44] D'Arcy Osborne, the British Minister to the Holy See, when discussing with Pope Pius XII three months later the overtures put forward by Beck, Canaris and Oster (p. 146), pointed out that even if they were genuine and the plans of the sponsors could be carried out successfully, there was no guarantee that the German Government to be dealt with would be any more trustworthy or less aggressive than the existing one.[45] For reasons explained above (p. 85), a government which overthrew Hitler would need, as part justification to its home public for its action, to demand favourable terms and, if it were headed by officials and soldiers, might be more dangerous, since more influenced by reason, than he.

(*vi*) By the end of 1939 Britain was spending a higher proportion of her national income on armaments than Germany, while her monthly output of aircraft had just begun to exceed the German.[46] During the eighteen months between the autumn of 1938 and the summer of 1940, the equipment which was to prove crucial in repelling the German onslaught – all-metal monoplane fighters, anti-aircraft guns, radar and Ultra – would become available in adequate quantities. The British Government had therefore reason for thinking that time was on its side. The validity of this thesis has been challenged[47] but it was apparently shared by Hitler and was reinforced by intelligence reports about the economic difficulties into which the German Government was supposedly running (p. 36).

(*vii*) British air intelligence seriously misled not merely the public but also ministers and their own chiefs as to German capabilities. They knew well that the Royal Air Force did not have the aircraft or the crews or the bombs to mount a sustained attack on Germany (and did not fully acquire that capacity till 1942–3). They knew that the Luftwaffe, in accordance with German strategic thought, had been largely developed as a supporting arm to the Army and did not have many aircraft suitable for long-range bombing. But they did not seriously question the ability of the Germans to mount a heavy attack on British ports and cities without, as an essential preliminary, overrunning the French and Belgian coasts. Extrapolating from 1918 figures, they expected as many people to be killed in Britain during the first two months as were in fact killed during the entire war. If it had been generally appreciated in 1938 that the Luftwaffe had no plan to bomb Britain, the public would have been much readier to see the Government adopt a strong line.[48] Before and at the Munich Conference, Göring knew that the Luftwaffe could not hope for any decisive result from an air offensive against Britain and, although he did not admit the fact openly, it led him to warn Hitler against going too far.[49]

(*viii*) The Chiefs of Staff took the view that nothing Britain and France could do in the military field would prevent a quick victory over Czechoslovakia (they probably exaggerated the quickness).

(*ix*) The French, having gone to war in 1914 with a strategy of attack when the need proved to be for one of defence, prepared for war in the 1930s by a strategy of defence, the Maginot Line, when the need proved to be for one of attack. They were thus badly placed to exploit Hitler's weakness on his western front where in 1938 he had only 12 divisions to resist 66 French ones.[50] Their commander Gamelin was accurately informed about the German order of battle but for some reason as yet unexplained harped on the difficulty of an offensive across the Rhine.[51] In the air they had rearmed too early with the result that they only had a handful of planes comparable with the Luftwaffe and were having to start on a completely new programme.[52] If the British had been keen to fight they might have been able to make the French do more but as it was they used French weakness as another reason to avoid fighting and tried to counter the influence of any Frenchmen who showed signs of aggressiveness.

(*x*) The considerations described in (i) and (ii) above operated even more strongly in the Commonwealth and the United States than in Britain itself. Until 1939 it was problematic whether the self-governing Dominions would follow Britain's example should she declare war; they put pressure on her in 1938 and 1939 to make concessions to Germany.[53]

(*xi*) In the United States the Johnson Act prohibited loans to states which had defaulted on previous debts (as Britain had done in 1934 after her own debtors had defaulted) and the Neutrality Act banned the sale of arms or the granting of credit to belligerents. Roosevelt, it was true, was more disposed to be helpful but his chances of being supported by Congress depended in part on his appearing to have his hand forced. Chamberlain told the Cabinet in December 1937 that 'the Power that has the greatest strength is the United States but he would be a rash man who based his calculations on help from that quarter'[54] – although help might have come quicker if Chamberlain had encouraged instead of obstructed proposals made by Roosevelt in 1937–8 to hold a world conference about peaceful change and if he had not persistently frustrated American attempts to open doors for world trade. Subsequent events were to demonstrate that, if the American attitude had remained unchanged, Britain would have been compelled by lack of funds to end within two years any war on which she ventured with a compromise peace in Germany's favour. Yet it was the US Senate which, by refusing to ratify the Treaty of Versailles, had undermined the preponderance of force which alone had made possible the imposition of the Treaty.

(*xii*) Although the German General Staff had expected in 1938 that, in the event of war, the Soviet Union would immediately side with the Western Powers,[55] those Powers were by no means so sure of it themselves and were in any case doubtful as to how Soviet help could reach Czechoslovakia in view of the refusal of Poland to give passage to Russian troops. The effectiveness of the Red Army after Stalin's purges was widely questioned. In any case the German fear and dislike of Communism was shared by many British Conservatives. They were afraid that the suffering and destruction caused in Europe by a war of any length would give excellent opportunities to the Communist parties. Some of them hoped that Nazi aggression could be diverted eastwards and two tiresome menaces be thus induced to destroy one another. Soviet awareness of this desire played a part in bringing about the Russo-German Non-Aggression Pact of August 1939.

If the British Government had known for certain that a decision by Hitler to attack Czechoslovakia would lead to his removal by a group of German Army leaders, they would probably have taken a firmer line than they did. Complications would have followed but no situation is without them. September 1938 may well have been the moment at which the democratic West had its best chance of displacing Hitler without loosing off a long war. But how sure could they have been, and how sure can historians be in hindsight, that a putsch would not only have been made but would have succeeded? As to determination, it is reasonable to give the benefit of the doubt, although by no means everyone in British official circles did so. But the chances of success are more questionable since it is hard to feel that the conspirators knew enough in detail about the situation to have taken all the obstacles into account. They would not seem to have obtained plans of the Chancellery until 24 September.[56] They had no accomplice inside the building who could help them to find Hitler. When in the autumn of 1939 Oster at Halder's behest revised the orders which Witzleben had drawn up in September 1938, he is said to have found a number of gaps. On 20 July even apart from the failure to kill Hitler, enough went wrong to dispel assurance that success earlier would have been automatic. A German military historian has written, à propos of the Schlieffen Plan in 1914, that 'a formula for victory needs a surplus of reasonable chances of success if it is to inspire confidence, a surplus which tends to be used up by frictions in the day-to-day conduct of events.'[57] Events of this kind are at the hazard of accident (which may admittedly work for as well as against).

Chamberlain and his Cabinet had however to take their decisions on the assumption that firm resistance to German demands might lead to a war which they could not be sure of winning. Hitler must be presumed to have realised their dilemma, even if he did so more by intuition than by reading documents. He pushed his luck because he sensed that these were men who were not going to fight. Perhaps they should have bluffed him into thinking that they were. But it is easier for a dictator to bluff than for a body of responsible men.

If British statesmen had foreseen that Hitler would have to be checked by force, they should have set about organising a coalition against him no later than 1935. But the proposition has only to be stated for its absurdity to be evident. The National Government was trying to reduce its international commitments, not add to them. Whether the countries whose help it would have needed would have given it aid on terms acceptable to it is doubtful. But it had no desire to ally with them; 1935 was the year in which it destroyed whatever future the League of Nations might have had as a focus of international order. Yet it could not bring itself to renounce all interest in the course of world events. Hitler's sense of the incompatibilities in British policy was a main reason for his confidence in forcing the issues in 1938–40.[58]

Thus in 1938 Britain, after several weeks of agonized heart-searching and with much misgiving, made a compromise at Czechoslovak expense to preserve peace. I look back on the period as the most unpleasant in my life. In 1939 a similar compromise could probably have been found if the British Government had been prepared to force the Poles into negotiating with Hitler by withdrawing its March promise to uphold Poland's independence. It not only refrained from doing so but came under strong public pressure to stand firm. War broke out in consequence. The event which more than anything else caused this change of attitude was Hitler's seizure of the rump of Czechoslovakia in March 1939. What made this step so influential was not essentially the cynicism and speed with which he went back on his word about the Sudetenland having been his 'last territorial demand'; if moral indignation had been all that was needed to induce Britain to fight, the *Kristallnacht* should have been sufficient. What proved decisive was the feeling that he had been given the benefit of the doubt and had abused it. His justifications were pretexts, his word could not be trusted and there was no knowing where he would stop. To give such a man a chance of dominating Europe was incompatible with the security of Britain. Plenty of people had of course said this before but the objections to war were so deep-seated that events and not mere words were needed to convince.

The 'Ides of March' were seen as pre-eminently the doing of Hitler himself so that for a time the change of attitude was directed against him more than anyone else. During the process which has been called 'the unwinding of appeasement' in the winter of 1939–40, the key figures in the British Government did not exclude reaching agreement with other Germans, even including for a time Göring, provided that the leader was removed.[59] But this readiness did not endure beyond the outbreak of 'real' war in April 1940 and the accession of Churchill to power. From then on the attitude of the British Government towards the Germans reverted to much what it had been in 1918.[60] A belief became widespread that no reliance was to be placed on promises of anti-Nazi Germans to reform, not necessarily because they were deceitful but because they might well prove impotent. Germany needed not merely to be beaten beyond any possibility of doubt but effective action must be taken to prevent her from inflicting a third war on the world. The British Government did not fully realise the implications of its turn-round. Hitler did not fully realise that in marching into Prague, he had destroyed his last chance of achieving his once cherished aim of winning British acquiescence to German expansion in Eurasia. And his opponents in Germany did not fully realise either the gravity of the British change of climate or the difficulties which it would create for their efforts to forestall the verdict of war by achieving a compromise peace between Britain and Germany. The lesson which the British learned from the experience of 1935–9 was that they could not afford to disregard Central Europe. They therefore became unwilling to end the war on terms which might in time allow an over-strong power to dominate that area. Appeasement thus led to the demand for unconditional surrender.

CHAPTER VI
The aims of the *Widerstand*

The primary aim of all those who disagreed with or disapproved of Hitler and the Third Reich clearly was to get rid of Hitler and those working for him. But, as was shown in the last two chapters, there was a wide variety of opinion as to how this could best be done. There was also a considerable difference of opinion as to what system should be set up after it had been done. The main division was between Communists and non-Communists.

(a) Communist aims

As has been said the Communists had before 1933 refused to work with anybody else (except on occasion the Nazis). For some time after Hitler gained power, the Communist leadership, under the directions of Moscow, continued to think that the German working class could be mobilised for a campaign which would throw him out. Bitter experience gradually convinced them that this strategy was futile. After the Comintern World Congress and the 'Brussels' Conference of the German Communist Party in 1935, comrades in Germany were instructed to co-operate in a United Front with anyone else who was against Nazism (p. 50). This involved substituting democratic socialism in place of a proletarian dictatorship as at any rate the nominal aim. But suspicions died hard, especially as there were several reasons for thinking that everyone who had dealings with Communists was likely to be caught by the Gestapo. The Social Democratic Executive Committee in the emigration steadily refused to enter into dealings with the Communists, convinced that the so-called United Front was merely a device for bringing non-democrats to power. Events after the war ended suggest that this conviction was well-founded. The German Communists brought from Moscow in May 1945 to set up a 'People's Democracy' in the Russian Zone were told 'the result must look democratic but the reins must really be in our hands'.[1]

A distraction occurred in July 1943 when the Russians finally persuaded twenty-two prisoners-of-war to form a 'National Committee of Free Germany', carried forward in the following September by a 'League of German Officers' which included two generals. The Committee began to issue over

Soviet radio, in leaflets and through other channels publicity material which gave detail to the broad distinction between Hitler and the German people drawn by Stalin in two speeches in 1942. The hope was held out that, if the German army were to stop fighting and retire in good order to the German frontier, they would win the right to decide their future for themselves. Nor would organised military force in Germany be destroyed. Here was a hint of an alternative to unconditional surrender.[2]

The Russians must be assumed to have had three possible aims simultaneously in making this change of policy. If by any chance the Wehrmacht had acted on it, the war in the east would have been over. As the Wehrmacht would have remained intact and undefeated, it should have been in a position to see that the promises about self-determination were carried out (which answers the question 'Did Stalin make the offer in good faith?') Alternatively an attempt to act by some units of the Wehrmacht but not others would have precipitated civil war in Germany and made victory easier for the Red Army. But thirdly the possibility of either of these two aims being realised might so frighten the Anglo-Americans as to make them fall in with Stalin's wishes about a second front and territorial changes in Eastern Europe. In the event, neither of the first two aims was realised, so that the Russians could treat the offer as withdrawn and make the National Committee revert to the older line of exhorting members of the Wehrmacht to desert. Meanwhile at the Moscow and Tehran Conferences the Russians got from the West the promises which they wanted. Even before the later meeting took place, the Russians had told the Americans that all official announcements showing friendship to the German people were mere propaganda.[3]

The policy initiative represented by the Committee was received with mixed feelings by the Communists inside Germany. The order to reach a United Front with the Socialists and anyone else willing to join in had been accepted because the damage done by the previous disunity was too obvious to dispute. But to work with officers and nationalists was repugnant. The implication seemed to be that, in the new Germany, Communists might not be in command. The difficulties of communicating with Russia were great so that the reasons behind the new policy could not be explained to the comrades inside the country. The justification usually given was that, after victory, a democratic republic would be set up to enable the German people to decide their own future. The underlying hope was that, in such a republic, Communist influence would be strong enough to create an opportunity for setting up a state on Soviet lines. Once it became clear that the Wehrmacht was not going to retire of its own will in good order to the frontiers, the two likely scenarios became a civil war, in which the German Communists would hope to seize power, and the occupation of Eastern Germany by the Red Army after the Wehrmacht had been defeated, in which case the decision as to the political shape of the successor state would rest with the Russians. Not surprisingly the German Communists preferred the first of these alternatives. (See case-history on Saefkow, p. 206.)

The non-Communist *Widerstand*, and in particular the military leaders, were always suspicious of the NKFD and made no attempt to get into contact with it. But its creation called their attention to the need to win popular support for their own post-Nazi government.

Socialist planning for a post-Hitler Germany was conducted almost entirely outside that country by emigrants from it in the West (except for Mierendorff as described below, p. 106).

(b) Non-Communist aims

When the Americans, British and French set about re-establishing central self-government in their Zones in 1948, they gave the job of devising a constitution (called a 'Basic Law' so as not to prejudice the possible future inclusion of the Russian Zone) to a 'Parliamentary Council' composed of delegates elected by the nine Land Parliaments which had already been established. These delegates were chosen from the six parties which had already been allowed to form. The Occupying Powers had already indicated that the democratic constitution must be of federal type. The result was that the shape of the Basic Law was decided by the political parties and was largely influenced by Western political ideas. Konrad Adenauer, who was elected chairman of the Council, allowed little say to the Ministers-President of the *Länder* or to the officials working in the Bizonal Economic Administration. Very few persons associated with the *Widerstand* belonged to the Council – and in any case most of the leading figures were dead. Those survivors who did have a share in the reconstruction, such as Gerstenmaier and Steltzer, held important positions but not key ones. Consequently the ideas of the *Widerstand* had little influence on the shape of post-war Germany. A minor confirmation of this is curiously provided by Article 67 of the Basic Law which lays down that the Bundestag can only pass an effective vote of 'no confidence' in a Chancellor if it at the same time nominates a successor. This article was taken from the Constitution for Baden-Württemberg where it had been suggested by Carlo Schmid who during the war had become a friend of Helmuth von Moltke. The Kreisau document *Fundamental Principles for the New Order*, for which Moltke was largely responsible, contained such a provision and the inference that Schmid had taken it from there would be natural but for the fact that in 1972 Schmid told me he had up to that moment been unaware that the Kreisau document had put the proposal forward.

A good deal of discussion has gone on during the last twenty years as to whether the aims put forward by the *Widerstand* should be regarded as reactionary or progressive. But the fact that they had little influence on Germany's future makes it unnecessary to submit them to any exhaustive analysis here.[4] One of the reasons for the decision to fight the war to a finish was the desire of the Allies to have a say in the shape of post-war Germany. The first governments to be set up were bound to be dependent on the

Occupying Powers, particularly the United States in the west and the Soviet Union in the east.

Aims were formulated in five milieus:

(*i*) One group was formed by those whom the Germans called *Excellenzen* or *Honoratioren* ('The Establishment'). They were older and had more experience of carrying responsibility. The military leader among them was Beck, the civilian leader in home affairs Goerdeler and in foreign affairs von Hassell. In 1941 Beck and Goerdeler drew up a memorandum, based on earlier drafts, which they called 'The Goal' (*Das Ziel*). On the whole this group was more conservative, although it did not fully deserve the description applied to it from the left of a 'grey-haired government' which aimed merely at a restoration.[5]

(*ii*) Closely linked but distinct was a group led by Popitz who remained (since he was not allowed to resign) Prussian Minister of Finance. In 1942 he, his former pupil Jessen, Erwin Planck, Langbehn and von Hassell, drew up a draft Basic Law.[6] Popitz's contacts with Himmler have been described (p. 81). Their views were more reactionary than those of the first group, although it must be said that their constitution was only to be regarded as an emergency and temporary arrangement.

(*iii*) A group centred on Freiburg consisted of people who were primarily economists, including Lampe, Eucken and Müller-Armack, although they did not confine themselves to economics. Their connection with the military conspiracy was tenuous and they none of them lost their lives. They are of interest chiefly because it was their ideas about a 'Free Market Economy' which began to be applied in 1948. Ludwig Erhard was a junior member.

(*iv*) A younger group was to be found in the 'Kreisau circle', so-called by the Gestapo after 20 July because three of its discussions were held by some of its members at Helmuth von Moltke's country cottage at Kreisau in Silesia. But there were many more discussions in Berlin while some of the more important members could not manage or did not dare to come to Kreisau. Moltke, who was the moving spirit and decided who was to be invited, insisted on including representatives of the workers and Churches, as the two anti-Nazi bodies which had most to contribute to a post-Hitler Germany. The group numbered about 20 people, although there was no such thing as formal membership and at least 30 more were loosely connected. The main document produced was the already-mentioned *Fundamental Principles for the New Order*, of which the latest draft dates from August 1943; to it were attached two subsidiary *Instructions for the Land Commissioners* (who were to take temporary charge in each German Land after the Nazis had been overthrown, so as to counter the charge that the new Government was a military junta). This group was younger, less experienced and more progressive.[7] They had close connections with the Religious Socialists.

(*v*) To complete the picture, a fifth group should be mentioned – those who were sceptical about the value of planning at all. Among these were Fritz Dietlof von der Schulenburg[8] (who did however produce plans including a map suggesting how the new Germany should be subdivided), Leber and, up to a point, Stauffenberg. The question which they posed has already been discussed (p. 69).

The two most elaborate plans were produced by groups (i) and (iv) and therefore discussion will be confined to these.

(c) Points on which there was agreement

(*a*) First and foremost came insistence that the rule of law must be restored. If a cynic were to suggest that the high proportion of Doctors of Law among the conspirators made this inevitable, one cannot too often emphasise that the rule of law is so fundamental to German thinking as to make it the distinctive form which the Liberal State has assumed in the country, and more particularly Prussia. A more searching criticism is that the Rule of Law had not been abandoned in the Third Reich to the extent which is often supposed but had been harnessed to evil purposes. Germans of Jewish blood were deprived of their citizenship and forbidden to marry Aryans by the laws passed quite constitutionally by the Reichstag at Nuremburg in 1935; the People's Court was set up by an authority duly constituted by the Reichstag and had its files in meticulous order, even though a lawyer in 1938 said that its task was not to pronounce the law but to destroy the opponents of National Socialism[9]. What needed observation was not the Rule of Law but the Rights of Man. The Weimar Constitution had had a list of such rights in its closing clauses but had provided no procedure for enforcing them. The solution found in the Basic Law was not simply to list them in the first nineteen Articles but to lay down that any law inconsistent with them should be automatically invalid and to provide the Constitutional Court to say whether a law fell into that category. The *Widerstand* while keenly alive to the importance of such rights never hit on the idea of entrenching them in this way, which clearly derives from US experience. It is surprising that Moltke never developed the idea since Curtis had inculcated to him respect for the US Founding Fathers and Kennan has described finding him reading *The Federalist* during the war.

(*b*) The rejection of 'Weimar'. This, as has been seen (p. 25), was one of the widespread sentiments which brought Hitler to power and the system for which the term stood had even fewer defenders than it deserved. Even the National Committee for Free Germany said in its 1943 manifesto that 'a Free Germany means a strong democratic constitution which has nothing in common with the powerlessness of Weimar'.[10] What was principally meant by 'Weimar' was the divisive effect of political parties and of the employer–worker antagonism, which combined to deny governments the consensus without which it is hard to pursue a consistent and effective policy. What the critics of Weimar were really concerned with was not a defective constitution but the lack of a *Volksgemeinschaft*. The aim of both Nazis and anti-Nazis (and indeed of the leaders of most political communities) was to reduce dissension. But dissensions arise from deep-seated divergences of interest. These can only be removed by increasing the material benefits which the society brings to all its members or by achieving agreement that certain long-term non-material benefits are more important than the pursuit of material sectional interests. Weimar had failed to do either. The Nazis for a time succeeded in doing both, raising the standard of living and putting greater emphasis than ever on the idea of Race/Nation. The anti-Nazis had to find some substitute for that idea which they hoped to do in a realisation induced by experience in the Third Reich that certain values such as individual freedom and respect for human personality were more important than sectional interests. But they would also have to do something to satisfy those sectional interests in an economy which seemed likely to be dislocated and impoverished.

(c) The aversion to Weimar gave the *Widerstand* a distaste for parliamentary democracy which, at the time they started planning, had virtually vanished from Europe so that they can be excused for having disregarded it as an outmoded form. But as they equally rejected authoritarianism, they were left in something of a dilemma as to what kind of constitution they should recommend instead. Considerable attention was paid to the ideas of von Stein and Hardenberg at the beginning of the nineteenth century, which might have led to something like a corporative state. Parties were regarded as something to be eliminated altogether or allowed as little influence as possible. The planners would have done better to spend more time investigating the function which parties perform in clarifying by discussion the issues which face a country and providing rules by which choices can be made between alternative solutions. They would also have done well to consider the reasons why the party system proved unsatisfactory in the Weimar Republic. These were (i) there were too many parties; (ii) a considerable proportion of the electorate were hostile to democracy in principle and as a result unwilling to subordinate their sectional interests to the common good. The Basic Law sought with success to combat these defects by (i) denying parties which win less than 5 per cent of the votes any seats in the Bundestag (in addition historical developments have eliminated the Catholic Centre Party and reduced the Communists to insignificance); (ii) banning as unconstitutional parties which by their aims or the behaviour of their members set out to impair or overthrow the free democratic state; (iii) declaring as inadmissible constitutional amendments which would affect the federal character of the state or the rights of man; (iv) making the validity of a vote of no confidence in a Chancellor dependent on whether it names his successor. Only the last of these requirements was mentioned in the Kreisau *Fundamental Principles* and *Das Ziel* included none of them (although Goerdeler while in prison proposed that the number of parties should be reduced to three without explaining how).

Instead, both documents set great store by a system of elections from the bottom upwards, with each deliberative unit (parish, district, Land) choosing the members of the one above it, so that each elector would have personal knowledge of the people available for him to elect. Such a cumbersome system would have made it difficult to get change effected quickly, and would probably have been unsuitable for the conditions existing in West Germany after 1948. On the other hand the Basic Law might not have worked successfully without the prosperous economic conditions in which it has operated and which have induced individuals to make concessions in order to maintain it.

(*d*) Decentralisation was widely favoured both by the Germans and by the Occupying Powers as a reaction to the excessive centralisation of the Third Reich. Bigness was taken to be a disease encouraged by totalitarianism. Little attention was paid to the saving of resources which can be brought by economies of scale or to the inequalities which can arise when common problems are not handled in a uniform way.

(*e*) Greater interest in social affairs by the Churches was sought in the hope that, by advocating brotherly love and deprecating emphasis on personal gain, they would help to integrate the community on a non-authoritarian basis. This roused some opposition among Social Democrats who found it hard to believe that the Churches (and particularly the Evangelical ones) would really become a progressive force. The Kreisau Group (or at any rate some of their lay leaders) wanted to separate the Churches from the state. They also hoped to bring about closer co-operation between Protestants and Catholics.

(*f*) Those who had committed crimes under Hitler were to be brought to trial and punished. Goerdeler was emphatic that this must be done by Germans, as part of the process by which Germany was to make amends for the Third Reich. Moltke wanted to use the International Court of Justice. The victors were to disregard both ideas.

(*g*) Europe, or at any rate Western Europe, was to be brought into closer political and economic unity. Here agreement did not go much beyond broad principle, so the matter is best discussed at the point where divergence began.

(*h*) There was a general hope, if not an assumption, that the Allies would, on victory, at once allow the *Widerstand* to set up an alternative Government and give it wide freedom of action, treating it on a more or less equal footing with other 'respectable' Governments. The idea that the government of the country would be taken out of the hands of Germans altogether would have been a considerable shock to the *Widerstand* leaders. The Kreisau Group in particular assumed that they would be able to take part in putting their plans into practice.

(d) Points on which there was disagreement

(*a*) Although there was general agreement that the support of the workers would be of vital importance to the new state, there was disagreement as to how it should be mobilised. Goerdeler, largely influenced by Leuschner, took it for granted that trade unions should be restored, membership being made compulsory. The previous Christian and other unions would be absorbed into a single organisation which would undertake wide responsibilities in the field of social insurance. The elected representatives of both white-collar (*Angestellte*) and blue-collar workers would negotiate wages and conditions of work at various levels on a regional basis with the representatives of the employers; only if agreement could not be reached would the state step in. These proposals came close to the system established on German initiative in the Federal Republic.

The Kreisau Group by contrast extended their dislike of divisive influences to bodies in which employers faced employees at all stages of the hierarchy; these they wanted to abolish. Each factory (whether on its own or a part of a larger firm) was to elect a Works Council, representative of all groups inside it; at higher levels this Council would be represented by persons whom all its members had elected as best qualified to speak for them. Thus the employer–employee conflict of interests would be eliminated above the local level. Such an arrangement not only foreshadowed co-determination but was reminiscent of the system which the National Socialists had purported to set up in the factories after the abolition of trade unions in 1933, only to allow the employers to obtain an excessive share of influence in the new bodies. In both cases the object was to get a body in which conflict would be reduced but whereas the Nazis were prepared to suppress it by force if agreement could not be reached, the Kreisau hope was that in the new atmosphere agreement would be reached. This was to be achieved by giving the workers more influence than the Goerdeler solution contemplated; Leuschner and Leber were sceptical as to whether it would happen. Nothing was said as to how wages were to be fixed or hours of work regulated, except that the share of the labour force in each firm's profits would be agreed between the owners and the workers' representatives.

(*b*) One of the ideas running through *Das Ziel* was the need to place responsibility on the individual and at the same time give him as much freedom as possible. Government regulation should as a result be reduced as far as possible (although it was recognised that in the immediate post-war situation this might be difficult to achieve). Kreisau, although laying just as much emphasis on the responsibility of the individual, wanted it to be exercised in a communal context. They considered the economic crisis to have shown the need for business to be controlled and for utilities and other key firms to be publicly owned.

(*c*) The older men took it for granted that the Europe of nation states in which they had grown up would continue. It followed that Germany should keep the shape she had assumed in the nineteenth century. Hassell wrote in August 1943 of the need to do everything possible to rescue the essentials of Bismarck's Reich.[11] At about the same time Goerdeler was suggesting as the future limits of Germany the frontiers of 1914 in the east (i.e. including East Prussia, the Corridor and Posen), Austria, the Sudetenland and the South Tyrol.[12] The problem was how a Germany of these dimensions could be fitted inside the European Confederation (*Staatenbund*) which was to be created. In effect the answer was that this body would be under German leadership but that that leadership would be exercised with moderation in the spirit of (the elderly) Bismarck, ample consideration being given to the views of the smaller members. They were to be reconciled to German hegemony by the advantages flowing from a Common Market and the existence of an organising power (*Ordnungsmacht*) in Central Europe. The latter phrase was a euphemism for the part which such a Germany would play in keeping out Communism.

The external views of the Kreisau Group were dominated by the complete disenchantment of Moltke and the Socialists with the nation-state, which they regarded as the main cause of war. They were therefore anxious to see the existing states merged in a Federation (*Bundesstaat*) where the central government had a preponderance of power; Moltke even advocated dividing Germany and France into a number of smaller states so that they did not outweigh the other minor members. They overestimated the willingness of states to make voluntary surrenders of sovereignty. The Kreisau thinkers were more realistic as to the amount of territory which Germany would have to surrender as compensation; so far from hoping to keep East Prussia and Posen, Moltke had before the end of 1941 told Kennan that he expected Silesia to go to the Poles or Czechs.[13] That a Russian advance should be threatening her eastern provinces was the price which Germany had to pay for Hitler's unprovoked attack. In visiting occupied countries, Moltke and Trott tried to establish contact with the local Resistance movements and convince them that there were at any rate some people in Germany anxious to atone rather than to dominate.

The documents are curiously reticent on the subject of the Jews. It must have seemed to their authors to go without saying that the repeal of Nazi laws and the reaffirmation of human rights would put an end to all racial discrimination in Germany. A memorandum, which Pastor Schönfeld gave to Bishop Bell in Sweden in May 1942 and which broadly expressed the views of the Kreisau Group, contained a promise that a new German government would at once 'reinstate the Jewish part of the population to a decent status, give them back the stolen property and co-operate with all other nations for a comprehensive solution of the Jewish problem'. *Das Ziel* contained a long paragraph admitting that the Jews constituted another race. The world would never be at rest until they had a state of their own, perhaps in Canada or South America. (The Nazis had talked of finding them such a home in Madagascar.) Once they had it, most Jews in Germany would become nationals of that state and would be treated exactly like any other foreigners. Nothing specific was said about restitution. It is relevant that when Goerdeler was writing, there were probably only about 140,000 Jews left in Germany who by the end of the war had dwindled to 15,000. Many of these would have come into the categories whom he was prepared to see remain as full German citizens.[14]

There was some fear on the part of the younger members that a 'Kerensky' solution would be adopted, i.e. that the first government set up after the Nazi overthrow would, like the Kerensky Government in Russia in February 1917, be insufficiently radical, with the result that it would in due course be overthrown by Communist or other radical leaders, as Lenin had overthrown Kerensky in October 1917. The phrase was put around by Moltke towards the end of the only serious discussion between the two groups which took place on 8 January 1943. If it prevented a half-way policy being adopted, it also prevented any clear agreement on policy at all.[15]

Since a revolution organised by the workers from below was out of the question, the initiative had to come from above. Increasing importance was attached by the conspirators to the question of how quickly and how completely popular support could be obtained for it. This concern was illustrated by a *Programme of Socialist Action*, a non-party popular movement to free the German people from Hitler's dictatorship, to restore the national order and to give freedom in a Socialist order.[16] The manifesto was written by Carlo Mierendorff on Whit Monday 1943 when considerations of security made it too dangerous for him to join his eight friends who were deliberating at Kreisau. The nine points in the programme did not go much beyond the Kreisau *Fundamental Principles* but the general tone of the document would have been too radical for Goerdeler and his friends to accept. It contemplated co-operation with Communists, to which at that stage Kreisau was opposed. On the other hand it called for 'respect in face of the foundations of our culture which is unthinkable without Christianity'; this, while wholly in keeping with Kreisau thought, would have been unwelcome to the radical left. The exact purpose of the document is unknown and no practical use appears to have been made of it. The same line of thought was illustrated by Stauffenberg's desire for a 'National Rising' (*Erhebung*) on the lines of 1813. But the older conspirators refused to see the danger which it was designed to counter.

There has been much discussion as to how far the Kreisau Group seriously tried to establish contact with the Russians. In the memorandum which professed to report the views expressed by Moltke during a visit to Istanbul in December 1943, the opponents of Nazism were said to be divided into an eastern and a western wing of which the former was the stronger, the inference being that it was likely to prevail.[17] In the following spring, Trott warned Dulles of the danger that Hitler's opponents would turn to the east. These hints were undoubtedly the mirror-image of Stalin's flirtation with the NKFD; they were intended to frighten the Americans and British with the spectre of Communism and induce them to pay more attention to the approaches of the conspirators. Another ploy was to say that so many Germans had lost so much property by bombing that they were no longer afraid of having it confiscated by Communists. A Foreign Office official described such tactics as 'very transparent'.[18] One of the chief ways in which Hitler's Government sought to avoid defeat was by sowing dissension between the Soviet Union and the West, so that all the conspirators succeeded in doing by their tactics was to foster suspicions that their emissaries might be acting as disguised Nazi agents. There is anyhow no conclusive evidence that any of the conspirators ever had discussions with a Soviet diplomat or agent, although Trott at one point arranged through Willy Brandt (who was working as a journalist in

Stockholm) to visit the Russian Embassy but called it off when he heard that the Nazis had penetrated that office (p. 186). On the whole the probabilities are against there having been any such contact.

As time went on the views of the two groups drew closer together. The *Fundamental Principles* contained the sentence 'The Reich remains the highest authority of the German people', thereby setting a limit to decentralisation. The *Honoratioren* for their part scaled down their expectations of what Germany could expect to keep, substituting federation for German hegemony. But a fundamental difference remained. Goerdeler, Beck and Hassell were concerned to salvage as much as they could and avoid unconditional surrender, at any rate to all three enemies simultaneously. They never fully rid themselves of the outlook which they had acquired when Germany was at her zenith. Moltke, by contrast, was prepared for his country to be defeated because only by such a humiliation would it be possible to get the clean slate which he thought was necessary for a satisfactory reconstruction. In 1941 he wrote that the end of the war would see a readiness for reflection and penitence which had not existed since 999. In the Istanbul memorandum (above) it was said that

> unequivocal military defeat and the occupation of Germany is regarded by the members of the [Kreisau] group as a moral and political necessity for the future of the nation. The group is convinced of the justification of the demand for unconditional surrender and realises the untimeliness of any discussion of peace terms before this surrender has been accomplished.[19]

Neither the older nor the younger men can be said to have been fully realistic. The elder statesmen deceived themselves about the speed with which occupied and satellite Europe would let bygones be bygones in their relations with post-Hitler Germany. They also deceived themselves about the attitude which Britain and the US would adopt prior to surrender as to the relative merits of Germany and the Soviet Union as an ally after surrender. They took it for granted that the British would see the need for a strong and healthy nucleus in Europe to maintain the balance of power against the extension of Communism and recognise in Germany the only possible source of such a nucleus. They overlooked the possibility that, after 1914 and 1940, the British might feel a greater need for Russian help against Germany than for German help against Russia. They assumed that the West would be prepared to trust Germans who shared its values, leaving out of account the widespread British conviction that, although 'good' men might occasionally come to power in Germany, they were incapable of holding it for long, so that concessions made to them were apt in the end to benefit people quite unlike them. For all these reasons the seniors formed erroneous expectations as to the treatment which they might receive from the West while they were planning and after they had executed a putsch. Their disappointment left them with a sense of grievance.

The younger men were apt to propose doing away with the phenomena which they disliked, such as national sovereignty, excessive centralisation and mass society, without paying enough attention to the forces which had brought such things into existence. Consequently they underestimated the difficulty of getting rid of them. They disregarded the part played by collective selfishness and power in internal and external politics and assumed too easily that this could be replaced by altruism. Their ideal was a paternalist government run by wise and benevolent technicians. They were ready and indeed anxious to draw such philosopher kings from as wide a social circle as possible. But they left out of account the American saying, 'Sure, we all want to vote for the best man but he's never a candidate.' Goerdeler described them as 'Parlour Bolshevists'. A better name would have been 'Social Romantics'. But it must be remembered that of the twenty who may be said to have formed the inner circle (a potentially misleading term because the setting of the number at twenty is the result of post-war analysis and not a distinction made at the time) nine were in their thirties. Moreover, they did not regard their proposals as final but foresaw a need to modify them in the light of changing conditions.

(e) Idealists or realists?

The accusation has however been made that all groups of the conspirators were not inspired by noble concepts of humanity so much as by the more sordid desire of enabling Germany to escape the consequences of defeat. Osbert Lancaster in 1944 published a cartoon showing three generations of a German military family with the caption, 'If we don't get out of this war soon, we'll be in no position to start another in ten years' time.' Such a formulation involved a cartoonist's licence but was not altogether unfair. Hassell's remark about rescuing at least the essentials of the Bismarckian Reich has already been quoted. Stauffenberg is said to have dropped on the night of 20 July a document containing the words

> The most important aim after a change of régime should be to see that Germany continues to count in the interplay of Powers and in particular that the Wehrmacht remains an instrument for its leader to use.[20]

What they feared was precisely what happened when occupation and disarmament left Germany without a Government of her own and without armed forces. If they had been able to foresee partition, they would have been even more disturbed. The wisdom of the Western policy will be considered in the next chapter; what we are concerned with here is the accuracy and adequacy of the charge.

In the first place a considerable reordering of customary values is required if we are to regard as ignoble such remarks as von der Schulenburg's claim that love of the Fatherland had been his driving force. Nor is there any reason to doubt that he meant it. And we should give him the credit of genuinely believing that Germany, in proper hands, had a valuable mission which no other country could perform so well, namely the organisation of Central Europe. A characteristic feature of the writings of Goerdeler and von Hassell is the recurrence of the words 'moral virtue', 'moral strength', 'order', 'conformity' in discussions of a Europe organised by Germany.[21] To be able to write like this may have revealed a certain lack of empathy but did not necessarily involve conscious hypocrisy. The phenomenon is not after all confined to Germany.

One of the earliest collective books about the *Widerstand* was however entitled 'The authority of conscience' (*Die Vollmacht des Gewissens*) and there can be no question but that a number of those who risked their lives in the movement to overthrow Hitler and his supporters did so because they believed not only that he was ruining their country by mismanaging the war but also that the rulers of Germany were evil men committing crimes. When men like von Moltke and Bonhoeffer admitted to hoping for their country's defeat, the very thing which the others so much feared, they did so not merely because they believed that only thus could an adequate break be made with the past but also because they considered defeat to be the punishment which Germany deserved. Elsewhere the motive of conscience was mixed with that of patriotism in varying degrees; the second half of this book gives some examples (see especially von Tresckow's statement on pp. 131). But all wanted to show that there was 'another Germany'. They went ahead with their plans in spite of failure to get any encouraging statements from the enemy, in spite of very questionable prospects of popular support and in spite of all the logistical obstacles to killing Hitler. They recognised that the odds were against their success.

It has been said that, whereas Hitler was a revolutionary posing for much of the time as a democrat, the members of the non-Communist *Widerstand* were democrats posing as revolutionaries. Leaving aside the question of how far they were democrats in the western sense of the word, there is much truth in this. They were not, like the Neapolitan *Carbonari* or the Serbian Black Hand, the IRA or the Basque Eta, fanatics who were not merely prepared to lose their own lives but who did not much mind how many other people they killed in order to reach their goal. They were, to their credit, too conscious of their responsibilities, too torn by moral qualms to achieve the necessary degree of ruthlessness. Early in the war, Moltke said to a member of the von Stauffenberg family, 'We're not conspirators, we're not capable of being, we've not learnt how to do it, we shouldn't try to make a start now, it would go wrong, we should make an amateur job of it.'[22] There were limits, as Beck pointed out (p. 144), to the German officer's vocabulary. The Communists, by contrast, were ready for self-sacrifice without asking whether it would achieve anything. People whose motivating influences are patriotism and Christianity are not nowadays likely to wade through rivers of blood in the hope of reforming society.

Were they then progressives or conservatives? There are two difficulties about answering this question. For one thing, such a variety of opinions were represented in the *Widerstand* that any generalisation must be inaccurate. Conservatives there certainly were amongst them in plenty. But the range ran from a reactionary like Kleist-Schmenzin who wanted to free the executive from all parliamentary control[23] to Moltke who said that what was needed was a revolution, not a coup d'état,[24] and Mierendorff who wanted a socialist economy. Secondly, much depends on how the terms progressive and conservative are defined. There has been a tendency recently to describe as 'conservative' anything which is not Communist.[25] But such a rigid dichotomy is hardly conducive to clear political thinking. Not only does it have no room for 'liberal democracy' but it leaves out of account those who were looking for a 'German way' to progress. If a common denominator must be found, it can only be the desire for more freedom. In 1933 that had been something which the German people had not been concerned to conserve. Its recovery was therefore in some sense a 'restoration'. But such labelling is perverse. It is up to those who insist on talking about the 'conservative *Widerstand*' to tell us what they would have considered a 'progressive' but non-Communist one.

CHAPTER VII
The West and the *Widerstand*

Once the turning-point of the war had been reached between the Alamein victory in October 1942 and the surrender of the German Sixth Army at the end of January 1943, the Anglo-Americans might at any time have enabled the *Widerstand* to succeed, restored peace, avoided a lot of damage and saved many lives by offering to make a compromise peace. Instead Roosevelt and Churchill ended their meeting at Casablanca by announcing on 23 January the demand for unconditional surrender, to which they stuck until it had been accepted by all three enemy Powers.[1]

Roosevelt's subsequent story that the formula had suddenly popped into his mind at the Press Conference has been shown to be as untrue as Churchill's story that its announcement at the Conference had taken him by surprise.[2] A State Department Advisory Committee had recommended it as early as May 1942 and the President had sent a message in the following August telling the Prime Minister that he would be content with nothing else.[3] The US Chiefs of Staff had endorsed the proposal and had been assured on 7 January that it would be supported at the meeting.[4] Three days before the announcement was made, Churchill had asked the Cabinet for their views on it.[5] The President spoke at the Press Conference from a written text containing the two words and one of the surviving drafts for this text contains emendations said to be in Churchill's hand.[6] Why both leaders should have chosen to cover their tracks remains a mystery.[7]

There had therefore been plenty of opportunity to consider the demand (even if that opportunity was not much used) and the initiative clearly came from America. Roosevelt all along took a hawkish attitude towards the Germans[8] while Churchill was too conscious of Britain's present and future dependence on the United States to challenge him on such an issue; he needed to keep his limited stock of influence for use in more immediate matters. In any case, he had often enough coupled 'Prussian militarism' with Nazi tyranny as the elements in German life which needed to be destroyed.[9] The President had been given a clear warning by his Chiefs of Staff as to the significance of what he was doing but insisted that the United States could not be expected to protect Western Europe from the Russians as well as from the Germans.[10]

If his attitude had been different, he might never have instituted Lend-Lease or signed the Atlantic Charter or given priority to the Atlantic over the Pacific, i.e. enabled Britain to win an outright victory. It is relevant that 1942 was the year in which knowledge spread in the West about the way in which Germans were treating Jews in Eastern Europe.[11]

Those who criticise the policy as misguided presumably think that peace should have been concluded on the basis offered on a number of occasions by a variety of German groups, Nazi as well as anti-Nazi. These would have been quite prepared to remove Hitler and the leading National Socialists, to do away with the more notorious Nazi laws and institutions, to re-establish the rule of law and to withdraw German forces to the frontiers of 1937 (or perhaps 1914). Subject to these limits the Germans would have been left free to decide on their own political and social reorganisation and would have retained an appreciable military capacity, thereby being enabled (possibly with Western help) to defend their eastern frontier against the Russians.

But for the Americans and the British to have made such a peace would not merely have involved breaking the promises made in their treaties with Russia and the other exiled governments and created an awkward dilemma as to Poland but would have been incompatible with the objects for which they professed to have been fighting the war and would have been bitterly attacked by public opinion (as were the Allied dealings with Darlan and Badoglio).[12] It may be true that what made Britain go to war was concern for her own security (p. 95). But public endurance of the hardships of war could not have been obtained by appeals to national interest alone. A considerable volume of moral enthusiasm was generated as well which could not be disregarded immediately victory was in sight. The view became established that Germany had twice precipitated war by seeking to enlarge her position in the world and that, in the interests of both security and humanity, she must be prevented from doing so again. There were broadly speaking three ideas as to how this might be achieved. (1) Dismemberment, the solution ultimately adopted as a result of disagreement after it had been openly agreed on at Yalta and a few weeks later abandoned by tacit agreement. (2) Pastoralisation, as recommended by Morgenthau, removing the capacity to aggress. (3) 'Re-education', i.e. reforms designed to remove the desire to aggress, based upon the idea that external policy is largely the result of internal conditions.

All three policies, however, required the transfer of power from German to Allied hands. They meant the disbanding of German armed forces and (since order would need to be maintained) the occupation of the entire country. They meant, in other words, the elimination of Germany as a power factor in Europe, if not permanently, then for a considerable time. Not only were the Nazis unwilling to consider such a reversal of their aims but, for reasons explained in the last chapter, so were the armed forces and the leaders of any government likely to come to power after an army-supported coup. This was not just a question of soldiers being reluctant to lose their jobs. They considered that they could only justify the overthrow of Hitler both to their own consciences and to the public if as a result the country obtained better terms than would follow from fighting to the bitter end. But even if the Allies had been willing to discuss conditions for surrender, the terms which they would have offered, as Churchill said in April 1944,[13] would not have been such as German generals would ever have accepted voluntarily.

The Americans and British however were not strong enough by themselves to bring about the complete defeat of Germany (unless the war had gone on until nuclear weapons became available). For that, Russian manpower was essential. Hence to insist on achieving it meant keeping the Russians in the war right to the end. The highly-suspicious Russians wanted assurances that the West were not going to do what most critics of unconditional surrender say should have been done – namely break off the war in the West, so as to prevent a decisive Communist victory in the East. The primary Russian aim in setting up the NKFD may have been the political one of intimidating the West into agreeing to Russian aggrandisement in Eastern Europe but that does not mean that, if the West had refused to be intimidated, the threat would never have been implemented. Moreover the British Government and people were acutely aware that Russia had (involuntarily but none the less effectively) saved them from defeat and their gratitude was tinged with shame that the bulk of the losses were falling on their saviours. Until 1945 any governmental move which involved a break with Russia would have led to the Cabinet's defeat in parliament. Meanwhile the demand for unconditional surrender reduced the opportunities for dissension as to what should be done after such a surrender.

In addition the Germans suffered from the back-lash of the two arguments which they had deployed with so much success between 1919 and 1939. First came the allegation that the terms imposed at Versailles violated the undertakings which the Allies had given to induce Germany to ask for an armistice in 1918. Sherwood has given a vivid description of how the portrait of Woodrow Wilson in Roosevelt's Cabinet Room acted as a perpetual warning against repeating Wilson's mistakes.[14] This cautiousness was heightened by the awareness that the world after the war would be in such confusion as to make it difficult to convince the defeated that any promises were being carried out to the best of the victors' ability. The result was a disinclination to make any commitments whatever. The closest that the Allied leaders came to giving hostages to fortune was Churchill's statement in parliament on 22 February 1944:

> Unconditional surrender does not mean that the victors have a free hand. It does not mean that they are entitled to behave in a barbarous manner nor that they wish to blot out Germany from among the nations of Europe. If we are bound, we are bound by our own consciences to civilisation. We are not bound to the Germans as the result of a bargain struck. (For full text see p. 260.)

Roosevelt had already said that 'we mean no harm to the common people of the Axis nations' and that 'we wish [the Germans] to have a normal chance to develop in peace as useful and respectable members of the European family.' Seven similar statements were made between 1943 and 1945 (see Annex B). It hardly need be said that they were all sedulously publicised through the BBC and other available channels.

The question is whether anything more should have been said. Dr Visser 't Hooft of the World Council of Churches suggested to Allen Dulles in January 1943 a statement that

> if a complete change comes in Germany, it may not be necessary to continue the war. We will judge a new government by its acts and if it takes a constructive line, we will be ready to offer conditions of peace which will allow Germany to survive and to have its normal place among the nations.[15]

At first sight this does not seem to go much further than Roosevelt and Churchill. But it fails to make clear the point on which the Allied leaders were emphatic. Terms would not be discussed until the Germans had been beaten. This was precisely what the Germans wished to avoid because they would then be unable to bargain. And the terms which they would have been offered would not have been regarded in Germany as allowing her 'to have her normal place among the nations'. Gerhard Ritter, the distinguished historian and biographer of Goerdeler, wrote in 1964 that

> The Tehran agreement was to sacrifice Germany to the friendship which Churchill and Roosevelt hoped for from Russia. To attain that end Germany was robbed of her eastern provinces, divided up into occupation zones, completely destroyed as a power factor and, with half her territory gone, left to the mercy of the Russians. To-day no German can read the Moscow–Tehran negotiations without deep indignation.[16]

He could not however claim that Germany had been tricked into surrender.

Possible further Allied statements were discussed in February, May, July and November 1944. All were discarded on the ground that they might do either too little or too much to raise German expectations.

Unconditional surrender is often said to have been a god-send to Goebbels and to have prolonged the war by making the Germans afraid of giving in. But this is disputable. For one thing, Goebbels and the other German propagandists do not seem to have made nearly as much use of the slogan as is popularly supposed (see note).[17] Moreover he did not need a particular phrase to build up a terrifying picture of what defeat would mean. That had been a persistent feature of Nazi publicity for a large part of the war. 'If we lose this war', said Göring in 1939, 'may God have mercy on us.'[18] The sort of thing which Goebbels was predicting was the castration of the entire male population, the removal of all children into captivity on the pretext of 're-education' and the deportation of many millions to forced labour in Siberia.[19] The retraction of the term 'unconditional surrender' would not by itself have undermined the credibility of such stories. The only way to have done so would have been to offer the same sort of conditions as the NKFD and such a concession the Western Allies, for reasons which should by this time be clear, were not prepared to make.

The second back-lash came from the argument that in 1918 the German armed forces had never been defeated in the field but had been 'stabbed in the back' on the home front. The best way to guard against a repetition of this legend was to continue the war until the German armed forces had no alternative but to surrender unconditionally or (to use the translation officially sanctioned by the State Department) make a *bedingungslose Waffenniederlegung.*[20]

History suggests that the negotiation of compromise peace during war runs into difficulties when each side has different estimates of what the outcome of a continued war is likely to be. Churchill has described how his immediate reaction to the news of Pearl Harbor was, 'So we have won after all.'[21] A year later the problem on the Allied side had become how to prevent the public from expecting victory too quickly; Alamein was not the beginning of the end but the end of the beginning.[22] But for some time longer it was still reasonable for a well-informed German to see a chance of obtaining a compromise peace brought about by mutual exhaustion. Only after the Anglo-Americans had succeeded in opening a Second Front in the west and after Hitler's secret weapons had turned out to lack decisive effect did it become wishful thinking to expect anything other than complete defeat. But by then the Allies had no inducement to change their view that a more lasting peace could be built on an outright victory than on a marginal one.

The German answer to this reasoning is, of course, that it was a fatal mistake to insist on eliminating German power, not merely because that is something which in an interdependent industrialised world cannot be done but also because German power was needed to keep the Russians out of Central Europe and the prospects of peace lasting would have been better if that had been done. The *Widerstand* grew exasperated at what they took to be a British failure to see this when it was in fact a British refusal to give it the same priority as they did themselves. The British attitude can be illustrated by Sir William Strang's remark that 'it is better that Russia should dominate Eastern Europe than that Germany should dominate Western Europe',[23] and by the conclusion of an official committee:

A strong Germany in the sense really desired by the [Russophobes] i.e. a Germany strong enough to counterbalance Soviet Russia but not so strong as permanently to dominate Europe – is no longer a feasible proposition. Either Germany is permanently eliminated as a major military power or she will permanently dominate Europe. There is no half-way house.[24]

At the end of the day, the question was whether Germany could be trusted to use power with restraint. The story of Wilhelm II and the spectacle of Hitler did not encourage an affirmative answer.

This is a matter on which historians cannot be expected to agree for several decades, perhaps for several centuries. We must wait until events have moved forward enough to bring within range a consensus of opinion as to how far each view was right. For one thing, we need to see whether the ability to make such a judgment is removed by nuclear war or facilitated by the absence of it. In the interim however we can at least avoid assuming that the state which would have emerged from a compromise peace would have combined the political and social characteristics of the Federal Republic with the frontiers of the 1937 Reich.

British and American politicians can be criticised for not thinking deeply enough about the likely results of assisting the Russians to join in the running of Germany (assuming that the Germans unaided could have stopped them from entering the country). Some of them underestimated Russian power and took too favourable a view of Russian intentions (although others, and notably Allen Dulles, did the reverse[25]). By 1944 Roosevelt was incapable of sustained thought and Churchill preferred to make certain of winning the war. The desire for Russian help against Japan played what proved an unnecessarily important part. Dick Crossman said in October 1945 that unconditional surrender was 'not only a formula for a tough policy towards Germany [but] a formula to avoid discussing the future of Germany.'[26] But a more extensive attempt to plan the future might only have ended in bewilderment and confusion. The underlying differences between East and West may have been such as to make a pragmatic rather than an explicitly formulated solution the only practicable one.

As things were, the policy adopted had three advantages:

(*1*) It enabled the consequences of Hitler's policies and the utter military defeat of Germany to be brought home unmistakably to every German. The sight of foreign troops moving unresisted throughout the country and government by a foreign control commission with officers in every district was a personal experience in a way a mere signing of documents by a small group could never be. The suggestion is sometimes made that Adenauer's 1949 Government was not so very different from that which Beck might have formed in 1944, so that nothing was gained by fighting on for nine and a half more months. This overlooks the traumatic effect of occupation and partition.

(*2*) By assuming government responsibility inside Germany the Allies not only eliminated the risk of civil war. They took onto their shoulders the blame for the state of Germany after the war and thus saved the first German post-war administrations from being discredited by failure to cope with a situation to which there was no quick or easy solution. They allowed the German politicians to draft a constitution at leisure and provided an answer to the question of legitimisation. This may have been more true of West Germany than of East but the administrators in the East did not have to depend on popularity to survive, while those in the West might have attracted more popular opposition sooner if it had not been for the mutual desire to stand together against Communism.

(*3*) The policies pursued ended in partition. This is now seen inside the

Federal Republic and outside in the Western world as a tragedy which should be reversed (by turning East into West rather than vice versa). But if it is in this respect an incentive to conflict, it is also a contribution to peace in that a united Germany would be strong enough (especially if it acquired nuclear weapons) to give the upper hand to whichever of the Super-Powers it chose to support. As has been shown above, the main reason why the West refused to co-operate with the *Widerstand* was that they did not want an over-powerful Germany in the middle of Europe. In the words of François Mauriac, '*J'aime tellement l'Allemagne que je suis heureux qu'il y en a deux.*'

PART TWO

A Portrait Gallery

Introduction

The twenty-five people whose case-histories follow have not been chosen as the twenty-five 'best' resisters. They are a cross-section designed to show the various ways in which it was possible to stand up to Hitler – or refrain from doing so. I have also tried to avoid making it a Gallery reserved for what the Germans call *Honoratioren* and we the Establishment.

But that is easier said than done. We are rightly reminded nowadays that the working-class adversaries and victims of Nazism were considerably more numerous than the better-born ones. But there was little that people born in humble positions could do and what one of them did tended to be much the same as the others. Moreover they did not leave so many documents behind. And the sword made a broader sweep among them. Fewer friends remained to describe their characters or quote their sayings. For this reason Anton Saefkow in particular has to stand for many more.

Some candidates for inclusion like Halder and Hassell were rejected on the ground that their companions were already represented, so that much of what could be said about them would involve repetition. The same applied to Popitz, Yorck and Mierendorff. I was tempted to include Schacht but decided that too much of what there was to say about him would concern what he did to help Hitler and that there was not enough to be said about what he did to hinder. Rommel was a similar case. I would like to have included Wurm but could not find enough material easily available. Faulhaber and Galen are names that occur in most accounts of the *Widerstand* but it seemed to me that Preysing was more substantial. I preferred telling what Lichtenberg did rather than what Delp thought. If I had put in more big fish, there would have been no room left for the smaller fry. I contemplated adding, as an appendix, a list of other deserving figures, giving perhaps five lines to each. But it soon became clear that the question of whom to include would be even more invidious.

1 Georg Elser[1]

Elser was a small, taciturn, innately sceptical man who was born in 1903, the son of an indigent small-holder in a Württemberg village. He was a non-practising Protestant. Thanks to Germany's system of technical education, he became a skilled cabinet-maker. He had however his own ideas of how things should be done and as a result wandered from one employer to another. For some time he worked at a clock-factory in Konstanz. He regularly voted Communist and belonged to the Red Association of Front Fighters but, except for playing in its brass band, did not engage in party activities. About 1938 he came to the conclusion that things had got worse for the average worker since the Nazis came to power and that war was inevitable. He therefore decided to kill Hitler, as an essential step towards bringing more moderate men to office.

He decided that one of the great Party occasions would provide him with the best opportunity of doing what he wanted and settled on the meeting held every year on 8 November at the Bürgerbräukeller in Munich to celebrate the 1923 attempt at revolution, a ceremony which Hitler always attended and at which he stood still for some time. In 1938 Elser came to Munich for the occasion and had a good look at the site. He decided to insert explosives into a pillar close to the platform and detonate them at a suitable time through a previously set mechanism. He went back home and got a job in a quarry, where he found it a simple matter to steal the necessary explosive and fuses. He made a number of sketches to settle how to instal the machinery and how to set it off; as regards the latter, his experience in clock-making proved invaluable.

He came back to Munich at the beginning of August 1939 and set about his preparations, living on his savings. In the day-time he worked on the clock and the bomb in his lodgings; in the evening he went to the Keller for over thirty nights and had a modest meal, after which he hid himself in an obscure corner of the balcony until the restaurant was shut and empty. He first cut the cladding of the pillar and turned it into a door which, when shut, was unnoticeable. He hollowed out the space behind it, removing the bricks and mortar so as to leave no trace. Security was lax; he was mostly left undisturbed and on the one occasion when he was challenged managed to pass it off. A waitress who may have given him some help had no idea what he was up to, any more than did the four craftsmen who made separate bits of equipment to his specifications.

On 1 November he began to instal his machine, found various adjustments necessary but got everything finished by the night of 5–6 November. He took his belongings, such as they were, to his sister in Stuttgart, intending to go on across the Swiss frontier. But on the night of 7–8 November he came back again to make sure that the clock of the machine was working. On 8 November he travelled to Konstanz and set out to cross the Swiss frontier by a little-used path. But for once he did not take sufficient care to make sure that the coast was clear and was caught by two German customs officials who by an ironical accident were listening to Hitler's broadcast from the Keller. It is tempting to suppose that he may have stopped to listen himself so as to hear the bomb go off. They found on him a postcard of the Keller, a pair of pliers (to cut any wire on the frontier), a badge of the Red Front Fighters Association, various bolts, springs and screws and a list of German factories making armaments, which he said was intended to dissuade the Swiss authorities from extraditing him. This miscellaneous and superfluous collection aroused suspicion, especially when news of the explosion came through. He was transferred to Munich and then Berlin where he gave a detailed account of his activities which still exists. For a number of reasons it can be accepted as true.[2]

Elser never read newspapers or indeed anything except an occasional technical journal. Had he done so, he would have learnt on 6 November that Hitler was not coming to the reunion. How this might have affected him is hard to guess but in the end the Führer changed his mind and did attend. But, instead of speaking from 20.30 to 22.00, he only spoke from 20.10 to 21.07 and then, instead of staying on to chat with the old comrades, left to catch his special train back to Berlin. (This was all in line with his practice of not having his movements advertised in advance and not following a set routine.) The bomb went off about 21.20, killing 8 and wounding 63. There is no need to invoke a special intuition to explain Hitler's action, although he did afterwards claim that an inner voice had told him to get out; the decision about launching a western offensive was due to be taken in Berlin the next day and he may well have wanted to be on the spot in good time.

The opponents of the Third Reich at home and abroad were convinced that the attack was a put-up job to boost Hitler's popularity (and perhaps to justify a western offensive). But there are cogent arguments against such an explanation.[3] Hitler, Himmler and 'Gestapo Müller' however refused to believe that a single man on his own could have brought off such a feat and sought evidence to connect Elser with the dissident Nazi Otto Strasser or the incident at Venlo on the Dutch frontier on the following day when two members of the British Intelligence Service, Major Stevens and Captain Best, were lured into a trap by Schellenberg of the Reich Security Head Office (p. 157). Elser was lodged in Sachsenhausen camp but given favourable treatment; he built a replica of his 'infernal machine', did carpentry for the jailers, played billiards on a table of his own making and strummed on the zither. He is thought to have been kept for use as a witness in a trial directed against the British, in which the link with Venlo must surely have broken down. At the end of 1944 he was moved to Dachau, where he was given the same privileges as Schuschnigg, Halder and Schacht. But on 5 April 1945 the Gestapo gave up hoping for an opportunity to stage an anti-British trial and announced that Elser had died in an air raid on the camp.

During his interrogation Elser took pains not to incriminate any of the people he had dealt with. He justified the killing of bystanders by saying that the total deaths would be far fewer than the lives lost if the war went on. During the months of preparation, he used to go into churches to pray. But he afterwards said that the failure of his plan convinced him that his appreciation of the situation had been wrong and that providence had not intended his attempt to succeed.

The case of Elser shows how much could be done by a single man who had no fellow-conspirators to consult and did not need to bother about what would happen next. His qualifications for the job were humbler than those of the other would-be murderers but they corresponded more closely to what was needed. The fact that he was a 'loner', not given to talking, saved him from attracting the attention of the authorities. He would not however have got as far as he did if the security precautions of the authorities had been as thorough as those of Hitler and their tightening-up, with all the difficulties which this brought to his successors, was in the end his main achievement.

2 Henning von Tresckow and Fabian von Schlabrendorff[1]

Von Tresckow was born in 1901 into a Pomeranian family which had provided the Prussian Army with 21 generals, including his father. His mother was the daughter of Count Robert Zedlitz-Trützschler, a Prussian Minister of Education under the Kaiser. He himself entered the Army at the age of seventeen and fought as a lieutenant in the final battles of the 1914–18 war. For two years after the Armistice he stayed in the 9th Infantry Regiment (destined to be a seed-bed of anti-Nazism). But in 1920 he left it to study law and economics at a university, to work in a Jewish banking house, and to travel through Britain, France and South America. Perhaps it was this experience which led him to adopt moderately liberal political views; provided that 'a mad rush into modernity' was avoided, he was not opposed to 'pragmatic socialism'. A desire to serve the state rather than to make money brought him back in 1926 to his old regiment. A fortnight before rejoining it he married a daughter of the debonair and chauvinist General von Falkenhayn who had taken over from General von Moltke as Chief of the General Staff in October 1914, to be superseded by Hindenburg two years later.

Tresckow regarded the Republic with as much distaste as most of his comrades and was at first attracted by National Socialism. Like so many, he hoped that Hitler might restore the nation's self-respect, provide leadership, revive prosperity and win the allegiance of the working classes to the national cause. But the events of 30 June 1934 disillusioned and the limp reaction of the Army High Command disgusted him; his deepest religious convictions were offended. Four months later, he was chosen to enter the War Academy, where officers were trained for the General Staff. In 1936 he left it as the best of his year and was promptly posted to a key division of the War Ministry, where he worked in close contact with Beck, Fritsch, Manstein and Heusinger. In 1937 he did the spade-work for, without approving the principle of, an attack on Czechoslovakia. The intrigues which led in February 1938 to the removal of General von Blomberg as Minister of War and to the prevention of the appointment of General von Fritsch as successor (p. 31) filled him with indignation. He and his colleague Baudissin obtained an interview with von Witzleben, the commander of the Berlin Military District. When asked whether he thought that the Army leadership should have acted against the régime, he said he did and was then told it would be best for him not to leave the Army in disgust, since plans for action were in train and helpers for them would be welcome. His knowledge of the outside world had by this time convinced him that any attempt by Germany to expand further would be met with force by other states. He doubted (correctly) the economic value of absorbing Austria and was against a military seizure of Czechoslovakia. He was only distantly involved in the plans against Hitler in September 1938 but was speechless with anger at the *Kristallnacht*. By the time he was posted, in the normal course of promotion, to command an infantry company in January 1939, his hatred of the Third Reich had made him physically ill. 'This cannot end happily,' he went about saying. 'Hitler is going to war.'

In July 1939 he arranged a first meeting at his family home with his cousin Fabian von Schlabrendorff. The visitor was six years younger, son of a Brandenburg landowner and great-grandson of Queen Victoria's adviser Stockmar; he was married to a Bismarck. While he was at the university a study of Nazi literature and acquaintance with Nazi students had convinced him that 'they went against everything my own upbringing represented and the traditions, principles and histories of families like mine.' He was much influenced by Ewald von Kleist-Schmenzin (p. 11). He himself wrote in March 1933 in the *Information Bulletin* of the Conservative Party that the new régime had, by their acts of illegal terror, broken with the old Prussia whose motto had been that 'justice is the foundation of government'. A second article of his later in the same year led to the *Bulletin* being shut down.

After 1934 Schlabrendorff spent much of his time in provincial cities in the course of qualifying as a lawyer and then settled as a private attorney in Wiesbaden. But he kept in touch with similarly-minded conservatives and in 1938 got to know Hans Oster. The latter arranged for him to be sent to London in the summer of 1939 to warn Lord Lloyd that a German attack on Poland could only be prevented if Britain made it clear that the result would be a large-scale war. He also saw Churchill who asked him what guarantee there was that, if Britain did as he suggested, Hitler's German opponents would be able to overthrow him. Schlabrendorff was honest enough to give a negative reply. He was fresh from this trip when he met Tresckow; it did not take them long to find themselves in whole-hearted agreement. Schlabrendorff was from now on to provide the link between Tresckow and Oster, for surprisingly enough the two men who (with Goerdeler) were to be the driving force of the anti-Hitler crusade during the next four years never seem to have met. Long ago it had been said of Tresckow that his ambition would cause him to end up as Chief of the General Staff or on the scaffold.[2]

When the Army mobilised against Poland, Tresckow became chief operational staff officer to a Division. A revision of the Polish Corridor was the only territorial change which he thought imperative but he could not approve of the way it was being brought about. He was profoundly shocked that Blaskowitz should have been the only general to protest to Hitler about the atrocities committed by the SS in Poland and that the protest should have been dismissed as 'childish'.[3] But if he was to succeed in eliminating Hitler, he had to remain undetected until a suitable opportunity arose and that meant performing his military duties to the best of his ability. Moreover the Army could not afford internal dissensions if it was to gain control in a post-Hitler Germany. He often quoted St Matthew's Gospel: 'I send you forth as sheep in the midst of wolves. Be ye therefore wise as serpents and harmless as doves.' He succeeded well enough to gain an unusually high grade of the Iron Cross. Schlabrendorff had meanwhile joined up but spent the next eighteen months in insignificant jobs.

At the end of October 1939 Tresckow was posted to be the direct assistant of Manstein, the Chief of Staff of one of the three Army Groups which were to conduct the campaign in the west. He shared the apprehension of his superiors about the proposed attack but could merely look on while they failed to talk Hitler out of it or to agree in defying him. He seems to have known nothing of the feelers which were being put out towards Britain. Ironically he was largely responsible for the detailed planning and execution of Manstein's 'sweep of a sickle' which cut through the Ardennes behind the British and French Armies. Great was his indignation when the leading Army Corps was halted short of Dunkirk. He helped to plan the invasion of England but saw it to be hopeless once the attempt to gain air supremacy had failed. In October he said in Paris to a secretary (later to become Jodl's wife), 'If Churchill can induce America to join in the war, we shall slowly but surely be crushed by material superiority. The most that will be left to us then will be the Electorate of Brandenburg.' He went on to quote the words on the monument to the theologian Schleiermacher, 'Let me seek this as fame – to know that there will come a point on my path which will swallow me up and yet that there will be nothing for me to do when I see it – not even to slacken my pace.'

It was in this mood that in December 1940 he took up the post of head of the Operations Section of the Central Army Group in the forthcoming Russian campaign under his uncle, Field-Marshal von Bock. He found on the staff three kindred spirits, von Lehndorff, von Hardenberg and Berndt von Kleist; he managed to add to them von Schlabrendorff and von Gersdorff. But not only did he have the most gloomy expectations about the campaign. He was appalled by the orders which were coming from Hitler about the treatment of Russian prisoners, not merely because they were inhumane but also because they ruled out any chance of establishing a non-Communist Russian régime. He is reported to have remarked, 'If international law has to be broken, the Russians shall do it, not us.'[4] When he learnt what was intended from

Gersdorff, he insisted that the two of them go at once to Bock and on the way said, 'If we don't succeed in getting the Field-Marshal personally to move heaven and earth to get these orders withdrawn, Germany will have lost her honour for good and all. The consequences will last for centuries and men will lay the blame, not exclusively on Hitler but on you and me, your wife and my wife, your children and my children, that woman who is crossing the street over there and that child playing with its ball.' But Bock would not face the Führer personally and Gersdorff, whom he sent instead, did not even get into Hitler's presence. The best that could be done was to find ways of preventing the orders from being carried out, in which Tresckow was abetted by a number of subordinate commanders.

When in December the German attack came to a halt outside Moscow, Tresckow told Bock that the Army was going to suffer a defeat from which it would not recover. When Bock asked for a remedy, Tresckow said there was only one – get rid of Hitler. 'I won't stand such remarks,' came the reply. 'I won't have the Führer abused.' But Hitler's remedy was to get rid of Bock and replace him by von Kluge who, as he acquired experience of working with the Supreme Commander, became more sympathetic to the idea of revolt.

A few days earlier Tresckow had been in Berlin where he told Karl Silex, the editor of the last paper to preserve a little independence, that the war was lost and Hitler must be removed. Could he have the names of some Englishmen who might be approached? Silex replied that such an approach would be seen by the English as a confession of defeat and would spur them on to win the war on the battlefield. There was also the danger of creating a 'stab-in-the-back' myth, of which Tresckow was well aware. There was nothing to do but to convince Kluge of the need to act and this aim was pursued steadily through 1942. The links between the front and the conspirators in Berlin were drawn closer. In April Gersdorff procured via the Abwehr supplies of captured British explosives and fuses. In the autumn a visit to the front was engineered for Goerdeler, who deeply impressed Kluge, already unnerved by the failure of the 1942 offensives. At a meeting in Berlin in December Goerdeler and Olbricht, head of the General War Office in the Replacement Army, agreed to have plans ready in six weeks for action inside Germany, after which Tresckow would persuade Kluge to raise the standard of revolt at the front. In March 1943 a visit by Canaris and other Abwehr officers to Kluge's Army Group headquarters enabled Tresckow and Oster's assistant Dohnanyi to arrange for mutual notification and support. Six days later Hitler gave the plotters the very chance for which they had been looking by agreeing, in response to a request by von Kluge for consultation, to stop at the Army Group on a journey from the Ukraine to East Prussia.

Kluge however explicitly forbade an open attack: 'For Heaven's sake, don't lay anything on today.' The officers who had declared themselves ready to make a combined pistol attack had to be called off. No attempt was made to use the cavalry battalion under Boeselager (p. 87). In any case Hitler's security precautions were formidable. Tresckow therefore asked a Colonel Brandt who was flying in Hitler's aircraft (and was later to be killed by the explosion on 20 July) to take a couple of bottles of Cointreau back to a friend at OKH.[5] On Brandt agreeing, Schlabrendorff handed to him a square parcel containing two of the British 'clam' explosives along with a silent pencil-shaped time-fuse set to explode in half an hour. He did this by breaking a capsule containing acid which then ate through a wire holding back the firing-pin; as soon as the pin was released, it should have impinged on and activated a detonator. But for some reason (probably the low temperature in which the aircraft was flying) this failed to happen and after more than two hours, the disconsolate conspirators heard that Hitler had landed safely.

Tresckow telephoned Brandt to say that by mistake the wrong parcel had been given to him and sent Schlabrendorff to OKH next day to retrieve it, substituting genuine Cointreau bottles instead. After being terrified at the careless way in which Brandt tossed the original package to and fro, Schlabrendorff took it off to the train in which he was travelling to Berlin and gingerly unwrapped it in his sleeping compartment.[6] After telling Oster what had gone wrong, he kept the explosive for a week and then handed it in the Eden Hotel to Gersdorff, who had come to Berlin in order to conduct Hitler round an exhibition of captured equipment. Gersdorff had agreed to activate the fuse (retimed to work in about ten minutes) and at the right moment (which would not have been easy to judge) throw himself on Hitler so that both died together. The plan failed because Hitler went through the exhibition too quickly, Gersdorff retired hastily to a lavatory and detached the fuse. His intentions were never discovered and he survived the war (p. 151).

The attention devoted to the bomb which did go off in 1944 has led to neglect of the one which did not in 1943. Yet if ever there was a case of the course of history depending on a horse-shoe nail, this was it. At the time the front on the east was still 300 miles inside Russia and although Rommel, on leaving Africa, had warned Hitler that the German position there would soon become impossible, the Anglo-Americans had still to cross the Mediterranean and, in Churchill's words, it was only the beginning of the war which had ended.

Two questions call for answers:

(1) What would have happened in Germany?

Göring would presumably have claimed the succession and it is hard to see who could have challenged him immediately with success. To judge by the evidence from 1944 (p. 57), the German public would have reacted violently against the perpetrators. Suspicion would have fallen on the Wehrmacht. If the part played by Tresckow, Schlabrendorff and Gersdorff had come to light, the generals would have faced a choice between putting them on trial for treason or, by protecting them, provoking a clash with the SS, who would have had much of the public on their side. But, while Göring's capacities in a crisis should not be underestimated, it is hard to believe that he would have proved as intransigent as Hitler. The generals would probably have told him how small the chances of outright victory had become.

The possibility of an early armed clash between the Army and the SS cannot be ruled out. The Army could hardly have failed to maintain its authority inside the field of operations but, having relatively few units inside Germany itself, and those half-trained, could only have hoped to prevail at home by weakening its strength at the front. Such a situation would have made it difficult to go on fighting the enemy. But the safer assumption is that an uneasy truce would have been established between the Party and the Army-cum-civil administration, that thanks to reciprocal mistrust, the military situation would have deteriorated even faster than it in fact did and that before long authoritative peace feelers would have been put out.

(2) How would the Allies have reacted to such feelers?

Although it was only seven weeks since the intention to demand unconditional surrender had been announced, it is hard to believe that the statesmen would have stuck by this formula for long or that the British and American publics would have allowed them to do so (the situation in 1944–5 was different because by then the prospects of winning in battle had much improved). But what terms would have been demanded? Territorially a return to Germany's 1937 frontiers might have provided a basis, although difficulties might have been expected over Austria, the Sudetenland, the Polish Corridor and possibly Alsace. Stalin might have demanded the gains which he had made in 1939 (and lost two years later); if he had, Roosevelt and Churchill could hardly have agreed to his having them, yet could hardly have prevented him from taking them (unless they had invoked the help of the Wehrmacht!) There would have been plenty of support in Germany for the reestablishment of the rule of law, the release of political prisoners and the cancellation of specifically Nazi measures. A thoroughgoing removal of Party Members from key positions and punishment for inhumanities would have been harder to carry through as would measures of disarmament. The first negotiations would almost certainly have ended in deadlock. Yet once the knowledge spreads that negotiations are being seriously considered, the willingness of men to die for a country or a cause diminishes. It is hard to believe that, if Hitler had been killed in March 1943, the war would have gone on for another 26 months or that German power would have been reduced to its level after Potsdam. A number of lives would have been saved, a good deal of physical destruction avoided. Many Germans would once again have refused to accept that they had been really beaten. Germany would have changed substantially less than it has done and would have stayed united. The Reich would have remained more and the Soviet Union less of a potential menace to the rest of Europe.

Try as they might, Tresckow, Schlabrendorff and their comrades never again got within killing range of Hitler. The elimination of Oster's office in April 1943 (p. 158) was a major set-back. Just as the long campaign to win over Kluge seemed on the verge of success (p. 150), the Field-Marshal was put out of action by a bad motor smash. Tresckow tried hard to get appointed head of the Operations Section at the Führer's headquarters but instead was posted, a move perhaps deliberately accelerated by the Personnel Department, to the command of a battalion at the front, where he was further than ever from the centre of events. Even his promotion a month later to be Chief of Staff of the Second Army did not bring him much closer. In November 1943 and February 1944 two officers, Axel von der Bussche and Ewald-Heinrich von Kleist-Schmenzin (son of Ewald von Kleist-Schmenzin) volunteered to sacrifice themselves in the same way as Gersdorff while displaying equipment to Hitler but this was destroyed prematurely in an air raid. In March Captain von Breitenbuch agreed to make an attempt with a pistol when he went to an interview with Hitler in attendance on Kluge's successor, only to be stopped by an SS man from entering the room. Three appeals to Manstein had no effect. By this time, Hitler seldom visited the front. The only encouraging development was the posting of Stauffenberg to the Replacement Army. Tresckow had met him briefly in Russia in 1942 and may have had a hand in his appointment. Here at last was someone as determined as himself. During August and September 1943 Tresckow took a long leave in Berlin and in company with Stauffenberg overhauled the plans which Oster had made for action in the event of a putsch and found them seriously deficient. About this time he asked Gersdorff if it was not monstrous for two of Germany's best staff officers to be discussing how to get rid of their Supreme Commander. 'But this is the only way to save the Reich and the German people from the greatest catastrophe in their history. We must kill him like a mad dog who is a public menace.'

In April 1943 Tresckow's two sons were confirmed in the Garrison Church at Potsdam (where Hitler ten years earlier had staged the ceremony designed to capture the loyalty of the old élite). He took the occasion to define what in his view the old élite stood for:

> Never forget that you have grown up in Prussia and been nurtured in Prusso-German ideals. Today you are dedicating yourselves at the most sacred of Prussia's ancient shrines. That in itself carries with it a great obligation, the obligation to truth, to inward and outward discipline, to the fulfilment of duty to the utmost. But one should never talk of the Prussian spirit without pointing out that that is not the whole of it although it is often taken to be. The idea of freedom can never be dissociated from the real Prussia. The real Prussian spirit means a synthesis between restraint and freedom, between voluntary subordination and conscientious leadership, between pride in oneself and consideration for others, between rigour and compassion. Unless a balance is kept between these qualities, the Prussian spirit is in danger of degenerating into soulless routine and narrow-minded dogmatism. Only when they are put together is the true German and European task of Prussia to be found. There lies Prussia's dream.

The conspirators had long agreed that they must act before the Allies landed in the west, since they would otherwise be accused (as they have been) of only having done so to forestall or mitigate a military defeat. But lack of opportunity frustrated them until Stauffenberg's appointment, decided on in May, as Fromm's Chief of Staff, to take effect on 1 July. Soon after D-day Stauffenberg asked Lehndorff to find out whether Tresckow felt there was still any point in making the attempt. Tresckow, recently promoted to Major-General, replied that the attempt must at all costs be made. For what was at issue now was not the practical effect so much as the demonstration in the eyes of the world and history that the *Widerstand* was ready to stake its all. Compared to this, everything else was a side-issue. There could hardly be clearer evidence that the main instigators of the attempted assassination were not primarily motivated by the desire to avoid paying the full penalty of defeat.

Tresckow was not in a position to take any direct part in the events of 20 July. He spent the day at his Army Headquarters on the frontier of East Prussia. In the afternoon one of his colleagues told him of a report that an attempt on Hitler's life had been made and failed. Soon afterwards Schlabrendorff arrived from Army Group Headquarters, having had a telephone message from Berlin that the attempt had succeeded. But first a news bulletin at 18.25, announcing Hitler's escape, then the notice about his intended broadcast and finally the broadcast itself in the early hours of 21 July convinced them that their hopes were vain. Tresckow said that he was going to take his own life. He told Schlabrendorff, on saying good-bye,

Now the whole world will set on us and abuse us. But I am as much convinced as ever that I have done the right thing. I believe Hitler to be the arch-enemy not only of Germany but of the whole world. When in a few hours' time I appear before God's judgment-seat to render account of my actions and omissions, I think I can with a clear conscience stand by all I have done in the fight against Hitler. Just as God once promised Abraham that he would spare Sodom if ten just men could be found in it, I too hope that for our sake he will not destroy Germany. None among us can complain about dying. Anyone who joined our group thereby put on the shirt of Nessus.* A man's moral worth only starts from the point at which he is prepared to give his life for his convictions.

He then drove to the front line and staged a suicide in no-man's-land, so as to give the impression that it had been the work of Russian partisans (an impression which his driver later discredited). Schlabrendorff took the body back to Germany and buried it in the family grave.

Schlabrendorff was himself arrested on 17 August and taken to the Security Police Headquarters in the Prince Albrechtstrasse in Berlin. At his first interrogation two days later he got the impression that, although the SD strongly suspected him, they had no definite evidence against him. His activities in 1943 never came to light at all. What the authorities wanted to extract from him were the names of other people involved. He was shackled night

---

* Nessus was a centaur who tried to rape Hercules' wife Deianira and was killed by a poisoned arrow from the hero's bow. The dying centaur told Deianira that, if she kept his blood, it could act as a potion to keep her husband's love. Suspecting soon afterwards that Hercules was having an affair with Iole, she steeped in the blood the garment in which he was about to sacrifice. Immediately he put it on, the poison from the arrow began to cause him agony. He was only saved from death by the intervention of his goddess mother Alcmena.

and day. Besides being hit by clubs, he was tortured by a device which pressed pins against his finger-tips, by another which drove nails into his bare legs and by a third which resembled a medieval rack. He lost consciousness but divulged nothing material. He was then taken to Sachsenhausen camp and made to watch while Tresckow's coffin was opened; the SD believed it contained the body of a Russian soldier, used to conceal the fact that Tresckow had deserted to the enemy (as the staff-officer who went with him on his last ride had afterwards done).

Tresckow's wife was arrested on 15 August and her children taken away but early in October she was released again. Schlabrendorff was finally put on trial before Freisler, the presiding judge in the People's Court, on 3 February. Just as the case had been called, the sirens sounded for the heaviest American daylight attack on Berlin. In the course of it Freisler, hit by a falling beam, died clutching the files on the case. The trial was resumed before another judge on 16 March, when the accused protested that he had been tortured. He was accordingly released, only to be arrested immediately by the Gestapo who a few days later included him in the convoy to Flossenburg camp which also contained Canaris, Oster, Bonhoeffer and others. Probably owing to a mistake, he was not executed there but taken on 12 April to Dachau, since American troops were at hand. A hundred or more prominent people obnoxious to the Nazis but not directly involved in the plot, such as Niemöller, Schacht, Halder and Schuschnigg, had been assembled there and all were taken off into the South Tyrol where on 4 May American troops saved them from being killed by Italian partisans.

After the war Schlabrendorff resumed his legal practice in Frankfurt. From 1967 to 1975 he was a Judge of the Federal Constitutional Court. In that capacity he supported in 1973 the judgment that the Basic Treaty with East Germany was compatible with the Basic Law of the Federal Republic – a somewhat surprising stand for someone with his generally conservative opinions and strong aversion to Communism. He died in 1980.

3 Claus Philipp Maria Schenck, Graf von Stauffenberg[1]

Stauffenberg was born in November 1907, so that he was 27 years younger than Beck and 6 than Tresckow. His father was the Chief Court Marshal of the King of Württemberg. He could trace his paternal ancestry back to 1382; through his mother, born an Üxküll, he descended from Gneisenau, Prussia's general in the Napoleonic War of Liberation. The children were brought up as Catholics like their father but taught to respect their mother's Protestantism. Until Claus was 11, he lived on the fringe of a modest but self-satisfied court. After the King's abdication in 1918, Count Alfred remained responsible for the royal estates and therefore divided his time between Stuttgart and his country home at Lautlingen 50 miles to the south. Like Ernst von Weizsäcker, Claus went to the Ludwig Eberhard Gymnasium in Stuttgart which, with 250 years of history behind it, was Württemberg's equivalent to Eton. If his home life instilled in him the belief that noblemen had a right to lead, it also taught him that they had a duty to serve.

In 1924 his twin elder brothers, Berthold and Alexander, brought him into contact with Stefan George. George, then 55, set out to be the poet of Germany's future by writing in a sententiously opaque style and printing his nouns without capitals. He rejected with disdain the society which he saw round him on the hardly novel ground that it was materialist and bourgeois. He looked for it to be renewed by a select band of his own disciples whose driving force must be action rather than conventional morality. He sought to develop among German youth a new nobility of spiritual beauty and to transform life through art. Exactly what his followers were to do was never clearly explained since the master believed that, if each could not see by instinct where his duty lay, there was no point in telling him. But the revolution which he sought was not a liberal one. Pacifism and Marxism were abhorrent, as was internationalism except in so far as Germany could provide Europe with inspiration. Christianity had had its day. But although he stressed that his Reich was to be a new one, he did not give it a number. He admitted that National Socialism had positive aspects but was too much of an élitist to let himself be patronised by it, dearly though its acolytes would have liked to make him their patron. By no means all those who professed admiration were admitted to the inner circle but the Stauffenbergs qualified without question for the privilege.

Some of Claus's contemporaries expected him to become a musician. Gneisenau is likely to have had as much influence as George in deciding him to become a soldier. He enlisted in a Bavarian cavalry regiment with which his family already had connections; it was stationed in Bamberg and affected to take its inspiration from the thirteenth-century statue of a rider, possibly of the Emperor Frederick II and much admired by George, in that city's cathedral. After a year as an ensign, Claus was posted away on training courses. Returning to the regiment he quickly established a reputation for himself as a competent technician and leader with wide interests; he was criticised for excessive self-assurance and unconventional dress. He was promoted First Lieutenant earlier than usual.

The story has gone round that on 30 January 1933 Lieutenant von Stauffenberg put himself at the head of a Bamberg crowd which was celebrating the appointment of Hitler as Chancellor. For a variety of reasons, including the absence of any first-hand evidence, this is most improbable. He is more likely to have greeted the event with hope that it might bring in the sort of national revival which he wished to see, combined with some doubt as to whether that hope would be realised. George's reaction was ambiguous, but when he died in Switzerland in the following December, his funeral was hurried forward so as to deprive Hitler of any chance to be represented. The roster of friends who watched by his body was drawn up by Claus von Stauffenberg.

In 1936 he was sent on the regular two-year course at the Berlin War

Academy; his outstanding performance made it certain that he would be taken on to the General Staff. He was then posted as quartermaster to the First Light Division (later renamed Sixth Panzer) with which he served during the occupation of the Sudetenland as well as in the Polish and French campaigns. Like most officers, he approved of the reintroduction of conscription, the remilitarisation of the Rhineland and the absorption of Austria into the Reich. Like many, he was disturbed by the Röhm affair, the Blomberg–Fritsch affair, Beck's resignation and the *Kristallnacht*. Although his duties kept him away from Berlin, he seems to have heard early in 1939 something of plans for an overthrow. In the spring of that year he was heard to say, 'The fool is going to war.' When Britain and France declared war, he said that, if Germany was to win, she must be prepared to hold out for at least ten years. Soon after his Division returned from Poland, he was visited by his uncle Colonel Count Nicholas von Üxküll and his friend 'Fritzy' von der Schulenburg who told him of the Party's excesses in Poland and tried to enlist him for the conspiracy, urging him to seek an influential post such as that of adjutant to General von Brauchitsch, the Army Commander-in-Chief. But he replied that 'we haven't got as far as that yet.'

In the middle of the French campaign however Stauffenberg was posted to the Organisation Branch of the High Command of the Army (OKH) where he was to remain for two and a half years. Here he had a close view of how the war was conducted and here his doubts about Hitler's military genius began to grow. He also suffered from the tension between the OKH and the High Command of the Armed Forces (OKW) which had been developing ever since Hitler created the latter on taking over as Supreme Commander in February 1938 on the departure of Blomberg. Stauffenberg thought that this tension broke all the rules of good organisation and it helped to lose the war for Germany. But having his subordinates at loggerheads was Hitler's way of ruling.

As soon as the Russian campaign started, Stauffenberg became restive at the Nazi policy towards the Russian people. One of his chief jobs was to manage the replacement of the Army's heavy losses by fresh reinforcements. It soon became obvious that those forthcoming from inside Germany would run short and local commanders took increasingly to using prisoners for non-military and even for low-grade military duties. But although Hitler was induced to let Turks and Caucasians be recruited into the German ranks, he was never happy about it and more than once ordered a halt to be made. Stauffenberg not merely chafed at this refusal to face facts but also grew convinced that Germany could not hope to win unless she succeeded in enlisting the aid of the Russian people by offering them a non-Communist state of their own. At the end of 1942 he submitted a paper on the handling of Russian civilian workers which ran counter to basic Nazi ideas and was disregarded; even a draft proclamation restoring collective farms to private hands was vetoed. In an address to staff officers in October 1942, he said that the Germans were sowing seeds of hatred which would be visited on their children. All the same when in the spring of 1942 Berthold von Stauffenberg sounded out his brother about joining Moltke and his friends, he got the reply that during the war one must not do anything of the kind, above all not during a war against the Bolsheviks. 'But when we get back home we will get rid of the brown plague.'

Events during the rest of 1942 however convinced him that the war could not be won unless the brown plague was got rid of first. Hitler not only refused to realise the extent to which losses had weakened the Army, and in consequence set it tasks beyond its strength. He gave priority to the SS and Air Force as regards supplies and reinforcements and, by refusing to allow the Sixth Army to retreat before it was surrounded at Stalingrad, sealed its doom. By the autumn Stauffenberg was heard to say that, 'It isn't a question of telling the Führer the truth but of killing him and I'm ready to do the dirty work.' He also said he hated Hitler and his whole gang. He was led to realise the importance of the rule of law by his brother Berthold, who was an international lawyer. But as a relatively junior officer in the OKH (not even the OKW) he had no access to Hitler. Tresckow, whom he first met at this time, arranged an interview for him with Manstein, who told him that a war was only lost when the leaders thought it lost – not 'the answer which I would have expected from a Field-Marshal'. He would not seem to have known of the Tresckow–Schlabrendorff–Gersdorff plans.

In any case he had left the east before they came to grief. Zeitzler, the new Chief of Staff, was impressed with his capacities and decided to give him experience with troops. He was therefore posted in January 1943 to North Africa as senior staff officer in an armoured division. But Africa was as depressing as Russia. Rommel had already told Hitler that continued resistance was futile and by mid-March there was no alternative left but a steady rearguard action. The success of the Anglo-Americans was largely due to domination of the sky and on 7 April one of their fighters caught Stauffenberg on the road. He lost his right hand, the third and fourth fingers of his left hand and his right eye; he had to have operations on his knee and ear. Although hardly fit to travel, he had been evacuated to Munich by the time of the final surrender on 13 May.

The many visitors to his bedside included his Üxküll uncle who again asked him to join the conspiracy. This time, after consulting Berthold, Claus agreed. 'Since the generals have so far done nothing, the colonels must go into action.' He was offered a wide choice of posts but the one which he accepted came from Zeitzler and was that of Chief of Staff to General Olbricht, head of the General War Office in the Replacement Army housed in the Bendlerstrasse in Berlin. He appears not to have known, any more than did Zeitzler, that, since Oster had in the previous April been ordered to keep clear of his own Abwehr office in the Tirpitzufer next door, Olbricht was the key man in the conspiracy. He realised however that the post was one which should give him opportunities for action. He told his wife of 'a feeling that I must now do something to save the Reich'; he told a friend that he would 'never be able to look the wives and children of the fallen in the eye if I do not do something to stop this senseless slaughter.'

He did not take up his appointment until 1 October but visited Berlin in August and spent most of September there, meeting such key figures as Beck, Goerdeler and Leber and taking advantage of Tresckow's presence to work out with him a cover plan for the action necessary immediately Hitler was dead. This was based not only on Oster's plans from 1939 but also on a contingency plan prepared in 1941–2, on Olbricht's initiative but with Hitler's approval, for the action to be ordered in the event of trouble from the 7.6 million foreign workers and prisoners-of-war in Germany, of whom by this time 140,000 had escaped and were living at large.[2] 'Operation Valkyrie' provided for military action to protect key points in Berlin and the main provincial cities; it could without much difficulty be adapted to an emergency caused by the death of Hitler and/or a rising by the SS against the Army. Although an up-dated version was complete by the end of September, it needed continual adjustment to changing circumstances and in particular to the shifts of personnel which were inevitably taking place.

Everything however hinged on Hitler being eliminated. There was growing agreement that his mere arrest would lead to civil war and that he must therefore be assassinated. There was also growing agreement that the best opportunity for assassination was offered by the daily 'situation conference', although the idea of using an inspection of material was not abandoned until the spring of 1944. But there remained the problem of finding someone who could get access, along with his explosive, to the conference room and had the necessary strength of mind to use it when he got there. Stauffenberg at first underestimated the gravity of this problem which was only brought home to him by the disappointments of the winter of 1943–4 (p. 130).

The delay made everyone restive. All realised the need to act before the Eastern Front collapsed or a western front was created. The Americans, British and Russians must be prevented from meeting in Berlin; delay might make it impossible to play the several enemies off against one another.[3] Lack of occupation and instinctive lust for action led Stauffenberg to turn his attention from the military plans to the civilian ones. Beck and Oster, true to the tradition of an unpolitical Army, had been ready to leave these to Goerdeler, Popitz and Hassell. Stauffenberg instead followed Gneisenau in considering that the Army carried a responsibility for the fate of the country and thus must not disregard politics. He had always had wide-ranging interests outside his profession and his move to Berlin meant that he was continually talking with civilians to an extent he had had no chance to do at military headquarters. Goerdeler, who was critical of the soldiers for not getting on with their side of the job, resented them claiming a right to a voice in his.

Stauffenberg left few documents behind him so that it is often difficult to be sure about his views and secret actions. He had had no training in political thought and at the outset was largely feeling his way, with the help of Berthold and their friend Rudolf Fahrner. He started like most of the others from a determination not to repeat the experience of Weimar. He was as a result averse to parliaments, parties and pluralism, hoping instead to build on such 'political realities' as communities, professional bodies and interest groups. Romantic desire for a society which would be free from internal conflict reinforced the inclination which he had absorbed from George towards paternalist rule by an élite. Anticipating that their project might end in disaster, he and Berthold drafted a document to leave behind them as their creed:

> We desire a new order which makes every German an upholder of the State and which guarantees him law and justice but which despises the heresy of equality and reverences the ranks created by nature. We want a people rooted in the soil of their homeland, in close contact with the forces of nature and finding happiness and satisfaction in doing their duty in the states of life to which they have been called, overcoming in proud freedom the lower instincts of envy and ill-will. We want leaders drawn from all classes and in close touch with the divine powers who will go ahead of the rest with good judgment, integrity and self-sacrifice.[4]

In all this he was not far from Goerdeler. When asked about the NKFD, he said that whereas he was committing *Hochverrat*, they were committing *Landesverrat* (p. 70). But during the winter of 1943–4 his views were modified by contact with Leber, Yorck and Trott who regarded Goerdeler as a reactionary. He had almost no contact with Moltke who suspected him of being over-anxious to act.[5] Leber in particular stressed the need to get the support of the workers for any new régime and argued the merits of a parliamentary system. Trott, on the strength of what he had learnt abroad, showed that Goerdeler's appreciation of Germany's external situation was far too optimistic. The Shadow Chancellor's volubility caused him to be regarded as a security risk and he began to be kept at arm's length. Stauffenberg queried whether he was really the right man for the top job. Goerdeler noticed and resented this; he replied by denouncing Stauffenberg as a 'self-willed crank'.[6]

Altogether there was ample occasion for rejoicing when in May 1944 General Fromm, the Commander of the Replacement Army and Olbricht's immediate superior, decided to make Stauffenberg his Chief of Staff. Once when Olbricht had held forth to Fromm about the gravity of Germany's position with the implication that something ought to be done about it, the reply had been 'That was very interesting. Well then, Heil Hitler.' His already quoted remark about not forgetting Keitel in a putsch (p. 87) shows that he had a shrewd but imprecise idea of what was going on. But he was one of those who were only going to join in after somebody else had done 'the dirty work'. He certainly did not choose Stauffenberg in order to assist the conspiracy nor realise how much he was doing so. For Fromm's chief job was to provide replacements for the casualties at the front and in that capacity he or his Chief of Staff had from time to time to attend the 'situation conference'. Moreover not only was Fromm a commander who (unlike most staff officers) could give orders to troops but his deputy was entitled to do the same on his behalf. At long last someone with the will to make the attempt was being given the opportunity to do so. Satisfaction at this progress was allowed to outweigh the two vital disadvantages of Stauffenberg's physical handicaps and the need to combine in one man two functions which common sense dictated should be kept apart.

There were many reasons making the need for action urgent. On 6 June came the invasion in Normandy. In mid-June a Colonel Staehle, who acted as intermediary between Goerdeler and the Dutch Resistance, was arrested and it became known that Goerdeler himself was being watched by the police. A Russian offensive which began on 23 June made it doubtful whether the front in the east could be held at all so that those who still had lingering hopes of doing a deal in the west before it collapsed saw that there was no time to lose. On 5 July came the arrest of Leber and Reichwein (p. 199); not only was it desirable to rescue them before too much information had been extracted but Stauffenberg felt a duty to help the man whom he was increasingly thinking of as the new Chancellor. On 16 July Hofacker, the conspiracy's man in Paris, came to Berlin with the news that the Western Front would collapse in six weeks at the most. On 17 July news leaked through that Goerdeler was to be arrested as soon as he could be found. Stauffenberg was looking for ways to establish contact with the West. Through Otto John of the Lufthansa he obtained a link with the American Military Attaché in Madrid, while he is said to have told Goerdeler that he had found a way of getting messages to Churchill although it is not clear how much this amounted to. He sent Trott to Stockholm to see what could be found out there about Allied readiness to negotiate. His preferred method of reaching an armistice would have been by direct contact between commanders. It is hard to tell what solid ground, if any, there was for these hopes. He also sent Lehndorff to Tresckow, who gave the advice which has already been mentioned (p. 131), while Stauffenberg himself said that

> It is now time something was done but he who has the courage to do it must do so in the knowledge that he will go down to German history as a traitor. If he does not do it, then he will be a traitor to his own conscience.

The first meeting to which Stauffenberg took the British-type explosive which the Abwehr had provided was at Berchtesgaden on 6 July but he made no attempt to use it because neither Göring nor Himmler were present and the aim was to kill them too so as to reduce the danger of civil war. After Himmler's absence had again prevented action on the 11th, it was decided to drop this requirement. At the next meeting, on the 15th in East Prussia, Stauffenberg's freedom of action was limited by Fromm's presence and by the fact that the conference ended early. But on this occasion the preliminary warnings called for in Operation Valkyrie had been sent out and had to be countermanded. This was likely to arouse suspicion so that a second false alarm could not be afforded. It was decided that next time the officers in Berlin would wait for a message from the headquarters.

On 20 July these mishaps were not repeated. But Stauffenberg was interrupted by an officious sergeant-major before he could, with his remaining thumb and two fingers, set the fuse of a second bomb and place it, along with the first, in his brief-case. As the headquarters were being reconstructed, the meeting was held in a room with a cavity below the wooden floor; it was a hot day and ten windows were open. The brief-case was so placed that a thick wooden table-leg stood between it and Hitler. All these things combined to blanket the force of the explosion so that, although four of the twenty-four persons present died of their injuries, the main target escaped with slight bruises and burns, damage to his ear-drums and severe damage to his new trousers.[7] Thus a contingency had arisen for which the plotters had made inadequate provision. It had proved possible to explode the bomb, thereby calling the attention of the world – and the security services – to the conspiracy but without achieving the result on which so many people had made their help dependent, namely the death of Hitler.

In spite of a suspicious sentry at the gate, Stauffenberg and his adjutant Werner von Haeften succeeded in reaching the airfield, throwing the unused explosive out of the car en route, and took off half an hour after the explosion which he had heard before he left the headquarters enclosure. One of the problems of the conspiracy had always been that there was no central communications point in the headquarters so that although General Fellgiebel, the head of both OKW and OKH signals, was a prominent member of the conspiracy, it had all along been clear that a complete communications black-out would be impossible. (For example, Dietrich, Hitler's Personal Press Officer, had a direct line to Goebbels, of which Fellgiebel was totally unaware.) Nevertheless for a variety of reasons something close to it did occur between 13.00 and 16.00. Before it began, Fellgiebel spoke to Hahn, his Deputy in OKH forward headquarters near by, who passed the information on to OKH rear headquarters outside Berlin. He said to Hahn, 'Something fearful has happened – the Führer's alive.' When Hahn asked him what to do, he said, 'Block everything!' He probably gave the same instructions to his deputy in the Replacement Army, Thiele. But Thiele lost his head at this unforeseen development and went out for a walk to clear his thoughts. When he came back he informed Olbricht of what had happened, which Olbricht may have heard already through other channels. Fellgiebel had realised correctly that, once the bomb had gone off, the only remaining chance for the conspiracy lay in immediate execution of the Valkyrie plans. But Olbricht and Thiele were frightened of repeating the false alarm of four days earlier. Moreover they were not authorised to issue the orders themselves and from all that they knew, Fromm would not issue them until he received proof of Hitler's death, which could not be provided.[8]

Thus when Stauffenberg landed at about 15.30 and immediately telephoned to the Replacement Army in the Bendlerstrasse to find out what was happening, he discovered the answer was 'nothing'. Two and a half precious hours had been wasted. On his assurance that Hitler really was dead, Olbricht asked Fromm to give the orders for Valkyrie. Fromm refused to do so without more evidence, was allowed to ring up Führer Headquarters and learnt from

Keitel that the attempt had failed. He therefore remained unwilling to move. All the same Olbricht and Colonel Mertz von Quirnheim (Stauffenberg's successor as Chief of Staff to Olbricht) began to put Valkyrie into execution – a lengthy business as separate orders had to be teleprinted to each destination. (The plotters had failed to discover that the teleprinter circuit automatically dropped a copy of each order at Hitler's Headquarters.) When Fromm heard what was happening, he ordered Mertz to be arrested. This was the position at about 16.45 when Stauffenberg reached the Bendlerstrasse, having been delayed because the car which should have met him failed to do so. He took command of the situation, told Fromm that Keitel was lying and ordered his superior's arrest.

Two further mischances sealed the fate of an otherwise forlorn hope. The officer who was sent to occupy the Berlin equivalent of Broadcasting House was no technician and failed to discover that the studios and control switchroom were no longer in the main building, so that in fact transmissions were never interrupted. He did not communicate with the Bendlerstrasse so that the technical officers who should have been sent from there to control them never received an order to move. Goebbels had been in touch with Dietrich since about 13.15 and although they took rather longer in settling the terms of an announcement than pleased Hitler, it went out by radio teleprinter to the press at 17.42 and was broadcast in the German Home Service at 18.25. It reported the attempt and Hitler's survival.[9]

Secondly when Hase, the Berlin Chief of Police and a conspirator, ordered Major Remer, the commander of the Berlin Guard Battalion, to cordon off the government quarter, one of Goebbels' Army Propaganda Officers, Lieutenant Hagen, happened to be in Remer's office. Stauffenberg had been advised to have Remer replaced on the ground that he was a convinced Nazi, but had not got around to doing so. Remer listened readily to suspicions which had been aroused in Hagen by the apparent sight of Marshal von Brauchitsch driving through Berlin in full uniform.[10] Hagen insisted on going to report Hase's order to Goebbels, who had not until then realised that anything was happening in Berlin. The Minister had Remer brought to him and put him through to Hitler on the private line. Remer was ordered to make himself responsible for the safety of the city until Himmler, just appointed Commander-in-Chief of the Replacement Army, arrived. He withdrew his troops from the government quarter and concentrated them at Goebbels' house.

Stauffenberg resorted to every device he could think of, protesting that Hitler was dead and stories to the contrary untrue. In particular he tried to get action started outside Berlin; Paris was the only place which looked at all hopeful but even there Kluge's attitude made success out of the question. But even if he had managed to set off outlying revolts, it would have made no difference to his position in and around Berlin, where more and more commanders were refusing to accept his orders and loyal troops were closing in. At about 22.00, a group of loyal officers in the Bendlerstrasse building obtained weapons, freed Fromm and held Stauffenberg, Beck, Olbricht, Mertz and Haeften at pistol point. There was some shooting. Fromm ordered the conspirators to surrender their weapons and conducted an immediate court-martial which, no doubt to prevent inconvenient evidence from being given to the SD later on, condemned them to be shot. Beck was allowed to commit suicide. The others were taken down to the courtyard and executed. As Stauffenberg fell, he shouted, 'Long live sacred Germany.'[11]

It is a humiliating reflection on the ability of human beings to determine the future course of events that a plan prepared by two of the ablest staff-officers in one of the world's most efficient armies should have met with so many mishaps. This reinforces doubts about the chances of earlier plans, particularly that of September 1938. But let us suppose that Thiele and Olbricht had acted immediately, that Fromm had agreed to issue the Valkyrie orders (a risk he could have afforded to take, since he was destined to be executed anyhow for complicity), that the government had been denied access to the Berlin transmitter (and not fed their announcement into the Reich network from some other station such as Königsberg instead), that Hagen had not called on Remer or that Remer had been replaced by someone sympathetic to the plot. How much would have been changed? Suppressing the revolt would have taken longer but it is hard to believe that the government would not have come out on top (although the disturbance might have handicapped the resistance offered to the enemy during the crucial weeks of August and early September). The attempt failed at the outset when Hitler survived (as he probably would not have done if Stauffenberg had had time to put in the second bomb). Its failure was a natural consequence of the conditions in which it had to be mounted. As has been said (p. 33) there were 2000 generals in the Wehrmacht in 1944. Only 22 are recorded to have lost their lives as a result of the conspiracy (and several of those were retired). To explain why that number was so low is one of the chief tasks of this book.

4 Ludwig Beck[1]

Beck was born in 1880, son of a distinguished civil engineer in Hesse. His father was a Protestant who voted National Liberal but took no active part in politics. He himself entered the Prussian Army in 1898 and was rapidly appointed to the General Staff; only 8 of his 40 years of service were spent with troops. His views were largely formed before the 1914–18 war, during which he became assistant to General Friedrich von der Schulenburg, the Chief of Staff of the Crown Prince's Army. In that capacity he was present at Spa on the melancholy day in November 1918 when his superior vainly tried to prevent the Kaiser from abdicating.[2] He retained an undeserved loyalty to the Crown Prince. His wife died early leaving him an introspective and somewhat ascetic man.

In spite of what he had seen in Army Headquarters he at first accepted the 'stab-in-the-back' myth, but came later to realise that too much had been asked of German rank-and-file and civilians. This insight shaped his view of the Army's place in the state. He saw that industrialised war involved not just the armed forces but the whole population; economics and psychology had a part to play as well as strategy. Ludendorff had drawn from this the conclusion that soldiers must have the last word in government. Beck preferred a theory of two pillars, military and civilian; each must consult and listen to the other and preferably be co-ordinated by an impartial head of state. Beck realised that Wilhelm II had failed to perform this task and his grandfather Wilhelm I had only half succeeded but he all the same believed it could be done. It could not in his view be provided for adequately by putting the Army under a civilian minister (even if that minister, as in the last five years of the Republic, was an ex-general). A leader-figure was needed to integrate the nation. The hope that Hitler might serve this purpose was one reason why Beck for a time looked favourably on National Socialism and in 1930 urged General von Schleicher to get its leader made Chancellor. This helps to explain why in the same year he gave evidence at Ulm on behalf of three subalterns in his regiment whose open sympathies for the Führer-principle had led to them being charged with high treason.

Partly as a result he won Hitler's favour and was in October 1933, by now a Lieutenant-General, made head of the *Truppenamt*, the name under which until 1935 the Reichswehr concealed the General Staff forbidden it by the Treaty of Versailles. The appointment was generally approved of, out of respect for his intellect and integrity. His view of the post was neither modest nor up-to-date. Its holder should be the man who, through the Commander-in-Chief, should brief the government on all matters involving the exercise of military power. For Germany's wars were expected to be primarily land wars, so that the Navy's voice should be secondary, while the new element of the Air Force (which did not officially exist until 1935) was regarded first and foremost as a kind of artillery and intelligence-collecting unit supporting the Army. Beck recognised the growing need for defence policy to be considered as a whole but thought that the Army was capable of providing for this by itself at a time when major states were moving towards the creation of combined Ministries of Defence. The German Reichswehr Ministry included a Ministerial Office from which von Schleicher, both before and after he became Reichswehr Minister, had exercised his influence over the whole field of policy. When Blomberg was made Reichswehr Minister by Hitler, he put the Office in the charge of General von Reichenau and then in 1936 of General Keitel. In March 1934 it had been rechristened the Wehrmacht Office and enlarged by a section responsible for the Defence of the Country under Colonel Jodl. This was the nucleus from which sprang the High Command of the Wehrmacht (Oberkommando der Wehrmacht, OKW). Beck looked down on the newcomers but he was bound to lose out in competition with them, especially when in February 1938 Hitler took over the post of Defence Minister and made Keitel his chief staff officer.[3] The Führer however failed to exploit the potential advantages of the new structure since he never issued a directive dealing with overall Wehrmacht rearmament prior to 1939 nor even one which would necessitate a loose co-ordination of the armament measures taken by the individual services.[4]

As has been explained (p. 30), it was the Army Command which was primarily responsible for the decision to rearm by a series of unilateral steps instead of by international agreement. This aggravated and extended the risk period through which Germany had to pass during her rearmament until she became strong enough to make other powers think twice before embarking on a 'preventive war'. The more Germany rearmed to a level which suggested aggressive intentions rather than mere defence, the more did other countries, particularly Britain and France, take steps to catch up. But this meant that Germany had to enlarge and accelerate her programme in order to keep her advantage. Soon however that programme came up against the limits of material practicability. To expand a force of 100,000 men to one of 520,000 within five years and get it trained was an organisational challenge of the first order. But to get its equipment, and the machines for making that equipment, designed and made was not something which could be done simply by giving orders (especially as the two other services were also equipping themselves and Hitler was not prepared to make life unduly austere for the consumer). In 1935 Beck calculated that he could have the Army ready by 1940 and the amount achieved to meet that deadline was remarkable.[5] But he was well aware of what had still to be done and of the likelihood that, on any rational calculation, time was running against Germany. He wrote in May 1938 that Germany was still weaker than she had been in 1914 as regards personnel, equipment and morale.

This was the dilemma which came to a head in 1937–8. Until then relations between Hitler and his generals had been relatively harmonious. Beck's dislike of the SA (who put his name on their list of candidates for elimination) must have modified his misgivings about the events of 30 June and he seems to have turned a blind eye to what he knew to be in progress. When, shortly after, the Army was hustled into taking an oath of allegiance to Hitler personally, Beck is said to have described it as 'the blackest day of my life'.[6] But in general Hitler was doing what the Army wanted and Beck was too busy to argue.

This situation was changed by Hitler's remarks at his celebrated meeting on Guy Fawkes Night 1937 (p. 31). Beck agreed that Germany's aim must be to recover a position of dominance in Central Europe and that for this purpose Austria, Czechoslovakia and Poland must be absorbed or rendered subservient. 'Czechoslovakia in its present form is intolerable for Germany.' But he was convinced that Britain and France would come to the rescue of any of these states which was attacked. Germany could not therefore move in the east until she was strong enough to defend herself at the same time in the west. Hitler however seemed to intend disregarding this danger, gambling that the Western Powers were not prepared to fight and that even if they did they would not in the short term be serious foes. He proposed to break out of the dead end into which the arms race threatened to drive Germany by taking risks which appalled his Chief of Staff. When lecturing in Hitler's presence in October 1935, Beck quoted with approval Field-Marshal von Moltke's saying that cautious evaluation was to be preferred to bold adventuring (*das grundliche Wägen vor dem kühnen Wagen*). Hitler however said on the eve of war that he had been a gambler all his life (*Va banque spielte*).[7] But the weakness of Beck's position was that it was beginning to look as though, on any cautious evaluation, Germany would never have an adequate preponderance of force to embark with any confidence on a two-front war.

This was the context in which the Blomberg–Fritsch crisis occurred. Beck's high-minded ideas about how public affairs should be conducted made him slow to realise the unscrupulousness with which they actually were being conducted. Even when the truth began to dawn on him, he blamed Göring and Himmler rather than Hitler. This explains his famous answer to the suggestion of his deputy Halder that the Army should intervene, 'The words mutiny and revolution do not occur in the vocabulary of the German soldier.' To which he got the reply, 'I know from the 300-year tradition of my family exactly what occurs in that vocabulary.' Beck then said, 'Don't you see that a legal process is going on and that during such a process no officer can interfere?'[8] The result was that the bulk of the generals never learnt the full truth and accepted Hitler's explanations.

Beck was in a situation for which neither his temperament nor his experience fitted him. He saw his trusted superior Fritsch being removed on scandalous charges which those bringing them knew to be made up and the post of Commander-in-Chief being given instead to a 'Yes-man' Brauchitsch, who had accepted public money to pay for a divorce. He saw the power of influencing, let alone taking, decisions slipping progressively out of his hands into those of people like Keitel whom he distrusted. On 28 May he was notified of Hitler's 'unalterable decision to destroy Czechoslovakia by military action within a foreseeable time' and told to have everything ready by

1 October. The Army on which he had expended so much effort was thus going to be used in a way of which he disapproved. Except for a chance conversation of five minutes in March, he never had an opportunity to expound his views to Hitler.[9] Instead he submitted seven memoranda to Brauchitsch during the summer, of which only the military part of the first was sent on to Hitler who rejected it as far too pessimistic. Realising that he was getting nowhere, he arranged an indoor war-game to study the course of a German attack on Czechoslovakia on the assumption that France would intervene. It showed that, whereas German forces might win a campaign against Czechoslovakia on its own, they could not win against France as well, let alone Britain and America. This conclusion was however challenged by some junior officers and Brauchitsch was not prepared to face Hitler about it.[10]

Beck then proposed that Brauchitsch should call a meeting of the commanding generals so that they could agree on a common view, and, if that was unfavourable to Hitler, force him by a threat of collective resignation to change his plans. 'Unusual times call for unusual methods.' He claimed that such an action would be taken in Hitler's own interests, to save him from bad advisers.[11] Such a meeting was held on 4 August. At first Beck's arguments seemed to carry the day but after von Reichenau and another general had opposed them, the sense of the meeting was less clear. Brauchitsch moreover had not used the speech which Beck had drafted for him and said nothing about a collective resignation; Beck complained later that Brauchitsch had let him down.[12] But the proposal was unrealistic. Even supposing that all those present had agreed to threaten resignation, which was most unlikely, there were plenty of younger generals who were convinced Nazis to whom Hitler could have turned instead, even without bringing in SS leaders.[13] The only way in which the situation might have been affected was that changing the guard would have taken time, and thus put off mobilisation.

Reichenau leaked Beck's behaviour to Hitler, who demanded his instant dismissal; earlier in the year the Führer had said, 'The only man I fear is Beck. That man would be capable of starting something,'[14] and no doubt he would in any case have been removed before long. But before Hitler's demand could be carried out, Beck himself had on 18 August offered his resignation. On 21 August he was told it had been accepted by Hitler who refused to receive him before he left. He has often been criticised for allowing an announcement of it to be held up till 19 October. But no German publicity organ would have been allowed to publish it and news of it did leak by two channels through to and out in London by 9 September. His successor Halder said to him, 'Now you see for yourself where you get with ingenious documents and elegant resignations. That's not how to overcome Hitler. We must use methods which would have been impossible in the past.' Beck replied, 'I am inclined to think you are right. But now it's up to you.'[15] He is said to have been plagued during the rest of his life by regret that he had not acted earlier.

At the end of July Beck gave some thought to the question of what might happen if the generals were to combine against Hitler and Hitler were to refuse them a hearing. 'It will be necessary for the Army to be prepared, not only for possible war but also for upheaval at home which it should be feasible to confine to Berlin. Get Witzleben (C-in-C of the Berlin Military District) together with Helldorf' (Police President of Berlin). Stülpnagel, a Deputy Chief of Staff who in 1944 was to be the Military Commander in Paris, was also told to work out plans. These steps show how far Beck had moved under the pressure of events from his position of the spring. But as things stood, he had been nominated to command, in the event of war, the First Army in the West, and although he was kept informed about the plans which Halder, Witzleben and Oster were preparing for the seizure of Hitler, he took no detailed part in them or indeed in any of the plans up to and including Valkyrie. He was much relieved by Chamberlain's journey to Berchtesgaden and by the Munich Agreement. He had always hoped that the Czechoslovak problem could be settled in some such way without recourse to fighting. The actual removal of Hitler was not for him at this stage an essential.

After the Polish campaign he protested to Brauchitsch about SS atrocities and was ignored. He was informed about the plans for removing Hitler in November 1939 and agreed to assume command of the Army if they came to fruition. His was also the deciding voice behind 'Ochsensepp' Müller's journeys to Rome in the winter of 1939–40 in the hope of obtaining with the help of the Pope (whom Beck had known as Nuncio in Berlin) a promise from the British that they would not take advantage of a rising against Hitler to march into Germany.[16] At the end of April he insisted that the Vatican must be given warning of the impending offensive so as to prevent it being thought that the earlier approaches had been intended merely as strategic deception. In January 1940 he wrote to Brauchitsch that Germany could not hope to win a general war and that the final result of the present one would be unconditional surrender. Soon afterwards he persuaded Halder to take a long walk with him by night through the suburbs of Berlin (so as to prevent their meeting being noticed) and plied him with similar arguments. But when in the previous November Brauchitsch had ventured to air to Hitler his doubts about a western offensive, he had received such a dressing-down about defeatism in the General Staff that he never dared to repeat the attempt. Halder was from then on loath to take any action against Hitler because he did not believe it would get enough support from the public; although he remained Chief of Staff until September 1942, he and Beck never met again. How much Beck knew about Oster's communications to the Dutch Military Attaché is uncertain.

Beck's chief occupation between his retirement and the revival of the conspiracy in 1942 was to put on paper his views about the place of the armed forces in the state and the purposes for which they should be used. He did this partly on his own, notably in a talk to the prestigious Berlin Wednesday Club in June 1942 on 'The Lessons of Total War', but partly in two papers 'The Goal' and 'The Way' written in collaboration with Goerdeler who was primarily responsible for the views on home politics which are therefore best discussed in relation to him (p. 169).[17] In the passages on external politics the main influence is bound to have been Beck's.

Beck had begun by accepting, like most thinking soldiers, the traditional German view that war was an indispensable element in international relations. 'A good army is a precondition for political security.' He always emphasised, however, that wars should not be fought for their own sake and that the gains to be expected from them must be big enough to justify the expenditure of human and material resources which would be involved. Above all a war should not be started unless there was a high probability that it could be won. He quoted with approval the elder Moltke's view that every war, even a victorious one, was a national disaster. From this standpoint, he had thought it justifiable that Germany should use the threat and, if necessary, the actual deployment of force to recover her hegemony in Central Europe. It was over the circumstances in which force could be wisely used that he clashed with Hitler.

But as that clash developed and as he reflected in retirement, Beck began to have second thoughts. As far as Central Europe was concerned, he originally believed that Germany could never win a war to re-establish her position as long as France and Britain were opposed to her, while if they were not opposed a war would be unnecessary. Even after Hitler had shown him that France and Britain could not prevent Germany from dominating Europe, he doubted the durability of the victory, especially after Hitler added Russia to Germany's enemies. When Schlabrendorff told him that the war was lost he said, 'Who do you think you're talking to? This war was lost before the first shot was fired.' In commenting on the November 1937 meeting, he had written that in the course of a thousand years and more the population question as such had so stabilised itself in Europe that far-reaching changes no longer appeared to be attainable. National groups were no longer going to submit contentedly to be ruled by aliens. He therefore drew a distinction between growth of territory and growth of power (*Raumzuwachs und Machtzuwachs*). Germany should aim at the latter and not the former. On the other hand he came to think that technical development called for big economic units. He sought to reconcile the two in a European Confederation (*Staatenbund*) under German leadership. But from 1942 onwards he came to realise that Hitler's policy was destroying any willingness on the part of the minor European States to be led by Germany. Territory could not permanently be conquered and without good-will power could not be converted into influence. Even before the era of nuclear warfare opened, the doyen of Europe's military thinkers, realising the self-defeating character which war had assumed, was formulating a strategy of deterrence.

In March 1942 the Berlin group of conspirators formalised an already existing position by agreeing to make Beck their leader and co-ordinator; he was the only man trusted by both the soldiers and the civilians. But when he took the chair at the meeting with the Kreisau Group in January 1943 (p. 106) his associate Hassell criticised his handling of it as weak[18] and he was becoming regarded as too academic. In April 1943 he underwent an operation for cancer of the stomach (which may explain the lack of energy) and did not recover properly until the year's end, although he took part in August in conversations with Kluge and others. In September he met Stauffenberg for the first time in the house of his surgeon Sauerbruch. Beck tried to mediate between Stauffenberg and Goerdeler but there was little else he could do until someone solved the problem of how to assassinate Hitler, an action which he had come to recognise as essential. In the spring of 1944 he made more than one attempt to secure through Gisevius in Switzerland and John in Madrid a promise from the Western Allies that, if a putsch was staged in Germany, the resulting régime would not be required to negotiate with the Soviet Union. Detailed proposals were made for getting American and British forces into as large a part of Europe as possible before the Eastern Front collapsed. But the reply was discouraging; the Western Allies would make no promises and it was most unlikely that they would act without consulting the USSR.

Beck continued to toy with the idea of a 'Western Solution', i.e. an opening of the Western Front, especially when it began to seem doubtful whether Stauffenberg would ever succeed in exploding his bomb. On 18 July Goerdeler put up a wild proposal that he and Beck should together fly to France and prod Kluge into action but Stauffenberg ruled this out. Beck however was insistent that action of some kind must go forward: 'The only point now is that action against this criminal régime should come from within the German people. Germany must suffer the consequences of all that has been done and not been done.'[19]

On 20 July Beck arrived at the Bendlerstrasse just as Stauffenberg got back from East Prussia; he was wearing civilian clothes to avoid giving the impression that the putsch was exclusively military. He spoke on the telephone to General Wagner at OKW Rear Headquarters, saying that he had assumed command and that Witzleben would be arriving shortly at Zossen to take control there. When argument arose as to whether Hitler had really been killed, he took the line that 'for me the man is dead'. At 18.00 he spoke to Stülpnagel in Paris and a little later to Kluge; when he failed to get any commitment out of the latter, he said, 'There's Kluge for you.'[20] He issued orders to General Kinzel, commander of the Northern Army Group in Russia, to withdraw from a hopeless situation. When Witzleben arrived in a highly critical mood, he and Beck had an argument which lasted for an hour. After he had been arrested by loyal officers, and condemned to death by Fromm's court-martial, he was allowed to keep his pistol and made two attempts to kill himself. Neither was completely successful and in the end he had to be finished off by a member of the Guard Battalion. His corpse was brought down into the courtyard and taken away on the same lorry as those of the other officers who had been executed there.

5 Günther von Kluge[1]

Kluge was born in 1882, two years after Beck, in what is now Poland but was then a province of Prussia. He was proud of being said to look like Frederick the Great but used to repudiate any pretensions to aristocracy. 'I am a peasant from the Marches, not a big man like one of your Silesian magnates.' He was a gunner (as was Beck). By 1935 he was the Lieutenant-General commanding the Hanover District, where he established excellent relations with the Gauleiter; in 1936 he moved to Münster. He was put in charge of the 4th Army in 1939, was promoted Field-Marshal after the French campaign, and transferred to the 6th Army at the start of the Russian campaign. When that campaign reached its first crisis in December 1941, Kluge was appointed to relieve the discredited Marshal von Bock in command of the Central Army Group.

Although Hitler's treatment of Fritsch made him indignant, he was won back by the victories of 1939 and 1940. When in February 1940 Himmler was invited by Brauchitsch to give a talk to senior officers about the aims of the SS, he said he would prefer to talk to a few commanders whom he trusted, such as Bock, Reichenau and Kluge. On the other hand Kluge protested against the behaviour of the SS in Russia and under the influence of Tresckow, who was head of his operations branch, began to have doubts about Hitler's military abilities. His method of dealing with Hitler was to report rapidly on the telephone, giving many details. Whenever Hitler cited his own experience in the First World War, Kluge pointed out that special circumstances applied in Russia.[2] But he lost the upper hand after Hitler turned down a proposal for a general retreat by saying that the existing line must be maintained for political reasons. When Hoepner, one of Kluge's subordinates, withdrew his troops against orders, Hitler ordered Kluge to dismiss him. Tresckow said that such a summary expulsion was illegal under military law and Kluge reported this to the Führer who in a fury demanded unconditional obedience, whereupon Kluge backed down. On the Marshal's sixtieth birthday, however, Hitler gave him a cheque for RM 250,000 and a handsome supplement to his pay. When Tresckow urged him to reject the present, Kluge said he could not bring himself to do so and, to judge by other cases, he would never have been allowed to turn such an offer down. Tresckow told him he would only be justified in keeping the money if he started to work for Hitler's overthrow; he replied that the time was not yet ripe.

In the autumn of 1942 Tresckow engineered a visit from Goerdeler, who had much impressed Kluge when they met in Münster in 1938. Goerdeler treated him to an exhaustive survey of the situation, particularly as regards foreign affairs (where the Marshal proved sadly ignorant) but although at the time the lecture seemed to have sunk in, it left no lasting impression.

When Hitler was expected at Kluge's headquarters in March 1943 (p. 127) and a collective attack on him was forbidden, nothing was said to the Marshal about the smuggling of a bomb on to the aircraft. But soon afterwards, in the course of a walk with Tresckow and Gersdorff, he said, 'The man must go.' They accordingly told him of the two attempts which had failed. He asked, 'How could you do such a thing?' 'Herr Feld-Marschall, because we take the view that this is the only way to rescue the German nation from complete downfall.' After a long silence, Kluge embraced them both and said, 'Boys,* count me in.' Tresckow told him that he could not go back on that. But he certainly showed no anxiety to go forward on it immediately. In July 1943 Goerdeler wrote him a long letter appealing to him to act but he replied that he 'was not interested'. In August he told Major-General Stieff, head of the Organisation Division at OKH, that he would try to get Hitler to change the military organisation but not resort to any attempt at compulsion.

In September 1943 Kluge came to Berlin on leave; he met Beck and Goerdeler at his own request and told them that in his opinion the war was lost unless somebody took 'drastic decisions'.[3] After an extremely optimistic sketch by Goerdeler of possible terms for a compromise peace, the Field-Marshal said that Hitler must be eliminated, if necessary by violence. Goerdeler, who naively imagined that it was merely a matter of enough generals talking to the Führer firmly enough, in the end left it to the soldiers to decide what was to be done. But before Kluge could consult his military colleagues, he was involved in a bad car crash which put him out of action for nine months. His successor in the east, Field-Marshal Busch, had no political views and would take no political action.

On recovery Kluge was in July 1944 appointed Commander-in-Chief in the west, in succession to Rundstedt who had made his loss of hope in victory all too clear; when Keitel rang up after the Anglo-American landings and asked what they should do, Rundstedt replied, 'Make peace, you idiots. What else can we do?'[4] The optimistic assessment which Kluge brought with him from Germany was drastically modified after a conversation with Rommel who was commanding Army Group B under his supervision. When an emissary from Tresckow urged him to open his front so as to allow an enemy break-through, he said that the problem was how to avoid the enemy breaking through. The most he could promise was to act as soon as Hitler had been eliminated; he was as yet too unsure of his troops and his staff, while his armies were engaged in heavy fighting. On 12 July Kluge and Rommel agreed to ask all their immediate subordinates how long the line could be held and, in the light of the replies, present demands to Hitler with a time-limit. On 14 July Rommel drafted a teleprinter message for Kluge to send to Hitler which, after making a blunt analysis of the situation in the west, ended:

> Our troops are everywhere fighting like heroes but the uneven struggle is nearing
> its end. [The Americans were to break through at Avranches on 31 July.] It is
> in my opinion necessary to draw the consequences from this situation.[5]

There is good evidence that, if Hitler had refused to draw these conse-

---

* *Kinder*, the habitual address of a Prussian officer to his subordinates.

quences, Rommel would have sent an offer of capitulation to Montgomery. Kluge however delayed the onward transmission of the message; as he is known to have agreed with its contents, he was presumably waiting to see what Stauffenberg might achieve. Consequently it had not been despatched when, on 17 July, Rommel was put out of action by Allied fighters and Kluge was given charge of the Army Group in addition to the overall command. On 19 July Kluge visited Stülpnagel, the Military Governor of Paris and leader of the conspiracy in the west; he apparently promised to open the front if the assassination succeeded.[6]

On 20 July Kluge was, by accident or design, away from his headquarters and only returned at 18.00. He was then told of the attempt on Hitler's life and of the rumour that it had failed. About 19.00 he was rung up by Beck who assured him that Hitler was dead and asked whether they could count on Kluge's co-operation. Beck's disgust at the answer he received has already been described (p. 148).

Contradictory stories continued to come in, making the Marshal more than ever unwilling to act. When Stülpnagel and Hofacker arrived for a conference at Kluge's request and called on him to take the lead, he procrastinated and, on hearing that Stülpnagel had already on his own authority given an order for all SS and SD in Paris to be arrested, said it must be countermanded. As he saw Stülpnagel into a car, he advised him to vanish somewhere in civilian clothes. He later reported Stülpnagel's activities to the High Command and sent a telegram of congratulation to Hitler. When a few days later Gersdorff said that he could not understand such an act, Kluge replied that it had been a choice between his pistol and the pen which his Chief of Staff had been pressing into his hand.

Although Hitler told Guderian on 21 July that Kluge had been 'in the know' (*Mitwisser*) about the attempt,[7] he was not immediately superseded, possibly for fear of the blow to morale which two changes of command in under three weeks would have caused. He was making frequent journeys to the front at this time and on 23 July may have tried to get himself killed.[8] He called Gersdorff to him on that day and was told not to be too hasty. A dead Field-Marshal would be no good to Germany; a live one was the only person who could ward off catastrophe. It was up to him to take a bold decision. On 26 July he told Falkenhausen, the Military Governor of Belgium, that he stood by the views in the message which he and Rommel had intended to send to Hitler (whether it had ever got sent off is uncertain). On 27 July he asked Gersdorff what the latter had meant by 'a bold decision'. Gersdorff said that Kluge should immediately use radio to open comprehensive negotiations with the US General Bradley about evacuating to Germany's 1919 frontiers in the west. Reliable units should be sent to Germany to assume control there. Power should be taken out of the hands of the Nazis. All available forces should be moved to the east, so as to reach an armistice there too. Kluge's reply was that, if things went wrong, he would be the biggest villain in history. Gersdorff told him that all the world's great men had faced the choice between going down to history as villains or as saviours in the hour of need. 'Gersdorff,' came the reply, 'Field-Marshal Kluge is not a great man.'

Early in August he advised Hitler to withdraw to the line of the Seine. He was told instead to attack westwards towards the coast so as to cut American communications; he was in no position to disobey. The attack failed for lack of strength and thus jeopardised the entire German position, since the troops were threatened by encirclement in the Falaise 'pocket'. On 15 August Kluge entered this to visit the 7th Army and General Eberbach, its SS Commander. On the way his escorting vehicle was destroyed by Allied fighters and his own radio put out of action. When he finally arrived, he said he had been repeatedly held up by the need to take cover and by traffic jams: 'Imagine it, a Field-Marshal having to spend an entire day acting as a traffic policeman!' Hitler heard that he had got lost, suspected immediately that he was trying to negotiate a surrender,[9] and appointed Model to succeed him. Kluge only heard of his supersession on 17 August, a few hours before Model arrived.

He started back to Germany on the 19th but took poison and died *en route*. He left behind him a letter in which he implored Hitler to end the war:

> The German people has borne such unspeakable suffering that it is time to end this horror. My Führer, I have always admired your greatness. If fate is stronger than your will and your genius, that is the doing of providence. You have fought an honourable and great fight. History will provide evidence of this. Now show yourself great enough to put an end to the hopeless struggle. I part from you, my Führer, as one who stood close to you in his consciousness of having done his duty to his utmost, as you perhaps have realised.[10]

'Clever [i.e. *kluger*] Günther', as he was called by his fellow-officers, was the man who had the best opportunities of anyone for removing Hitler and thus changing the course of history. Unfortunately cleverness was not enough. In directing battles, he no doubt acted with firmness and effect, along the lines instilled into him by his training. But he was faced with a situation for which that training had been inadequate and his own resources were insufficient for coping with it. He was not one of the Christian generals and his willingness to accept Hitler's bribe points to a certain lack of moral fibre. The qualities involved in civil courage are not the same as those needed for success as a soldier.

6 Wilhelm Canaris[1]

Canaris was born near Dortmund in 1887, the son of a steel industry technician. The family had come from Italy several centuries earlier; it amused Wilhelm to play up a connection with another branch which had provided Greece with a national hero and he was often known as 'the little Greek'. He himself went into the Navy and, as a First Lieutenant on the light-cruiser *Dresden*, took part in the defeat of Admiral Cradock's squadron by that of

Graf von Spee in the Battle of Coronel in November 1914. When the rest of von Spee's ships were sunk a month later in the Battle of the Falkland Islands, the *Dresden* managed to escape and, thanks largely to the ingenuity of Canaris in procuring fresh supplies of food and fuel, to lurk for three months in obscure Chilean bays. It was he again who, when the British finally caught up with the fugitive, managed by a show of negotiation to secure enough time for the Germans to scuttle their own ship. Six months later he managed to get home on a Chilean passport. He was then sent to Spain to organise a clandestine supply service for U-boats and afterwards sank two British ships near Gibraltar as captain of a submarine operating from the Adriatic. This was the only time he ever commanded a ship at sea.

He got back to Germany in November 1918 to find the Navy in a state of anarchy. What he regarded as a lack of patriotism on the part of the crews and the resulting break-down of order instilled in him an enduring aversion to Communism and in the next few years he had much to do with those who organised right-wing para-military forces to frustrate alike Germany's democrats and her conquerors. He was close to the murderers of Rosa Luxemburg and Karl Liebknecht even if he did not join in the actual operation. Having got himself on to the court-martial to try the accused, he actively assisted their leader to escape. He was hand-in-glove with the murderers of Erzberger and Rathenau and the instigators of the right-wing Kapp Putsch in 1920. In 1926 he spent a considerable time in Spain helping to bring off a deal by which German ship-builders would provide the Spanish Navy with submarines and thereby prevent the art of turning out such vessels from being forgotten in Hamburg and Kiel; he got to know not only the Spanish secret service but also many people destined to hold high positions ten years later under Franco. In between times, he more or less pursued a naval officer's normal career. But not only did he have difficulty in getting on with his superiors and winning the confidence of his men, but his past kept on catching up with him, either in the shape of the Luxemburg–Liebknecht murder or of financial scandals connected with Spain. Although he had reached the rank of Captain by 1934, his prospects of rising higher seemed to have vanished, when he suddenly found himself, as the kind of man who appealed to Hitler, being made on 1 January 1935 head of the Abwehr.

German Security and Intelligence Services dated back to Frederick the Great but had had to be wound up in 1919. In 1920 however a unit was set up again to protect (*abwehren*) the armed forces from enemy spies and radical agitators; it became part of the Army's 'Statistical Department', a cover name for Military Intelligence. In 1928 Naval Intelligence was brought in and in 1932 one of their officers, Captain Patzig, became head of the whole outfit. The end of Allied control and the rightwards trend of German governments in the early 1930s resulted in a steady build-up even before Hitler came to power. But the work remained that of collecting information; action to protect national interests involved calling in the police. But the police, like much else, was centralised by the Nazis and in 1934 control over its entire network passed to Himmler. He extended the Prussian Secret State Police (*GEheime STAats POlizei*) to cover the entire Reich and amalgamated it with the Security Service (*Sicherheitsdienst*, SD) which since 1931 had been one of the three main components of the SS and was particularly concerned with collecting intelligence about internal conditions.[2] He put the whole under the command of an ambitious 30-year-old called Reinhard Heydrich, who in 1936 was made Chief of the Security Police. One of their main ambitions was to make the Security Police Headquarters the central intelligence agency of the Reich by taking over responsibility for military and foreign intelligence from the armed forces. Patzig's moves to resist this not merely won him the hostility of the policemen but lost him the favour of the Reichswehr Minister Blomberg. He was removed but allowed to suggest Canaris as a successor. However a second sailor would scarcely have been appointed if he had not been well regarded in high quarters.

Canaris's qualifications for the job lay not merely in his intelligence, his resource in devising fresh initiatives and his ability to talk opponents round. A subordinate said that, 'The Admiral may not be much to look at but he has what it takes in the upper storey.' He had in addition an unusual qualification. Heydrich had begun his career in the Navy where he had as a cadet enjoyed the favour of his ship's second-in-command Canaris. When he was expelled from the service for trouble over a girl, respect for his patron was one of the few things excluded from a general dislike of things naval. It was therefore hoped that he would refrain from engaging in the intrigues which he would undoubtedly have deployed against anyone else. While this hope was not wholly realised a strange relationship developed between the two. They took to riding together through Berlin's greenwood in the early morning and soon the Heydrichs came to live next door in Schlachtensee; the artistic Erika Canaris welcomed the company of a man who had inherited from his half-Jewish opera-singing father and actress mother considerable talent on the violin. A dividing line ('The Ten Commandments') was quickly. reached between the activities of the Abwehr abroad and those of the *Sicherheitsdienst* at home, although each side not merely poached itself but resented poaching by the other.

At this stage there is no evidence of Canaris having turned against the Nazis. Their objectives still corresponded too closely to his own to make their methods objectionable. He is even said to have been the person who suggested, in 1935–6, that Jews should be made to wear a distinctive star. An article which he wrote in 1938 expressed how the Nazis were to be regarded as the inheritors in spirit of those who had fought in the trenches during the war (which of course he himself never did). In any case he was too glad to get his job to make trouble over its inherent drawbacks.

Three months after taking over he used his sources to assure Hitler that the reintroduction of conscription would provoke no dangerous reactions abroad; his reward was promotion to Admiral. A year afterwards it was a document claimed by Canaris to have been filched from the French (but later found to have been a forgery) which decided Hitler on risking the reoccupation of the Rhineland. It was first and foremost the promptings of the expert on Spain which led Hitler in 1936 to rescue Franco's tottering putsch by sending the air-liners needed to transport vital troops from Morocco to Seville. When the French and after them the Russians sent volunteers and arms to the Republicans, it was again Canaris who negotiated the despatch of the German 'Condor' Air Legion which won such fame at Guernica. And it was his arrangements for co-operation with the Italians which spurred Mussolini into talking in November 1936 about a 'Rome–Berlin' Axis.

What first turned Canaris's stomach would seem to have been the cold-blooded way in which in February 1938 the SD used evidence of homosexuality which they knew to be trumped up in order to discredit Fritsch (p. 31). Canaris was the first to tell Beck of the plot to oust Fritsch and is said to have been the channel by which Beck and Keitel learnt of the Fritsch–Frisch confusion.[3] The efforts which he made to get Fritsch rehabilitated and the Gestapo discredited brought him into closer touch than before with Oster in his own office, with Hans von Dohnanyi, at that time personal assistant to the Minister of Justice, and with Karl Sack, a military lawyer who later became Judge Advocate-General to the Army. At the end of September 1938 he reorganised the Abwehr so as to create, besides the Divisions for intelligence gathering, subversion and counter-espionage, along with the *Amtsgruppe Ausland* set up in June 1938 to evaluate incoming intelligence, a central group responsible for administration. Oster was put in charge of this and nominated Chief of Staff in the event of war.

How far Canaris carried his hostility to Hitler's Reich is a controversial question which cannot be fully discussed in the space available here. There are three ways in which he is said to have sought to help the enemy.

(1) During the months before the war, a number of rumours about German intentions reached London, some of which were taken seriously. One of the main initiators appears to have been Canaris, who was trying to goad the British Government into vigorous reaction with a view to convincing Hitler that Britain, if pressed too far, would fight.[4]

(2) On several occasions during the war, some of which will be mentioned later, Canaris and the Abwehr gave Hitler information about coming events which proved inaccurate. On the strength of these, he has been accused of incompetence.[5] The possibility cannot be excluded that in some cases at least it was done deliberately to hasten Hitler's downfall.

(3) There are stories of his having during the war passed secret information to the British. In particular he arranged, in the autumn of 1939, for the wife of the former Polish Military Attaché in Berlin, Colonel Szymanski, to be brought from Poland to Berne where she was given a part-time job in the Polish Legation. On various occasions he met her in Berne, Paris and Italy. Representatives of the British Secret Service were in regular touch with her. Canaris arranged a post in Zurich for Gisevius who also visited the lady.[6] There is said to be no evidence in British secret files that 'high-grade intelli-

gence'[7] passed through this channel and she has said that Canaris only told her about 'general intentions'[8] but there must have been some serious purpose behind the whole arrangement. Canaris was certainly anxious at one or more stages of the war to meet his British opposite number Stewart Menzies, who was apparently willing to respond but forbidden to do so by Eden.[9] On the other hand the story of a meeting at Santander in August 1943 between Canaris, Menzies and Colonel Donovan of the American OSS is considered a fabrication by those who should know.[10]

Like so many of Hitler's serious opponents, Canaris could only hope to work effectively against the régime if he managed to retain his job, which involved spending much of his time in carrying out Hitler's wishes or winning his favour. It must not be supposed that the whole Abwehr was a hotbed of subversion. In a staff of some 13,000 perhaps 50 were fundamentally anti-Nazi.[11] Many of the remainder were professional security officers who regarded it as their duty to uphold whatever government was in power and who collaborated actively with the SS and other Nazi organisations, so that there are many black marks on their pages. Canaris could only do a limited amount to put spokes in their wheels without drawing too much suspicion on himself. His position would have been untenable if it had not been for the ability of any secret agent to plead that apparently treacherous acts were done to mislead the enemy or gain his confidence. Thus in the weeks preceding the Munich Agreement, Canaris divided his time between organising subversion in Bohemia, encouraging first Beck and then Halder to oppose Hitler, keeping the Army Command informed of what he could gather from the AA about Hitler's intentions (so that they could judge the right moment to strike), visiting Rome and sending an emissary to Budapest to persuade Germany's main allies to deny her their support, sending Kleist-Schmenzin to London, and warning Hitler that Britain and France were not going to climb down. While this was the only plot for an overthrow in which he took an active part, he was careful not to know too much about Oster's activities.

Perhaps Hitler noticed a certain lack of enthusiasm and this might explain why it was that the underground preparations for breaking up the rump Czech state in March 1939 were entrusted to the SS rather than to the Abwehr. That autumn came the turn of Poland, which could probably have reached a not too humiliating agreement with the Reich, assuming that that country kept her promises. But nobody any longer believed that she would, a distrust which Poland's Foreign Minister, Josef Beck (perhaps assisted by Canaris) turned to advantage by spreading the story of an imminently impending German attack and using it to obtain from Britain a guarantee of his country's continued independence. Hitler's reaction was to make the imaginary attack a reality.

The Poland recreated in 1919 had been such a red rag to German nationalists that for once few officers doubted the wisdom of the decision, although some like Canaris believed that this time Britain would keep her word. The

Abwehr not only planned sabotage operations of its own to smooth the path of the troops but with some misgivings assisted the SD to lay on others, such as the faked attack on the Gleiwitz transmitter which provided the pretext for declaring war.[12] Canaris pulled strings to get a clear statement from Italy that she was not ready to fight and this was one of the things which delayed the attack for a week. But the Russo-German Non-Aggression Pact deprived Poland of any hope of effective help.

The actual outbreak of war filled Canaris with apprehension. '*Finis Germaniae,*' he said to Gisevius.[13] When he learnt how the SS were treating the Poles, he said to one of his staff, 'A war which is waged at the complete expense of morality can never be won. There is such a thing as divine justice.' But the Abwehr (upgraded as part of the OKW *Amt Ausland Abwehr*) and the SD (also upgraded to become the *Reichssicherheitshauptamt*, RSHA) worked closely together in Poland and the excesses were not confined to either body. Canaris helped to rescue one or two Poles but his only recorded protest at the general policy, made to Keitel, was so muffled that it easily went unheard. It was the Abwehr also which made the original contacts leading to the kidnapping of the two British secret service officers, Best and Stevens, at Venlo on the Dutch frontier on 9 November 1939, although the actual operation was handled by Walter Schellenberg, the thrusting new head of police counter-espionage in the RSHA.[14] He had purported to represent the 'German Resistance' and the deceit made the British unreceptive thereafter to any approaches which used such a label.

Hitler's decision to embark on a war in the west immediately the Polish campaign was over put Canaris once more into an ambivalent position. On the one hand the Abwehr were ordered to prepare and conduct various acts of deception and sabotage which were to introduce the attack. But on the other hand he sympathised with the widespread view that so rash a venture ought to be stopped by removing Hitler. The prospect of doing so disappeared however after the Brauchitsch fiasco (p. 146). Canaris knew and approved of Oster's action in sending the Bavarian Josef ('Ochsensepp') Müller to the Vatican to sound out the British (p. 146) but never at this stage met him. On the other hand he knew nothing of Oster's contacts with foreign military attachés or of the final message to Rome giving the date of attack. The recipients of some of those warnings were careless over the ways in which they were passed on so that the messages were intercepted. Hitler ordered Canaris and Heydrich to co-operate in finding the 'mole'. Fortunately it was the Abwehr investigator who decided that all the indications pointed to Oster. Canaris disregarded the findings. When an Abwehr officer's wife wrote to him with the same story, he got her shut up in an asylum! He thus saved Oster. But it had been a narrow shave and from then on he kept at a greater distance from the conspirators.

During much of the second half of 1940 Canaris was occupied, on Hitler's orders, in trying to secure Spanish co-operation for the capture of Gibraltar. But he also gave Franco ground to wonder whether Germany was in fact going to win the war so that the latter preferred not to expose his exhausted country to the ravages of further fighting. Canaris had equally little luck in trying to bring about an armistice between the Greeks and the Italians. Ever since the previous summer Hitler's hankering after a Russian adventure had filled him with alarm; apart from anything else, he knew that the Abwehr did not have the information about Russian resources which he would be expected to produce (partly because he had since 1939 been forbidden to offend the Russians). But once again he was put in charge of deception and sabotage to ensure the success of a campaign which he expected and wanted to fail. Once again he was sickened by what he heard of SS and Army behaviour behind the lines but once again the only action he took was to sign the minute drafted by Helmuth von Moltke which Keitel put aside (p. 69). But he nearly lost his job when Schellenberg complained to Hitler about the way in which the Abwehr were helping Jews to escape to Switzerland by pretending they were going as agents. Heydrich's murder in Prague in June 1942 meant surprisingly enough the loss of a friend; he may have been an unscrupulous empire-builder but his successors Kaltenbrunner and Schellenberg were worse ones and were not inhibited by any ties of past comradeship. The clouds were gathering on the horizon for the Abwehr as well as for the Führer. The organisation had grown too big, Canaris was too tired, too pessimistic and too little interested in administration. It was suffering from the corruption, nepotism and other abuses which develop in an organisation screened from outside scrutiny by the need for secrecy.

Prominent among the shady operators was a character called Schmidhuber who was loosely attached to the Abwehr office in Munich where he held the cabaret-style post of honorary Portuguese consul. Schmidhuber managed to arouse the suspicions of a German customs official in Prague and a long train of events thereafter led to his being arrested in October 1942. It had been Schmidhuber whom Müller and Oster had employed in May 1940 to pass to the Vatican the exact information of the timing of the western offensive; he had also been involved in smuggling into Switzerland money for the Jewish 'agents' to live on. He talked uncomfortably freely under interrogation. There was no denying that Oster and Dohnanyi (who since 1939 had been Oster's assistant) had broken the currency regulations and Dohnanyi had into the bargain been involved in some questionable financial transactions in Hamburg. Revelations by Schmidhuber led, by another long train of events, to the arrival in Canaris's office on 5 April 1943 of a senior military lawyer Roeder and a Gestapo official Sonderegger with a warrant for Dohnanyi's arrest. They proceeded to search Dohnanyi's room in the presence of Canaris and Oster and caught the latter trying to extract from a file and conceal three incriminating documents from Dietrich Bonhoeffer, Dohnanyi's brother-in-law (p. 223). Why such papers should have been kept, in spite of a warning on the previous day, has never been adequately explained. Dohnanyi was taken to SD headquarters; Bonhoeffer, Müller, Frau Dohnanyi and Frau Müller were arrested later in the day. Oster was ordered to go home and stay there.

As in other cases the Gestapo were using minor offences as a pretext for arresting people whom they suspected, without evidence to prove it, of having committed bigger ones.

A dejected Canaris was cross-examined but left in post; there is evidence that the SS from Himmler downwards still had too much respect for the 'Spy-Master' to want to topple him. He did not exert himself on behalf of the prisoners as actively as they had hoped but neglected his paper work and the office suffered. A group of senior officers persuaded Keitel that, in the interests of the war effort, the Abwehr chief must either be replaced or, if there was no firm evidence, cleared. Mussolini's downfall precipitated a decision for the second alternative. Canaris hurried off to meet his opposite number in Venice and came back reporting that there was no likelihood of Italy surrendering to the Allies; this was in fact the opposite of what he had learnt and the misrepresentation came to the knowledge of Schellenberg. Bad luck continued to dog the Abwehr. Two agents in Turkey absconded and a third, Erich Vermehren, went over with a good deal of publicity to the British. The Abwehr failed to give advance warning of the Allied landing at Anzio in January 1944 just as it had failed over the North African landing fifteen months earlier. But it was oranges which finally upset the apple-cart. Spain was doing a thriving trade with fruit-starved Britain which the Abwehr sought to disrupt by inserting time-bombs into the boxes. The British pressed the Spanish Government to get the practice stopped and the German Embassy, frightened lest Spain increase the amount of help she was giving to the enemy, called a halt to all Abwehr operations in the country and blocked an effort by Canaris to rescue the situation by a personal visit. But it was one thing to give high-level orders, another to get them carried out by low-level saboteurs; the explosions went on and Ribbentrop complained to Hitler. On 12 February 1944 a Führer order created a single German intelligence service under Himmler's control.

Keitel and Jodl called in person on Canaris to break the news and told him that he was to be put under house arrest in a Thuringian castle which the Abwehr had been using as a forgery factory. There he stayed while the details of the take-over were worked out in his absence. On 1 July 1944 he was allowed back to become chairman of the special staff for economic warfare, a body which had been of considerable importance during the early months of the war but was now a sinecure. Soon afterwards two of his former officers gave him an idea of what Stauffenberg was up to so that the bomb attempt did not come as a complete surprise; he had always been against assassination and Stauffenberg had not impressed him in the few meetings which they had had in the previous autumn.

On 20 July he learnt at about 17.00 from Sack both about the attempt and its failure; he went to his office and sent a telegram of congratulations to Hitler but this did not stop him from being arrested three days later. He was given, but did not take, opportunities for escape or suicide. His name kept on cropping up in evidence obtained from others but he showed so much resource in providing respectable explanations for apparently questionable activities that the SD found it hard to pin a precise charge on him. It was the extraordinary rashness of Oster and Dohnanyi in keeping, in a safe in the OKW Headquarters at Zossen, for use in a possible trial of Hitler, papers about past activities, including twenty pages of Canaris's diaries for 1939–40, which made his position untenable. All that he absolutely denied was having committed *Landesverrat* (p. 70) by passing to the enemy information about impending operations.

But the cross-questioning took time and Germany's defeat was clearly not far off. On 7 February Canaris was evacuated, with Oster, Halder and four others, from Berlin to Flossenburg camp to prevent him from being killed by an Allied bomb before his fellow-countrymen had decided whether he deserved death. Probably he would have been done away with anyhow since the authorities were convinced, even if they could not prove, that he had been at the heart of the *Widerstand*. But his chances of surviving were reduced by a further stroke of bad luck. The massing of troops to defend Berlin had led to empty rooms at Zossen being occupied again and in one of them were found more of Canaris's diaries which he had fancied were out of harm's way. The mere sight of them infuriated Hitler who on 5 April gave orders for the conspirators at Flossenburg to be eliminated. Before an improvised tribunal, Canaris argued tenaciously that he had only gone along with the conspiracy so as to be able to give it away at the last moment. But that story was demolished by Oster, who was brought in to confront his old chief. They died together next morning. In his cell Canaris had been reading Kantorowicz's biography of Kaiser Frederick II – a book which Hitler once claimed to have read twice.

Von Weizsäcker said of Canaris that he was 'one of the most interesting phenomena of the period, a type brought to light and perfected under dictatorship, a combination of disinterested idealism and shrewdness that is particularly rare in Germany. There one rarely finds the cleverness of a snake and the purity of a dove combined in one character.'[15]

7 Hans Oster[1]

Oster was born in Dresden in 1887, son of the Alsatian pastor of the French Protestant Church. He entered the artillery in 1907 and served in the field in the west until 1916 when he was appointed as Captain to the General Staff. After the war he was well enough thought of to be kept in the reduced Reichswehr; its nominally 'a-political' stance suited the unregenerate monarchist well. In the course of service he came to know Witzleben, Brauchitsch, Halder and Olbricht. He also served for five years in an artillery regiment commanded by Fritsch. In 1932 however he got into trouble because of an indiscretion during the Carnival. The licence habitually allowed during that season in the Rhineland might have been expected to protect him but his lapse appears to have occurred in the demilitarised zone which Reichswehr officers were supposed not to enter. He was considered to have shown a serious lack of discretion and required to resign from the Army, although he was allowed to keep his pension.

He did not take long to find a job in the new organisation which Göring had set up under the Prussian police for tapping telephone conversations and from there he moved on 1 October 1933 to the Abwehr. He soon came across Gisevius who was then working in the Gestapo and who introduced him to Nebe. Patzig thought him a tactless intriguer, 'careworn and shabby', but Canaris soon recognised him as a kindred spirit and made him a confidant. The welcome which he initially had given to the Third Reich faded when Schleicher and Bredow were done to death in the Röhm putsch. He told his interrogators in 1944 that 30 June 1934 had afforded the first chance of nipping in the bud the methods of a set of bandits.[2] But Himmler and Heydrich had managed to emerge from the contest as victors over the Wehrmacht. Thanks to Canaris, Oster was allowed into the Army again in 1935 but never on to the General Staff.

His antipathy to the régime was fostered by what he learnt from Gisevius and Nebe and converted into fanatical hatred by the Nazi treatment of Fritsch who had during their period of common service become a personal friend. In the course of the crisis Canaris took him to meet Beck for the first time. He saw in it the eclipse of the Army which stood for everything he respected, whereas the SS incorporated the lack of principle and order of which he disapproved. He was heard to say, 'We must clear out the whole Gestapo outfit and take over control. Hitler has always been ready to recognise accomplished facts.' His position at the centre of the intelligence service gave him exceptional opportunities for knowing what went on; he developed a close link with the AA through Count Wilhelm Ulrich Schwerin von Schwanenfeld. He maintained that lack of adequate knowledge had been one of the main reasons why the Army had been outwitted by the SS and Gestapo.

Through the summer of 1938 Oster did his best by continual contact with Beck to stiffen the latter. He was instrumental in getting passports for Ewald von Kleist-Schmenzin and Böhm-Tettelbach to go to London so as to persuade the British Government to act up to the role for which the German General Staff had cast it. He was one of Halder's first visitors after the latter had assumed office on 1 September; it is uncertain which of the two took the initiative in arranging the meeting. Previous dealings with Oster had made Halder doubtful whether he had the qualities needed for success in a revolt, doubt which turned into frank dislike where Gisevius was concerned. All the same, Halder commissioned Oster in agreement with Witzleben to prepare a detailed plan for occupying the government quarter of Berlin, seizing the main centres of communication, isolating the SS command-posts and capturing Hitler. Oster had got Witzleben, as Berlin military commander, to say that he would if necessary issue orders on his own responsibility without waiting to receive them from his superior Brauchitsch (who almost certainly would have refused to take an initiative in issuing them). But unknown to Halder,

Witzleben and Beck, Oster had also provided for a commando-type force of some sixty young officers, students and workmen under Major Heinz, a former Stahlhelm commander. When the signal for action was given they were to invade the Chancellery, overcome the guards and seize Hitler; if the latter resisted or tried to escape, he would be shot. But of course the Four-Power agreement to hold a conference at Munich on 29 September meant that the signal was never given. Oster was one of the relatively few people who were disappointed by the Munich settlement.

Oster's next opportunity for action arose in the autumn of 1939 in connection with the movement, led by Halder, to prevent Hitler from launching a western offensive. He received orders from Halder through Groscurth, a former head of the sabotage section of the Abwehr who had become liaison officer between that body and the OKH, to update his plans of the previous year, an operation which brought to light the fact that for various reasons the situation had become less favourable in the interval. But the effort expended was nugatory because within days Hitler gave Brauchitsch his dressing-down (p. 146) and Halder, who thought for a moment that the whole plan had been discovered, was too unnerved to make another move.[3] Next day Oster got himself and Gisevius invited to Witzleben's Army Group Headquarters in West Germany in the hope that they could there work out some way of bringing pressure to bear on Halder. But Witzleben was discouraging. When the two visitors spent the night in Frankfurt on the way home, Oster would seem to have allowed his frustration to get the better of him. He became drunk in the mess and launched into open criticism of the régime until led outside; he was going about with two copies of the proclamation which Beck was to make on taking over after a putsch. A messenger was sent to Halder asking him to call Oster to order. He not only did so but refused to receive Oster again. Between September 1939 and February 1940 it was Oster who, on Beck's general instructions, carried through the despatch to the Vatican of 'Ochsensepp' Müller in the hope of obtaining with the help of the Pope a promise from the British that they would not take advantage of a rising inside Germany to march into that country. Such an assurance was intended to remove the last doubts of the High Command against action to get rid of Hitler.

If anything was to come of the negotiations, full-scale war had to be stopped from breaking out in the west until there had been time for them to mature. The hope of preventing a German attack by inducing the Dutch and Belgian authorities to make clear that they were ready for it was one of the main initial reasons which led Oster to give the information to the Dutch Military Attaché in Berlin, Sas, which has already been mentioned (p. 72). Throughout the episode, Oster's aim was to secure the removal of Hitler rather than the defeat of Germany, since he was so convinced that Hitler's continuance in office would lead to such defeat as to justify risking catastrophe from one direction in order to prevent it from another. As he told Sas

People may well say that I am a traitor but in reality I am not. I regard myself as a better German than all those who are trailing along behind Hitler. It is both my purpose and my duty to liberate Germany, and with her the world, from this plague.

It is however noteworthy that, although Oster went to such lengths in the effort to evict the Hitler régime, he does not appear to have expressed any views about what should succeed it. His political ideal seems to have been the Germany of his boyhood under Kaiser Wilhelm II (to whose funeral he accompanied Canaris in 1941).

From May 1940 until 1942, Hitler's standing in the eyes of the German people was such that all thoughts of removing him were patently futile and Oster had to strain his patience like other conspirators. In the autumn of 1941 Schlabrendorff, whom he had known since 1938, put him in touch with Tresckow. He also drew closer to Olbricht and with the help of Gisevius they again in the spring of 1943 worked out plans for action in Berlin on the assumption that one of the attempts to assassinate Hitler would succeed. Oster had hardly had time to take stock of the situation created by their failure when the Gestapo arrived in the Abwehr office to arrest Dohnanyi (p. 158); Oster was ordered to leave the office and remain at home (actually, at his sister's house in Saxony), an unemployed Major-General. On 31 March 1944 he was dismissed from the Wehrmacht.

Arrested on general suspicion on 21 July, he managed at first to conceal the extent of his activities fairly well, although at some expense to his relations with Canaris. It was the discovery of the documents lodged by Dohnanyi at Zossen which proved his undoing.[4] Thereafter he seems to have made little attempt at holding things back and perhaps was left alive in the hope that he would reveal more. Like Canaris he was moved on 7 February 1945 from Berlin to Flossenburg and there on 9 April executed. The judge who presided over the summary court which condemned him said afterwards, 'He was the true type of the higher German officer, behaved in a soldierly manner, correct and also courageous.'[5] But he also refused to support Canaris's story of only having gone along with the conspiracy in order to give it away at the last moment.

He said to his son on his confirmation

To our last breath we should remain the upright men we were taught to be in childhood and in our training as soldiers. Come what may, we fear only the wrath of God that will fall on us if we are not clean and decent and fail to do our duty.

To a colleague he said

It is far easier to take a pistol and engage in a shooting-match, it is far easier to walk into a hail of machine-gun bullets than to do what I have set myself to do. If you ever get the chance, I hope you will as my friend testify after my death as to how matters stood with me and what motivated me to do things which other people cannot understand or at any rate would not have done themselves.

His friend Sas called him the most courageous and daring man he had ever known.[6]

8 Arthur Nebe[1]

Nebe was born in 1894, the son of a Berlin teacher. After serving as a Lieutenant through the First World War, he joined the Prussian police and made his name as a detective. Acquaintance with the Berlin underworld disillusioned him with democracy and in 1931 he joined the Nazi party. In 1937 a Criminal Police Department was created for the whole Reich and made, along with the Secret Political Police, one of the two main components of the Security Police Headquarters. Nebe was left at the head of it under Heydrich (p. 154). He systematised its methods and increased its efficiency; he prided himself on being more competent than the Gestapo, reaching his objectives by research and logic rather than crude violence.

In October 1933 he was ordered by Rudolf Diels, the then head of the Gestapo, to arrange the liquidation of Hitler's rival Gregor Strasser.[2] This began the process of turning him against the Nazis. With the absorption of the Kripo into the Security Police Nebe became an SS General (and as such the highest SS officer in the conspiracy) but his aversion to his colleagues, particularly Himmler and Heydrich, grew on closer acquaintance, even though he continued to lunch regularly with them.

In 1933 he came to know Hans Bernd Gisevius, then an official in Berlin Police Headquarters. Gisevius introduced him to Oster, who in 1939 obtained for Gisevius a job in the Zurich office of the Abwehr, with the cover title of Vice-Consul. Through the link to Nebe, the conspirators obtained an accomplice at the very heart of the machine of repression and were often warned of trouble ahead so that they could take steps to avoid it. Meanwhile Nebe increased his reputation with Hitler and Himmler by clearing up the Fritsch and Elser cases. (When he embarked on the second, he could not be sure that the explosion in Munich had not been the work of his own friends.) It was said that, when faced by some criminal puzzle, the first question that the top authorities asked was, 'Where is Nebe?'

In 1941 he was ordered to work in occupied Russia in charge of one of the 'Einsatz Commandos'. Foreseeing the crimes in which he would be involved, he tried to get out by asking for a move to the International Police Commission but is said to have been persuaded by Beck and Oster to stay in a position where he could give them such unique help. He worked with Tresckow and Schlabrendorff to reduce the atrocities committed but there is no doubt that he was involved in a good many, thus being a notorious example of someone who did evil in order to prevent worse. He came back from Russia convinced that the war would end in a German military defeat.

As part of the Stauffenberg plot, he was going to lead a team of twelve policemen to kill Himmler but the signal to move never reached him.[3] For a day or two he pretended to be vigorously searching for Stauffenberg's accomplices but when Helldorf, the Berlin Police President, was arrested, he had to go underground. On 24 July a warrant was issued for his arrest but he managed to evade capture until 16 January 1945. He was condemned to death on 2 March. Gisevius, who had been in the Bendlerstrasse on the evening of 20 July, got out across the Swiss frontier on 23 January with forged papers smuggled to him by the Americans.

9 Carl Goerdeler[1]

Goerdeler was born in 1884 in West Prussia, on the edge of what was later to become the Polish Corridor; his affection for the area was illustrated by the fact that it was thither he chose to return when he was on the run after 20 July. His forebears over four generations all became Prussian civil servants, as he did himself. His father sat in the *Landtag* as a Free Conservative, a party whose essence was support for Bismarck. After taking a doctorate at Göttingen and qualifying in 1911 as an assessor, he obtained a post in the Bürgermeister's office at Solingen in the Rhineland. Conditions there were very different from those in his eastern homeland and his dealings with Social Democrats left him with a lasting respect for skilled workers, although he continued to vote conservative. He spent the First World War on the staff at the Eastern Front and at the end of it engaged in various unsuccessful attempts to prevent the decisions of the Versailles Treaty about Danzig and the Corridor from being carried out.

In 1920 he became Deputy Bürgermeister of Königsberg, where he won a great reputation as an administrator with immense energy, a sound grasp of rational principle and an eye for practical detail. This led to his appointment in 1930 as Chief Bürgermeister of Leipzig, where there was a Social Democratic majority on the City Council. Throughout his life he was noteworthy for self-confidence and optimism, with unfailing faith in the power of reason (especially when put on paper!) and the benevolence of human nature. His friend Schacht called him a motor which ran too noisily. Someone else said that whereas Adenauer (at that time his opposite number in Cologne) trusted nobody, Goerdeler trusted everybody. He was insensitive to the political and other pressures which lead men to act irrationally. He joined the DNVP in 1922 and was elected to its council but disapproved of Hugenberg's opposition to Brüning and resigned in 1931.

His views, particularly as regards the need for deflation and economy, corresponded closely with those of Brüning. He was not only firmly anti-socialist but also anti-Keynes. He wanted to reduce wages and thereby create more jobs. In December 1931 he was appointed Reich Commissioner for Price Control and at once cut all prices by 10 per cent. Four months later he produced on request a programme to combat unemployment, which included the extension of the (voluntary) Labour Service scheme and the institution of public works but transferred such matters as social insurance from the state to the private sector in order to revive the personal responsibility of the individual. Brüning had regarded him as a possible successor. When Papen was chosen instead, Goerdeler was pressed to join the Cabinet as Minister of Economics and Labour. He refused, partly because Papen rejected his advice to include two or three Nazis, partly because he did not expect Papen to last long and hoped that the President would then turn to him. He was later to regret this miscalculation.

Leipzig was one of the few German cities which had the same Bürgermeister at the end of 1933 as at the beginning, although Goerdeler refused in October an invitation from Hitler to join the Party. He was one of those conservatives who hoped to enlist Nazi support for a policy of retrenchment, which would be impracticable as long as each of the laws implementing it had to obtain parliamentary approval separately. In any case he had long wanted to break the power of the parties and strengthen the executives at the expense of the legislatures both as regards the Reich and in all the federal states. He therefore welcomed the Enabling Act of March 1933 which authorised Hitler to pass laws for four years without reference to the Reichstag. He also agreed with the Nazis about the eastern frontier (calling the Corridor 'an arrow in the flesh of German honour and prosperity') and the need to escape from the other limitations imposed at Versailles. He even spoke in 1934 of the need to arm the German people for their eventual war of liberation. But he refused to let the swastika flag fly over Leipzig's City Hall, he blocked all attempts to remove the statue of Mendelssohn in front of the Concert Hall and he went out of his way to protect Jewish shop-keepers from treatment not sanctioned by law (while professing readiness to see the laws extended). But he came off the worst in a clash with the local Gauleiter over energy policy.[2]

Papen had sacked him from the price control job but Hitler, afraid of inflation, reappointed him in November 1934 and paid considerable attention to his advice about local government reform (which however took in the end a more centralised form than he thought desirable). He collided with Darré over the system of guaranteed prices introduced by the Reich Food Estate, saying that it helped inefficiency to survive and prevented distribution costs from being lowered, but he failed to get it abolished. With typical optimism, he hoped to talk the Nazis into keeping down expenditure and staying in the world market but such a policy was incompatible with Hitler's insistence on fast and massive rearmament. The introduction of the Four Year Plan showed that the mighty were not going to listen to him and it may well be that he seized on the removal of the Mendelssohn statue when his back was turned as a pretext for resignation in April 1937.

Instead he got a job as Financial Adviser to the Stuttgart firm of Bosch, whose Chairman Robert was a broad-minded Liberal, antipathetic to Prussians, nobles and generals. Krupps, who had been headed off by Hitler from making Goerdeler a director, paid him compensation. He was thus able to spend most of the next three years in journeys to Western Europe, North America and the Near East. The reports which he wrote on these trips were shown not merely to friends who shared his views but also to Göring and to Hitler's adjutant, which suggests that he did not entirely despair of exercising a moderating influence on Nazi policy even though his experience abroad made him increasingly critical of it. His message was that the outside world – and particularly Britain – desired peace and had no intention of attacking Germany who could therefore expect to get her demands met on such things as frontiers provided she did not ask for too much at once.

Long before February 1938 Goerdeler had warned Fritsch that he would be the régime's next victim. When the crisis broke, under the influence of Gisevius, whom he had recently met for the first time, Goerdeler tried to get List, the Commanding General in Leipzig, and his deputy Olbricht, to act against the SS, while at the same time seeking in an interview to make Brauchitsch aware of the dangers threatening the Army from that quarter.[3] On the following morning however a report reached Brauchitsch through a chain of five intermediaries to the effect that Goerdeler had said, in a supposedly confidential gathering in the Bank of England, that a major change, in which Brauchitsch would play an important part, was imminent in Germany. Brauchitsch vowed never to speak to Goerdeler again and repeated the story to Hitler. The result was a Gestapo investigation in which Goerdeler was only saved by Schacht.

Goerdeler had represented himself in Britain as belonging to a moderate party, which included Göring and was trying to counter the noxious radical influence of Himmler and Heydrich. The British Foreign Office took his story with a considerable dose of salt, noting that Goerdeler claimed to have held an important position in the Nazi government for three years and was still allowed to travel abroad. His pessimistic utterances about Hitler's economic policies were however accepted by many people as authoritative evidence that Germany was in no position to fight a sustained war. His advice that the British should make clear their determination to refuse Hitler any further concessions was hard to reconcile with his warning that Germany would have to be allowed to recover the Sudetenland. Elaborate proposals which he put forward in December 1938 for an agreement which Britain might make with a post-Hitler government were, after careful consideration, not pursued, partly because of scepticism as to whether Goerdeler could bring such a government into existence, partly because they did not differ by very much from what Hitler seemed to want.[4] The most hostile British attitude was expressed by Vansittart, who refused all along to believe in the existence of any serious opposition in Germany:

> I have known Dr Goerdeler for some time. I have also suspected for some time that he was merely a stalking-horse for German military expansion and by military expansion I mean the expansionist ideas of the Army as contrasted with those of the Nazi Party. There is really very little between them: the same sort of ambitions are sponsored by a different body of men and that is about all. Do not trust Dr Goerdeler except as an occasional informant. I do not count Dr Goerdeler as a moderate.[5]

During the crisis over Czechoslovakia he was abroad and during that over Poland he stayed on the side-lines. But during the winter of 1939–40 he duly contributed to the flood of memoranda suggesting how peace could be re-established and Hitler overthrown. He went to Sweden three times and had interviews with Roosevelt's emissary Sumner Welles, with a representative of Daladier and with the King of the Belgians. After the fall of France he tried to keep up his own spirits and those of his friends by denying that Hitler's success meant the end of the war and by foretelling future disasters. Hitler, in his opinion, could never rule defeated peoples intelligently enough to get them to accept him for long (a view shared by Beck, p. 147). He even gave August 1941 as the date by which economic collapse might be expected! Late in 1941 he completed what was for one who professed to disapprove of planning his most comprehensive sketch of his ideas about the shape of a post-Nazi Germany in the memorandum 'The Goal' (*Das Ziel*) written in close collaboration with Beck.

Goerdeler was a type of Liberal more common in the nineteenth than in the twentieth century and more common in Germany than in Britain. His starting-point was freedom for the individual, who was however expected to use it with a sense of responsibility. The aim of economic and social organisation should be to maximise contributions to the common welfare by making achievement easy and attractive (*Leistungsprinzip*). State interference in economic affairs should be kept to a minimum. He was not much concerned with equality. Whereas before the war he had regarded trade unions as a menace to the autonomy of management, he became under the influence of Leuschner and others ready to develop into an 'estate of the realm' a single united union, divided into twelve sections and with compulsory membership. The main purpose of this body would be to negotiate wages and conditions of work rather than to join in managing. He was insistent that social conflict must be eliminated but he was not clear about the sources of that conflict and provided little machinery for securing compromises between conflicting points of view.

Goerdeler, with his local government background, was keen to give communities power to rule themselves. He accepted universal suffrage but only when tempered by second votes for heads of families and only at the lowest level, councils at higher levels being chosen by the members of those on the level directly below. While Bürgermeister were to be chosen by the communal councils, he nowhere specified how the administrative officers at higher levels were to be appointed, the inference consequently being that this would continue to be done by the central Government. Experience had shown that as a result much hung on the character of that Government. But although Goerdeler devoted three paragraphs to discussing the alternative types of head of state, coming down in favour of a monarchy (if it was practicable, which it probably was not[6]), he failed to say how the first monarch was to be chosen (if by the leaders of a revolt, was there to be no later confirmation?) Nor did he say how the Chancellor was to be appointed, only providing that, if the two Houses of Parliament were in agreement, they might demand a Chancellor's removal. Again the inference must be that Chancellors were to be appointed by and responsible to the Head of State, even if they had to get parliamentary approval for many of their doings. This would have involved a return to the conditions of Goerdeler's boyhood. He was not in short prepared to carry his belief in human reasoning and benevolence to the point of allowing the common man an equal right to a direct say in the government to which he subjected himself.[7]

Where foreign policy and peace terms were concerned, Goerdeler's thought was dominated by his fear of Communism and his love of East Prussia. As late as the autumn of 1943 (and possibly even May 1944) he hoped to retain for Germany Austria, the Sudetenland and the South Tyrol, as well as her 1914 frontiers in the east, while suggesting that Poland might be compensated for the loss of Posen by annexing Lithuania.[8] (It must however be remembered that some of these plans were intended to secure the support of hesitant generals for a putsch and for that reason could not afford to be modest while one intended expressly for the English may have been pitched high as the starting point for bargaining.) He failed to realise the effect which Hitler's broken promises in 1939 and Russia's function in diverting German armed power away from Britain after 1941 had had on the British. He remained convinced that they would realise how vital it was for them to prevent Russia from gaining power as a result of the war. He said that certain proposals which had come to his ears, such as Poland's demand for East Prussia and parts of Silesia, made him take a black view of the future of Europe and the white peoples. On several occasions he asked his Swedish friend Jacob Wallenberg to discover through his brother Marcus[9] what terms (if any) the British would offer to a post-Hitler government. He paid no attention however when Jacob advised him not to seek assurances which he would not get in advance but take a chance on the probability that a Beck–Goerdeler régime would be in a better position than Hitler to circumvent unconditional surrender or, if it failed to do so, to continue the war.

A similar refusal to recognise realities made him fundamentally opposed to the assassination of Hitler, to which he offered the usual moral objections. He refused to believe that the various obstacles to a rising in which Hitler would be taken prisoner were as serious as he was told. To his mind it was merely a question of convincing a few generals. His two meetings with Kluge (pp. 149, 150) seemed to him to confirm this, since he disregarded the fact that their effect did not last. At one point he suggested that a meeting should be arranged between him and Hitler at which he would convince the Führer of the need to resign! When he discussed the assassination question with Beck and Kluge in August 1943, he ended by saying that he must leave the decision to the military.

The agreement that Goerdeler should be made Chancellor, as the person with the most suitable experience, was taken at the beginning of 1943. In November 1943 Beck asked him to draw up a list of ministers for the new Cabinet; in the following year he helped to draw up a list of the civilians who, as 'political commissioners', would advise the commanders of the various military districts. If conservatives preponderated in both lists, it was partly because too little was known about potential working-class candidates. Compiling the lists involved much travelling and numerous approaches to people who had not hitherto been privy to the plot; Goerdeler described himself as an 'itinerant preacher'. Some of the other conspirators, and particularly Stauffenberg, came as a result to fear that Goerdeler was becoming a security risk. Details of the military plans were accordingly withheld from him. As has been said (p. 137) he sensed this and took offence. He considered that Stauffenberg's lack of political experience disqualified him from intervening in the political aspects of the conspiracy. Stauffenberg for his part began to wonder whether Leuschner or Leber would not make better Chancellors. The process of selecting people for particular jobs inevitably brought out differences of outlook latent in the anti-Hitler coalition and these were made more acute by the strain of waiting. It is sad that the two people who (after the elimination of Oster and Tresckow) did most to inject dynamism into the planning should have fallen out with one another but the very fact that someone is vigorous makes him want to have his own way.

On 17 July Gisevius heard from Nebe that, after an outsider had been heard talking about Goerdeler as the future Chancellor, the Gestapo had decided to arrest him. On 18 July he had a talk with Stauffenberg who explained why he had not used his bomb three days earlier but made clear his intention to have another try at some unstated date in the near future. On 19 July Goerdeler was, for his own safety, taken out of Berlin by a friendly police officer and played no part in the events of the following day so that, even if Hitler had been killed, the new civil government could not have begun to function immediately. On 25 July he came back to Berlin and stayed there, in a variety of hiding places, till 8 August. A reward of a million marks was offered to anyone identifying him. He decided that escape was in the long run impossible and went off to East Prussia. There on 12 August he was recognised by a former servant of his family and arrested.

Although he was tried and condemned to death on 8 September, he was not executed until 2 February 1945 and his time in captivity was remarkable for two reasons. Whereas other prisoners tried to cover up their tracks and those of their comrades, he showed himself as voluble as ever and is said to have incriminated some people who might otherwise have escaped (although he helped to divert attention from others). He regarded the failure of the plot as a sign of divine disapproval so that he may have felt an obligation to make amends. He may also have wanted to bring home to Hitler the number of those who by this time condemned the policy of the régime and its refusal to consider capitulation. In this he saw eye-to-eye with the RSHA officials who were leading the investigation and in particular Otto Ohlendorff who sought to use the reports of cross-examinations in the same way as he had used public opinion reports during the war,[10] to get across to the top leaders how the German people were really thinking. Lastly Goerdeler may have hoped, by increasing the number of trails which the SD felt compelled to follow up in conditions of growing chaos, to survive until the war was over, which in the early autumn of 1944 seemed likely to be sooner than proved the case.

But there was another more extraordinary aspect to Goerdeler's captivity. He was commissioned by Ohlendorff and the Interior Ministry to draw up proposals for the reconstruction of Germany after the war in the fields in which he was expert, such as price control and local government. A conference was even held at the end of 1944 at which one of Ohlendorff's assistants lectured to relevant officials on 'The Plans of the participants in the July plot about reforming the state and the administrative structure'. These Nazi intellectuals had clear respect for Goerdeler's expertise and wanted to draw on it while he could still write memoranda. They did the same with Popitz, whose close collaborator Professor Jessen had been Ohlendorff's teacher. Perhaps both would have been kept alive if this could have been done without reference to higher levels. But at those levels too there was interest.

Mention has already been made (p. 81) of the meeting between Himmler and Popitz which took place in August 1943. A report of this was intercepted by Göring's deciphering service with the result that nothing came of it (except that Langbehn was arrested and a close watch kept on Popitz). But a year later Himmler would seem to have had the idea of using Goerdeler's contacts (particularly with the Wallenbergs) to get from the Anglo-Americans a promise of personal immunity in return for having Hitler removed. Goerdeler may have insisted on being released as a preliminary or he may have refused to aid a man whom he regarded as one of the roots of evil. At any rate the overtures came to nothing and it may have been fear of them leaking out which precipitated the decision to execute both Goerdeler and Popitz. In the face of death, Goerdeler's optimism deserted him. The RSHA headquarters where he was confined were without a chaplain. His family were all in protective custody so that there was nobody to visit him. His last days were unusually miserable.[11]

10 Ernst Freiherr von Weizsäcker[1]

Weizsäcker was born in 1882, the grandson of a Professor of Religious History and son of a Württemberg official who from 1906 to 1918 was Minister President of that state. After attending the Eberhard Ludwig Gymnasium at Stuttgart (as Stauffenberg was to do after him), he served in the Navy from 1900 to 1920. In 1913–14 he worked under Admiral Müller in the Personnel Section of the Kaiser's Naval Secretariat[2] (in which position he received much kindness from the monarch) and from July to November 1918 was a liaison officer at Supreme Headquarters. He was thus able to judge the Second Reich at first hand. He regarded the Tirpitz 'Risk Theory' and the adoption of unrestricted submarine warfare in 1917 as costly mistakes and, although he still believed as late as the spring of 1918 that the Central Powers would prove stronger than the Entente, he had realised by the autumn that Germany had been beaten in the field and rejected the 'stab-in-the-back theory'. Although not accepting that Germany was wholly responsible for the war, he certainly did not think her guiltless and regarded the Versailles Treaty as a misjudgment likely to cause another war rather than an injustice. While he preferred the Württemberg system by which level-headed officials were responsible to a public-spirited monarch, he was not an inveterate enemy of the Republic and respected some of its leading figures, notably Brüning. In

1920 he left the Navy and joined first the Consular and then the Diplomatic Service, working successively in Basel, Copenhagen, Geneva and Berlin. He was for three and a half years in charge of German relations with the League of Nations, in whose aims he had little faith. Hitler's accession to power found him Ambassador to Norway; he put half the blame for it on France and half on faulty internal policies.

His first reaction was that patriotism required men like him to stay in their posts so as to maximise the good effects of the change and limit the bad ones; he expected Hitler to come to grief soon for economic reasons. After four years as Ambassador to Switzerland (at a time when Swiss good-will was important for the Third Reich), he returned to Berlin in 1937 as head of the AA's Political Department. It was a critical moment. For four years the Nazi leaders had been chiefly occupied in making changes at home and building up their arms. Now they turned to aims which could not be achieved peacefully without the complaisance of other countries. In 1938 the post of State Secretary had to be filled and Weizsäcker was widely recommended for it. The new Foreign Minister Ribbentrop asked his private secretary, Erich Kordt, for advice; the reply, carefully phrased to appeal to the recipient, was 'he will not be an easy subordinate but he has been a sailor and knows how to obey'. He was offered the job on condition that he was ready to accept the Führer's 'Grand Design', which could not be achieved without war in three or four years' time. Weizsäcker also knew that Ribbentrop was recommending to Hitler a policy of building up a coalition which would force Britain either to ally with the Third Reich or wash her hands of Central Europe. He himself however regarded friendship with Britain as the key to successful German expansion. He therefore had his eyes open when he accepted the post, believing that he could exercise a restraining influence on two men who would be open to rational argument.

This belief was first put to the test in the Sudeten crisis. Weizsäcker disliked both the Czechs and their President Benes. He said that, if inside the Reich, they would be a louse in the fur; if outside, a pain in the neck. He was as keen as anyone on the Reich acquiring those parts of Czechoslovakia which had a German majority but he did not consider them to be worth a major European war and believed that, if Germany were prepared to wait, the Czechoslovak state could be made to 'decompose chemically' by which he seems to have meant exploiting the idea of self-determination, organising the holding of plebiscites and exercising economic pressure. At first Hitler seemed amenable to this course but when the Czechs mobilised at the end of May to meet mysterious rumours of an impending German attack[3] and Britain came to their support diplomatically, he was provoked into an irrevocable decision to 'destroy Czechoslovakia through military action in the foreseeable future'. Weizsäcker, convinced that this would lead to war with Britain and France, tried to talk Ribbentrop into pointing out this danger to Hitler. But '*Monsieur de trop*' (as Weizsäcker sometimes called him) was more bellicose than his master, of whom Weizsäcker did not yet despair, so that it became a question of finding a channel of access to the Führer which by-passed the Foreign Minister. He first tried Hitler's deputy Hess without much success; then the Swiss High Commissioner for the League of Nations in Danzig, Carl Burckhardt, whom he asked to impress on the British the need to make their intentions unmistakably clear, and finally Erich Kordt's brother Theo at the German Embassy in London.

The dilemma about such tactics was that a secret approach was liable to be disregarded by Hitler while a public one might again provoke him into forceful action. Whereas the Kordts favoured publicity, the British Ambassador in Berlin, Sir Neville Henderson, was strongly against it and Weizsäcker agreed with him. Chamberlain's preferred solution was of course a personal visit but again the effort to avoid appearing to threaten made it look like capitulation. When Hitler exploited this to raise his demands and war seemed inevitable, Weizsäcker brought in Göring and Mussolini, working on the latter through his Berlin Ambassador Attolico. As soon as the holding of a conference at Munich had been agreed on, Göring, Neurath and Weizsäcker formulated a possible basis for a settlement. Ribbentrop, bent on war, so amended it as to make it unacceptable to the British. But Weizsäcker had already passed it to the Italians and Mussolini produced it as his own, so that its discussion became inevitable. As three of the parties were willing to accept it, Hitler could not well refuse, especially as the German public was clearly in no mood for war, his only ally Italy said she could not fight, and the British at last took steps which made their intention to do so clear beyond doubt. Weizsäcker's crisis-management had thus succeeded in avoiding war at what was probably, with hindsight, the optimum moment for it (p. 94). But in case he should fail he had been steadily feeding information through Canaris to Beck and Halder so that they could decide when to give the signal for the putsch which he knew them to be contemplating but did not really want.[4]

After the Conference he acted as Chairman of a Committee with the three Ambassadors to settle the details and pressed his colleagues into a number of concessions, since he was himself being accused of weakness by Hitler. After the war he was evasive as to the date at which he first heard of Hitler's intention to invade the rump of Czechoslovakia but Hassell recorded him as reporting ten days after the Conference that Hitler had said the Czech problem would have to be 'totally liquidated' within a few months.[5] There was therefore an element of deceit as well as of realism in his answers to his British, French and Italian colleagues when between December 1938 and February 1939 they pressed him to settle the question of the proposed Four-Power Guarantee of Czechoslovakia's independence. For he replied that he did not see any point in such a guarantee since Czechoslovakia's existence now depended entirely on Germany and the other states had no intention of fighting to preserve it. After the German invasion of Bohemia and Moravia on the Ides of March, he took an abrasive line with the French Ambassador whom he told to stop talking about things where French participation did not promote peace. (The British Ambassador got a strong hint to convey his protest by letter rather than word of mouth.) Weizsäcker in fact thought the invasion a mistake since its results could have been achieved later without violence, but he rightly foresaw that it would not lead to war and therefore, so far from trying to stop it, he devised the political plan which was used to start it. He failed to appreciate, at any rate at once, the disastrous effect on foreign, and particularly British opinion of Hitler's departure from arrangements which had been agreed to with so much heart-searching such a short time before.

The immediate result was of course the British guarantee of Poland's independence which Weizsäcker, like the British Chiefs of Staff,[6] criticised as putting the decision between peace and war into the hands of a government over which Britain had no control. He saw the task as being to warn the Poles without encouraging Hitler and warn Hitler without encouraging Poland, a finesse which could only be achieved by secrecy. He wanted Britain to maintain *une silence menaçante*. He had no direct hand in the Russo-German talks and until about 20 August did not think they would succeed but then welcomed them as a way out of the dead-end into which, as he thought, the Führer had led Germany. Hitler had expected Britain to be intimidated by the Russo-German Pact into abandoning Poland. When instead the two countries signed a formal agreement, Weizsäcker brought into play the techniques which he had used in the previous year. He believed Hitler to be bluffing, but although some of the Führer's remarks support that interpretation,[7] he is more likely to have been gambling. Weizsäcker's main aim was to get the Poles to the negotiating table and it was he who drafted the sixteen-point plan which was to be presented to them when they got there. But this time the British were too disillusioned to press their ally very hard to negotiate and Ribbentrop's refusal to pass the plan to the British Ambassador in writing suggests that he did not want it to be used for negotiating. Consequently Munich was not repeated.

Weizsäcker at one point said to Hassell, 'Must we really be hurled into this abyss because of two madmen?'[8] When Erich Kordt asked him if there was no way of preventing war, he replied, 'Do you have a man with a pistol? You may call it a weakness but I can't kill a man.' He talked of resigning and returning to the Navy but did not insist on being allowed to do either. His remark that war meant opening the gates of hell was borne out by the death of a son in action on the second day of the campaign.

During the winter of 1939–40 Weizsäcker took the view that the only solution was intervention by the soldiers. 'But how?'[9] He sent a verbal message through Goerdeler to the German Ambassador in Brussels, which resulted in a joint offer from the sovereigns of Belgium and Holland to start peace negotiations. This was highly inconvenient to Hitler who, as Weizsäcker knew, was planning to attack their countries a few days later, an intention from which only the weather and not their gesture deterred him. Two months later Weizsäcker used the Norwegian Bishop Berggrav, whom he had known since his time in Oslo, to carry a message to the British Foreign Secretary Halifax:

'We must continue to work for peace. What must be considered is the fearful responsibility we take on ourselves if we have not attempted what we could attempt without doing damage.' He helped Adam von Trott to get to the United States (p. 182). He encouraged Theo Kordt, who had been posted to Berne on the outbreak of war, to find out from the British Government, through a private intermediary, what their terms for a settlement with a post-Hitler government would be. He got as answer an extract from a speech made by Chamberlain in parliament but failed to realise that he could have read it in a newspaper. He knew, distantly, of the parallel approach to the British made by Müller through the Vatican but almost certainly did not see the faintly encouraging reply which it elicited. When Sumner Welles visited Berlin in March 1940 on behalf of Roosevelt, Weizsäcker, disregarding instructions not to discuss with him the possibility of peace, drew his chair into the middle of the room, motioned to his visitor to do the same and then told him that no peace overtures would have any chance of success unless Hitler was approached directly or through Mussolini rather than through Ribbentrop who would do his best to block them.[10]

Weizsäcker was against almost all the military adventures in which Germany engaged in 1940–1, arguing either that they were unnecessary to the country's prosperity or else likely in the long run to do it harm. He did not believe, any more than Beck or Goerdeler, that a German political domination over other nations could last. At first, in the light of what the Luftwaffe told him, he rated Britain's chance of survival low but later became sceptical about the practicability of an invasion. He underestimated the resources, unity and determination of the British but was emphatic that the right strategy for Germany was to concentrate on knocking them out. He argued that, once they had been beaten, an invasion of Russia would be unnecessary. In April 1941 he told Ribbentrop that an attack on Russia would only give Britain new moral strength. It would be interpreted there as German uncertainty about victory. 'We would not only be admitting that the war was going to last much longer but might actually prolong it. . . . [Even if] we advanced to Moscow and beyond . . . we [should] have to reckon with a continuation of the Stalin system in eastern Russia and Siberia.'

Weizsäcker stayed on in his post partly because he could not leave it without permission but also in the hope of being able to contribute constructively to a post-Hitler settlement. But by 1942 the powers of the AA proper had been much reduced. German diplomats in the occupied countries reported directly to Ribbentrop or to a new 'German Department' under a character inappropriately named Martin Luther, who also had direct access to the minister. But one matter on which the original office was consulted concerned the deportation of Jews from French internment camps to the east in retaliation for actions of the French Resistance; the only question put to it was whether it saw any political objections to this, to which the answer given was 'no'. Weizsäcker had been told by Canaris in the autumn of 1941 that mass murders of Jews and Russians were going on in the east.[11] In several cases he had come to the help of individual Jews. A determined opponent could surely have found objections on the ground of international law or of Germany's long-term relationship with the rest of the world, as Helmuth von Moltke did in connection with the Commissar Order (p. 69). Whether Weizsäcker would have gained any more attention than Moltke may well be doubted but, as things turned out, an attempt would have saved him a good deal of trouble later.[12]

Early in 1943 Ribbentrop discovered a plot, instigated by Luther, to oust him as a prerequisite for peace negotiations. He suspected Weizsäcker of having encouraged it and decided to replace him by someone who would not have a mind of his own. In accordance with a desire which Weizsäcker had more than once expressed, he was made Minister to the Vatican. His superiors do not seem to have had in mind that he might be well placed to initiate peace feelers and, although he had such hopes himself, the only thing of the kind which came his way was a personal move by Ribbentrop in the spring of 1945 which was passed on to the Pope without comment and without sequel. His most notable achievements were a warning in October 1943 of Hitler's intention to deport Rome's Jews, which led to 8873 out of 10,000 being got out of harm's way, and an arrangement by which German troops withdrew from the city in June 1944 instead of fighting through it.[13] There is no evidence that he knew anything of the conspiracy after he left Berlin in May 1943. By July 1944 Rome was in Allied hands and he was ensconced in the neutral Vatican City, unable to participate but immune from retaliation. He antagonised the British by taking in a radio transmitter with him which was strictly speaking incompatible with the City's status and had not been done by the British Minister between 1940 and 1944.[14]

In May 1946 he was taken to Nuremburg to give evidence on behalf of Admiral Raeder and at the same time was cross-examined by American War Crimes investigators. He then went back to Rome which he did not finally leave till August. After further cross-examination, he was made the chief defendant in the so-called Wilhelmstrasse Trial, one of the series held of Germans who were considered to have aided and abetted the main criminals. He was accused on seven counts. The most serious of these concerned complicity in various acts of aggression; on these he was ultimately (and after appeal on the issue of the Ides of March) acquitted. But on the charge relating to the deportation of the French Jews, he was found guilty and condemned to seven years' imprisonment, reduced on appeal to five. He was in fact released in October 1950, only to die nine months later.

His elder surviving son is one of the more distinguished scientists in the Federal Republic; his younger son is now its President.

Weizsäcker was an outstanding example of the men who stayed on at their posts in the Third Reich in the hope of thereby being able to reduce the evil which it brought. To hold those posts, such men had to convince their superiors that they were more assets than liabilities, and this inevitably meant lending themselves to some extent to the purposes of those superiors, even if they were clandestinely seeking to frustrate them. Attolico, Italy's Ambassador in Berlin, who was in somewhat the same position himself, gave a clear exposition of the difficulties:

> Everything else is easier. The easiest is to emigrate and protest, but to start insurrections or make plots requires less strength and courage than to wring the most from hard reality, without self-pity, again and again defeated, always starting afresh, apparently sanctioning things one loathes, tough and without selfish gain, prudent, with constant watchfulness and tension. Imagine for a moment what it means to have a chief like Ribbentrop, a man without background, who is aware of nothing, who knows little about international law and economics, a pure dilettante, with less than average abilities, dangerous because he feels his own inadequacies, so that he abuses power to find compensation, always tempted to terrorise. Inclined always to drive things to extremes, to intensify the primitive inclinations of his sick chief Hitler. Day in and day out a Weizsäcker has to reason with this man, his ignorance and his rages. You asked what Weizsäcker wants – well, first of all he wants to avoid war.[15]

The Nuremburg Tribunal acquitted Weizsäcker on all counts except the Jewish one and even there it must be said that the legal case was slender. Had all the evidence of his anti-Nazi activities which has come to light by now been available at the time of his trial, he would probably not have been prosecuted at all. When his counsel asked senior officials of the British Foreign Office to testify to all the approaches which had been made to them at his instigation in 1938–9, Vansittart, Cadogan and Kirkpatrick came close to denying that any such approaches had taken place; it is a shameful story.[16]

But that is only half the answer. Wider issues call for consideration. The Tribunal hinted at them when it said that, although none of the documents (concerning the occupation of Bohemia and Moravia) legally justified a verdict of guilty, they did not put Weizsäcker in a favourable light, contained many statements which he knew and admitted later to be false and were official attempts to justify what he afterwards agreed had been unjustifiable.[17] Beck could never forgive him because on bidding good-bye to the American diplomats who had been in internment after Pearl Harbor, he said, 'We stand behind the Führer. His will is ours.'[18]

Up to a certain point his differences with the régime were ones of method rather than aim. Although he felt less emotional about the Treaty of Versailles than many of his fellow-conspirators, he wanted to get virtually all of its provisions regarding Germany reversed and saw nothing objectionable in Germany organising an economic federation of Central and South-east Europe provided she kept politically within her linguistic frontiers. He merely thought that the use of force was an inefficient way of reaching these objectives (although agreeing that, without force in the background, Germany could never achieve them). It was because he approved of so many of the aims that he was not prepared to make objection to some of the methods a breaking-point. He wanted to get rid of Hitler but keep Germany a Great Power.

He stayed at his post, as he was urged to do by many of his friends, in order to prevent worse from happening. Yet it is hard to point to anything which he did prevent, except the questionable achievement of avoiding war in 1938. Although he often asked himself whether he would not do better to move away, he never brought himself to insist on doing so and in the end only went because he was turned out. Hassell, whom he scolded for garrulity and who as a result had a grudge against him, accused him of being weak. 'It is noteworthy that when one scrutinises Swabians carefully [Hassell was a Bavarian!] one finds a lack of firmness in their character and a peasant's slyness which is covered up by bonhomie.'[19] This was perhaps unfair. Weizsäcker was of a type not uncommon in the higher reaches of administration; some of his traits are reminiscent of his opposite number Cadogan. He had intelligence, culture and principle but he had lost too many illusions. He was inclined to believe that whatever happened would be for the worse. This did not stop him from trying to improve things but, to immunise himself against disappointment, he did not indulge in much hope of being successful. Such a man is more inclined to compromise with than to stand up to the world in which he finds himself and the fiercer that world becomes, the harder is it for him to emerge with credit. That he should have been made to endure the hardship of trial and imprisonment may have helped to trim the balance of historical judgment in his favour just as it seems to have contributed to his ultimate peace of mind.

11 Adam Freiherr von Trott zu Solz[1]

Trott was born in 1909, second son of a Hessian baron who in the same year was made Prussian Minister of Culture by his friend Bethmann Hollweg. He had married a daughter of General von Schweinitz, Bismarck's Ambassador in Vienna and St Petersburg, who in his turn had married a daughter of an American Ambassador in Vienna. Adam was thus one-quarter American and descended from the first Chief Justice of the United States. He had an English nurse and spoke the language from an early age. The Trott family had lived for six centuries at Imshausen, near the little town of Solz in the middle of a forest called the Trottenwald. Adam was dominated by the love of his home, which he extended to his homeland. 'That he was a patriotic person before all else was patent always.'[2] His father impressed on him the family tradition of service to the state as a duty of the privileged. He studied law at Munich, Göttingen and Berlin, passed his *Staatsexamen* and obtained a Doctorate *summa cum laude* in 1932 for a thesis on Hegel and international law. If he was to hold an official post, he should then have started on a training course as a *Referendar*. Instead he became for two years (1931–3) a Rhodes Scholar at Oxford (which he had already visited in 1929).

Here he read Philosophy, Politics and Economics in six terms instead of the usual seven. But Oxford's nineteenth-century enthusiasm for Hegel had waned and its flirtation with Logical Positivism was beginning; its examination system, which puts a premium on quick thinking and concise writing, is ill-suited to someone trained in Germany to respect thoroughness (*Grundlich-keit*). For a student who had a lot of ground to cover in a short spell, he devoted a high proportion of his time to 'extra-curricular activities' and was considerably preoccupied by all that was going on in his native country. Thus it should cause no surprise that he only got a second class. For his part he came to think, with some justice, that Oxford was living in a self-contained world.[3]

But if his time at Balliol College was undistinguished academically, he was a great social success. He was not only tall but had striking features, a ringing laugh and tremendous personal charm. He got to know not only the outstanding personalities of his own generation but also a number of the university's senior members. One of the two girls who became close acquaintances said of him that 'he made human contacts remarkably easily but then devoted so close a scrutiny to their nature and meaning that the relationships themselves often wilted.'[4] The other referred to his 'carelessness and frequent laughter which were only part of his general assurance.' It may have been these qualities which led him astray, for 'his judgment, both of politics and personalities, was often at fault.' A tendency to base relations on emotion led him to belittle differences of opinion. He expected his friends to show sympathy for his views without recognising much need to reciprocate.[5]

In 1930 he had voted Social Democrat and he acquired a reputation in Oxford of being further to the left than he was. Soon after 30 January 1933 he spoke out against National Socialism at the German Club and was reproved by his mother. 'As far as I understand the movement, I reject it. Nevertheless it is a national movement which you should not denigrate or belittle outside your own country.' Taking that advice to heart, he treated criticism of Germany as many treat criticism of their relations – something which may be indulged in by oneself but not by others. He was wont to say in reply to attacks on the Third Reich either that the outside world, by its treatment of Germany since 1918 (or even earlier), had forfeited its right to criticise or else that Nazi behaviour was not as widespread or as reprehensible as foreigners were claiming. His mother once said that he was a Don Quixote, apt to rush into battle without having considered the consequences.[6] In one of these moods he wrote two letters to the *Manchester Guardian* in 1934 not only denying anti-semitic prejudice in the Hessian law-courts (which the paper had reported) but asserting that 'active storm-troopers' to whom he had talked 'turned with indignation from the suggestion of atrocities being committed in their presence.' His British friends regarded this statement of personal experience as wilful blindness to acts which violated all their canons of civilised behaviour. They found it hard enough to understand why he did not quit the country in disgust. That he should plead for favours to it outraged them. They could not understand the position of someone who both loved and hated what he belonged to. He could not comprehend the exasperated indignation which the Third Reich was progressively arousing among the British and it therefore seemed to him reasonable to seek in the long-term interests of Europe for concessions which they were not prepared to support. They for their part suspected anyone who asked for such concessions as allowing himself to be used as a tool.

After leaving Oxford he took up again the regular training for German lawyers. In spite of pressure he refused to join the Nazi Party or even the Nazi lawyers' association. But he also refused to accept that such behaviour would exclude all possibility of his serving his country as long as Nazism lasted. With characteristic optimism he denied that it would last long. He did not actually engage in underground activities such as producing literature but he associated with people who did and more than once intervened to protect or rescue friends who were in trouble with the authorities. He also edited in 1935 a selection from the writings of Heinrich von Kleist (1777–1814) which served as a cover for vindicating 'the right of men to live candid lives for the sake of the individual's own greatness and thereby the greatness of his country.' But he was still reluctant to accept that such an attitude was bound to frustrate his determination to serve the state. He scraped through the final examination only to find that nearly all the careers for which it qualified him were either closed or unpalatable.

Instead he prevailed on the Rhodes Trustees (largely through their Chairman Lord Lothian) to let him spend the third year of his scholarship on a journey to China and Japan. The nominal object of the trip was to study Confucius with a view to bringing a 'unique and dynamic contribution' to the Germany of the future. A more practical objective was to qualify himself for a teaching post in a university. In the background was the hope of finding an answer to his key problem by looking at it from the other side of the world. That problem was how a patriotic German could pursue a useful career in Germany without compromising himself or helping Hitler. The chief result was a strengthening of the conviction which he all along felt that emigration was not the solution. Two years earlier he had said to a friend who did emigrate, 'Someone must stay behind. I shall lead a double life getting a post from which I can fight secretly against National Socialism. But I shall do it from here, not from abroad.'[7] He came back with his mind made up to help overthrow the régime from inside it, regardless of what temporary concessions that course might involve.

He was out of Europe during the Munich crisis and admitted afterwards that he had failed to realise how much it had done to exacerbate the situation. He heard of the *Kristallnacht* on his way home and wrote that 'it is we [Germans] who are humiliated by what has passed.' He had not been back long when the seizure of Prague made Anglo-German relations still more difficult. A war seemed hard to avoid but Trott, convinced that it would solve no problems, set himself to avoid it.

During his time in England he had inveighed against what he called 'the lid theory', the argument that the right way to counter Nazi Germany was to offer uncompromising resistance, to hedge Germany in materially and morally;

in his view such a course would only lead to an explosion which would destroy Europe. But after the reoccupation of the Rhineland he had found it hard to get up an enthusiasm for Britain's passive acceptance of it. After Munich, he felt uneasy.[8] During a visit to England in February 1939 he said that, unless Britain and France stood up to Germany, war would come and Hitler would win it.[9] Yet only a little while later, at the prompting of friends in the AA, he paid three visits to England to enlist support for an idea which was not necessarily his own. By it Britain, in return for the restoration by Hitler of self-government to the Czech areas of Bohemia and Moravia, was to withdraw her opposition to German expansion in Eastern Europe (as exemplified by the guarantee given to Poland). The way to weaken Hitler in his view was to show that German aims could be achieved by discussion rather than violence. He also hoped, by spinning out negotiations, to get past the favourable season of the year for an attack. In other words, 'appeasement' was to be revived, although Germany was to make her contribution.

By exploiting all his English social contacts (notably the Astors) he managed to put this proposal personally to Halifax, the Foreign Secretary, and to Chamberlain, the Prime Minister, who did not turn it down out of hand. Whether British Ministers would or, given the state of public opinion, could have agreed to such a deal is highly doubtful. But they were never required to consider it since Ribbentrop refused to put it to Hitler and it was in any case soon upstaged by the Russo-German Non-Aggression Pact. In order to launch it without bringing down on himself the wrath of the German authorities however he had to pose as much more of a Hitler supporter than he really was, and thus incurred further suspicion among his English friends, not to mention hostility among his English enemies. Considerations of security kept him in most cases from explaining that the real object of his proposal was to create an opportunity for an existing group of Hitler's opponents to stage a putsch. When he did hint at such a possibility to an Oxford friend, Maurice Bowra, and was asked what a new German régime would do about Hitler's territorial gains, he replied that it would keep them and indeed seek more. He was thereupon asked to leave the house. By overeagerness to do good, without paying enough attention to the complexities of the situation, or even indeed being adequately aware of them, an honest man incurred a reputation for double-dealing which was not dispelled until after his death.

Three weeks after war broke out, Trott left Genoa on an Italian ship for New York, ostensibly to lecture on China at a meeting of the Institute of Pacific Relations. His main achievement during the three months which he spent in the United States was to convince the Federal Bureau of Investigation that he was the man running the Nazi spy-system in the country! After Pearl Harbor all his friends were for a time interned or kept under close police supervision. The FBI could not believe that anyone who managed to travel outside Germany in wartime was disapproved of by the Nazi authorities and one or two accidents combined to give a bad impression. The fact that on one or two other occasions he more or less publicly expressed anti-Nazi views was regarded as a deliberate attempt at strategic deception. In talks with several Englishmen (including Lothian, by then Ambassador), he argued for some early formulation of war aims. Even after he had been brought to admit that such a statement would be untimely as long as Hitler retained power, he made the first of many attempts to extract from the Western Powers (at a time when the USA was not yet a belligerent) some assurance that, if Hitler were overthrown, Germany would not thereafter be too implacably treated. He managed to get a memorandum to this effect put in front of Roosevelt but he also aroused the enmity of one of the President's most trusted advisers, the Jewish Justice Felix Frankfurter who, having been warned against him by Bowra, received the sound but tactless advice that Jews should not be given much part in American propaganda to Germany.

He fell ill on the journey home through Siberia and did not become active again until April 1940. His first step was to marry Clarita Tiefenbacher. He had made many friendships during his wanderings but now that he had decided to remain in Germany, he wanted to make a home there. In June he started work in the new Information Department of the AA, which rapidly became a focus for Hitler's ill-wishers. His immediate superior was Hans Berndt von Haeften whom he had met in Oxford in 1933; the ultimate head was Weizsäcker. At the end of May he re-established contact with Helmuth von Moltke whom he had met in Oxford in 1937 and again in Berlin in 1939.[10] Their chief private task during the rest of 1940 was to keep up their spirits in a world where evil seemed to have secured an outright triumph. His first official task was to collect documentation for the force which was to invade Britain! But there is evidence that during this time Trott on several occasions managed to rescue victims of the régime. As cover he applied for, and was granted, membership of the NSDAP, and he sent a message to one of his American friends saying that German war aims must include annexations in both east and west.

In April 1941 he was given an extra job. Subhas Chandra Bose, the head of the violent left wing of the Indian Congress Party, arrived in Berlin and Trott was made leader of this Bengali bear. Bose's twenty-two months in Germany were an unhappy interlude. He was never given the support to which he thought himself entitled and got on badly with almost all the Germans he met, from Hitler downwards. Trott disliked Bose but it has never been suggested that his Anglophile associations led him to make things difficult for the Indian. All the same, he must have felt a conflict of loyalties when in March 1942 Stafford Cripps was sent by the Cabinet to negotiate a compromise with Indian nationalism and as a result was denounced by Bose on the German Radio Free India, for in addition to many other kindnesses Cripps had helped to finance Trott's trip to the Far East.

During this time the group round Moltke was gradually clarifying its views as to the shape which they would like Germany after Hitler to take. Haeften and Trott were given special responsibility for foreign affairs where Trott was considerably less prepared than Moltke to see the country dismembered or absorbed into a supranational body. He is on record as having had 6 talks with Moltke in 1940, 12 in 1941, 15 in 1942 and 28 in 1943, when he attended the third meeting at Kreisau (p. 00). He also took advantage of his official position to make 8 trips to Switzerland, 4 to Sweden, 4 to the Low Countries and 1 to Turkey. Notable among them was one to Geneva in April 1942 when he entrusted to Dr Visser 't Hooft (Secretary of the Provisional Committee of the World Council of Churches and a friend of his mother's whom he had known since 1928) a letter for onward transmission to Cripps who by that time had returned from India and was a leading minister.[11] This document seems to have been put on paper in Switzerland in the light of discussions which had been going on throughout the previous winter in Berlin; it indicated how members of the group were thinking but could not in the nature of things have been shown to or approved by them in its final form. The letter stressed the danger to civilised life involved in a continuation of the war. It said that the forces working inside Germany for an overthrow were impeded not merely by Gestapo terror but also by the need to defend the nation against the Soviet Union and the complete uncertainty about the British and American attitudes towards a change of government in Germany. It outlined some of the ideas which were being developed in Germany by a coalition between the workers, the churches and influential circles in the Army and bureaucracy (as described in Chapter VI above). It ended with a plea for discussion coupled with a common recognition of 'our' failure to deal in a Christian manner with the historical, geographic, economic and psychological factors which had brought the world to its present situation.

Cripps showed the memorandum to Churchill who wrote on it 'Most encouraging'. A verbal answer was sent back welcoming further communication but ruling out all prospect of negotiating the lines of a post-war settlement until Germany had been defeated militarily. This exchange of messages set the tone for the debate which was to be continued through various channels until July 1944. The Germans stressed the genuineness of the *Widerstand*; the British replied that they would believe in it when it produced some results. This scepticism may have displayed an underestimation of the difficulties of withstanding a totalitarian régime but it had a valid base; the movement would have produced results sooner if more Germans had been ready to give it whole-hearted backing. The German reply was that it would get more backing if the Anglo-Americans would promise to treat a post-Hitler régime with clemency. The Anglo-Americans, remembering 1917–19, were reluctant to make promises as to how they would treat a régime about whose character they could not feel certain in a situation containing many elements which could not be foreseen. The authors of the messages reaching the West from Germany might be honest and decent men but the fact that they had been unable to get the support needed to overthrow Hitler raised the question how far they would get the support needed to instal and maintain a liberal régime after Hitler's overthrow. They might be allowing themselves to be used by men of much less good-will whose sole concern was to save Germany from the full consequences of defeat. In this connection the existence of suspicion in both Britain and America about Trott's own *bona fides* was unhelpful. His misjudged encounter with Felix Frankfurter proved disastrous when a document representing the views of his friends reached Roosevelt via Istanbul, because it was to Frankfurter that the President turned for advice and on the strength of that advice refused to treat with 'these East German Junkers' – a description which was of course totally erroneous.

Trott seems to have been slow at realising how arguments which he used were going to strike the people to whom they were addressed. Mention has already been made (p. 107) of the way in which most Germans took it for granted that America and Britain would give top priority to keeping Communism out of Central Europe. Trott's warnings about the possibility of the *Widerstand* turning to the Russians may have been genuinely felt but it does not seem to have occurred to him that it was the kind of thing which a spokesman of Goebbels might have been expected to say. The same applies to his argument that continued bombing would promote Communism (p. 106). In talking to a Swedish woman in November 1943, when he knew that what he said would be passed on to the British, he told her that the Germans were not much interested in British and American plans for post-war Germany since it was the Russians who were going to defeat them. But there was a considerable risk that in certain cases Germans might be uncritically receptive to English ideas and try to bite off a larger piece of British Liberalism than they could chew.[12] In June 1944 he told an American journalist in Stockholm that the Allies would find a serious revolutionary situation when they reached Germany. The Allied administration would be largely in the hands of American military officials whose understanding of and respect for the honour and feelings of Germans were lower than those of the Russians![13] That there may have been grains of truth in these remarks did not make them ways of winning over those who heard or read them. The tragedy was that this should have cancelled out so much courage and enthusiasm.

During a visit to Geneva in April 1944 Trott suggested to Dulles a number of announcements which he wanted the Anglo-Americans to make in order to win the confidence of German workers and keep them from falling under Communist influence.[14] The general effect of these would have been to assure German labour that it would be given a privileged place in a post-war Germany and allowed to settle its own affairs without interference. A promise was also to be given that the Allies did not intend to set up a puppet government to promote their interests at the expense of the German people. Just at this time the European Advisory Commission set up at the Moscow Conference was considering post-surrender arrangements in Germany which Trott would probably have regarded as a puppet régime. In any event post-war experience hardly confirms that the danger of German labour going Communist was great enough to warrant the Anglo-Americans departing in these ways from their established policies.

In 1942 and 1943 Trott met Peter Kleist (p. 71) in Stockholm and learnt at least something of his talks with Edgar Clauss who claimed to be a spokesman for the Russians.[15] In June 1944 he arranged through Willy Brandt, who was then working as a journalist in Stockholm and had contacts with the Soviet Embassy, for an interview there (apparently to convey news of the impending assassination) but called it off because of rumours that the Russian mission had a German mole.[16] At the same time he rejected an earlier offer from the British Embassy to fly him to London because the condition was attached that he should not return and he feared with good reason reprisals on his family.[17]

Trott met Stauffenberg for the first time in the spring of 1943, if not earlier;[18] he met him for the last time on 19 July (p. 138). On 16 July he warned his fellow-conspirators that the Allies were likely to insist on unconditional surrender on all fronts simultaneously, making futile the hope which he had long cherished of negotiating a surrender confined to the west. He did however say, presumably on the strength of something he had heard from Dulles or in Stockholm (or even of the message sent to him by Cripps in 1942), that there was a good chance of the enemy being ready to negotiate as soon as the precondition of a complete change of régime had been accomplished.[19]

He spent the day of 20 July in his office; about 15.00 he got a message that the bomb had been exploded and that Hitler was dead. A rumour that Hitler had survived reached him three hours later. He, Haeften and others watched from their window how troops arrived to seal off the area round the Wilhelmstrasse, only to be withdrawn again afterwards. All attempts to ring up the Bendlerstrasse failed. At 23.00 Trott went to the Foreign Press Club where he heard Hitler's broadcast at 01.00. He then met Haeften in the middle of the Grunewald Forest to settle a common line of defence after they were arrested. On the 21st he was asked by a friend whether he had any hope for the future. 'No,' he replied, 'there is no hope left now or for the future. This is the end. The disaster must take its course till no stone is left upon another. Hitler will carry on this madman's war until everything is destroyed. And yet it is good all the same that there were people ready to break this reign of terror. It remains a historical fact and, more than that, a symptom.'[20]

On 25 July Trott was arrested, having refused several offers of help in escaping. But surprisingly enough the SD had no incriminating evidence against him beyond his friendship with Stauffenberg. He was tried before the People's Court on 15 August in company with Haeften and others from the AA. He was condemned to death more for guilt by association than anything else. The SS man who had recently become head of the Information Department represented to his superiors the desirability of sparing the lives of those accused from the AA, so that they could help in the negotiations with the Allies which were clearly impending. Although Himmler agreed, Hitler raged at the mere idea of negotiations, shouting that the diplomats were the worst of the lot and should be hanged as soon as possible. This fate overtook Trott on 26 August. His wife had been arrested after forcing her way into his trial; their children, aged 2½ and 9 months, were lodged in a Nazi orphanage. But she was released in the autumn and the children were returned to her soon afterwards.

In one of his last letters to her he wrote:

> What hurts most is that I may never now be able to put at the service of our country the special faculties and experience which I have developed by concentrating, perhaps too exclusively, on its standing among the Powers. Here I could really be of use. I would so much have liked to put my ideas and suggestions at the disposal of others in systematic form. But this will remain denied me. It was all a developing attempt, springing from the visual influence of our native land, which I am always grateful to my father for having inspired in me, to maintain and speak for her enduring rights, no matter what changes and difficulties recent times may have brought, and for her deep indispensable contribution against the encroachment of alien powers and ideas. That is why I have always hurried back from foreign countries, despite the temptations and possibilities which I found there, to the place where I thought I was called to serve. . . . A sower does not easily leave his seedlings for others to tend, since so much can happen between seed-time and harvest.[21]

12 Helmuth James Graf von Moltke[1]

As a reward for his contribution to victory in the Austro-Prussian War of 1866, Field-Marshal Helmuth von Moltke (whose family came from Mecklenburg and Holstein rather than Prussia proper) was given a bounty of £30,000. He used it to buy an estate at Kreisau in Silesia, west of the Oder and about half-way along the province's south-west frontier with Bohemia. As the Field-Marshal and his English wife were childless, Kreisau passed on his death to Wilhelm, the eldest son of his younger brother. Wilhelm's eldest son, who duly succeeded him, married Dorothy, the only child of Sir James Rose-Innes the Chief Justice of South Africa.[2] Helmuth James von Moltke, born in 1907, was their eldest son. The father was a rather ineffectual person and it was the views of the mother, derived ultimately from Scottish liberalism, which dominated the household. Kreisau, with only about 1000 acres, was a relatively small estate by East German standards. Consequently it is not surprising that a south German anti-Nazi, on meeting Helmuth James for the first time, should have said to himself, 'What an astonishing sort of Prussian!'[3]

The young Moltke attended grammar schools in Silesia and Berlin, went for a time to a boarding-school and in due course got his leaving certificate (*Abitur*) but lessons did not much interest him and he never studied seriously at a university. Greater influence was exercised, in addition to that of his mother and her father, by Dr Eugenie Schwarzwald, a remarkable Jewess from the Bukovina living in Vienna, and Eugen Rosenstock (p. 60), then a Professor at Breslau whom he helped to run a prototype work-camp in an industrially derelict area near his home. In one way or another he came to know a number of outstanding people such as Brüning. He started to train as a lawyer but just as he was getting down to work, two distractions intervened. Kreisau found itself on the verge of bankruptcy thanks to Germany's economic difficulties and his father's mismanagement. He had to take charge and six years of hard work were needed to get things straight; amongst other economies, the family moved from the Hall to a cottage on the estate. Secondly he became engaged to Freya Deichmann, the daughter of a Cologne banker whose finances were in crisis too. They married in the face of possible penury in September 1931, Helmuth arguing with characteristic realism that they would have to live on something even if they did not marry and there was no reason to think it would cost them more to live together than separately.

All along he viewed the Nazi menace with the utmost gravity; he was one of the few members of the upper class who never felt any sympathy for its objectives. In the presidential election of 1932 he voted Communist; on 30 January 1933 he passionately challenged the view that accession to power would show Hitler to be so incompetent that he would not last long. From the start he said (like the Social Democrats) that 'voting for Hitler means voting for war'. He had close links with Dorothy Thompson and Edgar Mowrer, two American journalists who did much to alert their country to the danger which Hitler and National Socialism meant for the world. In 1934 (and again in 1936–7) he and his wife visited South Africa and he paid a first visit to England. In 1935 his mother died suddenly. He completed his legal training and started to practise privately in Berlin (since his views made any public appointment out of the question). Much of his work consisted in helping victims of the Nazis, and particularly Jews, to emigrate. But in 1935 he started to work for the English bar so as to have an external qualification in case he and his wife decided life in Germany to be intolerable (p. 61). Thanks to the respect enjoyed by his South African grandfather and the impression which he made himself (he was even taller than Adam von Trott), he met a number of prominent Englishmen in London and Oxford. He visited England at least seventeen times between 1935 and 1939 and was called to the bar in 1938. He stuck to the view that Germany must be resisted and not appeased. After an interview with Lord Lothian, he wrote to his grandfather's Oxford friend Lionel Curtis:

> I fear [his policy of appeasement] will prove to be misleading for Germany. It will induce our government to believe that we can count on the English neutrality while in truth, should a European war break out, England would fight on the side of France. . . . England is not really an arbiter but the party to the struggle, but its lack of rigid policy is what induces Germans to believe that she is an arbiter.[4]

In 1938, as has been said, he felt tempted to emigrate and arranged to spend much of the winter of 1939–40 in London. But war came before he could move. Accordingly he found himself a job as adviser on International Law to the Foreign Department of the Abwehr, without fully realising that he was entering the chief focus of the *Widerstand*. This meant living in Berlin; the letters which he wrote almost daily to his wife are a key record of his wartime activities. Up to this point, he had had to be content with doing as little as possible to help the Nazis and as much as possible to help their victims. His sources of information were already good enough in February 1938 to discover the truth about the Blomberg–Fritsch crisis within a month of its occurrence.[5] During the Munich crisis, he was in London taking his examination. In the course of the following winter (1938–9) he began to discuss with friends what kind of Germany they would like to see as successor to the Third Reich. In his Abwehr post however he at first confined himself to trying to prevent Germany's rulers from breaking international law, particularly at sea.[6]

His reaction to the depressing course of events in the summer of 1940 was to intensify his thinking about post-Hitler Germany, the value of which has already been discussed (pp. 69–70). His chief interlocutor now became Peter Yorck von Wartenburg, a distant relation and Silesian neighbour. Between them, they defined the purpose of the state as being to foster the free and rational development of all individual citizens. On this foundation they advanced to more detailed practical proposals. Other old friends to whom Moltke soon turned were his cousin Carl Dietrich von Trotha, Horst von Einsiedel (an economist) and Edward Waetjen. Moltke himself decided whom he should ask for advice and it was on his insistence that the churches and workers were brought in as the two groups most likely to make a valuable contribution to the new Germany. Their participation added a new dimension to a movement which to start with had been almost inevitably the activity of an élite. Otto von der Gablentz, Theodor Steltzer and Eugen Gerstenmaier were the main figures in the first category, Adolf Reichwein and Carlo Mierendorff in the second. Later Father Rösch, head of the Jesuits in South Germany, joined in for the Catholics, with Father Delp as his deputy, as did Julius Leber for the workers. As has been mentioned (p. 183) the task of framing goals in foreign affairs was entrusted to Hans von Haeften and Adam von Trott.

Moltke was well aware that he and his friends were not in a position to overthrow Nazism; his remarks about their being amateurs have already been quoted (p. 109). He looked to the soldiers to apply the force even if he had little confidence that they would do so. In 1942 he asked the Norwegian Bishop Berggrav (whom he and Bonhoeffer had gone to Oslo to rescue from imprisonment) whether it was compatible with Christianity to kill tyrants.[7] Berggrav, who later described the question as the most difficult ever put to him, replied that in certain cases it was, provided the murderer was clear that not only would the attempt succeed but that a satisfactory new government could be formed instead. He was inclined to think that by then it was too late for Germans to kill Hitler; his removal should be left to the Allies. Moltke himself was deterred not merely by the thought that resort to murder involved taking a leaf out of the Nazis' book but also by fear that it might prejudice the chances of making a fresh start in Germany afterwards. He could however conceive of circumstances in which such a course might become a duty. If it did, and if that duty fell on him, he would not shrink from it. But for the time being he held aloof, partly because the greater the number of people in the know, the greater the risk of a leak, partly to prevent the failure of an attempt from compromising the whole anti-Nazi network.

For nearly four years from the summer of 1940 until his arrest at the end of January 1944, Moltke was active in three directions. He continued to exert an influence for good in his office. To do this was harder than it had been earlier because success made the régime more contemptuous of the restraints of law and morality. The case of the Commissar Order has already been mentioned (p. 69). Later Moltke sought to protect from execution prisoners belonging to any of the 'free' forces fighting with the Allies or Allied personnel fighting with national resistance forces (whom the Nazis insisted on treating as guerillas). One such British officer captured in Yugoslavia was brought to Berlin to be shot; he was rescued by Moltke who got him handed over to the Army authorities as a prisoner-of-war and in the process gave him a breakfast of ham-and-eggs. On another occasion he said to Admiral Bürkner, his immediate chief, 'So long as orders exist for me which no order of the Führer can annul and which have to be acted on even in the face of an order from the Führer, I can't allow the latter to pass unchallenged because the difference between good and evil, right and wrong, is fixed for me *a priori*.' 'A surprising number of people are willing to make a stand as soon as anyone else does. But there always has to be somebody to go first; nobody will do it alone.' How far his efforts produced lasting results may be questioned. He told an assistant, 'Anyone who wants to see his proposals translated into reality had better not come to work for us.' Indeed the limitations on what he could achieve often filled him with deep depression: 'More than a thousand men are being murdered for a certainty every day and thousands more Germans are being habituated to murder. . . . How can I bear this and sit just the same in my warm room and drink tea? Don't I make myself into an accomplice by doing so?'

Secondly he pressed ahead with his plans. He can fairly be described as the 'moving spirit' among his companions. He started the whole process off, assigned particular jobs to particular people, chased laggards and arranged for the gradual assembling of the various pieces into a whole. After the three week-end meetings at Kreisau in 1942 and 1943 he drew up, in consultation with Yorck, a summary of conclusions which was then agreed with those of the participants who were within reach. He argued vigorously for his own views about the overall approach and certain details but there were other areas in which he frankly admitted ignorance and was content to be guided. At no stage did he try to impose his own views. Indeed it was intrinsic to the whole approach that views were not to be imposed but were to be evolved in the process of discussion. After the war his collaborator Gerstenmaier compared his position to that of a foreman in a gang of labourers who, while having the responsibility for overall direction, does basically the same work as the rest.[8]

The main ideas of the group have already been described (pp. 101–9) so no more than a brief recapitulation is needed here.

(*1*) National Socialism was not to be regarded as an isolated phenomenon (although it might have some characteristics which were unique) but as a symptom of a defect to which all densely populated industrialised societies are prone – undue centralisation and the denial to the individual of a say in the decisions affecting his own life. The remedy was to revive a spirit of true community and couple it with a sense of individual responsibility. Participation in communal affairs should be both a right and a duty. Two consequences followed. One was the need to decentralise and assign as much decision-making as possible to a local level, where the individual could appreciate its effects and know the men involved. The second was to bring into the community those, and especially the workers, who had hitherto been treated in Germany as outsiders. There were two further corollaries. One was the need to build economic and social life upwards from the smallest units. The second was a suspicion of political parties and even of trade unions as lobbies to promote the interests of sections of the community at the expense of the whole. In the letter which Moltke sent to Curtis via Stockholm in 1943 (see below), he said 'We need a revolution, not a coup d'état.'

(*2*) Experience of life in a society where law was disregarded led to great emphasis being placed on the need to restore the rule of law. Responsibility for judging crimes committed during the war was to be given to the International Court of Justice at the Hague. But the Court was to proceed on the principle of 'no penalty except as provided by law', thus ruling out retrospective legislation. Moltke was confident that most Nazi crimes would prove to have violated one of the basic principles of natural law, of the law of nations or of positive law generally current in the community of nations.[9]

(*3*) The belief that no community could make a success of its affairs unless it was inspired by a sense of purpose. For this reason great emphasis was placed on reviving the waning belief in religion and principally Christianity. Moltke had abandoned the Christian Science in which he was brought up but in 1942 he wrote to Curtis that 'the amount of risk and readiness for sacrifice which is asked from us now and that which may be asked from us tomorrow require more than right ethical principles.'

(*4*) Just as Moltke wanted to decentralise as many functions as possible, so he wanted to raise others to an international plane. The hypertrophied form which the nation-state had assumed in Germany repelled him and he felt little respect or affection for it – in this he resembled many young Englishmen of his own generation and was closer to his Socialist collaborators than to von Trott. But he was acutely conscious that after the war Germany must reckon with the hostility of her neighbours. 'Hunger, illness and anxiety spread all the while under our rule. No one can ever guess the consequences which that will have or how quickly they will develop. Only one thing is sure. The Horsemen of the Apocalypse are beginners compared to what is ahead of us.' He wrote to Curtis that 'for us Europe after the war is a question of how the picture of man can be re-established in the breasts of our fellow-citizens.'

Moltke's third main wartime activity consisted in travelling. He wrote to me in 1943 that, 'I have become a sort of travelling agent.' Pretexts for these journeys were mostly provided by legal disputes. The real aims were three. The first was to find ways and means of alleviating the effects of German rule in the occupied countries, especially as regards the taking and shooting of hostages. The second was to establish contact with the resistance movements in those countries and convince them that not all Germans were to be regarded as criminals. The third was to get messages through to his friends in England, for much the same reason. For these purposes he went to Norway and Sweden in April and September 1942 and March 1943. On the last occasion he took with him a copy of one of the Scholls' leaflets (p. 236) which he handed over to the Norwegian resisters and to a sympathetic editor in Sweden, with a long note explaining the background and suggesting follow-up action; it was almost certainly through this channel that first the outside world and then the German people heard about the Scholls.[10] In April 1943 he went to Poland, in May–June and again in September to Holland, Belgium and France, in July and December to Turkey and in October to Denmark and Norway. Except for the Scholls it cannot be said that these journeys had much result. Bishop Berggrav was released from captivity and most Danish Jews escaped from being sent eastwards but in both cases the main credit was due to other people. One long letter, and another in summarised form, reached Curtis in England but had no more effect on Allied policy than a document sent from Istanbul to Washington. His request that I should meet him in Stockholm in September 1942 was rejected after being referred to Churchill.

Another contact which he maintained until December 1941 was with the American diplomats Alexander Kirk and George Kennan and the American journalist Wallace Deuel. Kennan has paid him a striking tribute:

> I consider him in fact to have been the greatest person, morally, and the largest and most enlightened in his concepts, that I met on either side of the battle-lines in the Second World War. Even at that time – in 1940 and 1941 – he had looked beyond the whole solid arrogance and the apparent triumphs of the Hitler régime; he had seen through to the ultimate catastrophe and had put himself to the anguish of accepting it and accommodating himself to it inwardly, preparing himself – as he would eventually have liked to help prepare his people – for the necessity of starting all over again, albeit in defeat and humiliation, to create a new national edifice on a new and better moral foundation.
>
> The image of this lonely struggling man, one of the few genuine Protestant-Christian martyrs of his time, has remained with me over the intervening years as a pillar of moral conscience and an unfailing source of political and intellectual inspiration.[11]

He told Kennan that 'my own homeland of Silesia will go to the Czechs and Poles.' He told Father Rösch in October 1941 that the Russians would reach Berlin.[12] He invented an imaginary Russian called Serpuchoff who would manage the Kreisau estate after defeat (as Poles have actually done) and referred to him so often as to make him almost a family friend. These forecasts were not due to any liking for Communism; on the contrary, two of the documents sent to enemy countries during the war contain explicit warnings against the danger he considered it to be. If they illustrated a certain pessimistic realism, this was a shield which he adopted against disillusion; he never lost faith in the need to make higher qualities prevail. At the end of his 1942 letter to Curtis, he wrote:

> The hardest bit of the way is still to come but nothing is worse than to slack on the way. Please do not forget that we trust you will stand it through without flinching as we are prepared to do and don't forget that for us a very bitter end is in sight when you have seen matters through. We hope you realise that we are ready to help you win war and peace.

Being in the Abwehr Moltke was naturally in touch with Canaris who had a high opinion of him. He only mentioned Oster twice, on both occasions in the autumn of 1941. The first crisis in Russia was coming to a head and it was hoped that Brauchitsch would defy Hitler. Moltke appears to have tried unsuccessfully to find a general who would be prepared to initiate a revolt inside Germany. Otherwise contacts with the military conspirators were left to Yorck and Trott. Only one meeting with Stauffenberg is mentioned, in December 1943, and that was a social occasion (p. 137). His behaviour at the only meeting between the *Honoratioren* and the Kreisau Group on 8 January 1943, with his interjection of the phrase 'Kerensky solution' has been described (p. 106).

In January 1944 Dr Reckzeh's breach of good faith (p. 79) gave the Gestapo indirectly an excuse for arresting Moltke. His offence was a minor one and the authorities remained unaware of most of the activities in which he had been engaged. Early in July his release seemed imminent. While at liberty, he had consistently opposed assassination for the reasons which he gave Berggrav. On the first occasion his wife visited him after 20 July, while relatively open conversation was still possible, he said, 'If I had been free, this wouldn't have happened.' His last letter to his sons said that he had 'never wished for or contributed to acts of violence like that of 20 July . . . because I . . . believed that the fundamental spiritual evil would not be got rid of in that way.' It is always possible that he would have changed his mind if he had become convinced, like several of his friends, that assassination offered the only chance of securing a quick end to the war with all its losses and sufferings. Nobody can be sure. But inevitably, as the SD Commission obtained evidence, the extent of his involvement began to emerge. By 25 August a considerable dossier had been collected.

All the same, when it came to drawing up his indictment, the authorities found themselves in difficulty. As he had been in prison since January, he had obviously had no hand in the immediate plot and could point to the evidence that he had opposed murder. Few of his activities abroad came to light and the documents which his group had drafted, along with his letters to his wife, were well concealed at Kreisau (the letters in her bee-hives!). The charges actually brought against him came down to discussing what should happen after the war was over and failing to report the existence of a conspiracy of which he was well aware. In the two remarkable letters describing his trial which he wrote to his wife between sentence on 10 January 1945 and execution on the 23rd,[13] he said that 'we are to be hanged for thinking together.' This has been widely interpreted as an admission that he did nothing but think, whereas preceding paragraphs should have made it clear that he took action whenever a possibility occurred. His remark merely stated the reason for which he was condemned and he took pleasure in demonstrating the antagonism of National Socialism to anyone who did so much as think along dissentient lines. Freisler, the President of the People's Court, said in giving judgment that 'only in one respect are we [National Socialists] and Christianity alike; we demand the whole man.'

In his farewell letter to his sons,[14] Moltke said

Throughout my life from my schooldays onwards I have fought against a spirit of narrowness and subservience, of arrogance and intolerance, against the absolutely merciless consistency which is deeply engrained in the Germans and has found its expression in the National Socialist state. I have made it my aim to get this spirit overcome with its evil accompaniments, such as excessive nationalism, racial persecution, lack of faith and materialism. In this sense and seen from their own standpoint the National Socialists are right in putting me to death. . . .

Ever since National Socialism came to power, I have done my best to mitigate the consequences for its victims and prepared for a change: I was driven to do so by my conscience and in the last resort that is a task worth a man's while.

13 Julius Leber[1]

Leber was born in 1891, the illegitimate son of an Alsatian peasant's daughter. The father must have been a person of some position because he gave the girl enough money to make her an attractive match four years later for the day-labourer Jean Baptiste Leber. Her son, with the help of the parish priest, got to a primary school at Breisach on the other side of the Rhine and then to a secondary modern school in Freiburg. Before he left he had joined the Social Democratic Party, partly because of the support which it was giving to autonomy for Alsace. He started on a university course in economics but broke off to volunteer for active service in August 1914. After the war, when Alsace returned to France, he was to opt for German citizenship.

He was promoted Lieutenant in March 1915, was twice wounded and twice received the Iron Cross. In 1918 he remained in the Army to protect the eastern frontier. When in March 1920 right-wing units sought to defy Allied orders and overthrow the Republic (the 'Kapp Putsch') Leber sided with the local *Landrat* and workers rather than with his superior officers. For this 'disobedience' he had to leave the Army (just as the Social Democratic Minister of War Noske was made to resign for having supported the general strike which broke the revolt).

Leber went back to the university and took a doctorate on the function of money in capitalism. In March 1921 he started work as the political editor of the *Lübecker Volksbote*, where he won the admiration of an office-boy, also illegitimate, who was later to call himself Willy Brandt. He proved such a doughty fighter for the Socialist cause that he was elected to the City Council in the same autumn and to the Reichstag in 1924.

The basic problem of the Republic was that it did not contain enough republicans. The majority considered such a form of government, with a cabinet responsible to the Reichstag, unsuitable for German conditions and only accepted it in the face of Allied insistence after defeat. Some of those who believed in the constitution, like Leber, saw the need to get as many key posts as possible into the hands of people whom they could trust. But to do this they had to possess political power, which they could only obtain by allying themselves with other parties whose loyalty was skin-deep. If they refused to take part in such coalitions, they condemned themselves to futility; if they joined in, they had to share responsibility for many government actions of which they disapproved.

Leber took time to come to terms with this position. He began as a fervent Marxist who bitterly attacked all those who compromised their principles. But he decided that the Master's ideas had been too much influenced by the conditions of nineteenth-century England to be valid without modification in twentieth-century Germany. He criticised his leaders for being too absorbed in theory and day-to-day tactics. He criticised his comrades for being unable to speak without notes; 'he who learns to speak off the cuff quickly learns to think off the cuff.' He criticised the party organisation for having become too bureaucratic. By the time men reached the top, they had lost such ability to initiate as they might once have had. He looked for a new approach to the state which would combine democracy, socialism, pragmatism and compassion. Brandt said that he knew how to convince, cajole and, when necessary, to coerce. 'Even in politics, he was a front-line officer.'

This trend to realism was strengthened as he made himself the chief party spokesman on defence. On the one hand he disagreed with the militarist outlook of the Reichswehr and its concept of the non-political soldier (which meant loyalty to Germany rather than to the Republic). He anticipated the Federal Republic by saying that the soldier must be the citizen in uniform (although that would hardly have changed matters much as long as so many of the citizens were anti-democratic). But he saw that, if the socialists wanted to dominate the state, they must realise the need to have force at their command. Pacifism and attacks on the armed forces as an instrument of the possessing classes meant abandoning any attempt to impose their will. If they were to expect loyalty from the troops, they must show sympathy to the desire of those troops for recognition. But this realism won little sympathy and Leber was unable to exercise much influence in the party. He saw that Socialism needed a new programme with wider appeal but he did not himself manage to formulate one. He realised the need for new leaders with more dynamism and the capacity to rouse enthusiasm but he saw nobody among his comrades who had these qualities and doubted whether the party would give such a person the chance to exercise them.

In the circumstances he was not surprised by the rise of the Nazis, although he opposed it pertinaciously. 'When it is a matter of fighting for freedom, one does not ask what is going to happen tomorrow.' The idea of converting Germany into a socialist nation had much appeal for him. He would have been glad to see the Nazis break the power of the big landowners and industrialists. But he failed to foresee what power in Nazi hands would mean. In November 1932 he said that Hitler, if he became Chancellor, could no longer wade in blood but would have to march in the top boots (*Spanische Stiefeln*) of the constitution. His combative nature made it inevitable that this optimism would be disproved on his own person. On the very night of 30 January 1933 he was involved in a brawl in which he was badly beaten up and a Nazi stabbed to death. He was taken to the police station, released and rearrested. On 16 February he was again freed but his injuries were such as to compel him to confine his remarks at a big demonstration three days later to a call for 'Freedom'. But this was not allowed him; on 23 March he was once more arrested as he was about to take his seat in the new Reichstag. He was held in 'protective custody' till July, having in May been condemned to twenty months' imprisonment for his conduct in January. He began to serve his sentence in September but when it ended in 1935 he was again taken into 'protective custody' which in this case meant a concentration camp. Here he was roughly handled and spent three months without bed, chair, table, exercise, warm food or occupation. His final release in March 1937 owed much to the efforts of his wife Annedore whom he had married in 1927 against the wish of her school-teacher father and whom he had often pained by his addiction to wine and women.

It was a condition of his release that he keep away from Lübeck so he set up in Berlin where his neighbour, former Hamburg friend and co-socialist Gustav Dahrendorf (father of Ralf) found him a job as a coal merchant. Annedore meanwhile set up a successful tailoring business. In the winter of 1938–9 he established through Ernst von Harnack, the socialist son of the theologian, contact with Leuschner and Noske and agreed on the need for an all-embracing Popular Front. But beyond a fruitless attempt to enlist the help of General von Falkenhausen (who was to be thought of five years later as a possible successor to Hitler), nothing is known of any active steps he may have taken. However the urge to join in overthrowing the régime grew stronger as its difficulties grew greater. In the autumn of 1943 Harnack brought him into touch with Goerdeler and Mierendorff with Moltke who introduced him to Schulenburg who in turn introduced him around the end of 1943 to Stauffenberg.

He was welcomed by all these men as a representative of the workers who had practical experience in politics. He was repelled by the stress which was laid on his good military record in persuading Beck and Goerdeler to meet him. Although he too had dreamed of a cultural and social Germany which would stretch from Königsberg to Strassburg, Berne to Vienna and Eger to Bözen, he felt that they belonged to another world and generation to him. The Republic may have been a second-best to both sides but the directions in which each wanted to see it reformed were discrepant. He could agree that the results of exact proportional representation had been unfortunate but thought that Goerdeler's idea of indirect election from below would prevent the best men from getting to the top. The role foreseen for the workers in the new state was in his opinion far too modest. But his views made an impression on the others, who earmarked for him the key post of Minister of the Interior.

The ideas of the Kreisau Group might have been expected to have a greater appeal for him than those of Goerdeler but he seems to have found them more patronising than the authors perhaps realised. For him the workers were not merely to be an indispensable pillar of society but the body on which the whole fate of the country rested. There was a further clash over Moltke's idea of replacing employer–employee confrontation at higher levels by delegates chosen by both sides of industry at lower levels. Leber thought that this would impede the ability of the workers to look after their own interests and indeed Moltke wanted them to look after the interests of the country as a whole instead. Moltke considered that he was helping the workers by giving them equal status; Leber wanted a society in which they took the decisions. Mierendorff's *Programme of Socialist Action* (p. 106) corresponded more closely with his ideas and may well have been discussed with him. Mierendorff played a valuable role in reconciling the two points of view so that the situation was not eased when his death in an air raid in December 1943 left Leber as the chief link between Kreisau and the workers.

Moltke came to regard Leber as a 'convincingly good man who at any rate keeps a firm grip on the purely practical and attaches a good deal less importance to things of the mind than I do.' Both men were worried lest the first scheme of government set up after Hitler's overthrow would not be radical enough to have any chance of lasting but merely open the door to Communism. They did not however have as much in common as Leber found with Schulenburg and Stauffenberg, particularly after Moltke's influence had been removed by his arrest in January 1944. All these three had considerable practical experience and were more interested in planning for early action than in thinking about the long-term effects of action upon society. Leber's influence led Stauffenberg to give the workers more attention than he had previously done. The two Counts began to think the man of the people might make a better Chancellor than Goerdeler.

In mid-May at a meeting attended by Leber, Goerdeler, Kaiser, Leuschner and Schulenburg, there was an argument as to whether the attempt on Hitler's life was worth pursuing, especially as it was proving so difficult to bring off. Goerdeler stuck to his view that a separate peace could still be reached with the west, to be followed by a joint defence in the east. Leber, in the light of what he had heard from Trott, argued that the Allies would stick to their demand for unconditional surrender on all fronts simultaneously and that no change of government could stave off a total occupation of the country.

A month later Leber and Goerdeler had another stormy meeting. The successful invasion and the arrest of Staehle during the interval had made the situation more urgent. When Goerdeler repeated his hopes of a separate agreement in the west, Leber said they were based on illusions. The frontiers of 1940 could not be preserved; German negotiators must be prepared to renounce East Prussia, Alsace and the Sudetenland. Leber read proposals for a programme of 'Socialist action', which would seem to have run along the lines of the Mierendorff document. The Goerdeler group attacked the slogan as unduly radical and said it represented an attempt to revive the old policies of the SPD (which it did not). An angry Leber replied that Goerdeler's economic ideas were out-of-date and unduly influenced by heavy industry (which they were not). If the Russians were going to reach Central Europe, there was a risk that they would instal a National Bolshevist German Government on the lines being propagated from Moscow by the National Committee of Free Germany. The best hope of taking the wind out of their sails would be to obtain as wide support as possible for a Popular Front, a radical *Volksbewegung* which would obtain the adherence of the Communists in Germany. For this reason he favoured making an early approach to the Communists. They alone in his view could counterbalance the Army in the new state whereas the Socialist organisation had withered away. Leber then announced that, in the event of a military collapse, he would no longer consider himself committed to the plans which had been agreed. He was not prepared to sacrifice vital principles for the sake of unity. Against this background, a second meeting on the same day discussed the wisdom of establishing contact with the Communists. Leber's attitude was that he would join forces with anybody if he could thereby bring about Hitler's overthrow. What happened afterwards could be left to look after itself provided that the will to establish tolerable conditions of life was upheld.[2] Although the decision against making contact was attributed to considerations of security, there can be little doubt that considerations of policy played their part.

The question came up again however at a meeting in Yorck's house on 21 June. Leber reported a request for a meeting which he had received from two Communists known to him from life together in the concentration camp. Most of those present thought that the danger of being caught was too great. Communists were apt to get out of prison by agreeing to act as informers and their groups were particularly liable to infiltration by the SD. Stauffenberg was not there and his views are uncertain. Leber thought that this particular pair were to be trusted and he and Reichwein decided to take the risk. A meeting was held next day at the house of Reichwein's doctor, Rudolf Schmidt. Three Communists, Saefkow, Jacob and Rambow, turned up instead of the agreed two. No explanation of Rambow's addition has ever been forthcoming and it is now generally accepted that he was a spy (although it is possible that he or one of the others was already being followed by the authorities). The Communists claimed to be able to speak for their comrades inside Germany but to have no contact with those 'over there' (i.e. the NKFD). They declared themselves ready to join any alliance which would bring about the fall of the Fascist dictatorship. This would afford an opportunity to organise legally. After an interval a fresh form would be given to German politics. When Leber asked about democracy and private property, he got the answer that these would be permitted, subject to the abolition of big business and large estates. The Communists sought but were refused information about the nature and timing of the proposed assault on Hitler.

The Communist attitude was more conciliatory than had been expected, which roused Leber's suspicions. Reichwein however considered that it justified another meeting, to take place twelve days later on 4 July at a railway station (since Schmidt was going on holiday). But when he arrived at the rendezvous, he was arrested, as were the Communists. Leber was seized at his office next day. Stauffenberg was not merely anxious to rescue a friend from torture but did not wish to be without his services or allow the Gestapo to extract compromising information. Through a friend, he sent to Annedore a bunch of red roses and a message that he would 'do his duty'. It was another reason why the attempt had to be staged on 20 July.

Leber was passed through five prisons before he was tried by Freisler in the People's Court on 24 October. He was seriously beaten up and realised that his chances of survival were slim. Paul Sethe, an anti-Nazi journalist who was at the trial, wrote after the war

The man who stood before the powerful and angry Freisler had done more than merely discuss whether the war was lost. He had sought to overthrow the government and admitted as much. He had long known what his fate would be but instead of appearing nervous, he was calm and patient. He listened carefully to what his enemy said and then answered in a soft, clear and unhesitating voice. . . . Freisler's aim is to humiliate his victim and destroy him morally. He risks being reproached for cowardice. Will Leber bluster? Will he lose his temper in defending himself? And then be promptly shouted down, abused yet again, forced to shut up? No, the accused listens calmly to the outbursts and answers with composure, 'That is a mistake, Mr President, in reality it was like this.' It gradually emerges that in this duel of wits the positions are being reversed. The man sitting up there in his red robe begins to give way, to lose confidence, to run out of steam. He seems disconcerted, exhausted, vexed. He is still the man in authority. But the man who turns round and goes slowly back to the dock is the real victor. Isolated in the hall, his only friends accused alongside him, equally powerless. Everywhere he looks he sees hostile opponents, judges, lawyers, policemen, SS. He is facing certain death. Yet in the end he has outplayed his enemy.

When the sentence is pronounced, Julius Leber does not give his opponents the pleasure of seeing him wince. He stares into the distance, far beyond the walls of the court. The world will never know what his thoughts were but when the policemen take him away, he stands as upright as ever. We can be sure that he will walk the same way when he goes on his last journey, to a painful and bitter death.

Before he was executed on 5 January, he managed to convey to his friends the message that the cause was sufficiently just and good to be worth spending one's life for it. 'We have done all it was in our power to do. It is not our fault that things have happened as they have and not otherwise.'

14 Wilhelm Leuschner[1]

Leuschner was born in Bayreuth in 1890, the son of a stove-fitter. He was trained as a wood-carver, making dishes, lamps, tombstones and ornaments for furniture. He spent a term at the Academy of Graphic Art at Nuremburg where he won first-class marks. He turned himself into a competent black-and-white artist and kept up an interest in art history; during a spell in 'protective custody' at the beginning of the war he spent the time reading a book on Tilman Riemenschneider. He could speak French and English.

In 1911 he got a job in a furniture factory in Darmstadt, the centre of the *Jugendstil*, and soon became the District Leader of the Carvers' Union. During the war he was called up but graded unfit for front-line service. Afterwards his small guild became absorbed in the Woodworkers' Union and his own union activities developed, especially in wage negotiations. In 1923 he became chairman of the Darmstadt branch of the General German Trade Union (ADGB). He had joined the Social Democrats in 1914 and ten years later obtained a seat in the Hessian *Landtag*. In 1926 he became City Treasurer for Darmstadt and two years later Minister of the Interior for Hesse. After a year in office, he proposed a thoroughgoing rationalisation of the complicated political boundaries of the Rhine–Main area, to produce something like the post-war state of Greater Hesse. At the end of 1931 he and his friend Carlo Mierendorff, who was working as his Press Officer, obtained and published the minutes of a meeting which Werner Best and other Nazis had held at the Boxheim Hotel near Worms; it contained plans for seizing power and making radical changes (including the murder of opponents) on the pretext that the Communists were going to win an election. The High Court dismissed the ensuing charge of high treason for alleged lack of evidence but the episode did not endear the prosecutors to National Socialism.

By the end of 1932 it was clear that sooner or later the Nazis would come to power in Hesse and Leuschner looked round for a fresh job. On 21 January 1933 he was appointed Deputy-chairman of the ADGB and simultaneously representative of the German Trade Unions in the International Labour Office in Geneva. The hope was that the ILO would help the ADGB to ward off Nazi attacks. Leuschner was actually in Geneva on 30 January. He sought to unite the ADGB with the Catholic and Liberal unions and to relax their links with the SPD. His hope was that the creation of a single union would satisfy the Nazis' desire for co-ordination and induce them to leave the movement in peace. But they were not prepared to accept a body which was non-political and closed down the entire union structure on 2 May 1933.

Leuschner was arrested along with all other ADGB officials. Leipart, the elderly chairman, collapsed under the treatment he received and the members of the executive committee, while they were all still in custody, agreed that Leuschner should replace him. Ley, the Reich Organisation Leader of the NSDAP, was also head of the German Labour Front (DAF) and as such representative of the Nazi Government at the ILO. Before he could appear there, however, he had to be recommended by Leuschner. Leuschner agreed to go to Geneva on condition that he and his colleagues were released but on arriving there kept his mouth significantly shut in all plenary meetings, while making clear to the other delegates through informal contacts what the true position was. Ley had a frigid reception from the other unions, particularly the French, lost his temper in public and went home early. In the following October he saw to it that Germany walked out of the ILO as well as of the League of Nations. Leuschner was pressed to stay in Switzerland but said that his duty lay at home. He was arrested on re-entering Germany.

After four months in prison in Hesse, Leuschner was taken in November 1933 to a camp at Börgermoor on the desolate marshes near the North Sea and the Dutch frontier. It was here that the 'Song of the Moor Soldiers', a classic of the *Widerstand*, was written by two prisoners. But after a month he was moved to Torgau on the Elbe, where eleven and a half years later the Russian and American armies would meet. After six more months the authorities released him in order to avoid hostile comment at the 1934 conference of the ILO.

When war was impending in 1939, Leuschner wrote to an English trade unionist

> Tell our friends that we still are what we used to be. But we are completely incapable of preventing the catastrophe. We are prisoners in a great penitentiary. To rebel would be as suicidal as would be a rising by prisoners against their heavily-armed warders.

But while he saw no immediate chance of revolution from within, he remained convinced that National Socialism would not last indefinitely. He therefore regarded it as his duty to keep alive the idea of a single trade union and to keep the people who would be its officials in touch with one another so that when the moment came they could move quickly to take over. He himself founded a small factory in Berlin for making beer-barrel taps. This business gave him a good pretext for travelling all over Germany, visiting in particular the inns which local unionists had used as meeting-places. He further got an exclusive licence for using a special non-corrosive type of non-ferrous metal. Screws made of this rapidly became important for types of naval and air armaments, enabling him to invoke the help of the armed forces if anyone threatened to interfere with his production. He established good connections with the DAF which had to some extent been infiltrated by former trade unionists, and thus got access to confidential documents. When in 1938 the Gestapo wanted to know why he travelled so much, he was able to give a perfectly satisfactory answer without revealing anything connected with his secret political activities. He was adamant that nothing should be committed to writing; once when he saw Goerdeler beginning to take notes in a meeting, he walked out. His experience as Interior Minister had taught him how much help leaflets gave to the police in tracking opponents and as a result strenuously opposed their use. But one result of this emphasis on word-of-mouth communication is that few documents survive to testify to all that he did.

At first he favoured letting the Nazi system dig its own grave so that everyone could see what it led to. But as the war went on, he increasingly felt the need for action to bring the human suffering which it caused, particularly in the industrial areas, to an end as soon as possible. In September 1938 he was in touch with Heinz, the ex-Freikorps officer whom Oster had commissioned to capture and kill Hitler (p. 162), with a view to backing up that event by calling a general strike. But the experience of 1918 made him opposed to working-class action until the soldiers had committed themselves to the revolution; he was not going to have his companions accused again of stabbing their country in the back. He doubted in any case whether they would answer the call for a general strike until the régime was in real difficulty. He thought a general strike was a defensive weapon, to be used only in the last resort, rather than an offensive one.

He met Beck in the autumn of 1939, Goerdeler in the following summer and Moltke in December 1941. His influence led Goerdeler to give the workers a more important place in the plans than they would otherwise have received.

Whereas Goerdeler was inclined to retain the DAF as a system which would include both employers and employees from the lowest level, Leuschner insisted that the workers must have an organisation of their own but one which was united instead of being (as hitherto) fragmented. He deserves some of the credit for the success of trade unions in the Federal Republic. His basic aim for the workers was equality of social status, which he believed could be achieved by better education as much as by redistribution of wealth. He wanted central supervision of the economic system combined with local self-management. He was sympathetic to the idea of a corporate state (*Ständestaat*) with three 'estates' of workers, peasants and bourgeoisie. He would even have been prepared to go along with Goerdeler's idea of making the Kaiser's grandson Prince Louis Ferdinand Head of State, if the latter had been ready to accept the post. Moltke referred to him by the cover-name of 'the Uncle' and they had arguments, in which Mierendorff acted as intermediary, as to the relative merits of unions and works councils. In the later months, he left relations with the Kreisau Group increasingly to his assistant Maas who did not carry much weight in that quarter. He hoped to see the SPD develop after the war as it has in fact done, as a *Volkspartei* based on concept rather than class. On security grounds, he refused all approaches made to him by Communists and advised Leber to do the same. The intention was that he should become Vice-Chancellor.

During 20 July he was unaware of what was going on. Afterwards he tried to go into hiding in Berlin but had difficulty in finding anyone who would give him lasting shelter. He was betrayed by a female neighbour on 16 August, brought to trial on 7–8 September and executed on the 29th. His last message was 'Create unity' leaving those who received it free to decide whether the unity should be in the unions, in the Reich or among mankind – possibly even in all three.

15 Adolf Reichwein[1]

Reichwein was born in 1898 in north-west Germany, the son of a primary school teacher. As a boy he was active in the democratic Youth Movement (*Wandervögel*). He volunteered for military service as soon as he left school in 1916. On one occasion when he was ordered to join in an execution squad, he asked to be posted elsewhere, an act which was regarded as open disobedience and punished severely. In December 1917 a wound put him out of action for the rest of the war. He then studied history, philosophy and economics at Frankfurt and Marburg, and took a doctorate in 1923 with a thesis on the influence of China on Europe in the eighteenth century. Like many other young Germans of his time he wanted to bridge the gap between the middle and working classes. In 1921 he organised a camp which brought both sides together.

In 1923 he was put in charge of a new *Volkshochschule* in Jena where the firm of Zeiss were making enlightened provision for their younger employees. He was clearly an inspired teacher, arousing the interest of his students in their work and carrying them along with him. In 1926 his 2-year-old son was drowned and as a result his marriage broke up. He got a grant to visit the United States round which he travelled in a second-hand Ford. By dint of working as a seaman, he went on to China and Japan. On arriving home, he put the fruits of his research into a 639-page book on 'The Raw Material Resources of the World' – an early contribution to the North–South discussion.

He went back to Jena but in 1927 C. H. Becker, the non-party Prussian Minister of Culture and most distinguished German educationalist between the wars, asked him to work as a Personal Assistant, with special reference to teacher training. In 1928 he joined the editorial board of the periodical which was being founded by Paul Tillich and other religious Socialists, although he was by no means a conventional Christian.

In 1930 political difficulties caused Becker to resign and Reichwein left as well, to become Professor of History and Civics at the Teacher Training Academy at Halle, a type of institution which he had helped Becker to set up and which concentrated on a *studium generale* rather than specialised courses. In that autumn, having previously refused to adopt any party label, he joined the SPD as a gesture of solidarity with the workers, after the September 1930 election had suggested that the tide was turning against them. He never however took much share in party affairs nor was he involved in the trade unions. In today's terms, he would undoubtedly have been a 'Green'.

In 1931 he was foreseeing a period of 'overwintering'.[2] Unfortunately he underestimated the length of the cold spell. He was dismissed in April 1933, just after he had married again, but refused to emigrate because he did not want to cut himself off from his fellow-countrymen in what was going to be a difficult and decisive time. Instead he was allowed to become a primary school teacher at the little village of Tiefensee 40 miles east of Berlin. He sold the aeroplane which had given him three years of adventure, partly because he would otherwise have had to put a swastika on it, and bought a car to keep himself in touch with the outside world. He was able to put into practice his ideas about teaching, which made it, instead of being a matter of instruction, a process of helping children to use their own initiative to acquire information and experience. He emphasised the importance of conveying ideas visually by picture and film. He took his classes on frequent trips outside their village. As this shows, he was ahead of his time.

Yet in 1939 he left Tiefensee to become head of the Department for School and Museum at the Berlin Museum for German Folklore. He also accepted responsibility for a daily half-hour programme on the Educational Radio. It may seem surprising that the Nazis should have been prepared to give such a job to someone who made it clear that he was not one of themselves, especially as regards the rights and duties of the individual. But he had never up to that point engaged in any organised hostile activity and he was a master of a subject to which they attached great sentimental importance. His move to Berlin however may have been motivated by a feeling that a time was coming when he would want to be nearer the centre of things.

Although exact dates are lacking, he met up again about this time with Moltke and Mierendorff, whom he had admired in the early 1920s and now brought together. He ranked sixth in order of mention in Moltke's letters between June 1940 and January 1944, being at first the chief contact for the Kreisau Group with the workers. He was also the group's chief adviser on education. He attended two out of the three gatherings at Kreisau (where his wife and children were later given shelter after being bombed out in Berlin). He also allowed his office in the museum to be frequently used as a contact point. Since he left behind no papers on these activities, never mentioned politics in his letters and asked his correspondents to follow suit, it is impossible to tell exactly what his contributions to the discussions were. But it is likely that he played a large part in getting acceptance for the idea that state schools in the new Germany should be compulsory for all children and have religion as a common subject. He also pressed the case for his type of training academies for teachers but did not convince his companions. He was earmarked to become the new Minister of Culture.

More generally, he is likely to have been among those who wanted to reverse the trend towards centralisation, but instead to give as much freedom and responsibility as possible to the individual and the small community. He agreed with Mierendorff's *Programme of Socialist Action*, a phrase which he had himself used as early as 1932. Although his background was different from Leber's, they were both convinced Socialists – his own version was later described as having been 'emphatic and almost bitter'. He had for long been opposed to murdering Hitler but in the summer of 1944 gradually became resigned to the view that Nazism could not otherwise be overthrown from within. As he was wont to say, 'There is no way of evading decisions.'[3]

Reichwein once described Soviet Russia as 'the great and powerful land of the future without which or against which a European policy will be impossible.'[4] He thought Communism too materialistic and dictatorial. But he had had a number of Communist friends during his life and considered it so important to establish contact with the underground party that he was prepared to take risks. He seems to have established contact, perhaps through Communists in Jena, with a Berlin group in the autumn of 1943. A friend said that his guilelessness was sometimes alarming[5] – perhaps it was more a refusal to apply to others standards lower than his own. It led however to catastrophe, as has been described (p. 199). But even if he had not been arrested on 4 July, he almost certainly would have been at the end of the month.

He was severely tortured and at his trial on 20 October could not speak above a whisper. He was executed the same afternoon.

16 Anton Saefkow[1]

Saefkow was born in Berlin in 1905, of working-class parents. His wife Aenna was also a Communist. Little else is known about his private life.

In 1919 as an apprentice he led a strike in his factory. He joined the Communist Party in 1924 and was elected to the Young Communist Central Committee in 1927. In 1926 he was sacked from his job on returning from the annual meeting of his union and thereafter became a party official, first in Leipzig, then in the Ruhr and finally in the Elbe ports. In 1932 he became a deputy in the Prussian *Landtag*. In April 1933 he was arrested in Hamburg and condemned to two years' imprisonment; on being released, he was sent to Dachau. In 1936 he was condemned to a further two and a half years in prison for having organised a memorial meeting for a friend murdered by the Nazis.

Just before war broke out, he was released along with a number of other Communists. He found the Russo-German Pact something of a puzzle which he solved by emphasising that both parties to it were out to fight imperialism. If the German authorities had imagined that its conclusion would modify his attitude to them, they were mistaken. While working as a driver for a car-hire firm (which helped him to travel about) he managed to establish contact with the Schulze-Boysen organisation and with a Berlin Communist group led by Robert Uhrig, which is said to have numbered 200. The latter was infiltrated in February 1942, six months before the former was run to earth. Saefkow's network then became the biggest in Berlin, if not in Germany as a whole. At about the same time a Communist group in Hamburg which had been led by Franz Jacob (at one time Thälmann's secretary) and Bernard Bästlein was broken up. Jacob fled to Berlin where he managed to live illegally; Bästlein was sent to be imprisoned in the same city but early in 1944 escaped during an air raid. The two of them joined with Saefkow to form an approximation to a Central Committee. Cells were established in 30 of the main factories, links made with Magdeburg, Leipzig, Dresden and Hamburg and over 1000 workers recruited. Contact was also achieved with Communists in Sachsenhausen and other camps.

The German attack on Russia in 1941 enabled Communists to view the world through their traditional spectacles once more. But the establishment in 1943 of the National Committee of Free Germany confused the issues again for Saefkow and his colleagues. It represented in fact a return to the Popular Front policy which had been pursued in the late 1930s during the Spanish Civil War. But Saefkow and the others had been in prison at that time and had only a rough idea of what the party line had been. Communication with Moscow was almost impossible although a tenuous and indirect contact was set up through Sweden. Various agents who had been landed by parachute were quickly caught. Although those inside Germany talked of themselves as the 'Berlin Committee of the NKFD', it is unlikely that they had been formally constituted as such. The intentions of the Moscow leadership had to be deduced by analysing the NKFD propaganda. The prospect of having to reach a common front with Socialists was tolerable since the damage done to both parties by their quarrels before 1933 was widely recognised. But to work with officers and nationalists was at first repugnant. Jacob however said that 'things have now reached a point at which we are ready to conclude a pact with the devil himself.'[2]

In these circumstances Saefkow and his comrades devised a line which came close to what we can guess to have been Moscow's intentions. They stressed the paramount need to overthrow National Socialism, which they recognised that they could not hope to do on their own. All hands held out must therefore be grasped. The main immediate target of illegal work must be to recruit as many *Widerstandskämpfer* as possible and to persuade the most promising of them to become Communists. With this in view, a number of contacts were made in cultural circles. Jacob talked to various Catholic priests and members of the middle class. During the winter of 1943–4 a group in Leipzig led by Schumann made contact indirectly with Stauffenberg and Goerdeler.

But the workers still aimed at getting into a position where they could control everything which went on. Accordingly the most important long-term task was to mobilise the workers in the factories. As long as Nazi rule lasted, the Party should be kept small – NCOs rather than rank-and-file. For security reasons the organisation was based on cells of three, only one of whom knew which other workers in the factory were Communists. The contact men from the various cells were in turn to form *Kampfgruppen*, with only one man from each group being in touch with the Central Liberating Committee.

Members of the organisation were given the following tasks:

(*a*) The communication of news and instructions by word of mouth and still more by leaflets since these were evidence that an organisation existed.

(*b*) Sabotage, whether by wasting time and materials or producing defective goods.

(*c*) Contact with soldiers, especially those at the front, urging them to build up groups of the dissatisfied. Soldiers were not to desert individually and only to surrender in groups where this would hasten military developments. The main aim should be to have units which could make an orderly retreat into Germany and there form the core of a new People's Army. Petrol supplies were to be sabotaged.

(*c*) Contact with prisoners-of-war and foreign workers, both to encourage sabotage and reduce hatred of Germans collectively.

(*e*) Contact with peasants in the hope of producing a situation similar to that in Russia in 1917. It was recognised that Nazi land policy had induced many peasants to support the régime.

(*f*) Combatting the fear that the Russians would shoot or maltreat their prisoners, or send all Germans to Siberia. 'We shall not be able to escape responsibility for having supported the war for so long. But Germany will always exist because Europe cannot live without her.'

(g) Maintaining contact between the dozen or so groups existing throughout Germany.

The leadership continued to talk as though Germany's ultimate political form would be Communist. 'We are putting off the propounding of our socialist solution till the time when Germany's internal condition has advanced from the stage of development to that of action.'[3] The Communists inside Germany were more frank about this being the long-term objective than were those controlling the NKFD. But no matter how much was said or not said, the non-Communist left in Germany were well aware of what was likely to be attempted. Indeed the Communists could not cease to work for radical social revolution without abandoning their raison d'être. Yet the knowledge that it was their aim was bound to impede collaboration with those who did not share it.

Loose rather than intimate contacts with Social Democrats were a constituent part of this policy which explains why they welcomed Reichwein's approach in the autumn of 1943. The meetings arranged for 22 June 1944 and 4 July were a cautious step towards making common cause with the military conspirators. Saefkow and Jacob were tried on 10 August and executed, along with Bästlein, on 18 September. Saefkow's fellow-prisoners managed to procure paper and a pencil so that he could write his political testament with fettered hands. They then learnt the various paragraphs by heart and reconstructed the text after being liberated by Soviet troops on 27 April 1945. The main items of the testament were:

> 1. Root out Fascism. Factories belonging to Nazi Party members or war criminals are to be nationalised at once. Those responsible for Fascism and war must be made to pay compensation to the full extent of their means.
> 2. The factories are to be taken over by the workers, who must have power to make decisions and give orders. If the people are to rule, they must be armed. Organise an armed militia, with which to protect their representatives.
> 3. Allow only a single union and have only one branch in each factory.
> 4. Build the new Germany on people's committees.
> 5. The future belongs to the proletariat as the developing working class. Build your power up step-by-step and never relinquish it. If we Communists are to restrain our long-term aims for the time being, we will never give them up. Once the proletariat has constituted itself the ruling class, all the rest is merely a question of time.
> The German people have gone through hard times, but the hardest of all are still to come. Yet I say look forward with courage.[4]

Thälmann, the former Communist leader, who had been in captivity since 1933, was shot in Buchenwald camp on 18 August 1944. Twenty-four leading Communists were killed at Sachsenhausen in October. The liquidation of the Saefkow group is said to have involved 450 executions. The number of executions during the first three months of 1945 has been put at 1800.[5] It is hardly surprising that Communist activity came virtually to an end until Allied troops arrived, although a group in Saxony survived by doing no more than passing on news by word of mouth.

17 Harro Schulze-Boysen[1]

Schulze-Boysen was born in 1909, the son of a naval officer who was a nephew of Admiral von Tirpitz (and thus a first cousin of Tirpitz's daughter, Frau von Hassell). His mother, Marie Louise Boysen, belonged to a professional family in Flensburg. When only 14 he took part in underground resistance to the French occupation of the Ruhr. In revulsion against his middle-class background, he became involved in a right-wing nationalist movement, only to swing two years later to the left. In 1932–3 he worked for a periodical called 'Opponent' (*Gegner*) which was national-revolutionary but anti-Nazi and subsidised by the Russian Embassy. As a result, he found himself subjected in April 1933 to treatment in a concentration camp to which one of his companions succumbed. When, thanks to his mother's influence, he emerged, he joined what was still the clandestine Air Force. One of his passions was for sailing and in pursuing it on Berlin's Wannsee in 1935 he met a girl called Libertas Haas-Heye who was a granddaughter of the Kaiser's favourite Philipp Count zu Eulenburg; a year later they married. His mother was a friend of Göring's, who attended the wedding and helped to find Harro a job in the Press Section of the now overt Air Ministry. Libertas encouraged his appetite for living dangerously and fidelity was not a prominent feature of their ménage.

Harro had long thought that Hitler was heading for war and by 1938 was forecasting its outbreak in 1940–1 at the latest. In the years since 1933 he had acquired a group of literary and artistic friends whose sympathies were Communist even if they were not party members. From 1936 onwards he engaged steadily in the drafting and distribution of anti-Nazi leaflets, to which he soon added the unsolicited supply to the Russian Trade Delegation of information about Air Force activities in the Spanish Civil War. This service was soon discovered and consequently suspended but not before its author had aroused the interest of Russian Intelligence. They put him in touch in 1939 with another group centred round Arvid Harnack, a nephew of the theologian (and cousin of Ernst, p. 197) who had a post in the Economics Ministry and a radical American wife Mildred. Schulze-Boysen assumed the leadership while Harnack tried rather ineffectively to make him pay more attention to the need for caution in conspiracy. At least three other groups were joined up in what were not regular Communist cells nor under the orders of the Central Committee – Schulze-Boysen was not the kind of man who would take orders from anyone. Of the total 20 per cent are said to have been professional soldiers and civil servants, 21 per cent artists, writers and journalists, 13 per cent workers and 29 per cent academics and students.

Schulze-Boysen had in the meanwhile managed to get himself moved from the Press Section to the Attaché Group in Air Force Headquarters, which handled all the reports sent in by Air Attachés in German missions abroad, and then to the section concerned with intelligence about the enemy. He got access to and copied a number of reports. The contents were passed, along with information collected from other sources, to Moscow via the Trade Delegation which in mid-June 1941, foreseeing what was coming, provided him with three wireless transmitters. Many of Schulze-Boysen's collaborators had qualms about making it easier for the enemy to kill German soldiers. Any which he may have had himself were swept aside by indignation at a régime which had brought catastrophe on Germany and Europe as well as making the German Reich a synonym for barbarity and injustice. (He does not seem to have noticed, or at any rate been worried by, the Soviet record in this respect.) To a sceptical friend he said, 'If the Russians come to Germany, as they will, and if they have a role to play here, there has got to be a proof that there was a genuine *Widerstand*. Otherwise they can do what they like with us.'

His aim was to bring about, by one means or another, a Communist state in which he would hold the post of Minister of War. He expected the opportunity to come in 1943. In preparation for that time the various sections of the German public must be made to look into the future and realise that the military position was hopeless. Between July 1941 and the autumn of 1942 his group produced once or twice a month an underground newspaper, *Die Innere Front*, with a circulation of 600 copies. It on one occasion claimed that 'the inspired strategy of Stalin, the heroism of the Red Army and the resistance of Soviet workers have broken the backbone of Hitler's army.' He had no use for plots against Hitler's life, any more than he had for those who were trying to make life more bearable in occupied Russia.

The weak point of the set-up lay in the communications with Moscow. There was only one operator for the three transmitting sets and he was inadequately trained. Inevitably the authorities detected the transmissions and tried to pinpoint the source. As a precaution the sets were used in irregular order and at varying times; this led to messages in both directions going unreceived. In the crucial autumn of 1941 the recipients in Moscow became afraid that valuable information was failing to reach them. Never very security conscious, they now made the elementary mistake of instructing their second agent in Europe, a Russian known as Kent who worked from Brussels, to go to three named addresses in Berlin and discover why communications were faulty. This he did and put things back in order, only for them to break down again soon afterwards since the security monitors were hot on the track. Meanwhile the message from Moscow to Brussels was being worked on by the SD. It took them nine months to break the cypher and they then held their hands for six weeks in order to find out as much as possible about the group (to which they gave the name of *Rote Kapelle*, Red Orchestra) and thus ensure a clean sweep when they did finally close in. At the end of August 1942 however a member of the group who was inside the security monitoring service learnt of the interception from a talkative colleague and realised the danger. He tried to telephone Schulze-Boysen, who was not at home, and then left a message asking him to call back. By the time he did, the monitor had gone home and the call was taken by a senior officer to whom the name of the caller meant a lot. He guessed that the group knew they had been betrayed and were likely to scatter; the Gestapo moved without more ado and on 30 August Schulze-Boysen was arrested. Before his execution on 20 December he wrote to his parents that 'it is an old European custom that mental harvests are sown with blood',[2] while he left a verse hidden in his cell

> The final argument is not
> Ended by rope or axe
> And Judgment Day will give a chance
> To get the verdict changed.

Libertas was induced by an apparently sympathetic typist in the Gestapo office to reveal numerous names. She was not the only one to do so although others, particularly the Communist Party members, remained obdurate; 118 arrests were made and about 55 people, including 19 women, met their death for having been involved.

There has been much controversy as to whether Schulze-Boysen was a hero or a traitor. Correspondingly emphasis has concentrated either on his propagandist or his espionage activities. But it is clear that he regarded both as part and parcel of a single endeavour. And, although Germans have always distinguished *Hochverrat* from *Landesverrat* (p. 70), it is not clear why desiring the defeat of one's country in war is less reprehensible than taking active steps to bring it about. If the argument is that supplying information to the other side (which the supplier does not of course himself regard as 'the enemy') makes it easier for them to kill one's own compatriots, Schulze-Boysen could have replied that if he could shorten the war, he would reduce the numbers killed on both sides.

But did he in fact have any effect on the course of the war? There is no evidence that his propagandist activities inside Germany changed anybody's mind. The most important information which he supplied to the Russians – his warning of the impending German attack – was also provided by 82 other sources and disregarded. None of his other messages seem to have had anything like as much value as Sorge's information about Japanese intentions in December 1941 (p. 73). At best he merely supplemented what the Russians were learning from elsewhere and he did not save them from false appreciations.

The general issue of treachery has already been discussed in Chapter IV and will be dealt with again in Part III. Here it is perhaps sufficient to say that, although revolution is not necessarily immoral, the morality of revolutionaries must be judged by the quality of the régime which they wish to introduce.

18 Martin Niemöller[1]

Niemöller was born in 1892, the son of a Lutheran pastor in Westphalia. When he was 18 he became like many of his family a naval cadet and during the war saw service like Canaris with submarines in the Mediterranean. He left the Navy in 1918 after rejecting an order to take two vessels for surrender to the British. In 1920 he decided to be ordained and almost literally 'starved his way' through a training course at Münster University. During Communist troubles in the Ruhr in the next year, he commanded a battalion of the 'Academic Defence Corps'. He voted for the German National People's Party until in 1924 he transferred his allegiance to the National Socialists. He repeatedly stressed Germany's need for a leader and was a pall-bearer at the funeral of Schlageter, a young man whom the French shot for sabotage and whom the Nazis thereupon made into a martyr. For eight years from 1923 as manager of the Westphalian Home Mission he ran a chain of Christian social institutions throughout the province. In 1931 he came to Dahlem, the Berlin parish which was the richest in Germany, as its third pastor. Six months later he succeeded to the top post.

When the 'Young Reformers' movement began (p. 38), Niemöller joined them and within a week found himself on the managing committee. He was prominent in the effort to prevent Müller from being chosen as Reich Bishop. In the July election Dahlem was the only parish in Berlin and Westphalia the only province in Germany where the German Christians did not win a majority. Niemöller accepted defeat and helped to draft the first clause of the new Church constitution, which said that 'the Gospel of Jesus Christ was the unalterable foundation of the German Evangelical Church revealed in Holy Scripture and presented in a fresh light by the Confessions of the Reformation'.[2] The burning question was whether the views of the German Christians were, as they claimed, compatible with this basis. Niemöller, although not a profound thinker, saw that the best way to decide this question was to reformulate the faith in terms related to the problems of the day and see whether the German Christians were prepared to accept it.[3] But the first attempt to do this was frustrated by the inability of the remainder of the Protestants in Germany to agree on such a reformulation (p. 218).

Meanwhile the German Christians had been using their majority to oppress their opponents and in particular to dismiss non-Aryan pastors. Niemöller (after trying in vain to get two older men to take a lead) wrote to 2000 pastors on the mailing list of the Young Reformers inviting them to join a Pastors' Emergency League (*Pfarrernotbund*). Membership involved standing firm on the principle that the Bible and Confessions were the foundation of faith; protesting against anyone or anything which departed from that principle (as the application of the Aryan clause was said to do); and accepting responsibility for anyone suffering as a result. Niemöller ended his appeal for signatures by saying he was aware that the League would not rescue the Church or move the world 'but I am equally aware that we owe a debt to the Lord of the Church and to our brethren to do what stands in our power to do at present and that today cautious restraint amounts to failure since our brotherly support will be lacking to those who are oppressed.'⁴ While over 7000 signatures were obtained, only five men in senior positions joined the League. The telegram which Niemöller so soon afterwards sent congratulating Hitler on leaving the League of Nations was not, as might at first sight appear, inconsistent with his initiative over the other League but a sign that he still held to his nationalist political views and only differed on questions of Church government and the Aryan clause.

Needless to say Niemöller played a leading part in compelling the Reich Bishop to condemn the German Christian views which had been expounded at the *Sportpalast* (p. 38), to dismiss Hossenfelder and to resign as President of the German Christians. Müller retaliated with a 'Muzzling Decree' which forbade the introduction of Church politics into religious services and criticism of the Church leadership. He also, without consulting the people concerned, surrendered to the Hitler Youth control over the youth work which the Church had been doing. These actions and the alarm which not only foreign churchmen but also President Hindenburg had been showing at Müller's behaviour encouraged his opponents, including not merely the Pastors' League but also the three South German Churches which had hitherto held aloof, to think that they could persuade Hitler, at a meeting which had been organised for 25 January, to make a change of policy. Göring who was also at the meeting read out the intercept of a telephone call which Niemöller had made just before coming to it. Speaking off the cuff, he had made himself sound as though his aim was to drive a wedge between Hindenburg and Hitler. When he defended himself by saying that his only concern was the welfare of the Church, State and German people, Hitler replied, 'You confine yourself to the Church, I'll take care of the German people.' As Niemöller was going out, he went up to the Führer and said, 'We too, as Christians and churchmen, have a responsibility to the German people which was entrusted to us by God. Neither you nor anyone else in the world has the power to take it from us.'⁵ Such plain speaking was unusual in the Third Reich, although typical of the man, and his companions reproached him afterwards for having strengthened Müller's position. What he certainly had done was to excite Hitler's lasting animosity. On 26 January Niemöller was suspended from office and on 10 February superannuated. As his parishioners backed him however he was able to continue functioning.

He himself had compared the Hitler interview with the Battle of Jutland, where it had only become clear afterwards which side had won. This view seemed justified in the following April when Müller was misguided enough to turn against Wurm of Württemberg, who had bent over backwards to be conciliatory, and thus provoke the meeting of Protestants from all over Germany at Ulm (p. 39) which led on to the foundation of the Confessing Church. It was the Council of Brethren set up at Ulm which convened the Synod at Barmen. Niemöller, who once claimed that he had never read any of Barth's books, did not play a leading part in producing the Barmen Declaration but he defended it when accused by a National Socialist theologian of disturbing the German Churches by teaching false doctrines. When a further Synod in October 1934, held in Niemöller's own parish of Dahlem, declared the Confessing Church to be the only legal one in Germany and commissioned the Council of Brethren to act on its behalf, he was one of the six members of the Executive Committee which the Council set up.

But within two months the edifice collapsed as the moderates swung round to co-operation with the Government and the new Committee turned into a Provisional Church Government with Marahrens of Hanover, the weakest of the South German Bishops, in the chair. For two and a half years Niemöller fought obstinately on, denouncing official interference in Church affairs, denying that the doctrines of race were compatible with Christianity and defying the steps taken to shut him up. He was put in prison five times for short spells. In January 1936 a pamphlet 'The State Church is here' was published under his name although written by the deposed General Superintendent of the Prussian Church Otto Dibelius (the man who had preached at the Potsdam Garrison Church in March 1933, p. 27). Five months later he had a hand in composing a letter of protest to Hitler (although not in leaking it to the Swiss press with disastrous consequences, p. 41). The authorities, although their personnel and their tactics changed at intervals, remained implacable, determined to win for the Nazi state the unquestioning support of a united Evangelical Church. The number of pastors under one form of constraint or another gradually rose. In between the two extremes, the moderates tried to avoid confrontation only to find that their efforts met with no lasting official concessions. As they were not prepared to surrender completely, they too were harassed.

In June 1937 Dibelius, who had written an open letter denouncing attempts to dictate faith by state decree, was put on trial. Over fifty prominent churchmen were arrested and finally on 1 July Hitler ordered Niemöller himself to be detained. Imprisonment came in fact as a relief, since he no longer had the responsibility for leadership.[6] By November over 700 pastors were in captivity. Dibelius however was acquitted and when Niemöller came up for trial in February 1938, the judges showed enough independence to decide that the seven months which he had already spent in prison were ample punishment for the minor offences which were all they considered him to have committed. But Hitler, who had just removed Blomberg, Fritsch and Neurath, and was about to occupy Austria, was in a mood to defy the outside world. He immediately revenged himself by having Niemöller placed in 'protective custody' as his personal prisoner (since the Minister of Justice and others were unwilling to have any more formal legal action taken against him). He remained behind bars, at first in solitude at Sachsenhausen, then in company with three Catholic priests at Dachau, until the end of the war. In 1939 he asked to be allowed to rejoin the Navy but, although such a step would have scandalised many of his supporters abroad, permission for it was refused.

The direct influence which he could exercise from prison was small but his presence there constantly reminded the world of the Third Reich's character. The arrest undoubtedly weakened the staying power of the Confessing Church. Membership of the Pastors' Emergency League fell. The Reich Council of Brethren never met again (although provincial councils did). The leadership passed to the moderates and particularly to Wurm, partly because they were realising that compromise with a victorious Nazism was not to be had. The situation only changed when Nazism ceased to be victorious.

At the end of April 1945 Niemöller was included in the convoy of distinguished prisoners who were taken southwards from Dachau and finally rescued by American troops from being killed, first by SS men, then by Italian partisans. When the 27 German Churches met at Treysa in August 1945 to found the new Evangelical Church, he was made Vice-President to Wurm with special responsibility for foreign relations. In that capacity he, Barth and Dibelius were the moving spirits behind the Declaration of Guilt which was issued at Stuttgart in October (p. 249).[7] Later he and Dibelius were chosen as Germany's representatives on the World Council of Churches. He also became President from 1947 to 1968 of the new Church which corresponded to the new State of Greater Hesse. He once said that 'Germans must bear their post-war distresses silently, knowing that we have had our share in causing them.' But in practice he did not bear them at all silently, showing himself to be a congenital member of the 'awkward squad', persistently calling for changes in Allied policies over food supplies, treatment of prisoners-of-war, denazification and dismantling. He later opposed German re-armament, calling on the occupying forces to leave Germany and on the Americans to leave Vietnam. He became a nuclear disarmer and opponent of racial discrimination, confessing his own repentance for having once been an anti-semite. The stubbornness with which he had opposed Hitler now showed itself in a refusal to listen to explanations as to why the things he wanted done could not be done. He lived until 1984.

Niemöller was a practical man of action with considerable gifts of leadership and a strong will. His downrightness was apt to provoke opposition. While not much of a theologian, he was intelligent enough to get a clear grasp of the main issues. But neither integrity nor organising ability nor vigour of purpose nor a well-expressed definition of the principles at stake were adequate to the situation which confronted people who were both Germans and Christians. Niemöller once defined the mistake of his opponents as being to say 'first we are Germans and secondly Christians too'[8] instead of the other way round. But the crux of the problem was that the holders of power were not merely unwilling to be Christians at all but were not prepared to leave others to be Christian in any true sense of the word. For the latter, the choice was between reluctant compliance and various degrees of martyrdom which might satisfy conscience or secure acquittal at the bar of history but offered no hope of achieving more until someone else took the power out of Hitler's hands.

19 Dietrich Bonhoeffer[1]

Bonhoeffer was born in February 1906. His father was one of Germany's most distinguished psychiatrists, who in 1912 took up in Berlin the country's top chair in his subject. The family was not notably devout, although a great-grandfather on the mother's side had played an important part in developing German higher biblical criticism and been imprisoned for his liberal opinions. By the time Dietrich was 14 he was already talking of becoming a theologian and at school he learnt not merely Greek and Latin but also Hebrew. He took his doctorate before he was 22 with a thesis on 'The Communion of Saints', designed to show the practical consequences of revelation. He was gifted as a keyboard musician and played such games as tennis and chess with ardour. He could have won fame as an actor.

Berlin theology was until 1930 dominated by the liberal scholar Adolf von Harnack. But although they lived near one another and walked to the subway station together, in Harnack's seminar Dietrich was a dissenting voice for, like many others of his generation, he had fallen under the influence of Karl Barth (p. 17). Bonhoeffer by no means always saw eye-to-eye with Barth but was to play as important a part as his master in formulating the Dialectical Theology. And whereas the higher criticism had inadvertently opened the door to the *Myth of the Twentieth Century*, to Barth Bible and *Volk* were not to be mentioned in the same breath. Harnack, with a view to concentrating on the essentials of Christianity, had been ready to dispense with the Old Testament but Barth sought to bring the whole Bible alive by reading into it interpretations relevant to contemporary issues. Bonhoeffer, like a seventeenth-century Covenanter, made even such unpromising material as the 119th Psalm yield significances hitherto undetected. The danger of this close examination of texts is of course that one reads one's own ideas into them. Bonhoeffer maintained that no ethical question was really complex since each could be answered by looking for direction from God. But unless God is capricious, all serious Christians should then reach similar conclusions and that notoriously does not happen.

In order to qualify as a pastor, Bonhoeffer had to spend a year as a curate in a parish and unconventionally chose as the scene for this the German community in Barcelona. Here he not only sampled Spanish life and found emotional satisfaction in the elegance of bull-fighting but preached, lectured, visited parishioners and ran a Sunday school. He then returned to Berlin, to work for two years on a habilitation thesis about 'Act and Being' – the nature of God is revealed when the teaching of Jesus is put into practice. As he was still too young to be ordained, he spent the year 1930–1 at the Union Theological Seminary in New York, where one of his teachers was Reinhold Niebuhr. The mutual impact of these two leaders in the religious thought of the twentieth century deserves more study than it has received. Both were keenly interested in oecumenism. Bonhoeffer, with the brash confidence of youth, thought American theology sadly deficient by German standards.

Niebuhr was not interested in theology so much as in its practical results; he was a social scientist concerned with the interaction of religious ethics and political pressures. He may well have helped Bonhoeffer to forsake the pacifism which he had once embraced and to realise the inadequacy of a religion which was over-concerned with personal piety. In return Bonhoeffer's exposition of Dialectical Theology may have helped to prevent Niebuhr from becoming a religious modernist.[2] The challenge presented by Hitler may have made Bonhoeffer more sympathetic to Niebuhr's ideas than he had been on first acquaintance with them; it is noteworthy that when his life came to a crisis in 1939 Niebuhr was one of the people to whom he turned for help and advice.

Back in Germany in 1931, he began to teach in Berlin University, worked as a students' chaplain and, at a meeting in Cambridge, was appointed by the World Alliance for Promoting International Friendship through the Churches (the forerunner of the World Council of Churches) as one of their three European Youth Secretaries. At this juncture, which coincided with his ordination, he seems to have undergone something of a personal conversion. From the student primarily attracted to the intellectual side of Christianity, he became the dedicated man, resolved to carry out in the fullest possible detail the teaching of Christ as he found it revealed in the Gospels.

By the time that the Nazis reached power on 30 January 1933, therefore, his character had taken a shape which made collision with them inevitable. It was a symbolic coincidence that he made his one and only broadcast next day and was cut off just as he was asking how far emphasis on leading and being led was healthy, how far misleading. The whole Bonhoeffer family took the view that Hitler meant war. They had none of them been Communists or Socialists and had no Jewish ancestors, so that their personal positions were not immediately threatened. But Dietrich's twin sister Sabine had married a Jewish lawyer called Leibholz and it was the Aryan paragraph excluding Jews from the civil service on which he first fastened as demonstrating the incompatibility of Christianity with National Socialism. He wrote a paper in which, while still admitting that it was not the business of the Church to praise or condemn legislation, he asserted that the Church had a duty to ask the state whether its actions were essential to the maintenance of law and order and not merely the result of political expediency. He went on to claim for the Church an unconditional obligation towards the victims of any social order, even where those victims did not belong to the Christian community. Moreover he declared that if the Church were to see the state unscrupulously meting out either too little or too much law and order, it was her function 'not only to bind up the victims under the wheel but also to put a spoke in the wheel'. This amounted to a claim that circumstances could arise in which it became the duty of the Church to interfere with the state, a radical departure from the established Lutheran view. What he still left open was the question where responsibility for deciding on such interference should lie. Much of his energy in the next few years was devoted to seeking a body which could take that responsibility, only to decide in the end that it must rest with the individual.

In May he joined in signing a radical appendix to the initial manifesto of the 'Young Reformers' (p. 38). When at the end of July Niemöller set going the attempt to define what it was that a reforming Church should believe, Bonhoeffer was one of the two young theologians commissioned to draft such a document. But the rapidity with which it was watered down seemed to him ominous and he refused to sign the final text which anyhow failed to win general acceptance. The realisation that he was in a small minority was one of the reasons why in the autumn of 1933 he accepted a two-year appointment as pastor of a German church in south London. Barth regarded this as running away from the real battle: 'I can only reply to all the reasons and excuses which you put forward "And the German Church? And the German Churches?" '3 But it may well be that, if Bonhoeffer had stayed in Germany he would merely have got himself arrested just as Barth in the following year found himself forced to retire to Switzerland. The result however was that he took little part, except by telephone, in the developments which led to the foundation of the Confessing Church and to the acceptance by its Synod of the Barmen Declaration.

Bonhoeffer did not go to England simply to avoid trouble at home or to get a chance of thinking out his position in perspective. He believed it to be important that there should be someone outside Germany who was qualified to interpret (naturally, in his own terms) the struggle inside Germany to the Churches of the West. He also hoped to use the oecumenical movement in the interests of those Germans who thought like him. The Protestant world had no Vatican qualified to lay down rules of conduct for all its members. The nearest equivalent was the World Alliance of Churches. But this had only come into existence at a World Missionary Conference in 1910 and was, as its title implied, a collection of autonomous bodies, loosely organised into two groups, 'Faith and Order' and 'Life and Work'. The two chief English representatives of the former, Bishop Headlam of Gloucester and Canon Hodgson of Oxford, firmly refused to take sides in the internal controversies of participating groups, even if these did raise such basic questions of faith as the *Führerprinzip* and the Aryan clause; they were not prepared to exclude from conferences any delegation which produced proper credentials from its national Church. Bonhoeffer however nurtured a visionary hope that the oecumenical movement would produce a statement of Christian belief which would include a judgment that any Church accepting racial discrimination was in heresy and that accordingly the Confessing Church was the only body in Germany entitled to be recognised as a true Church. Such a pronouncement would strengthen his hand in demanding that the Confessing Church should expel the official Church as schismatic. But few Churchmen, either inside or outside Germany, were prepared to create new divisions when the temper of the time was to overcome old ones.

With 'Life and Work' it seemed at first to be a different story, since its

Chairman Bishop George Bell of Chichester also had a vision of a Christianity which would be internationally valid. He saw Nazi Germany as the complete antithesis to that ideal and therefore the chief religious issue of the day. Bonhoeffer quickly won the friendship and admiration of this large-hearted but obstinate man and returned it with an affectionate respect which he showed to few other people.[4] In vain did Bishop Heckel, the head of the German Churches' Foreign Department, pour scorn on the ideas of 'Life and Work' as the obsolete offspring of the humanitarian ideals of the Enlightenment and French Revolution.[5] Bell persuaded the movement in October 1933 not only to express grave concern about the anti-semitic laws and the restrictions on freedom in Germany but to authorise him to write in those terms to the German Government. Seven months later he again drew the attention of members to the gravity of what was going on. These warnings aroused resentment among orthodox German churchmen who not merely denied the right of the oecumenical movement to make such judgments but claimed that, after the way Germany had been treated since 1919, other countries had no right to make moral criticisms at all. When the Council of Life and Work, meeting at Fanö in Denmark in August 1934, began to discuss German Church affairs, the official German delegation refused to take part. The Council was however persuaded to accompany its demand that the Confessing Church be left free to preach the Gospel, and that Church's action in electing two of its leading figures (one of them Bonhoeffer) as full members, by a conciliatory statement that it wished to remain in friendly contact with all sides in the German dispute. This was not the resounding declaration of disapproval for which Bonhoeffer had hoped; even the support of Bell was not sufficient to turn the oecumenical movement into something which it was not intended, at any rate as yet, to be and from that moment onwards the amount of time which Bonhoeffer devoted to it declined.

The training of Protestant candidates for ordination had traditionally been done in Germany by the universities. But professorships were official posts and after 1933 only persons with views acceptable to the Government were allowed to hold them. The Confessing Church, being unprepared to put its recruits under the influence of such people, had to make alternative arrangements, with which officialdom was at first prepared to connive since otherwise the supply of new pastors might dry up. In 1935 Bonhoeffer was brought back from London and put in charge of such a training establishment at Finkenwalde near Stettin. Here he spent over two years of fruitful activity, writing his book *The Cost of Discipleship*, teaching, practising a semi-monastic communal life and influencing the men who should have led the Churches into the next generation but for the deaths of many of them in battle. In March 1936 he engineered an invitation from the Swedish oecumenical authorities to bring his students on a visit. He did not obtain official permission to leave Germany, shrewdly suspecting that it would have been refused; in revenge, he was forbidden to give any more lectures in Berlin. He was not a member of any of the bodies which negotiated with the official government of the Church but did all he could to encourage an uncompromising attitude on the part of those who were. But compromise was becoming increasingly difficult to avoid. The Government, having first failed to take over the Church and then to silence it, decided to throttle it by administrative action, against which high-sounding declarations of principle were hardly an effective support. In September 1937 Finkenwalde was closed down by government order.

For the next two and a half years Bonhoeffer contrived to continue teaching ordinands by hiding them in two vicarages in the recesses of Further Pomerania. He himself was almost continuously on the move, struggling to limit the ground gained by the authorities. He was in England in April 1939 when Dr Werner (p. 40) and the German Christians issued a Declaration at Godesberg denying that Christianity could be international or be regarded as compatible with Judaism. The 'Life and Work' movement was in process of being given higher status as the Provisional Committee of the World Council of Churches, with William Temple, then Archbishop of York, as Chairman and the Dutch disciple of Barth, Visser 't Hooft, as Secretary. Bonhoeffer never met Temple but at this point established a cordial relationship with 't Hooft in the course of pacing the platforms at Paddington station. 'T Hooft arranged for Barth to draft an answer to Godesberg which Temple and others then issued. It denied 'that the national structure of the Christian church was a necessary element in its life. . . . Recognition of spiritual unity . . . without regard to race, nation or sex belongs to the nature of the Church. . . . The Gospel of Jesus is the fulfilment of the Jewish hope. . . . The Church has to proclaim Christ's lordship over all spheres of life, including politics and ideology.'[6] Bishop Heckel demanded the immediate withdrawal of the manifesto as far exceeding the Committee's authority, proceeding from a wrong judgment of the German situation and representing an intolerable interference in German affairs.[7] The manifesto was not withdrawn and Heckel's demand only impeded his claim to be the sole official channel of communication between the new Council and the German Church, besides prejudicing the position of Schönfeld, the German representative at the Council's headquarters in Geneva. On the other hand it was still judged inadvisable to give the German seat in the Provisional Committee to a member of the Confessing Church, so that it remained unfilled.

As the position of that Church deteriorated, so did the international scene. Bonhoeffer saw that, while he could not possibly fight for a National Socialist Germany, refusal to do so would cost him his liberty, perhaps even his life, besides damaging the public image of the Church.[8] His first impulse was to find a post outside Germany. During his visit to Britain in April, he had taken advantage of Niebuhr's presence there to explain his problem.[9] Niebuhr immediately cabled to various people in America asking them to help in finding a job. As a result Bonhoeffer himself went to the United States in June 1939. But when he arrived there, he was unable to get the German situation out of his mind and realised that emigration was not for him. He wrote to Niebuhr

> I must live through this difficult period of our national history with the Christian people of Germany. I will have no right to participate in the reconstruction of Christian life in Germany after the war if I do not share the trials of this time with my people. . . . Christians in Germany will have to face the terrible alternative of either willing the defeat of their nation in order that Christian civilisation may survive or willing the victory of their nation and thereby destroying civilisation. I know which of these alternatives I must choose but I cannot make that choice from security.[10]

An alternative line of evasion was provided by the position held in the Abwehr (pp. 155, 158) by Bonhoeffer's lawyer brother-in-law, Hans Dohnanyi (son of the composer) as deputy to Oster. At the end of October 1940 Bonhoeffer became a member of the Abwehr attached to their Munich office. But this did not mean that he was paid by them or did routine work in any office. He purported to be a 'confidential agent' (*Vertrauensmann*) but it was not part of Dohnanyi's duties to enlist or employ such people and Bonhoeffer's name never figured in the files of the section to which they were responsible. His claim to be concerned with Church politics at home fitted badly with the fact that the Abwehr had made a demarcation agreement with the SD (p. 154) by which it was excluded from the home front. What membership of the Abwehr conferred on Bonhoeffer was the designation 'indispensable' (*unabkömmlich*) which meant that nobody else could make use of him. It was a short way of saving him from being called up and in 1943 one of the charges made by the judge who later investigated Dohnanyi was that he had improperly withdrawn the pastor from the Wehrmacht.[11]

Bonhoeffer spent much of his time at the Catholic Abbey of Ettal in the Bavarian mountains, working on a book about *Ethics* and writing letters to keep up the spirits of his former pupils. The pretext for his Abwehr membership was that he could through his œcumenical contacts help the unit in assessing the political situation in Switzerland, Britain, America and Scandinavia; the underlying purpose was that he should use those contacts to bring about an understanding between the *Widerstand* and the Allies. For this purpose he visited Switzerland in February and September 1941 and May 1942. Through Visser 't Hooft he passed to London messages saying that the *Widerstand* was still active and determined. It was to Visser 't Hooft's question as to what might be the object of Bonhoeffer's current prayers that the answer was given, 'I pray for the defeat of my country since I think that is the only way of paying for all the suffering that my country has brought upon the world.'[12] Two of his other wartime utterances were, 'If we claim to be Christians, there is no room for expediency. Hitler is anti-Christ. Therefore we must go on with our work and eliminate him whether he is successful or not,' and, 'There must be punishment by God. . . . Our action must be considered as an act of repentance.' Barth, whom he met for the last time in Switzerland, found it hard to understand how such an attitude could be compatible with membership of Germany's Secret Service.

The experience however gave a new turn to Bonhoeffer's thought. Even if the world had ceased to be religious, had 'come of age', the Christian must live in and not screen himself off from it, although living in the world meant being contaminated to some extent by it. His attitude to the Protestant conscientious objector Hermann Stöhr is said to have been 'unsympathetic, almost suspicious'.[13] He came to support the assassination of Hitler on the ground that new methods of oppression justify new types of disobedience. This by itself goes a long way to explain his failure to establish a close personal relationship with Helmuth von Moltke during their joint visit to Norway in April 1942 on behalf of Bishop Berggrav (p. 189). They never seem to have met again. This may have been due to the fact that their paths did not cross naturally. But the theologian and the international lawyer were not kindred spirits.[14]

A month later Bonhoeffer heard in Switzerland that Bishop Bell was in Sweden and persuaded the Abwehr to make a meeting between them possible. It occurred at Sigtuna on 31 May–1 June. The position was complicated by the simultaneous presence in Sweden of Schönfeld from Geneva who, in travelling through Berlin, had been given by Trott a picture of the situation which he embodied in a memorandum handed to Bell. Schönfeld was suspect as having, in Bonhoeffer's opinion, sat on the fence in his pre-war dealings with Heckel. The possibility of his meeting Bell had been foreseen and the conspirators round Oster clearly doubted his ability to convey a message which would create the right impression in England.

In fact the line taken by the two emissaries differed only in detail.[15] The picture which they gave of the prospects of the conspiracy leaves the impression that (as we cannot suppose them to have been deliberately misleading) they were imperfectly informed. They declared that key positions everywhere were held by members of the *Widerstand*, although all the five people whom Bonhoeffer (with the permission of Beck) named were private individuals without official jobs. Of the four Field Marshals described as 'reliable', Kluge, Bock and Küchler had all refused to get involved, while Witzleben had just been dismissed. Bonhoeffer cannot have helped his cause by mentioning Goerdeler and Schacht, seeing the suspicion with which they were viewed in London (p. 168). Both pastors put forward in slightly varying terms the standard *Widerstand* request for a public statement by the British and American Governments that they would be prepared to negotiate what would clearly amount to a compromise peace with a post-Hitler régime. A memorandum which Schönfeld brought with him from Berlin referred to a European Federation of Free Nations to include a Free Polish and a Free Czech state but there was no indication as to whether these were intended to include the Corridor and the Sudetenland and what is known from other sources makes it probable that they were not. A promise was made that the new government would gradually withdraw all its forces from the occupied and invaded countries but Austria, Alsace and the South Tyrol were not specifically included and, to judge by subsequent proposals of Goerdeler, would have been mostly excluded. The German Army was to remain in being, although it would be merged in a European force if one were established. Allied troops would be welcome as a help against reactionary forces, but not if they came as conquerors. British ministers may have been closing their eyes to the obstacles to action inside Germany when they asked the *Widerstand* to give evidence of its ability to do what it promised. But the prospectus on which they were being asked to commit themselves was hardly convincing or accurate.

Bell came back from Germany hoping for a mass rising, apparently on the strength of a written statement by Schönfeld that 'the strong opposition movement would have sufficient power to overthrow the present régime because of their control over large masses now having arms in their hands and, as regards the workers, at their disposal.' It is hard to attribute any meaning to this sentence which is not misleading. One of the things which the workers had conspicuously failed to do was to acquire arms and it is hard to see how they could have done so. Fifteen years later Bell quoted Schönfeld as having said that 'the likelihood of a British victory was not very great'. That a German should have thought this in May 1942 is hardly surprising. But in fact the tide of war had turned, although eight months still had to elapse before this became evident. This fundamental difference of opinion between the *Widerstand* and British ministers lay however at the heart of Eden's refusal to give the approach any answer.

Except for a fortnight's holiday in Italy with Dohnanyi later in June (when he explained to the Vatican what had gone wrong in the spring of 1940), Bonhoeffer did not leave Germany again and spent much of his time in Berlin where on 6 April 1943 he was arrested (p. 158). The papers which Oster was caught trying to conceal came from Bonhoeffer. One said that the Churches were determined to overthrow Hitler. The second was concerned with the position of the Churches in a post-Hitler Germany. The third mentioned that, as Bonhoeffer had learnt at Sigtuna, talks were going on in oecumenical circles outside Germany about the form of a post-Hitler world and suggested the desirability of trying to put a German Protestant pastor into touch with such talks.[16] Bonhoeffer had also had a hand in the smuggling of Jews into Switzerland under the excuse that they were Abwehr agents (p. 158). He was lodged in Tegel prison where he remained for eighteen months. Convinced though the police were that something irregular had been going on, they were unable to find any hard evidence on which to base a prosecution for crime. The cover-stories for Bonhoeffer's trips to Switzerland and for the smuggling of the Jews stood up to scrutiny; the Sigtuna meeting did not come to light at all. Had not Dohnanyi's health given way under ceaseless interrogation, so that a decision about him had to be postponed, Bonhoeffer might have been released in the spring of 1944 or merely prosecuted for avoiding the call-up. Instead he was allowed a considerable amount of liberty and carried on writing his *Ethics*. His letters to his parents and to his faithful disciple Eberhard Bethge provided the material for the posthumous book on which his reputation as a theologian and a man at first rested.

This relatively lenient treatment of course stopped when the arrests and searches provoked by 20 July greatly increased SD knowledge of all that had been going on since 1938. But Dohnanyi was more incriminated by this than Bonhoeffer. The available evidence suggests that, although the Sigtuna meeting came to light, it was accepted as an attempt to ascertain British attitudes, a matter which had become interesting to the German authorities now that defeat stared them in the face. Conversations about post-war plans, concealed as discussions of political ethics, were only marginally criminal. As Bonhoeffer had been in prison for over a year before 20 July, he could not be accused of any close connection with it. The Nazi hierarchy sensed that in him they had one of their most implacable opponents who was all the more dangerous because his antagonism was based on deeply-held principles. But the subversive character of what he had actually done was hard to document. As a result he was never brought to trial before the People's Court. Instead he was held at the RSHA headquarters for four months and then for another month in Buchenwald where he kept up the morale of the other prisoners by his imperturbable behaviour and by his conducting of services. On 3 April 1945 he was sent to the camp at Flossenburg; when, owing to a confusion, he was found to have ended up at another camp a hundred miles away, the German police machine, in spite of American guns being within earshot, still functioned well enough to have him brought back. The decision to put him (among others) to death would seem to have been taken by Hitler himself or Kaltenbrunner; the hasty trial improvised before the execution showed how hard the Nazis found it to get respect for legal procedure out of their system. At a late stage in Bonhoeffer's travels Payne Best of the British Secret Service, captured at Venlo in November 1939 (p. 157), crossed his path and was given a farewell message for George Bell: 'Tell him that for me this is not the end but the beginning.' 'He was,' wrote Best later, 'the finest and most lovable man I ever met.' The camp doctor said that he had never seen anyone on his deathbed so submissive to the will of God.

He died on the morning of 9 April along with Canaris, Oster and three others. Dohnanyi was executed in Sachsenhausen camp on the same day. A fortnight later Bonhoeffer's younger brother Klaus and his brother-in-law Rüdiger Schleicher, who had been condemned by the People's Court in February, were butchered by SS men on a dark Berlin bomb-site when Russian tanks were already inside the city. Schleicher's only offence had been not to have told the authorities what he knew about the plot against Hitler (in which he had no direct part). But the Nazi fanatics were determined to involve in their own ruin as many as possible of the kind of people whom they regarded as responsible for preventing their dream of Germany from lasting.

20 Bishop Konrad Graf von Preysing[1]

Count Konrad von Preysing-Lichtenegg-Moos came of an ancient and noble Bavarian family which had a palace in Munich within a stone's throw of the spot where Hitler's attempted rising came to grief in 1923. Born in 1880 he studied law at the university and joined the Bavarian diplomatic service, his first posting being to Rome. But in 1907 he left it to study theology and was ordained five years later. He wrote monographs on Thomas More and F.W. Faber. For four years he acted as secretary to the Cardinal Archbishop of Munich and then for eleven years performed the same service for Eugenio Pacelli, the Papal Nuncio, first in Munich and after 1925 in Berlin. In 1928 he was made a member of the Munich Cathedral Chapter and in 1932 Bishop of Eichstadt, a predominantly Catholic town in a predominantly Protestant part of predominantly Catholic Bavaria which remained a centre of opposition throughout the Third Reich.[2] In 1935 he reluctantly allowed himself to be translated to Berlin, a see which had only been created five years before as a result of the Concordat which Pacelli had negotiated with the Prussian state in 1925–9 (p. 18). The South German from the small town did not take kindly to the big North German city and for some time was known to his flock as the 'Marble Bishop' because he was said never to smile.

In 1933 Preysing was one of the two German Bishops who opposed the conclusion of a Concordat (the other being Schulte of Cologne). With the Archbishop of Munich, Cardinal Faulhaber, who also was uneasy, he went to Rome to warn the Vatican of the pitfalls which might be involved, but failed to shake the complacency of Papen. When Faulhaber told him that Papen was a statesman Preysing replied that he was a liar and bane to church and country. In a letter to Pacelli he said that while he would welcome the disenfranchisement of the clergy (since the right to vote no longer had any meaning), he would be deeply disturbed by a veto on all clerical intervention in politics since priests could then be accused of disloyalty if they spoke in public about any of the social matters which were of direct interest to Catholics. He went on to doubt whether a Concordat was possible in a country where things were done without any legal basis and leaders took the view that whatever served the Fatherland was right irrespective of whether it was morally justifiable. He also pressed that the Pastoral Letter which the Bishops were about to issue should reaffirm the dogmatic and ethical rejection of Nazi errors:

> The Bishops owe it to the Catholic people to open their eyes to the dangers to belief and behaviour which follow from the National Socialist world view. . . . We must be able to refer back to this Letter in the conflict which probably lies ahead.

He ended up by pointing out that terms such as God, Christian morality and law were being given a hollow and perverted meaning[3] (just as Bonhoeffer was to write from prison that 'for evil to appear disguised as light, beneficence, historical necessity and social justice . . . confirms [for the Christian] the radical malice of evil'⁴). In private he said that 'we are in the hands of criminals and fools'. One of his closest friends was among those murdered on 30 June 1934, while he helped another to escape to Switzerland.

His warning had little effect. The Concordat was not merely signed but signed before a number of details had been properly clarified. One of Preysing's first tasks, on arriving in Berlin, was to try, in company with two other Bishops, to negotiate, on behalf of the Vatican, an agreement on what the document meant. He got nowhere. It was part of his job, as Bishop of Berlin, to handle on behalf of the Fulda Bishops' Conference all matters relating to publicity and the Catholic press. Here he was in continual controversy. When the Propaganda Ministry insisted that all Catholic papers be subordinated to the Editors' Law, Preysing, foreseeing that this would lead to a steady adulteration of their contents, wanted to close them down instead but Bertram (p. 42) said that he could not do without his diocesan magazine and the majority of Bishops agreed with him. In 1936 private schools in Berlin began to be closed down on the pretext that parents no longer wanted them. In 1937 Preysing was one of the two Bishops (the other being Galen of Münster) called to Rome with the three Cardinal Archbishops of Breslau, Munich and Cologne to review the situation, a deliberation which led to the Encyclical *Mit brennender Sorge* (p. 43), the first draft of which was made by Faulhaber. In Berlin copies were cyclostyled in church premises so as to preserve secrecy, with the result that the authorities knew nothing of it until 20 March, the evening before it was read from the pulpits. In less careful dioceses printing firms were used and got shut down as a result. Preysing, who had visited Niemöller four days earlier, was quite prepared to find himself in custody. He told a friend, 'I said in 1933 that the time would certainly come when we would have to break away, the only question would be when to choose.'

Goebbels, Kerrl, Heydrich and others wished to see the Concordat abrogated and the Bishops prosecuted. But moderates, including Göring and Mussolini, persuaded Hitler that it would be more subtle to discredit the Church by headlining cases where priests were being prosecuted for immorality. Goebbels fell in gleefully with these tactics. Preysing however sent a skilfully-drafted letter to him and to the Minister of Justice, with copies to all other Ministers, setting out the relative infrequency of the cases and evidence that the attention given to them was inspired officially by ulterior motives. At the end of July Gürtner, the Minister of Justice, halted the trials. In the same month the Bishop issued a Pastoral Letter saying that a fight was in full swing between Christians and anti-Christians as to whether there was a heavenly authority higher than all earthly ones and whether men had certain inalienable rights including that of following their consciences. Another letter followed in October, seeking to counteract the effect of Church schools being closed. A further letter, also in October, backed up *Mit brennender Sorge* by urging the laity to stand firm in their faith.

The question of how the Church should in future deal with the state was one on which Bertram and Preysing did not see eye-to-eye. The Archbishop believed that, while the Party was irrevocably hostile, there were other groups in the Government who were not and that the wiser course was to strengthen these by showing a steady desire to be conciliatory. The Bishop held that the Party had no intention of keeping any undertakings which it might make so that before any negotiations were started, the Church should insist upon an 'armistice' in which official attacks on the Church would stop. Bertram countered that such an armistice would never be accepted and, even if it were, would not be long observed. Preysing called for an end to pretence and for franker speaking. The Concordat was becoming a farce. Appeals to it which did not at the same time show up the insidious tactics of the Party and their broken promises sounded ridiculous. The Bishops, in their dealings with the Government, must stop using the refined language of diplomacy and go over to forms of expression which were suited to the mental level of National Socialism. Bertram claimed that refinement was the best way of handling coarse people. Preysing resigned from the group of Bishops commissioned by the Fulda Conference to conduct negotiations.

In March 1938 the annexation of Austria brought a further clash. The Austrian Bishops sent a message to Hitler gratefully acknowledging the achievements of National Socialism and calling on the faithful to vote 'Yes' in the referendum over joining Germany. Goebbels ordered the entire German press, including religious papers, to print this. The Austrian blindness to the experience of the Vatican and German Catholicism in dealing with National Socialism angered Preysing and he wanted Goebbels's order to be disregarded as far as the religious press was concerned. But so general was the enthusiasm which had greeted the long-desired union that Bertram and other Bishops thought that the Church would do itself more harm than good by refusing to join in. Preysing found little support for his argument that the voting-paper called for approval of the entire National Socialist internal policy including its treatment of the Church.

There was further trouble in April 1940 when Bertram, without consulting Preysing, sent in the name of all the Bishops a letter of congratulation to Hitler on his birthday which came immediately after the German victories in Scandinavia. Preysing was so angry that he threw up the job of handling the press relations of the episcopate. He also offered his resignation to Pacelli (by this time Pope) who refused it and urged the Bishops to resolve their difficulties by an uninhibited discussion. But when Preysing proposed this at Fulda in the following August, Bertram walked out. From then on relations between Breslau and Berlin were glacial. When Hitler's death was announced in April 1945, Bertram had a Requiem Mass celebrated for him.[5]

Another thorn in Preysing's side was the Papal Nuncio, Cesare Orsenigo (p. 44), who was a Fascist at heart and anxious to propitiate the National Socialists. When on one occasion he had to take to the Government three Vatican protests in quick succession, he was said to have been so worried that he lost a night's sleep. Preysing's comment was that it would have been better if he had started having bad nights earlier. On 13 April 1940 Orsenigo felt himself bound to report to his superiors that

> some of the clergy have adopted an almost openly hostile attitude towards Germany at war, to the extent of wanting a complete defeat. This attitude arouses not only the displeasure of the Government but gradually also that of the whole people, as they are almost all enthusiastic about their leader, which makes me afraid that a painful reaction will one day follow which will divide the clergy and even the church from the people. . . . As long as it was merely a matter of domestic policy, it was easy for anyone to distinguish between anti-nazi and anti-national attitudes; the clergy might adopt the former but not the latter. Now, when it is a matter of external policy . . . there are only a few who can understand how one can be against Hitler without being a traitor.[6]

A year later, after the attack on Russia, he said that anyone who talked of peace was a Stalinist.[7]

Yet the actions of the state called more and more to be condemned. Early in the war it leaked out that, on Hitler's orders, the old and mentally ill were being quietly put away. Bertram contented himself with a protest to Lammers the Cabinet Secretary and Faulhaber with a protest to Gürtner the Minister of Justice. In March 1941 Preysing condemned the policy outright in a sermon. He quoted the Pope as laying down that no justification or excuse could be found on any economic or eugenic grounds for depriving the sick and weak of life. It was however the even more outspoken sermon of Preysing's cousin Count von Galen the Bishop of Münster in the following August which brought results. Bertram thought Galen 'too clamorous' and complained that he lacked subtlety. But Galen's habit of going straight to the point without beating about the bush roused a storm which the censors could not hush up and the authorities had to resort to less palpable methods and less frequented areas for achieving their ends. (It is significant that they did not stop completely.)[8]

In the autumn of 1942 Preysing was asked by his colleagues to draft their Advent Pastoral Letter (the only one during the year which went to all dioceses alike). Encouraged by Helmuth von Moltke, whom he had got to know in 1941,[9] he composed a powerful piece on the subject of *Recht* (which means in German 'law' as well as 'right' and 'justice'). It denied the right of any authority to deprive of their basic rights anyone at all, including those who were of different blood or spoke a different language. It thus went to the heart of the issues separating National Socialism and Christianity. It was in some sense a Catholic counterpart to the Barmen Declaration. Both documents had to keep to general terms but their implications were unmistakable. Preysing did not openly condemn the Nazi treatment of the Jews but what he said amounted to as much. The draft was too downright for some of his colleagues who made him tone it down. The text was leaked abroad and carried verbatim by the BBC German Service; the author, on being told this, said 'it will make my gallows all the higher'. An even more outspoken letter followed in 1943. As a more practical help, the Bishop had established a relief unit in the diocesan office (*Hilfswerk beim bischöflichen Ordinariat*) and appointed as its director Fr Bernhard Lichtenberg (pp. 229–31). When the Father was arrested on 25 October 1941, Preysing took over the post himself, so as to avoid risking the freedom of another of his assistants.

In the spring of 1944 Preysing received a visit from Claus von Stauffenberg who said nothing about an impending putsch or assassination, and still less asked for priestly condonation of such an act. But the conversation took a turn where the need for a drastic change came up and with it the question as to whether tyrannicide could be justified. The Bishop, who could see perfectly well what he was not being asked, told Stauffenberg's mother later that, although he had not on this occasion given her son the blessing of the Church, he had given his own blessing as a priest.[10]

On 22 November 1943 the Bishop's Palace was hit by a British bomb. Preysing escaped alive but was badly shaken and had to move to a convent in the northern suburbs where he spent the rest of the war. No sooner was it ended than he had to start fighting another totalitarian and anti-Christian régime. He was made a Cardinal in 1946 and died in 1950.

Preysing has claims to be regarded as the ablest and most determined of the German Catholic leaders, although he did not attract as much public attention as Faulhaber or Galen. More letters were addressed to him by Pacelli between 1934 and 1944 than to any other German bishop. He cannot however be said to have had much effect on the Government's actions. He was of course inhibited by the supposed need for the Catholic Bishops to show a united front and was therefore continually yielding to the views of his more conciliatory and timid colleagues. Yet even if he had been free to act on his own judgment, it is questionable whether he would have achieved much more.

21 Bernhard Lichtenberg[1]

Lichtenberg was born a Catholic at Ohlau, a mainly Protestant village in Silesia, in 1875. His father was a grocer and publican but it was the pious mother whose influence predominated. Bernhard got to a gymnasium, to Innsbruck and Breslau universities, and travelled in Europe (though not to Rome). He was ordained priest in Breslau in 1899 and moved next year to Berlin (which in those days was in the diocese of Breslau). He worked in a number of different parishes, mostly new ones which had to be developed. In 1913 he took charge at Charlottenburg. Next year he became chaplain to a Guards regiment and served with distinction throughout the war. After the war he returned to his parish, which had 36,000 Catholics and a church with room (until he enlarged it) for 467. An outspoken opponent of Social Democracy (on account of its association with atheism) he became a member of the Centre Party group on the City Council. But in 1931 he was abused by Goebbels in *Der Angriff* for having become a pacifist and sending out invitations to a showing of the film *All Quiet on the Western Front*. In 1931 he became a Canon of St Hedwig's, the Catholic Cathedral.

He was a pastor, teacher and organiser rather than a theologian. On one occasion he said in a sermon, 'How grateful we should be to the dustmen for taking such a dirty job off our hands.' When a workman criticised him for reading his breviary on the Underground, he replied, 'You read your Red Flag and that is your affair. I read my breviary and that is mine.' When a Gestapo official said that each individual should be allowed to be happy in the way he wants, Lichtenberg corrected him, 'In the way God wants.' When asked how he was, he habitually replied, 'Better than I deserve to be.'

On 31 March 1933 he sent Oscar Wassermann of the Deutsche Bank to Bertram with the request that he should intervene with Hindenburg to get the Jewish boycott abandoned. Bertram replied that he had no authority from his fellow-bishops to do so and was uninformed about the reasons for the boycott. Bertram then sent a letter to the five German Archbishops recommending that no action in aid of the Jews be taken; all save Grober of Freiburg agreed with him.

In 1935, when Lichtenberg was in charge of the Berlin diocese after Bishop Bares's death and before Preysing's appointment, he received a report on bad conditions in the concentration camp at Esterwegen. He insisted on taking it to Göring's office himself so as to ensure that the minister in charge of the Prussian police read it. For this he was described by an SS man as a 'turbulent priest' (*Hetzkaplan*).

In 1938 he was elected Provost of St Hedwig's. Soon afterwards there occurred the *Kristallnacht*. At the end of evening service on the following Sunday, he said, 'Let us pray for the persecuted non-Aryan Christians, for the Jews and for the poor prisoners in concentration camps.' This became his regular practice. He said to one of his helpers, 'If we priests keep silent, the laity will go all wrong and won't know where we have got to. We must preach the word no matter whether it is welcome or unwelcome.'[2] Preysing had already put him in charge of the episcopal *Hilfswerk* for the Jews, staffed by ten Christian Full-Jews. At first energies were concentrated on facilitating emigration; when this was forbidden in 1941, money, clothes and food were supplied. Efforts were made with varying success to enable those liable to deportation to avoid or at least postpone it.

In August 1941 the Provost addressed a letter to Conti, the Chief Medical Officer of the Ministry of the Interior, pointing out that no action had been taken against Bishop Galen for the charges he had made earlier in the month about the premature killing of invalids and old people. These charges must therefore be presumed to be true. That meant that not only were God's Commandments being disobeyed but also the law of the land which made it a punishable offence to know of a murder and not report it. He then quoted a case with which he was personally acquainted. He ended by calling Dr Conti to account for a crime committed on his orders or with his connivance.

Lichtenberg also drafted a letter for Bertram, as Chairman of the Bishops'

Conference, to send to the Reich Government in reply to a letter from Kerrl reproving the Bishops for exceeding their functions in their criticisms of euthanasia. The minister was to be told bluntly that the Bishops were themselves the people entitled to pronounce on questions of faith and morals. A request by the entire bench of Bishops in that field amounted to a command incumbent on any secular power which in an excessive claim to authority crossed the limits laid down by God. Not surprisingly Bertram did not use the draft which illustrated Preysing's remark that Lichtenberg could only see what was immediately in front of him. Instead it was found by the Gestapo when they arrested the Provost a few days later.

The charge against him was based on his Sunday evening prayers. He was further charged with having said that an anti-semitic pamphlet of the Propaganda Ministry broke the commandment to love one's neighbour as oneself by telling its readers not to commit treason towards the *Volk* by false sentimentality towards the Jews. The letter to Conti was not mentioned but there can be little doubt that it, coming on top of all he had done for Jews, was the real cause of offence.

When interrogated, he professed agreement with everything that Galen had said. When asked about his attitude to the Führer, he said, 'I have only one Führer – Jesus Christ. Adolf Hitler is only the Head of State. He is not my Führer as I don't belong to the National Socialist Party.' He was condemned to two years' imprisonment. Attempts by his seniors to get the sentence rescinded were unavailing. He asked that, when he was released, he might be sent as chaplain to the Jews in the Lodz ghetto. Instead he was sent to Dachau. While on the way there, at the age of 68, he collapsed and died. The considerations which led the Catholic Bishops to hesitate before a show-down with the state are illustrated by the fact that what most disturbed his last moments was the fear of it proving impossible to find a priest who would give him absolution and extreme unction.

22 Franz Jägerstätter[1]

Jägerstätter was born in 1907 at St Radegund in Upper Austria, about twenty miles from Hitler's birthplace of Braunau. His father, who was called Bachmeier, made an honest woman of his mother but was killed in action in 1915. Two years later his mother married a local farmer called Jägerstätter and the boy not only took his name but, as there were no other children, in due course inherited the small-holding. His school reports varied from 'good' to 'very good' and in his early life he was something of a lad – '*liaba Mensch*' was the phrase his neighbours used – being adept at dancing, bowls and cards. The first motor-cycle in the village was his.

About 1934 he went off to work in the Styrian iron-mines. Here he is thought to have fathered an illegitimate son. He came home in 1936, married a pious girl and took her for the honeymoon to Rome. In some way these events combined to effect a conversion. Although this was the point at which he took over the farm, he also became the village sexton, attended mass daily, gave food to the needy and sang hymns as he walked round the fields (although here one is inclined to suspect malicious gossip). According to the parish priest, he wanted to enter a religious order.

This religious fervour carried with it a rooted objection to National Socialism as 'the worst and most dangerous anti-Christian power which has ever existed.' He often referred to an article in the *Osservatore Romano* of October 1930 which said that belonging to the Party was incompatible with the Christian religion, just as belonging to Socialism of any kind was in general incompatible with it. 'Since Rome has not to this day rescinded that statement, I believe it cannot possibly be a crime for a Catholic to refuse the present [after 1938] military service.' He was the only man in the village to vote against the Anschluss in 1938. He compared it to the choice offered by Pilate to the crowd between Barabbas and Jesus. Thereafter he not only refused to contribute to Party funds but also to draw the subsidies which the Government offered to farmers.

He was over 30 when war broke out and a food producer which may explain his not being called up till 1943. At some previous stage he had done a spell of military service which convinced him that war was unjust and that life in the Army offered too many opportunities for sin, especially against the sixth commandment. When the need for replacements became acute after Stalingrad and he was ordered to report at Enns, he refused to serve, even as a medical orderly. All sorts of people from the Bishop of Linz downwards argued with him, but to no avail. To those who called on him to think of his wife and three small daughters (to whom he was deeply attached), he quoted St Matthew's Gospel, 'he that loveth son or daughter more than me is not worthy of me'. 'I cannot believe that, just because a man has a wife and children, he is free to offend God by lying (not to mention all the other things he will be called on to do).' To the argument that other convinced Catholics saw no need to behave as he was doing, he retorted, 'They have not been given the grace to see things otherwise.' 'For what purpose did God endow all men with reason and free will if, as so many say, the individual is not qualified to judge whether this war started by Germany is just or unjust? What purpose is served by the ability to distinguish between good and evil?'

'We cannot know God's mind or tell which of the many paths he leaves us free to travel is going to reach the right goal. As long as a man has an untroubled conscience and knows that he is not really a criminal, he can live at peace, even in prison.'

'Many have the idea that this war which Germany has started is a war pretty much like all the others that have already taken place. But it is not a war like the others in which simple greed for territory played the major role; it is one of a revolution which has already brought almost the whole world within its grasp. The Führer has himself said that the National Socialist state is the greatest revolutionary [institution] of all time. Since it is more of a revolution or a war of ideas, I could fight as much as I want for the German Fatherland and yet, if I refuse to acknowledge the National Socialist Volk community, they would still regard me as an enemy. . . . Is it not more Christian to offer oneself as a victim right away rather than first to murder others – who certainly want to live and have a good right to live – just to prolong one's own life for a little while? Can there be any [justification for] talk about defending the Fatherland when one invades countries which owe one nothing and robs and murders there?' 'That we Catholics must make ourselves tools of the worst and most dangerous anti-Christian power that has ever existed is something I cannot and will not believe.'

'Consider what efforts and sacrifices many are prepared to make to gain worldly esteem or to win prizes as athletes. If we were to make the same efforts to gain heaven, there would then be many and great saints.'

All the foregoing remarks were made privately, not in public.

Jägerstätter was taken to Linz and then to Berlin where he was tried by a military rather than a Party court. He was provided with a defence counsel who reasoned with him at length and if he had been prepared to make the least concession, his life would have been spared. But he remained adamant and was beheaded in August 1943.

When Jägerstätter's case was unearthed by the American historian Gordon Zahn in the 1960s, it was a considerable embarrassment to the Catholic authorites in Linz. How could they condemn someone who had died trying to carry out literally the teaching of Jesus, especially when the Roman Church was under fire for having compromised with National Socialism? What, on the other hand, would be the long-term result if people generally were encouraged to adopt the attitudes of Jägerstätter? In the end it was decided to treat him as having been 'a martyr to his conscience'. He represented an exceptional case, more to be admired than copied. In a letter in the local paper which reflected the views of the Bishop, the 'greater heroes' were said to be 'those exemplary young Catholic men, seminarists, priests and heads of families who fought and died fulfilling the will of God at their posts just as the Christian soldiers in the armies of the heathen emperors had done. All respect is due to the innocently erroneous conscience – it will have its reward from God. For the instruction of *men*, the better models are to be found in the example set by the heroes who conducted themselves consistently in the light of a clear conscience.'

Franz Jägerstätter had a cousin who was one of Jehovah's Witnesses (p. 277) and there was much the same kind of fundamental obstinacy in the nonconformity which that sect offered to National Socialism. But there is no evidence that their attitude had any effect on his.

23 'The White Rose'[1]

'The White Rose' is the name by which a group of students has gone down to history who in the summer of 1942 and early spring of 1943 distributed anti-Nazi leaflets in Munich. They were caught and five were executed, along with a professor who had encouraged them. Hans Scholl (25) and his sister Sophie (21) were children of an anti-Nazi small-town Bürgermeister in Swabia who was himself in trouble in 1942 for calling Hitler a 'scourge from God'. Alexander Schmorell (25) was the son of a well-known Munich doctor who had married the daughter of an Orthodox priest in Russia in 1915; she had died soon afterwards and the boy had been brought up by a Russian peasant nurse who came back to Germany with the father in 1921. Alexander could speak Russian fluently and was much influenced by that cultural background. Christian Probst (23) was the son of a connoisseur living between Munich and Salzburg; thanks to his father's private income, he had been to the nearest German equivalent to an English public school, had married early and had three children. Willi Graf (24) was the son of a wine wholesaler from the Rhineland. Thus all of them had comfortable cultured backgrounds and were happy in their homes. Schmorell and Graf had belonged to the *Bündische Jugend* or groups associated with it and were indignant when these were forcibly absorbed into the HJ; Graf continued to go on holidays and outings with ex-members and spent three weeks in jail in 1938 as a result. Hans Scholl by contrast had been fascinated by the HJ, in spite of his father's disapproval, and had only been disillusioned by a visit to the *Parteitag* in 1935, after which he too joined the BJ and was also jailed. Sophie Scholl rose to be a *Gruppenführerin* in the *Bund deutscher Mädel* before she too turned against it.

The men after doing their labour and military service opted to become doctors, in the belief that medicine was likely to be the career least subject to Nazi influence. But they were enrolled in the Wehrmacht and sent to serve as medical orderlies on various fronts. They were then however sent back to a Student Company in Munich so that they could pursue their studies. Thus it came about that in the winter of 1941–2 the four were all living in Munich and got to know one another. Sophie was also there, studying philosophy and biology. Munich at that time had had its official Nazi description 'City of the Movement' changed by wits to the 'City of the Anti-movement' (*Stadt der Gegenbewegung*). The students first met at the house of an elderly Catholic publicist Carl Muth and in the studio of an architect Manfred Eichemeyer. Here they gathered regularly, along with others, to talk and read aloud; they went to concerts and joined the Bach Choir. To one of their discussions there came a 51-year-old Professor Kurt Huber, a philosopher who had applied psychology to the study of folk-music. This interest had to some extent protected him from the persecution which his general views might have invited from the authorities. Excused military service as a cripple from birth, he was a born teacher and attracted to his lectures many who were not studying the subjects to which these were nominally devoted, including the Scholls and their friends. The evening discussions were at first cultural and philosophical rather than political but moral indignation with the régime gradually gathered force. To those who argued that opposition was impracticable, Huber replied that something needed to be done and done quickly.

The Scholl parents had already had put through their letter-box, possibly by a suppressed Catholic youth organisation in Würzburg, leaflets giving the texts of Bishop von Galen's sermons (p. 228). Hans, on reading them, said, 'At last someone has had the courage to speak out.' The example suggested to him how Huber's call could be implemented. He later told the Gestapo that the name 'The White Rose' under which his leaflets were sent out had been chosen arbitrarily but it seems in fact to have been borrowed from a novel about a Mexican farm which had escaped the corruptions of civilisation, written by a German under the pseudonym of B. Traven. The association with purity and plainness may even owe something to Shakespeare (*King Henry VI Part I*, Act II Scene 4). Hans Scholl was the main author but Schmorell was involved as well. Four texts were produced at this time, each with about 100 copies. They were sent through the post to residents in Munich whose names were mostly chosen from the telephone directory.

This batch of leaflets was written in high-flown language, with references to Lycurgus, Solon, Aristotle, Lao-Tse, Schiller, Goethe and Novalis. The contents however included such passages as:

> The state itself is never an end but is only important as a condition in which the end of man can be fulfilled and this end is none other than the development of all man's faculties.
>
> Since the conquest of Poland three hundred thousand Jews have been murdered in that country in a most bestial way [evidence that the treatment of the Jews was known in Germany].
>
> Why do the German people behave so apathetically in face of all these dreadful and inhuman crimes? . . . It is not only pity that we ought to feel but guilt. . . . Each will declare himself guiltless, each does so and then goes to sleep with an easy conscience. But he cannot declare himself guiltless, he is guilty, guilty, guilty.
>
> It is high time that we uprooted the brown horde. . . . We shall only do this by co-operation between many convinced and bold men who are agreed on how to achieve their aims. We have no great choice of means since the only one available to us is passive *Widerstand*. . . . Each must find his own way of carrying that out. Sabotage in armament and war-essential factories, sabotage in all gatherings, demonstrations and festivities organised by the National Socialist Party. Sabotage on all scientific and intellectual fronts. . . . Sabotage in all cultural events. Sabotage in all branches of the visual arts, in all writing and journalism.
>
> For the sake of future generations an example must be made after the end of the war which will stop anyone from having the least inclination to do such things again.

From July till November 1942 Hans Scholl, Schmorell and Graf were sent with their Student Company to the southern front in Russia as medical orderlies. There is no doubt that the experience made a great impression on them which they intensified by reading Dostoievsky to one another. Thanks to Schmorell, they were able to make contact with a number of Russians. But there has been some argument as to the exact character of this experience. East German writers have sought to make out that it gave them a favourable impression of Communism and sent them home determined to organise a revolution. But Schmorell's impression was that all the Russians he met hated the Russian Communist system. What really affected the visitors was the Russian landscape and what they took to be the products of traditional Russian culture. They became all the more anxious to end a war against a people whom they so much admired.

On getting home, they sought to establish links with similarly-minded people in other cities, of whom the most important were Falk Harnack, a brother of Arvid (p. 209), and a Hamburg group. Individuals among them made friends in Stuttgart, Freiburg and Saarbrücken. But before these reinforcements could achieve much, activities were brought everywhere to a halt by the dramatic course of events in Munich.

Early in January 1943 Hans Scholl wrote another leaflet 'A Call to All Germans' which Huber revised. It was shorter and more down-to-earth than its predecessors. When in the previous summer he had said under the influence of Muth and Huber, 'The end is upon us,' he cannot have carried much conviction. But now, after Stalingrad and Alamein, he had more justification for beginning

> The war is approaching its inevitable end. With mathematical certainty Hitler is leading the German nation to disaster. Now is the time for those Germans to act who want to avoid being lumped with the Nazi barbarians by the outside world.
> The idea of imperial power must be scotched for ever. A one-sided Prussian militarism must never again come to power. Only in broad-minded co-operation between the peoples of Europe can the basis be established for a new society. All attempts to centralise power, as Prussia did in Germany and Europe, must be nipped in the bud. The Germany of the future can only be a federation.
> Freedom of speech, freedom of belief, protection of the individual citizen against the arbitrary action of criminal power – these are the foundations of a new Europe.

Several thousands of these leaflets were distributed by hand or by post in Munich and Augsburg; others were sent or taken (sometimes only as examples to be copied) to Ulm, Stuttgart, Linz, Salzburg, Vienna, Frankfurt, Bonn, Mannheim, Karlsruhe, Freiburg and Berlin, so as to give the impression that the movement had more than one centre.

Meanwhile on 13 January the Munich Gauleiter Paul Giesler made a highly provocative speech at a big student meeting held to celebrate the 470th anniversary of the university's foundation. Among other things he told the girls that, instead of hanging round as students, they should be presenting sons to the Führer. When some sought to walk out in protest, they were stopped but the remainder of the meeting was such a fiasco that Giesler ordered the protesters to be arrested. Over a thousand students, many of them in uniform, lined up outside and prevented the arrests from being carried out.

The episode excited the Scholls who were already in a tense state, sleeping little and using stimulants. When Paulus's surrender at Stalingrad was announced on 2 February, they decided that the downfall of the régime was close at hand, and felt that a clearer call to action was needed. In the night of 3–4 February and again on 8 and 15 February, they painted slogans like 'Freedom' and 'Down with Hitler' on walls in central Munich and the university; surprisingly enough they were not caught. They decided to produce a new leaflet, specifically addressed to students, and Huber wrote it for them, comparing 1943 with 1813 and calling on its readers to liberate Europe from the slavery to which National Socialism had subjected it in a new confident bid for freedom and honour; 3000 copies of these were made. But while a few were distributed by post in the usual way, the rest were brought into the university by the Scholls on 18 February and scattered on the main stairs and window ledges. When the porter ran up, nobody made any effort to prevent him from leading the two distributors off to the Rector, an SS Oberführer; on the contrary, some of the students are said to have cheered him.[2] After the events of 13 January, followed by the disaster in the east, the authorities were clearly afraid of the situation getting out of hand. Freisler, the President of the People's Court, hurried to Munich and on 22 February held a brief trial at which the two Scholls and Probst were sentenced to death. Sophie told him, 'Many people are thinking as we have spoken and written, only they don't dare do so openly,' and again, 'You know as well as we do that the war is lost. Why are you too cowardly to admit it?'[3] They were executed the same afternoon. Fourteen others were arrested in the course of March; Huber and Schmorell were executed on 13 July, Graf on 12 October. The rest received sentences of imprisonment varying from ten years to six months.

A few groups similar to that of the Scholls, comprising perhaps 50 people in all, already existed in Hamburg. The main one grew out of a literary circle, organised by Erna Stahl, a progressive teacher dismissed in 1935. They disliked the Nazi régime but had no clear alternative. What they wanted was more personal freedom. 'Essentially the problem was not that we were against the Nazis but that the Nazis were against us.' When they heard about the events in Munich, they duplicated and distributed some of the Scholls' leaflets. Some planned sabotage including the destruction of a railway bridge but were unable to procure any explosives. The Gestapo infiltrated the groups and three executions resulted while five more died in captivity.[4] Thirty people were arrested for organising a collection in aid of Huber's widow; the man who took the money to Munich was arrested there and executed a year later.

Why was it that the Scholls went over from their relatively inconspicuous activities to steps which they must have known would lead to them being caught? Would they not have done better to realise that, as Saefkow once said, 'Patience too is a revolutionary activity'? A meeting had been planned for shortly after 18 February with Fr Delp of the Kreisau Group; had it taken place, he would have counselled caution. Was the impatience due simply to the fact that the leaflets seemed to be bringing no result, coupled with nervous tension and a belief that German defeat was imminent? According to one story they believed that the Gestapo was already hot on their heels, making it a question of 'now or never'. On 18 February their names were not on the lists of the Munich Gestapo; Hans may possibly have been betrayed in Ulm but there is no sign that the authorities in that city were about to move. The Scholls talked much about the need to light a torch (*Fanal*). If they had kept to distributing leaflets clandestinely, they would almost certainly have been caught before long and quietly suppressed, whereas their conspicuous action attracted attention. It would not have done so however if their leaflets had not been smuggled to England (p. 192). Most Germans who heard about it will have done so, initially at any rate, through the BBC. To point to any effect which it had on the course of the war would be hard. But it certainly provided an incontrovertible proof of the existence of 'another' Germany.

On the morning of Hans's death, his sister Inge went to see him in prison. After taking farewell, he turned and wrote on the white cell wall. Immediately afterwards the guards hustled him off to trial. The words on the wall were a quotation from Goethe, 'Remain yourself in spite of all the mighty do' (*Allen Gewalten zum Trotz sich erhalten*).

24 Kurt Gerstein[1]

Gerstein was born in 1905 in West Germany, the son of a judge who had engraved on his desk the German words for Justice, Honour, Calm, Certainty, Fidelity, Honesty, Fervour, Simplicity – whose capitals, if put together, made up his name and whose concepts, if put together, illustrate the virtues commonly admired in Germany, as well as the gaps in them. The son never achieved an easy relationship with the father, yet exemplified many of the listed virtues – except calm. He was a man of great height and immense energy, yet always a member of the 'awkward squad', a 'loner' whose unbalanced life was full of inconsistencies and contradictions. 'I was always out of line,' he said of his training.

The family's religion was superficially Protestant but Gerstein as a boy was much influenced by a Catholic nurse. Niemöller, who knew him over a number of years, called him 'a strange kind of saint' (*sonderbarer Heilige*). But, although he was active in student Bible classes, he often railed against conventional religion. To him belief was only legitimate if it found expression as compassion. The task of making religion effective in daily life needed to be taken over by the laity. He was capable of great kindness, assuming responsibility for the twin sons of a poor widow and taking them to live with him in Berlin. Yet he treated his own wife and three children with scant consideration, leaving them behind in Tübingen and only visiting them at intervals. He was attracted to young men and attracted them in return, although they sometimes reacted against his domination. His obsession with Honour and Purity points to a sexual basis for these relationships but all the evidence goes to show that they remained platonic.

He was clever and duly gained his school leaving certificate, although refusing to pay much attention to timetable and syllabus. He then decided to become a mining engineer and obtained a post in the Prussian Coal Mines in 1936 but his work was unmethodical and spasmodic. At one stage he had expressed approval of Stresemann and Brüning and at first fought hard to prevent the absorption of his Protestant youth group into the HJ. Yet in May 1933 he became a Party member. Twenty-one months later he got up in a theatre to protest against a neo-Pagan play, 'We will not allow our faith to be publicly insulted without protest.' In September 1936 he was arrested for sending at his own expense leaflets of the Confessing Church to all the jurists in Germany. Although his father secured his release after six weeks, he lost his job in the mines, was expelled from the Party and for two years was unemployed. He had however a private income from an engineering firm in Düsseldorf apparently owned by his mother's family.

He started to study theology at Tübingen but the hard intellectual slog was not for him. He switched to medicine but was made to give up after he had started to prescribe for patients before he was qualified, with unfortunate results. In 1937 Dibelius officiated at his marriage. In 1938 he was again arrested, although whether his offence was political or theological is obscure. Again his father came to the rescue and even persuaded the Party to change his expulsion into provisional membership. In July 1939 through the industrialist Hugo Stinnes he was found a job in a Thuringian potash firm but did not hold it for long. In the summer of 1940 he joined the SS who at first failed to notice his two arrests; by the time that they caught up, he had made himself too useful to be ousted. He later claimed that he had been led to this surprising step by the death of a female relative in the euthanasia operation but in fact his application for membership went in before her fate became known. He assured his Christian and anti-Nazi friends that the step involved no change in his basic views but was merely a matter of tactics. Only by going into the diabolical machine, by becoming 'a spy for God', could he hope to discover what was happening and put spokes in the wheel.

Inside the black guards he was quickly promoted to Lieutenant and appointed to the Waffen SS Institute of Hygiene in Berlin where he was welcomed for his combined if superficial knowledge of engineering and medicine. He was first concerned in decontaminating the Wehrmacht in order to counter a typhus epidemic in Russia. He went on to provide the same services for the concentration and extermination camps. In June 1942 he was ordered to procure 260 lbs of a special kind of prussic acid (Zyklon B) from a plant near Prague and take it to Belzec near Lublin in Poland. Here trainloads of Jews were being killed daily by being herded into an airtight shed and there asphyxiated by the exhaust from an old Russian diesel engine. The bodies were then buried in pits or burnt. The camp authorities felt that there ought to be some more efficient way of accomplishing their task and wanted Gerstein to advise them on the possibility of using prussic acid instead. He was given a front-seat view of the whole operation and later entertained at Treblinka where eight gas chambers were said to be operating satisfactorily, although by what method is not specified. Gerstein claimed to have got his Zyklon cylinders buried on the pretext that they were leaking and therefore unusable.

On the train back from Warsaw to Berlin Gerstein came into contact with Baron von Otter, Secretary to the Swedish Legation, to whom over ten hours sitting in the corridor he poured out the story of what he had seen. He asked Otter to transmit it to the outside world, suggesting that the British should print it as a leaflet and drop it over Germany. Otter did report to his superiors who forwarded the report to London. Gerstein called at the Nunciature in Berlin for the same purpose but not surprisingly was chased away. He later told the story to a number of other Germans and in 1944 to the Swiss Consul Hochstrasser who transmitted it to Berne.

Gerstein's activities during the last two and a half years of the war are obscure. He went to Ravensbrück and Oranienburg but there is no evidence of his having visited any of the Polish camps again. There is a story of his having been ordered early in 1944 to procure large quantities of prussic acid, for purposes undefined (but with a vague suggestion that they were to be used against civilians in the event of defeat), to have succeeded in getting them stored in Oranienburg or Auschwitz rather than Berlin and ultimately to have had them destroyed. He claimed to have been in touch with Goerdeler and others. But he is also reported to have said that there was no chance of acting successfully and that there was nothing to be done but wait for the Allies to occupy Germany. Many accounts suggest that his double life told on his physique.

He left Berlin in March 1945 and on 22 April, after crossing the lines near Reutlingen, surrendered to the French. He seems to have expected the Allies to accept him at his word and make him a leading witness against the Nazis. He was put into a hotel in Rottweil and there wrote a long report, first in French, then in German. He gave the French version to two intelligence officers, one American and one British, who came across him on 5 May; this was later used at Nuremburg. One copy of the German version reached his wife; another came, by an unknown route, into US intelligence files. At the end of May he was taken to Paris, where he was first put in a hotel, then into the house of an organisation investigating war crimes and finally into the Cherche-Midi prison. It slowly dawned on him that, instead of being used as a witness against war-criminals, he was to be prosecuted as the man who had invented the gas chamber. This was too much for him and he hanged himself in his cell on 25 July.

One is tempted to dismiss Gerstein as a romancer, one of those people who find it hard to distinguish fact from fiction, who embroider the circumstances of their past lives and who claim close acquaintance with people they barely know. The task of disentangling what was false from what was true has not been helped by Gerstein having been made a prominent character in Rolf Hochhuth's play *The Deputy*, where a good deal of artistic licence about his sayings and doings has crept in. Judgment about Gerstein's own behaviour is caught up in the question whether the Pope should or should not have threatened to put Germany under an interdict if the killing of the Jews did not stop. Even supposing that Gerstein was justified in joining the SS as a means of discovering what went on in the camps, should he not, when he had found the answer, have managed to escape from the organisation instead of continuing to abet the crimes? He must have realised that his actions were having no result. It was on those grounds that a denazification tribunal in the 1950s refused to pay his widow a pension.

On the other hand several authors have been at pains to trace people who knew or met Gerstein and their statements largely corroborate his own version of his story. Close acquaintances have asseverated that his religious beliefs were genuine.

His was not the only account of the camps to reach the West during the war. Among others a Pole, Jan Karski, who had visited Belzec, managed to give an account of what he had seen to President Roosevelt at first hand in 1943. Nor is it true that Allied publicity remained silent about the subject. In December 1942 the BBC were instructed 'to establish Hitler's plan to exterminate the Jews in Europe', and provided with evidence specifically naming Treblinka, Belzec and Sobibor as extermination camps. In April 1943 they carried a statement that the Oswiecim camp was equipped to burn 3000 corpses a day.[2] In the following month RAF planes dropped leaflets over Germany carrying similar information. This publicity had no observable effect on German actions, except possibly to accelerate the pace with which they were pushed forward. But Gerstein could not have been expected to have foreseen this.

PART THREE

Six Questions

This book has raised a number of general questions. They cannot all be discussed here. Yet I should not have been doing my job properly if I had not thought about them and I feel the reader is entitled to know the conclusions I have reached. I have therefore chosen six for discussion in this chapter. What I write is obviously a personal reaction and makes no claim to be a final word.

1. In what circumstances, if at all, does an individual have a right – or even a duty – to seek to overthrow by violence the government of his or her country?

This age-old question is intrinsic to the theme of this book but there is only space for a short answer. Some people would deny that anyone is ever entitled to rise against a government which has come into existence by due process of law. But the world would be an even less satisfactory place than it is if there had never been any rebels. Others would say, as the Brandenburg Church Administration did in July 1945, that 'the Church of Jesus Christ can never condone an attack on a human life for any reason whatever.'[1] The debate may not seem to be much advanced by saying that recourse to violent resistance is justified where a government is violating fundamental human rights since such an answer leaves to the individual the judgment as to what rights are fundamental and how far they are in fact being violated.

Yet it is with the individual conscience that the decision must ultimately rest. Where individuals come to the conclusion that vital moral principles are being disregarded by the government under which they are living, they have not merely a right but indeed a duty to consider what, if anything, they should do to remedy the situation. One of the remedies open to them is the use of force. Clearly they should not have recourse to it until other remedies have proved inadequate and even then they should not have recourse to it unless they have a reasonable expectation that its use will improve the situation. Much will depend on the quality of the alternative régime which they propose to substitute. Some would for this reason say that only persons in prominent positions, where they can get an overview of the whole situation, should resist forcibly. But this would exclude, for example, The White Rose.

If individuals' appeals to force fail, they cannot expect the government into whose power they come to give them any credit for the fact that their actions were based on high principles. They must console themselves with the conviction that they were right (unless, like Elser, p. 124, or Goerdeler, p. 171, they conclude that the very fact of failure is evidence of their having been wrong) and with the hope that future generations will think them praiseworthy.

Some would go on to say that, where manifest and gross evil is being done, individuals and in particular Christians have a duty to resist it by force, that the establishment of justice is a primary obligation regardless of the consequences which may be involved for them and others. But this is a difficult doctrine for a world in which the just cause could conceivably only prevail by the use of weapons which would put an end to civilisation, if not to life on our planet. Those who stood up to Hitler, whether inside or outside Germany, believed that he was evil and their own cause just. But were they therefore justified in adopting all the methods which they did, such as mass bombing, in order to defeat Germany? Can the price of making our own particular view of justice prevail be too high? Even those who accept that, in an inherently sinful world, resort to force is in certain cases unavoidable must admit that it is an unsatisfactory solution since it inevitably contains an element of self-will and leaves behind it resentments which a non-violent solution is less likely to do.

There is of course the possibility that someone who is energetic and warm-hearted will be unable to 'endure an hour and see injustice done'. But while this may make him honourable, it does not automatically justify him.

2 What is the right relationship between statesmen and soldiers?

We all know that war is too dangerous to be left to the soldiers – a view with which Hitler would cordially have agreed. But in May 1945 I heard General Dittmar, who had been the military commentator on the German home radio, say that war was too expert a matter to be managed by amateurs.

Ludendorff, basing himself on his experience between 1914 and 1918, had demanded that, in a Total War, the commander-in-chief must be allowed full power in the civilian as well as the military sphere. Von Seeckt, to justify his willingness to command the Reichswehr from 1920 to 1926 under the hated Republic, propounded the view that generals should be *nur-Soldaten*, mere executants of the wishes of their political masters. Beck's theory of the 'Two Pillars' has already been described (p. 142). But when Hitler displayed less than no intention of acting on it, the general was slow to face the question of what in such circumstances a soldier was entitled to do. For some time he preferred to attribute the Führer's behaviour to bad advisers. It was really only after his retirement that Beck came to put the blame on Hitler himself and decide that it was his removal which was essential. Churchill ruthlessly challenged the views of his generals and in turn pressed them to adopt his own. But when they stood firm, he did not override them. Beck would almost certainly have approved of this.

Tresckow and Stauffenberg, coming on the scene when Hitler's responsibility was still more evident, claimed like Gneisenau that the Army, and particularly the General Staff, had a special trust on behalf of the nation and a duty to act where the national interest was being disregarded.

But this is reminiscent of Spain, Greece, Chile, Pakistan, Uganda and elsewhere. World opinion has tended to condemn the soldiers in those countries for taking it on themselves to define the national interest.

But if it is to be left to civilians to decide when an established government needs to be overthrown, how are soldiers to decide which groups of civilians are to be obeyed? Yet the support of the military is nowadays likely to be essential if any dissident group is to gain power. In Germany this problem was solved by the civilians agreeing that a respected soldier, Beck, should head the new government and on the whole it is likely that a post-Hitler government, if successfully formed, would have been civilian-dominated (unless civil war had provided an argument for military leadership).

The answer may be that military interference in politics is only justified when it leads to an improvement. But to an improvement on what? More individual freedom may seem the answer. Yet where freedom leads to anarchy, an increase in law and order may be more important. The need to maintain order however has been used to excuse many tyrannies.

There is the further related question as to how far soldiers should obey commands given by their superiors, whether civilian or military, when these are illegal or immoral. When Keitel and Jodl were sentenced to death at Nuremburg for obeying Hitler, protests were made in Britain that the essential bonds of discipline were being undermined. But if this principle is strictly interpreted, only Heads of State, Prime Ministers and Defence Ministers can be prosecuted when major crimes are committed during a war. Sometimes the illegality only arises in the choice of means to carry out a legitimate decision; Churchill could not be condemned for ordering his Chiefs of Staff to do all they could in February 1945 to help the Russians but this did not automatically justify the decision to bomb Dresden. As has been seen, Prussian Military Law laid down that orders with a criminal content were not to be obeyed and that a soldier who did obey would be liable to punishment (p. 82). The US Military Code is said to contain a similar provision whereas the British does not.[2] The International Military Tribunal at Nuremburg justified its verdicts on the ground that those condemned had violated the principles of the general European code of laws.

The root of the problem is that in war certain acts are allowed which in peacetime would be crimes, notably the murder of individuals whose only fault is belonging to the enemy nation. International law has sought to restrict the circumstances in which this can be done, e.g. by limiting it to armed members of the enemy forces who are offering resistance. The totality of modern war tempts belligerents to disregard these limits. This is a trend which in the interests of humanity should be resisted. But resistance is likely to be regarded as disobedience by the order-giver and punished accordingly. Individuals may thus find themselves forced to choose between the immediate danger of being punished for refusal to obey orders by their superiors and the longer-term one of being punished for violating a law which those superiors do not recognise.

3 Does anyone who lives under an evil régime inevitably acquire some share of guilt for its misdeeds?

If after the Second German War there were no Points to be departed from and no backs to be stabbed, there was equally no Treaty to contain a 'War Responsibility', let alone a 'War Guilt' clause (p. 6). This has not prevented it from being widely taken for granted that by the end of the war the British and Americans had come to regard the entire German people as 'collectively guilty' and that this belief caused them to be more harshly treated than they would otherwise have been.

The reality, as so often, was more complicated. I have tried to set down in Annex C the main facts, as far as I have been able to establish them, regarding the language used on this subject by the British and American authorities which was either directed to the German people or used in contexts to which the German people might have had access. From this it will be seen that the term 'responsibility' was used as much as, if not more than, the term 'guilt'. Some deliberately chose the former term since they, like Burke, did not know how to draw up an indictment against a whole people and were well aware that some Germans, having opposed Hitler from the outset, could not be charged with the moral delinquency which the term 'guilt' contains. There was an explicit desire to avoid repeating the post-1919 argument about 'German war guilt'. At the outset this issue was not everywhere realised and there was some looseness in the use of terms. But the phrase 'collective German guilt' was practically never used.

Article A3(ii) of the Potsdam Protocol stated that one of the principles of the Occupation should be 'to convince the German people that . . . they cannot escape responsibility for what they have brought on themselves since their own ruthless warfare and the fanatical Nazi resistance have destroyed the German economy and made chaos and suffering inevitable.' The thought behind the term 'responsibility' is that events in any society result from the sum total of actions taken (or not taken) by all its members. As I wrote in the *British Zone Review* on 23 November 1946:

> A person who is held 'responsible' for an action with evil effects is not necessarily blameworthy; yet he is held to have contributed by his behaviour to the ultimate evil result. To say therefore that the German people were responsible for the rise and domination of Nazism is to imply that Nazism was the result of all the historical forces acting in Germany between 1919 and 1945, which historical forces are no less than the combined result of all the individuals living in Germany in that period. And it cannot be denied that, if all Germans had acted differently, Nazism would never have happened.
>
> Obviously some Germans bear a much higher degree of 'responsibility' than others, while some, such as those thrown into prison for resistance, may only bear responsibility in an indirect way. Yet none are wholly exempt. And if it is argued that this emphasis on an individual's responsibility for his surroundings, even when he struggles against them, implies a grim view of the world, the answer can be made that such an emphasis is both a democratic and a Christian point of

view. It is upon each individual that the responsibility lies for the world as he
finds it and as he leaves it. And although we may sympathise with the tragic fate
of those born into an epoch with dominant forces which they renounce yet are
unable to surmount, their very struggle to surmount them implies a responsibility.

The idea of personal responsibility before God for the course of this world
is one familiar to many Christians. Ironically it has often been those with least
cause to reproach themselves who have been most ready to admit their share.
The Scholls wrote (p. 235) that 'Germans should feel not merely pity (*Mitleid*)
for the victims of Nazism but guilt (*Mitschuld*). None can acquit himself of
this, each is guilty, guilty, guilty.' In a leaflet for circulation to front-line
troops late in 1943, Anton Saefkow wrote, 'Great is the guilt of the able-
bodied masses in Germany for having allowed the Fascist terrorists to gain
power. The atrocities of the Wehrmacht have increased this guilt.'[3] Adam von
Trott said in 1943 that he and his friends were ready to accept their share of
responsibility and guilt.[4] Helmuth von Moltke wrote in 1942 that 'it is beginning to dawn on a not too numerous but active part of the population, not
that they have been misled, not that they are in for a hard time, not that they
might lose the war but that what they have done is sinful and that they are
personally responsible for every savage act that has been done, not of course
in the ordinary sense of the word but as Christians.'[5]

In October 1945 the newly-formed German Evangelical Church, under the
influence of Niemöller, Barth and Dibelius, presented to a delegation from
the World Council of Churches at Stuttgart a declaration that

> we know ourselves to be with our people in a great company of suffering and in
> solidarity of guilt. With great pain do we say 'Through us endless suffering has
> been brought to many peoples and countries.' True, we have struggled for many
> years in the name of Jesus Christ against a spirit which found its terrible expression
> in the National Socialist régime of violence. But we accuse ourselves for not
> witnessing more courageously, not praying more faithfully, for not believing
> more joyously, for not loving more ardently.

A similar but personal declaration was made by Albrecht Haushofer, the
protégé and adviser of Rudolf Hess, in his sonnet 'Guilt'. He was clutching
the book containing this when, on 23 April 1945, he, along with Klaus
Bonhoeffer, Rudiger Schleicher and twelve others (p. 224), was despicably
murdered by the SS.[6] In a service of commemoration for the men of 20 July
in 1954, Peter von Yorck's brother asked pardon 'for that with which we are
collectively burdened. May our epoch's distance from God be reduced to
insignificance.'[7] Hans Lukaschek of the Kreisau Group said that, while he did
not believe in collective guilt, he, unlike the majority of his countrymen,
believed just as little in collective innocence.[8]

Some Germans have argued that a share of responsibility must fall on
people outside Germany, including Britain, for treating Germany unimagin-
atively after 1919 and for failing to stand up to Hitler after 1933. An acknowl-
edgement of such responsibility was made by Dr Geoffrey Fisher, Archbishop
of Canterbury in December 1945, as a response to the German Church

Declaration.[9] Similar acknowledgements can be found elsewhere including the article in the *British Zone Review* which has just been quoted. The concept could be extended to make all individuals collectively responsible for all the evil in the world. It then comes close to the theological notion of Original Sin.

4 Has the nation-state outlived its usefulness?

There are in fact three questions here which need to be distinguished:

(a) Have modern communications and nuclear explosives made the sovereign state a lethal anachronism?

(b) Does it still make sense for states to be based upon groups of people united by awareness of a common but distinctive nationality?

(c) If so, have all people possessing such a consciousness a right to live together in a single sovereign state, even if that means incorporating within that state substantial minorities of people without that awareness (but normally with awareness of some other nationality to which the right of cohabitation is being denied).

The answers to all these questions are complicated by the fact that any government which manages to maintain itself for an appreciable period inevitably creates (or, if they already exist, strengthens) certain common characteristics among its subjects — linguistic, social, cultural, political — which serve as badges, enabling those subjects to recognise one another and distinguishing them from the subjects of other states. Nationality is not immutable and states create nations more than nations create states. Where the reverse seems to have happened, as in nineteenth-century Germany and Italy, the nations are relics of earlier states which have broken up or been subjugated.

To maintain itself for an appreciable period, a government needs (i) to bring sufficient order and prosperity to enough of its subjects to make its overthrow from within unlikely and (ii) to remain strong enough to repulse, if necessary with the help of allies, any threat to its existence from outside. For both these purposes it needs to win and hold the loyalty of as many as possible of its subjects (if not to itself, then to the constitution on which the state is based). Its chances of doing this will be enhanced if those subjects share the awareness of common characteristics which not only obligates them to sacrifice narrow self-interest to a common cause (or at least to a wider conception of self-interest) but also distinguishes them from other states. And the chances are that the longer a government (or system of government) exists, the stronger will that awareness become. Of course, the process is reversible. A government or system which for some reason or reasons fails to maintain order and prosperity (as the system of the Weimar Republic did) will gradually forfeit loyalty. The consciousness of national membership is important, if not vital, to the effective functioning of any state in the industrialised world.

Governments are greedy of loyalty. To get support and thereby exercise power, they insist that their points of view are right so that to plan their overthrow is not merely intellectually mistaken but also morally (as well as legally) wrong. They claim that members of the nation have a duty to support its government and they regard with hostile suspicion any concept or institution which weakens that claim. They profess that their purposes are consonant with and further the interests of humanity at large but view with hostility any of their own citizens or any other government which disputes that profession.

Thus all states which do not disintegrate tend to become national states and all governments habitually invoke the right of their nation to self-determination, i.e. to sovereignty. If two sovereign states become involved in a dispute which one or both are not prepared to settle by mutual concessions, and which cannot be left unresolved, force remains the only way out. Technology has however transformed the amount of damage involved in armed conflict, making it likely that large-scale war would put the world back to its condition in the sixth century and perhaps even end human life. For that reason it has become urgent to find a system or systems by which sovereign states will settle their disputes according to generally and previously agreed principles. That however will not happen, at any rate fast enough, if a government can, by appealing to the patriotism of their citizens, persuade those citizens that the results of insisting on having their own way will be more satisfactory than accepting some form of peaceful dispute-resolution. Moreover it has so far proved beyond man's capacity to devise a way of coercing powerful states into accepting peaceful dispute-resolution against their will and it remains to be seen whether the fear of annihilation can become vivid enough to make them realise that such resolution is in their own long-term self-interest.

The result is that, although the independent sovereign state has become a lethal anachronism, the obstacles to transcending it are great, as the League of Nations, the United Nations and the European Economic Community have shown. Human selfishness has to be curbed if social life is to develop. Only states held together by the emotional force of nationality seem capable of exerting the necessary restraint. It is not enough to point out that large-scale war can no longer be to either side's advantage. The *Widerstand* were apt to overestimate what could be achieved by reason, as is illustrated in their *Observations on the Peace Programme of the American Churches.*[10]

There are of course states in which the awareness of common nationality is not shared by substantial elements of the population (usually the relics of some previous governmental system or the result of migration). Such a minority is unlikely to accept, either at all or to the same extent, the obligation to loyalty felt by the majority – and may even replace loyalty by passive or active antagonism (as with the Ulster Catholics, the Basques and the Tamils). The presence of such an element impairs the effectiveness of the government, which therefore seeks to weaken or eliminate it by assimilation. Experience however suggests that attempts at assimilation, if openly and deliberately pursued, are counter-productive. Success requires the exercise by the majority of a degree of forbearance which does not come easily to human beings organised in groups. The only other solution is to set the minority free to govern itself or transfer its members to another state which already contains a majority like themselves. Where groups with different nationalities live intermingled, the only permanently satisfactory solution may be a redrawing of frontiers combined with a transfer of populations.

This book began by asking why the National Socialist Government was ever allowed to happen. Part of the answer is that the German nation found itself in a crisis in which its accumulated possessions and inherited values seemed at risk. The causes and nature of the crisis were imperfectly understood and, in an atmosphere of panic, the Germans resorted to such solutions as were in their own power to apply. In the apparent urgency for drastic action, they allowed their norms of judgment and humanity to be swept aside. The forms which action took were largely determined by Germany's past history and the society resulting from it (which is not to say that everything was inevitable).

But the crisis to which the Germans were reacting was by no means exclusively a German one. Although they may themselves have been largely responsible for what happened, the treatment of the world situation by other nations had played its part, as Adam von Trott pointed out (p. 184). Elsewhere developments took different forms (in Britain a National Government, in the USA a New Deal) because the histories and societies were different. But in all cases the nations and their governments were adopting limited national solutions because, although the crisis was international, there was no adequate machinery for agreeing on international solutions. Each nation-state did what seemed best for itself without considering what effect its actions would have outside its frontiers, so that the difficulties of others were often exacerbated. This had been the practice of states since time immemorial. But industrialisation had greatly increased the interdependence of states. The rational solution would have been to develop an international political society to match the international economy. But nation-states have been largely consolidated by their difference from and antagonism to other nation-states. To ask national governments to transcend these antagonisms and allow themselves to be overridden by a majority of 'foreigners' comes close to asking them to deny their natures. Nor, if they were to do so, could they count on the support of their populations.

The phenomenon of National Socialism was therefore a notable example of the problem created for man by his nature. The processes of change in the world repeatedly confront him with situations which he does not fully understand but which seem to threaten the roots of his existence. He then tends instinctively to take the narrower selfish solution rather than use reason to search for longer-term solutions which involve co-operation with people who do not share the same outward badges (such as geographical situation, language and culture) indicating a community of interest. This reluctance to co-operate makes international action a slow and frustrating business, which in itself heightens the temptation to act nationally. Even when decisions are taken internationally, there is the problem of enforcing them without adequate instruments for international coercion. One hesitates to reconcile oneself to the position that man's limitations are so innate that they will end by undermining his achievements, especially when individuals are capable of noteworthy insight and altruism (as examples in this book show).

5 What did the Widerstand achieve?

It clearly failed to overthrow the Nazi régime or to shorten the war. It only modified the policies of the Nazi government in relatively minor matters, such as crucifixes in schools.

It had little influence on the form of the post-1945 Germanies. The vital decisions in that respect were taken by the Americans, British and Russians, while the Germans to whom they left the detailed execution of their decisions had not on the whole belonged to the active internal *Widerstand*, although some of the most prominent had been in captivity (Schumacher) or exile (Brandt, Ulbricht).

The *Widerstand* may certainly be said to have demonstrated to the world that there was 'another Germany' and to have 'redeemed the honour of the German people'. But to show that this had any effect on the way the victors treated Germany would be hard. There has even been a danger that the demonstration of the existence of 'another Germany' would be used by Germans who scarcely if at all belonged to it as an excuse for not facing up to the extent to which German society as a whole was responsible for Nazi misdoings.

Certain features of current life in West Germany can trace their origin back to the *Widerstand*. One is the improved relationship between the Catholic and Evangelical Churches which followed from their discovery of common interests in face of Nazi attacks. This has played some part in the creation of a single Christian Democratic Party to replace the DNVP (predominantly Protestant) and the Centre Party (entirely Catholic). This simplification of the party system has contributed to making stable government easier. The Evangelicals have become more ready to admit that the Churches may and in certain circumstances should criticise the state. Greater sensitivity to the use of violence has perhaps developed. The simplification and consolidation of the trade union organisation was worked out by its leadership while in exile.

There is a good deal in German life today, such as the importance attached to human rights and the appreciation of the value of pluralism, which represents learning from the experience of life under Nazi rule. Various parts of the *Widerstand* came to realise how much they had in common and thus replaced the splintering of Weimar by a broad consensus, partly embodied in the Basic Law. The workers have been accepted as full members of the community. It is hard to be sure that these lessons would have been learnt if nobody had set an example by standing up to Hitler. The fact that those who disagreed with Hitler proved right has contributed to the process of reinterpreting the German past and acquiring a more realistic view of Germany's place in the world.

If it is objected that 21 per cent of the population live in the Democratic Republic and do not therefore enjoy full freedom, it must be remembered that the sort of society in which they do live was precisely that for which the Communist 61 per cent of those executed for their part in the *Widerstand* gave their lives.[11]

Alfred Delp, the Jesuit who was executed for his share in the Kreisau discussions, wrote before his death that his time had been one of sowing rather than reaping. 'God sows and assuredly will also in due course reap. The least I can do is to fall into the ground as sound and fruitful seed-corn.'[12]

6 Has the Widerstand a lesson for today?

The lesson of the *Widerstand* is one familiar from history.

'Fascism' is something which must be prevented rather than cured. Ousting it once it has gained power is costly in human lives and material resources.

It wins support when an inadequately integrated society is subjected to excessive strains. The degree of a society's vulnerability to Fascism varies with

(*a*) the degree of its integration;
(*b*) the severity of the strains;
(*c*) the norms and values established in its culture;
(*d*) the goals which it holds up to its people.

The ways to prevent Fascism from gaining support accordingly are

(*a*) to foster integration;
(*b*) to foresee and forestall serious strains;
(*c*) to develop a culture which assigns high values to integrity, humanity and imagination;
(*d*) to refrain from claiming a place in the world disproportionate to the society's resources.

Strains arise when any substantial section of the population believes itself to be unfairly oppressed or deprived. The other sections of the society must, in their own long-term interest, show enough generosity of mind and money to prevent such beliefs from arising. The oppressed section must be prepared to respond to such generosity; where it does not, the society must not fear to be firm.

The generosity must be shown between nations as well as inside them.

Easy to say, hard to do. Farsightedness cannot be *installed* like television.

ANNEX A
Numbers

Many books about The Third Reich contain many statistics. Inevitably these have been built up for different purposes and on different bases. One source gives 4500 arrests for the first six months of 1944, another 200,917! No useful purpose would be served by trying to reconcile them all here. It may however be helpful to indicate some rough orders of magnitude.

Arrests

In July 1933 26,789 persons were said to have been in 'protective custody'.[1] The *Statistisches Jahrbuch* for 1935 gave a total of political prisoners for the whole of 1933 as 20,565. But this figure has been criticised as far too small.[2]

In 1936, 11,687 persons were arrested for 'socialist work',[3] in 1937 the figure was 8058, with a further 17,168 arrested for offences under the 'Malice Act'.[4]

In April 1939, according to Gestapo records, there were 162,734 persons in protective custody, 112,432 serving sentences for political offences and 27,369 awaiting trial for such offences, a total of 302,535.[5] (Total population of Germany in 1937 58 million.)

On 1 September 1939 there were 21,400 prisoners in the six main concentration camps and about another 3600 in other camps.[6]

In 1939 6284 persons were found guilty on 'political grounds'; in 1940 the figure was 10,963, in 1941, 17,344. In the single month of October 10,776 people were arrested in Germany and Austria. In the first half of 1942 the number fell to 9343, but in the corresponding period of 1943 rose again to 26,650.[7] Another source gives the number of those arrested for 'socialist work' in 1941 as 11,405.[8]

At the end of 1942 there were 88,000 in concentration camps inside Germany.[9] Thereafter the figures rose steeply but the majority of inmates were non-German.

August 1943	224,000
August 1944	524,286
January 1945	714,000[10]

It has been said that 3 million Germans saw the inside of a camp or prison during the twelve years of Nazi rule, an average of 250,000 a year.[11] Two-thirds of these are believed to have occurred during the war years. For such figures the number of arrests and prisoners would have had to be higher than the foregoing statistics indicate. There has probably been some double-counting of people arrested more than once, but this applies throughout.

Executions

The Ministry of Justice Register of Executions (which until 1933 had been confined to executions for murder) contained 11,881 names between January 1933 and December 1943, with a further 11,398 in the next sixteen months, a total of 23,279.[12] But this figure on the one hand includes ordinary criminals and on the other excludes persons killed without trial, 16,000 condemned to death by courts martial mostly for offences against discipline such as desertion[13] (12,000 of these after 1 January 1944) and persons dying from whatever cause in concentration camps (about 120,000 a year in 1942 but including non-Germans).[14] An estimate of 32,500 Germans executed for political offences during the Third Reich is in line with these figures and has been widely accepted.[15] Of these 20,000 were Communists (p. 50).

German Jews

There were 503,000 Jews in Germany in 1933.[16] By 1939 400,000 persons are said to have emigrated from Germany, of whom 35,000 were non-Jews,[17] but there is an alternative total figure of 250,000.[18] There are said to have been 15,000 Jews left in Germany at the end of the war.[19] This leaves between 253,000 and 123,000 unaccounted for who must be presumed to have perished in camps (although a few may have emigrated in 1939–41).

Total deaths

At the Nuremburg Trial, the SS Gruppenführer Wilhelm Hoettl claimed to have been told by Eichmann in August 1944 that the total number of Jews exterminated was 6 million.[20] The vast majority of these were non-German.

Brockhaus Encyclopaedia (in its article *Weltkrieg*) now gives the total number of persons who lost their lives as a result of the Third Reich and the war as 55 million. About 8 million of these were German.

Executions as a result of the 20 July plot

A figure of 20,000 was given (without indication of source) in the British *Annual Register* for 1944.

Among the German documents which came into the hands of the British Admiralty after the war were the reports which Admiral Raeder and his successor Admiral Doenitz filed at German naval headquarters about such matters affecting the Navy as had come up at those of Hitler's situation conferences which they attended. A South African journalist called Anthony Martienssen, who had served as a temporary naval officer during the war, was given a temporary post as a Press Officer in the Department of the Chief of Naval Intelligence so that he could prepare a translated text of these documents for publication.

The translation was published in mimeographed form in seven instalments during 1947. Copies were distributed to various newspapers and university libraries. Each chapter was given an introduction explaining to English readers the background to the subjects discussed in it. As newsprint was strictly rationed in Britain at that time, the press made little use of the material and a decision was taken to reprint it in the 1948 edition of the *Naval Annual* which had been started as a private venture in 1886 by Lord Brassey, a former Civil Lord of the Admiralty, to enlist public support for a stronger Navy. The *Annual* was subsequently taken over by the Royal United Service Institution, a semi-official body. The Editor of the *Annual* in 1948 was Rear-Admiral H. G. Thursfield, a former naval correspondent of *The Times*.

In 1948 Martienssen, who had by then left the Admiralty, published a book called *Hitler and His Admirals*, which made much use of the Admiralty material.

The Introduction to Chapter III of the Report for 1944, which dealt with the events on 20 July, contained the following passage, which was reproduced verbatim in Brassey's *Annual* and Martienssen's book:

> The plot miscarried. Firstly because Stauffenberg did not wait to make sure that Hitler was dead, secondly because the communications were not severed, thirdly because Fromm, uncertain of Hitler's death, betrayed the movement. The revolt was essentially a revolt from the top. It was impossible under the reign of terror of Himmler's Gestapo for ordinary people to take part but an indication of the extent is given by the fact that, according to one source, based on names and places, more than 4980 Germans were exterminated in the purge which followed.

The commentary was said to have been drawn 'partly from other German reports and partly from Admiralty sources'. But no document such as that referred to in the last sentence occurs in the list of documents supplied to Martienssen by the Naval Intelligence Division. The copy of the Brassey publication now held in the Ministry of Defence has a marginal note, made some time later by the then head of the Admiralty's Enemy Documents Section, that 'the figure must be considered very doubtful'.

Various attempts to trace Martienssen have proved fruitless. No scholar appears to have come across the document to which he referred. Dr W. Hammer in 1959 described the figure of 4980 as 'imported from America'.[21] But Prince von der Leyen wrote in 1965 that 'at the end of 1944 people were talking of 5000 dead and 20,000 arrests directly or indirectly concerned with 20 July'[22] while R. G. Graf von Thun-Hohenstein in 1982 spoke of 'the 5000 people who were handed over to the hangmen in the ensuing nine months'.[23] Chancellor Kohl also used the figure of 5000 in a speech on 20 July 1984.

The latest list of names of those executed would seem to be that made by

Ulrike Eich in R. Lill and H. Oberreuter, *20 Juli, Portraits des Widerstands* (Düsseldorf 1984), pp. 393–409. This spread its net fairly widely, including for example Kiep and Fräulein von Thadden of the Solf Circle who were condemned to death on 1 July 1944. It contains 213 names, of whom 157 men and 8 women died in one way or another before the end of the war. It is not complete: G. Beier, for example, in *Die Illegale Leitung der deutschen Gewerkschaften 1933–1945* (Cologne 1981) lists 11 victims at this period of whom only 6 are on the Eich roll. Hammer says that 39 persons were killed at Sachsenhausen on 4 January 1945. Nitzsche in *Die Saefkow–Jacob–Bästlein Gruppe* (East Berlin 1957) says that 400 were killed in the breaking up of the Saefkow group. If these figures are put together and no allowance made for double-counting, the total is 609.

On 16 August 1944 Party District Leaders were asked to inform Gauleiters of the names of all people who might have been connected with the putsch as well as of other persons whose behaviour, either in the past or the present, gave rise to doubt concerning their NS views or ideological integrity, including especially all Freemasons, 'Jewish lackeys' and leaders or officials of former political parties.[24] On 22 August, in an operation known as *Gitteraktion* ('Railing' or alternatively but less probably *Gewitteraktion*, i.e. Thunderstorm) the security authorities rounded up about 5000 people, chosen no doubt on the basis of the lists sent in. At the time the German armies in both west and east were in headlong flight and there was no knowing where they could be halted, if at all; the Nazi leaders no doubt wanted to reduce the problems they might have on their hands at home by getting behind bars all those likely to make trouble. Most of the people gathered in were released fairly quickly after the military situation had been stabilised; Adenauer, for example, was set free in November. But some were kept till the end of the war and a number died, although there is no evidence that they were deliberately killed.

Several officials from the Reich Security Head Office said after the war that under 1000 people were arrested as a result of 20 July and under 200 executed (although one of them had previously given the figures of 7000 arrested and 700 executed).[25] I suspect that the figure 4980 resulted from a confusion with the *Gitteraktion*. In any case it should not be regarded as a considered estimate approved by the British Government. The actual number of executions depends on how close a connection with the putsch is called for in order to qualify. The figure of 11,398 given above implies that on an average 23 persons were being executed every day between 1 January 1944 and 30 April 1945. Heinrich Müller, the head of the Gestapo, said to Freya von Moltke in the autumn of 1944, 'We are not going to make the same mistake as in 1918 and leave our internal enemies alive.'[26] Hence the rate of executions tended to rise as defeat came closer. It seems highly likely that at least 5000 people were executed between 20 July 1944 and 7 May 1945. But of these probably not more than 200 were closely involved in the plot or in sheltering those who had been. The figures of 5000 deaths and 20,000 arrests may well have been put into circulation by the security authorities *pour décourager les autres*.

(I am grateful to Mr R. M. Coppock of the Foreign Documents Section of the Ministry of Defence and to Mr T. C. Charman of the Imperial War Museum for help in establishing the circumstances in which the Brassey document was compiled.)

ANNEX B

Statements made committing the American and British Governments as to the treatment of Germany after Unconditional Surrender 1943–5

1 *Roosevelt* at Casablanca 23 January 1943. The elimination of German, Japanese and Italian war power does not mean the destruction of the population [of those countries].

2 *Roosevelt* 12 February 1943. We mean no harm to the common people of the Axis nations. We wish the Germans to have a normal chance to develop in peace as useful and respectable members of the European Community.

3 *Simon* 10 March 1943. An Allied victory is not going to mean the end of Germany, the extinction of the German race, the breakdown of society or a return to chaos. We are not seeking to deny Germany a place in the Europe of the future. [Simon was speaking on behalf of the Government as a whole in reply to a debate initiated by the Bishop of Chichester in the House of Lords.]

4 *Churchill* 21 September 1943. We do not war against nations as such.

5 *Roosevelt* 24 December 1943. The United Nations have no intention to enslave the German people.

6 *Churchill* 22 February 1944. The term 'unconditional surrender' does not mean that the German people will be enslaved or destroyed. It means however that the Allies will not be bound to them at the moment of surrender by any pact or obligation. There will be for instance no question of the Atlantic Charter applying to Germany as a matter of right and barring territorial transfers or adjustments in enemy countries. No such arguments will be admitted as were used by Germany after the last war saying that they surrendered in consequence of President Wilson's Fourteen Points. Unconditional surrender means that the victors have a free hand. It does not mean that they are entitled to behave in a barbarous manner nor that they wish to blot out Germany from among the nations of Europe. If we are bound, we are bound

260

to our own consciences to civilisation. We are not bound to the Germans as the result of a bargain struck.

7 *Roosevelt* 21 October 1944.   We bring no charge against the German race as such. . . . The German people are not going to be enslaved.

8 *Churchill* 18 January 1945.   The President of the United States and I in your name [the House of Commons] have repeatedly declared that the enforcement of unconditional surrender upon the enemy in no way relieves us the victorious Powers of our obligations to humanity, or our duties as civilised and Christian nations. . . . We may now say to our foes, 'We demand unconditional surrender but you well know how strict are the moral limits within which our action is confined.' We are no extirpators of nations or butchers of peoples. We make no bargain with you. We accord you nothing as a right. Abandon your resistance unconditionally. We remain bound by our customs and our nature.

9 *Roosevelt* 1 March 1945.   Unconditional surrender does not mean the destruction or enslavement of the German people.

ANNEX C
Did the British and Americans regard the Germans as 'collectively guilty'?

The answer to this question is widely assumed to be 'Yes' but no extensive or systematic examination of the evidence seems to have been made. This note is only to be regarded as a preliminary indication of the likely answer. That answer would be that two terms were used, 'collective guilt' and 'collective responsibility'. Whereas 'collective guilt' implied moral blame, the term 'collective responsibility' was deliberately chosen as indicating that, although all Germans adults must be regarded as having contributed to the history of their country, many of them did not recognise or foresee the consequences of their actions while others tried to make that history take a different course but were unsuccessful. They should not therefore all be regarded as morally blameworthy, although they must expect to have to share in the present and future consequences of their country's past. As time went on, 'responsibility' was more generally used than 'guilt'.

Pre-surrender statements

Eden May 1942.   The longer the German people continue to support and to tolerate the régime which is leading them to destruction, the heavier grows their own direct responsibility for the damage they are doing to the world.
Simon, replying for the Government in House of Lords 10 March 1943.   People must accept responsibility for the form of government which grows up in their country.
Attlee 7 July 1944.   If any section [of the German people] really wants to see a return to a régime based on respect for international law and the rights of the individual, they must understand that no one will believe them until they have themselves taken active steps to rid themselves of the present régime. The longer they continue to support and to tolerate their present rulers, the heavier grows their own direct responsibility for the destruction that is being wrought throughout the world.

The Handbook of Military Government issued by the British War Office in September 1944[1] and those issued by SHAEF in December 1944 and April 1945[2] do not contain the word 'guilt' while 'collective responsibility' only occurs in relation to acts of the German civilian population against the occupying forces after surrender.

Protocol of Potsdam Conference Para. A3(ii)

The purposes of the occupation of Germany ... are ... to convince the German people that they have suffered a total military defeat and that they cannot escape responsibility for what they have brought upon themselves, since their own ruthless warfare and the fanatical Nazi resistance have destroyed the German economy and made chaos and suffering inevitable.

Post-surrender statements to the German public in the British Zone

The Press and Public Relations Branch of 21 Army Group, which in August 1945 became the Public Relations and Information Services Control Group of the British Element of the Allied Control Commission, issued a series of directives to those British officers who were in charge of producing newspapers for the German public; they also applied to radio.[3] These are the clearest evidence of the view which the British authorities presented to the Germans, with the intention of getting it adopted.

12 May 1945   Five points were to dominate output. One was to be 'the common responsibility of all Germans for Nazi crimes. The moral responsibility for those crimes (especially Belsen and Dachau) must be laid wholly and solely on the German nation.

19 May 1945   Distinguish clearly between the active guilt of criminals which can only be atoned for by punishment and the passive guilt of the people as a whole which can be atoned for by hard work, restitution and a change of heart. .... We should convey to the Germans the impression that our interest is in reviewing the facts of history rather than waging a propaganda campaign on the subject of guilt. .... By accepting Germany's guilt as his personal guilt, the individual begins the task of spiritual reconstruction.

26 June 1945   The theme of collective moral (as opposed to legal or criminal) responsibility should remain as the undercurrent of our output.

1 August 1945 (in connection with Religious Affairs)   Particularly welcome are contributions [from Germans to the press] in which writers express or imply recognition of some degree of collective German guilt for the events of the past few years.

26 September 1945 (in connection with the Belsen trial)   There is a tendency to allow our readers and audience to forget their own share (passive or active) in responsibility for the NS régime. .... Opportunities should be taken to note incidentally the complicity or passive responsibility of the vast majority of Germans and to point out in connection with the need for responsible individual action in rebuilding Germany the results of leaving things to the Führer in the past.

1 November 1945   In comment on the Nuremburg trials and other subjects it is important to distinguish between the criminal guilt of those who may be condemned and the collective responsibility of those who supported, were indifferent to or opposed ineffectively the criminals of the 'Nazi conspiracy'. The conceptions of *Mitschuld* and *Mitverantwortung* must be kept distinct if our discussion of this theme is to have any effect.

20 February 1946   No leader on the guilt of Nazi leaders as exposed at Nuremburg should fail to mention the responsibility of the German people for having such leaders.

7 March 1946   Germans are not represented on the prosecution [at Nuremburg] because in spite of the bravery of individual opponents the nation as a whole was an instrument, however ignorant, of crimes and of the conspiracy against humanity.

The last extract comes from the last of these directives to be issued. For by the spring of 1946 responsibility for producing newspapers was in process of being transferred from the British authorities to Germans licensed by them and in consequence close control was no longer exercised over what was said in the press. The licences reminded the recipients that the German press had a particular responsibility in 'reorientating' the minds of German people. The papers were therefore required to direct the German public towards a fuller appreciation of the facts of recent history (including the origins and misdemeanours of the Nazi régime).

The *British Zone Review*

The 'house magazine' of the British Control Staff, published fortnightly from October 1945, contained a number of discussions on the subject of guilt and responsibility.[4] An article which appeared on 8 December 1945 and was signed by Major-General Bishop, the Chief of the PR/ISC Group, contained the following paragraphs:

> One problem of particular interest and complexity is the manner in which the 'war guilt' theme should be presented. The German people firmly believe that any responsibility attaching to Germany for the outbreak of war in 1939 rests on the shoulders of Adolf Hitler and the other prominent Nazi leaders. At present they resolutely close their minds to any argument that, by entrusting power to Hitler and allowing him to control their destinies, they thereby assumed a share of the responsibility for the crimes committed by Germany under the Nazi régime. Any statement which emphasises their collective guilt is dismissed as 'propaganda'. The lesson they draw is that 'it does not pay to lose a war'; they are not as yet prepared to accept the thesis that it does not pay to start a war.
>
> It seems likely that this problem can only be solved by letting the facts speak for themselves. . . . It is, in my belief, only through a gradual assimilation by the German people of the reasons underlying the sufferings which they, and the other peoples of Europe, are now undergoing, that they will be led to turn their thoughts inwards and search their hearts for their own responsibility in bringing this catastrophe upon themselves and upon the whole world.

After this, the subject dropped out of discussion for a while, only to be revived in the autumn of 1946 by the Nuremburg verdicts. The *British Zone Review* contained articles and letters on 28 September, 12 October, 9 and 23 November and 7 December 1946 and 1 March 1947. The main protagonists were myself and Dr Henry Dicks of the Tavistock Clinic, who combined long experience in psychiatry with deep knowledge of Germany; in the Control Commission he was helping to select suitable Germans for administrative posts in the new régime. I was arguing (p. 248) that the notion of guilt should be abandoned but that that of responsibility should be pressed home in spite of unfavourable German reactions. He argued that Germans who admitted guilt in their hearts would not be prepared to admit it publicly as long as their conquerors were pressing them to do so and that the occupation authorities would be depriving themselves of the help of a number of Germans who would be useful to them unless they were prepared, in these cases, to let bygones be bygones. I was much impressed by Dicks's arguments at the time and used them against critics in Britain who complained that our publicity was not getting across to the Germans. In retrospect, however, I think we were arguing at cross-purposes. He was primarily concerned with the effect of denazification proceedings on individuals, I with the desirability of bringing before the German public all the information which was coming to light about the ways in which Germans had behaved between 1933 and 1945. I think today that it was right to get that information on the record inside Germany even if little immediate attention was paid to it.

The US Zone

Until the summer of 1945 action was governed by the same SHAEF handbooks of December 1944 and April 1945 as directed the British Zone. On 21 May, in preparation for the hand-over from Military Government to the Control Commission, the Joint US Chiefs of Staff Directive No. 1067 was issued to all key personnel (although it was not published until October).[5] It made no mention of guilt, collective or otherwise, but Paragraph 4A, anticipating Potsdam, gave instructions for it to be brought home to the Germans that Germany's ruthless warfare and the fanatical Nazi resistance had destroyed the German economy and made chaos and suffering inevitable, and that the Germans themselves could not escape responsibility for what they had brought on themselves.

The Directive issued on 22 May 1945 by the Psychological Warfare Division of SHAEF said that the first steps of re-education were to be undertaken by arousing insight into the collective responsibility for the crimes of Germany. This was to confine itself to confronting the Germans with incontrovertible facts which would arouse an insight into German war guilt and the collective guilt for such crimes as the concentration camps.[6]

But a second directive six days later called for a distinction to be drawn between the active guilt of the crimes and the passive guilt of the entire *Volk*. In May and June American-controlled papers carried articles by prominent

German-speakers living abroad, such as C. G. Jung and the novelist Fritz Werfel, in which references were made to collective guilt. But a subsequent study of these papers reported that the German people were being held responsible but not guilty while a study made in 1956 of the American overt paper *Die Neue Zeitung* came to the same conclusion.

Notes

In these notes, full details are given about a book when it is mentioned for the first time. Thereafter, a reference is given to that first mention, e.g. 'as No. 3' refers to the third note to the same chapter, 'as I 5' refers to the fifth note to Chapter I in Part I, 'as Beck 20' refers to the twentieth note to the section on Beck in Part II.

Where no place of publication is given, London should be understood.

Wherever possible, references have been given to English translations of German books.

VfZ refers to the *Vierteljahreshefte für Zeitgeschichte.*

FRUS refers to *Foreign Relations of the United States.*

Chapter I Why was Hitler allowed to gain power?

1 E. Zeller, *Geist der Freiheit* (Munich 1965), p. 82, citing document of Nuremburg International Military Tribunal, vol. XLI 267. Schacht resigned on 26 November 1937 but the appointment of Funk as his successor was not announced until 4 February 1938.

2 I have developed my views on German history in *The Kaiser and his Times* (1964) and *West Germany* (1968).

3 T. Parsons, 'Democracy and Social Structure in Pre-Nazi Germany' in *Essays in Sociological Theory* (Glencoe 1964), p. 107; D. Ehlers, *Technik und Moral einer Verschwörung* (Bonn 1964), p. 13.

4 For a brief description of this process in Britain, see M. Balfour, *Britain and Joseph Chamberlain* (1985), ch. I.

5 R. Dahrendorf, *Society and Democracy in Germany* (1969), p. 61.

6 See especially F. Fischer, *Germany's Aims in the First World War* (1967); V. I. Berghahn, *Der Tirpitz Plan* (Düsseldorf 1971); V. I. Berghahn, *Germany and the Approach of War in 1914* (1973).

7 M. Gilbert, *The Roots of Appeasement* (1966), pp. 30–1.

8 Dahrendorf, as No. 5, ch. X.

9 H. V. Dicks, 'German Personality Traits and National Socialist Ideology. A Wartime Study of German Prisoners-of-war' in D. Lerner (ed.), *Propaganda in War and Crisis* (NY 1951), p. 157; H. V. Dicks, *Licenced Mass Murder. A Socio-psychological Study of some SS Killers* (Sussex 1972).

10 Dicks, as No. 9; E. Fromm, *The Fear of Freedom* (1960); N. Sandford, T. Adorno

et al., *The Authoritarian Personality* (NY 1950). See also criticism in Dahrendorf, as No. 5, ch. XXIII.

Chapter II How the various sections of society regarded Hitler's rise

1 D. Schoenbaum, *Hitler's Social Revolution* (1967), p. 15.
2 J. E. Farquharson, *The Plough and the Swastika: The NSDAP and Agriculture 1928–1945* (1976), p. 31.
3 T. Childers, *The Nazi Voter: the Social Foundations of Fascism in Germany 1919–1933* (Chapel Hill 1983), p. 111.
4 B. Scheurig, *Ewald von Kleist-Schmenzin. Ein Konservativer gegen Hitler* (Oldenburg etc. 1968), p. 95.
5 R. C. von Gersdorff, *Soldat im Untergang* (Berlin etc. 1977), p. 51.
6 M. Balfour and J. Frisby, *Helmuth von Moltke. A Leader against Hitler* (1972), p. 222.
7 M. Demeter, *Das deutsche Offizierskorps* (Frankfurt 1962), p. 55; H. C. Deutsch, *Hitler and his Generals* (Minneapolis 1974), p. 7.
8 Dahrendorf, as I 5, p. 254.
9 K. J. Müller, *Das Heer und Hitler* (Stuttgart 1969), p. 15.
10 W. Deist, *The Wehrmacht and German Rearmament* (1981), ch. I.
11 M. Messerschmidt, *Die Wehrmacht im NS-Staat* (Hamburg 1969), p. 150.
12 Childers, as No. 3, p. 165.
13 M. Geyer, 'Etudes in Political History: Wehrmacht, NSDAP and the Seizure of Power' in P. Stachura (ed.), *The Nazi Machtergreifung* (1983), p. 111.
14 K. J. Müller, *General Ludwig Beck* (Boppard 1980), pp. 50–7.
15 Dahrendorf, as I 5, pp. 233–5.
16 J. Caplan, 'The Politics of Administration' in *Historical Journal*, 1977.
17 M. H. Kater, *The Nazi Party. A Social Profile of Members and Leaders* (Oxford 1983), pp. 241–61; R. H. Hamilton, *Who Voted for Hitler?* (Princeton 1982), pp. 90, 121.
18 The title of a book by A. Mitscherlich and F. Mielke (Heidelberg 1949); A. D. Beyerchen, *Scientists Against Hitler* (New Haven 1977).
19 D. Lerner, *The Nazi Elite* (Stanford 1951).
20 J. Caplan, 'Civil Service Support for National Socialism. An Evaluation' in G. Hirschfeld and L. Kettenacker, *Der Führerstaat. Mythos and Realität* (Stuttgart 1981).
21 J. Noakes, *The Nazi Party in Lower Saxony 1921–1933* (Oxford 1971), p. 173.
22 H. Genschel, *Die Verdrängung der Juden aus der Wirtschaft im Dritten Reich* (Göttingen 1960), pp. 274–87; M. Kater, *Studentenschaft und Rechtsradikalismus in Deutschland* (Hamburg 1975), p. 147. Statistics like these were challenged by the Nazis as being too low. Approximately 10 per cent of Germans of Jewish faith converted to Christianity.
23 Hitler's anti-semitism had a special background owing to his having spent his early years in Austria–Hungary where from 1867 onwards Germans were steadily losing ground to Magyars, Slavs and (especially in Vienna) Jews. P. Pulzer, *The Rise of Anti-Semitism in Germany and Austria* (NY 1964).
24 H. A. Turner, *German Big Business and the Rise of Hitler* (Oxford 1985), p. 125.
25 The same, pp. 192–4.
26 R. P. Eriksen, *Theologians under Hitler, Gerhard Kittel, Paul Althaus and Emmanuel Hirsch* (Yale 1985), p. 104.
27 E. Bethge, *Dietrich Bonhoeffer, Theologian, Christian, Contemporary* (1970), p. 91; M. Broszat, E. Fröhlich and F. Wiesemann, 'Zur Lage der evangelischer Kirchengemeinden' in *Bayern in der NS-Zeit* (Munich 1977), vol. I, p. 370.
28 K. Scholder, *Die Kirchen und das Dritte Reich. I. Vorgeschichte und Zeit der Illusionen 1918–1934* (Frankfurt etc. 1977, English tr. vol. I 1987), p. 19.

29 J. R. C. Wright, *Above Parties. The Political Attitudes of the German Protestant Church Leadership 1918–1933* (Oxford 1974), p. 19.
30 A. Williams, 'Resistance and Opposition Amongst Germans' in S. Hawes and R. White (eds), *Resistance in Europe 1939–1945* (1975), p. 143.
31 Eriksen, as No. 26, p. 18; A. L. Drummond, *German Protestantism since Luther* (1951), p. 153.
32 Scholder, as No. 28, p. 198.
33 Scholder, as No. 28, pp. 84–90, 185.
34 Hamilton, as No. 17, ch. III; Kater, as No. 17, pp. 27–30, 44–50; Childers, as No. 3, pp. 264–9. In Bavaria, the figures were 55 per cent and 23.5 per cent (I. Kershaw, *Popular Opinion and Political Dissent in the Third Reich, Bavaria 1933–1945* (Oxford 1983), p. 115). The relative strengths of the three main sectors were in 1933: Elite 2.78 per cent = 752,000; *Untere Mittelstand* 42.65 per cent = 11.5 million; Workers 54.56 per cent = 14.75 million. Kater, p. 12.
35 Dahrendorf, as I 5, p. 393; T. Mason, *Arbeiterklasse in Volksgemeinschaft* (Opladen 1975), p. 51; H. A. Winkler, 'Der entbehrliche Stand. Zur Mittelstandpolitik im 3ten Reich' in *Archiv für Sozialgeschichte*, 1977, p. 2.
36 Dahrendorf, as I 5, ch. XXIV.
37 L. Kettenacker, 'Sozialpsychologische Aspekte der Führer-Herrschaft' in Hirschfeld and Kettenacker, as No. 20, p. 112.
38 Farquharson, as No. 2, p. 40.
39 Noakes, as No. 21, pp. 152, 215.
40 Kater, as No. 17, p. 74; Kettenacker, as No. 37.
41 H. J. Steinberg, 'Die Haltung der Arbeiterschaft zum NS-Regime' in J. Schmädeke and P. Steinbach (eds), *Der Widerstand gegen den Nationalsozialismus* (Munich etc. 1985), p. 868.
42 C. Fischer, *Stormtroopers. A Social, Economic and Ideological Analysis 1919–35* (1983), pp. 26, 46; G. Mai, 'Der NSBO' in *VfZ XXXI* (1983), p. 601.
43 G. Klotzbach, *Gegen den Nationalsozialismus. Widerstand und Verfolgung in Dortmund* (Hanover 1969), p. 126.
44 J. Stephenson, *Women in Nazi Society* (1975); D. Winkler, 'Problematik der weiblichen Erwerbstätigkeit in Deutschland 1930–1945' in *Archiv für Sozialgeschichte*, 1977; Childers, as No. 3, p. 260.
45 Kater, as No. 22, p. 63.
46 The same, p. 94.
47 The same, pp. 43–56, 68, 123.
48 V. Sheean, *Dorothy and Red* (1964).
49 G. J. Giles, *Students and National Socialism in Germany* (1986), pp. 1, 18; Kater, as No. 22, p. 11.
50 Kater, p. 92.
51 The same, pp. 115, 117.
52 Giles, as No. 49, p. 71.
53 P. Stachura, *Nazi Youth in the Weimar Republic* (Santa Barbara 1975), ch. VIII.
54 E. Mowrer, *Triumph and Turmoil* (1970), p. 208.
55 *Völkischer Beobachter*, 29 September 1935.
56 Noakes, as No. 21, pp. 148, 165, 170.
57 Turner, as No. 24, pp. 59, 115, 157, 347.
58 I. Kershaw, *Der Hitler Mythos. Volksmeinung und Propaganda in Dritten Reich* (Stuttgart 1980), pp. 28, 70–1; M. Kater, 'Hitler in a Social Context' in *Central European History*, 1981, p. 258; Deutsch, as No. 7, p. 23.
59 H. Pohle, *Der Rundfunk als Instrument der Politik* (Hamburg 1955).
60 Scholder, as No. 28, p. 123.
61 H. O. Malone, *Adam von Trott zu Solz. Werdegang eines Verschwörers*

1909–1938 (Berlin 1986), pp. 110, 267, citing H. Schneider, *Das Ermächtigungsgesetz vom 24 März 1933.*

62 M. Goehring, *Alles oder Nicht* (Tübingen 1966), p. 70.

63 G. Ritter, *Karl Goerdeler und die deutsche Widerstandsbewegung* (Stuttgart 1964), p. 93.

Chapter III The development of the *Widerstand*

1 Farquharson, as II 2, pp. 143, 155.

2 G.C. Boehnert, *The Jurists in the SS Führerkorps 1925–1939* in Hirschfeld and Kettenacker, as II 37, pp. 361–73.

3 See list on pp. 394–409 of R. Lill and H. Oberreuter (eds), *20 Juli. Portraits des Widerstands* (Düsseldorf etc. 1984).

4 *Die Zeit*, 20 June 1986.

5 For the following paragraphs, see in particular M. Geyer, 'The Dynamics of Military Revisionism in the Interwar Years, Politics Between Rearmament and Diplomacy' in W. Deist (ed.), *The German Military in the Age of Total War* (Leamington 1985), pp. 100–51; W. Deist, as II 10, chs I to III; K.J. Müller, as II 14.

6 K. J. Müller, as II 9, p. 120; N. Reynolds, *Treason was no Crime. Ludwig Beck, Chief of the General Staff* (1976), pp. 42–5.

7 The record of the meeting prepared by Colonel Hossbach can be found in *Documents on German Foreign Policy* (1949–66), Series D, vol. I, pp. 29–39. On the validity of the text, see W. Bussmann, 'Zur Entstehung und Ueberlieferung der Hossbach-Niederschrift' in *VfZ* XVI (1968), pp. 373–84. See also J. R. C. Wright and P. Stafford, 'Hitler, Britain and the Hossbach Memorandum' in *Militärgeschichtliche Mitteilungen*, December 1987. I am grateful to Dr Wright for letting me see this important paper in typescript. See further Deutsch, as II 7 and K.-H. Janssen, *Die Zeit*, 11 and 18 March 1988.

8 W. Schieder, *Zwei Generationen im militärischen Widerstand gegen Hitler* in Schmädeke and Steinbach, as II 41, p. 441.

9 *VfZ* II (1954), p. 435.

10 W. Treue, 'Hitlers Denkschrift zum Vierjahresplan 1936' in *VfZ* III (1955), pp. 184–210.

11 M. Messerschmidt, 'Militärische Motive zur Durchführung des Umsturzes' in Schmädeke and Steinbach, as II 41, p. 1027.

12 Müller, as II 9, p. 470.

13 As No. 3.

14 As No. 8.

15 B. Scheurig, *Henning von Tresckow* (Oldenburg 1973), p. 181.

16 Udet committed suicide when depressed over the failure of the Luftwaffe against Britain and Russia and afraid that the blame for it was going to be pinned on him by Göring and Milch. He was notorious for 'shooting his mouth' and had made a number of critical remarks about his colleagues which might have been used against him. But there is no evidence that he had taken any steps against the régime.

    For Mölders, see E. Howe, *The Black Game* (1982), p. 207.

    I am indebted to Professor Manfred Messerschmidt and Dr Guth of the Militärgeschichtliches Forschungsamt, Freiburg-im-Breisgau, for guidance about Udet.

17 H. Mommsen, *Beamtentum im dritten Reich* (Stuttgart 1966), pp. 39, 115, 147; J. Caplan, as II 20; K. Schönhoven, 'Der politische Katholizismus in Bayern unter der NS Herrschaft 1933–1945' in M. Broszat *et al.* (eds), *Bayern in der NS-Zeit* (Munich 1983), vol. V, p. 633.

18 M. Jamin, 'Das Ende der Machtergreifung. Der 30 Juni 1934 und seine Wahrnehmung in der Bevölkerung' in W. Michalka (ed.), *Die nationalsozialistische Machtergreifung* (Paderborn etc. 1984).
19 Williams, as II 30, p. 140.
20 J. Noakes, 'Oberbürgermeister and Gauleiter: City Government between Party and State' in Hirschfeld and Kettenacker, as II 37, pp. 194–225.
21 H. Boberach (ed.), *Meldungen aus dem Reich* (Neuwied etc. 1965), 20 April 1942.
22 Text in Z.A.B. Zeman, *Nazi Propaganda* (1973), p. 222.
23 M.G. Steinert, *Hitler's Krieg und die Deutschen* (Düsseldorf etc. 1970), p. 320.
24 For the following paragraphs, see Mason, as II 35; L. Herbst, 'Die Krise des NS Regimes am Vorabend des zweiten Weltkrieges' in *VfZ* XXVI (1978).
25 Farquharson, as II 2, pp. 262–4.
26 W. N. Medlicott, *The Economic Blockade* (1952), vol. I, pp. 47–52.
27 As No. 10.
28 Turner, as II 24; J. R. Gillingham, *Industry and Politics in the Third Reich. Ruhr Coal, Hitler and Europe* (1985).
29 Schoenbaum, as II 1, ch. IV.
30 H. Schacht, *Abrechnung mit Hitler* (Hamburg 1948), p. 19.
31 W. Treue, 'Widerstand von Unternehmern und Nationalökonomen' in Schmädeke and Steinbach, as II 41, pp. 917–37.
32 J. Bentley, *Martin Niemöller* (Oxford 1984).
33 W. Niemöller, *Der Pfarrernotbund* (Hamburg 1973), Introduction; Scholder, as II 28, vol. I, p. 684. The compensation payments made by the League to evicted pastors reached a peak in 1938–40. According to M. Niemöller (Wright, as II 29, p. 171) there were only 14,000 pastors in all.
34 A. C. Cochrane, *The Church's Confession under Hitler* (Philadelphia 1962), pp. 239–42; Scholder, as II 28, vol. II *Das Jahr der Ernüchterung*, p. 190.
35 M.D. Hampson, 'The British Response to the Kirchenkampf', paper read at Anglo-German conference at Leeds, May 1986, citing W. Temple, *Nature, God and Man* (1934), p. 396.
36 G. Klotzbach, *Gegen den Nationalsozialismus. Widerstand und Verfolgung in Dortmund* (Hanover 1969), p. 139.
37 W. Niemöller, as No. 33.
38 G. van Norden, 'Widerstand im deutschen Protestantismus 1933–1945' in C. Klessmann and F. Pingel, *Gegen den Nationalsozialismus. Wissenschaftler und Widerstandskämpfer auf der Suche nach historische Wirklichkeit* (Frankfurt etc. 1980), p. 107.
39 R. Southar, *Landesbischof Wurm und der NS-Staat* (Stuttgart 1968), p. 324.
40 E. Wolf, 'Political and Moral Motives Behind the Resistance' in W. Schmitthenner and H. Buchheim (eds), *The German Resistance to Hitler* (1970), p. 217.
41 G. Besier, 'Ansätze zum politischen Widerstand in der Bekennenden Kirche' in Schmädeke and Steinbach, as II 41, p. 268. See also essays by G. van Norden, K. Scholder and E. Bethge in the same volume, also Wolf, as No. 40, p. 199.
42 W. Adolph, *Geheime Aufzeichnungen aus dem nationalsozialistischen Kirchenkampf 1933–1945* (Mainz 1979).
43 Scholder, as II 28, vol. II, ch. VIII; L. Volk, *Das Reichskonkordat vom 20 Juli 1933* (Mainz 1973).
44 B. Schellenberger, 'Katholischer Jugendwiderstand' in Schmädeke and Steinbach, as II 41, p. 317.
45 R. Bleistein, *Augustin Rösch, Kampf gegen den Nationalsozialismus* (Frankfurt 1985).
46 W. Adolph, *Kardinal Preysing und zwei Diktaturen* (Berlin 1971), p. 74.

47 E. Klee, *Euthanasie im NS-Staat. Die Vernichtung lebensunwerten Lebens* (Frankfurt 1983).
48 Scholder, as II 28, vol. II, p. 154.
49 K. Mammach, *Widerstand 1939–1945* (E. Berlin 1986), p. 99. No source is given but as the author is a Communist, he may be presumed to be impartial as between Catholic and Protestant!; H. Hürten, 'Selbstbehauptung und Widerstand der katholischen Kirche' in K. J. Müller (ed.), *Der deutsche Widerstand 1933–1955* (Paderborn etc. 1986), p. 153.
50 B. Schneider (ed.), *Briefe Pius XII an die deutschen Bischöfe* (Mainz 1966), no. 37.
51 As No. 50, no. 355.
52 F. Gilbert, *Hitler Directs His War* (Oxford 1950).
53 D'Arcy Osborne cited in O. Chadwick, *Britain and the Vatican During the Second World War* (Cambridge 1986), p. 316.
54 J. Caplan, as II 20.
55 Boehnert, as No. 2.
56 J. Caplan, as II 16.
57 M. Balfour, *Propaganda in War 1939–1945. Organisations, Policies and Publics in Britain and Germany* (1979), p. 327.
58 As No. 57, p. 353.
59 A. J. and R. Merritt (eds), *Public Opinion in Occupied Germany* (Urbana 1970), p. 33. The figures for the British Zone were much the same. Neither set gave any indication of the sections of society in which the various percentages were found.
60 Farquharson, as II 2, p. 195.
61 G. van Roon, *Helmuth James Graf von Moltke: Völkerrecht im Dienste der Menschen* (Berlin 1986), p. 80.
62 Kershaw, as II 34, p. 58.
63 As No. 62, p. 48.
64 Kater, as II 17, p. 123.
65 T. Mason, 'Labour in the Third Reich' in *Past and Present*, no. 33, April 1966.
66 Mason, as II 35, p. 262.
67 Herbst, as No. 24; Steinberg, as II 41, p. 870.
68 Mason, as II 35, p. 173; D. Peukert, *Die KPD im Widerstand. Verfolgung und Untergrundarbeit an Rhein und Ruhr* (Wuppertal 1980), p. 316; Steinberg, as II 41.
69 Kater, as II 17, pp. 34–8.
70 C. Webster and N. Frankland, *The Strategic Air Offensive Against Germany* (1961), vol. II, p. 280, vol. III, p. 266.
71 The same, II, p. 225.
72 Gillingham, as No. 28, p. 56.
73 Steinberg, as II 41.
74 H. Rothfels, 'Adam von Trott und der State Department' in *VfZ* VII (1959), p. 524.
75 P. von zur Mühlen, 'Sozialdemokraten Gegen Hitler' in R. Löwenthal and P. von zur Mühlen, *Widerstand und Verweigerung in Deutschland 1933 bis 1945* (Berlin 1981), p. 67.
76 Klotzbach, as No. 36, p. 145.
77 K. Mammach, *Der antifaschistische deutsche Widerstandsbewegung* (E. Berlin 1984).
78 H. Duhnke, *Die KPD von 1933 bis 1945* (Cologne 1972), p. 101.
79 Mammach, as No. 77, p. 97.
80 Peukert, as No. 68, p. 233.
81 M. Broszat, E. Fröhlich and F. Wiesemann, 'Lage der Arbeiterschaft,

Arbeiteropposition, Aktivität und Verfolgung der illegalen Arbeiterbewegung 1933–1944' in *Bayern in der NS-Zeit* (Munich 1977), vol. I, p. 234.

82 R. Mann, 'Was Wissen wir vom Widerstand?' in Klessmann and Pingel, as No. 38.

83 The same, p. 46.

84 Duhnke, as No. 78, p. 525.

85 The same, p. 101.

86 Peukert, as No. 68, pp. 318–22.

87 The same. Mammach (No.77, p. 129) says there were fifty 'instructors'.

88 Schabrod, as No. 49, p. 143.

89 Broszat, as No. 81, vol. I, p. 240.

90 Kater, as II 17, p. 81.

91 Duhnke, as No. 78, pp. 459–62, 485–92. Some of the sub-totals in the figures for deaths look suspiciously round. One group managed to survive the war but only by confining itself to listening to broadcasts and passing on information.

92 Peukert, as No. 68, p. 348.

93 D. Peukert, 'Volksfront and Volksbewegung im kommunistischen Widerstand' in Schmädeke and Steinbach, as II 41, p. 886.

94 W. S. Allen, 'Die sozialdemokratische Untergrundbewegung' in Schmädeke and Steinbach, as II 41, pp. 859, 866.

95 For *Neubeginnen* see: D. Lehnert, 'Vom Widerstand zur Neuordnung' in Schmädeke and Steinbach, as II 41, p. 512; R. Löwenthal, 'Vom Wert eines hoffnungslosen Kampfes' in *Die Zeit*, 26 December 1986, reviewing J. Foitzik, *Zwischen den Fronten* (Bonn 1986); P. von zur Mühlen, as No. 75, pp. 62–7; E. Wolf, as No. 40, pp. 180–92.

96 B. Carroll, *Design for Total War* (Hague etc. 1968), p. 249.

97 H. J. Steinberg, 'Thesen zum Widerstand aus der Arbeiterbewegung' in Klessmann and Pingel, as No. 49.

98 Stephenson, as II 44, ch. II.

99 No two sets of statistics about female employment seem to correspond. Thus Schoenbaum, as II 1, says (p.190) that 11½ million were employed in January 1933 and later that the number of working women rose from 4.24 million in 1933 to 4.52 million in 1936. Winkler, as II 44, gives a figure of 14.6 million employed in May 1939 but also quotes the State Secretary to the Ministry of Labour as putting it in June of that year at 13.8 million.

100 Goebbels Diary, 10 May 1943.

101 Winkler, as II 44, p. 126, quoting figures from the *Statistisches Reichsamt* given by Kaldor in *Review of Economic Studies*, 1945/6.

102 R. J. Overy has recently (*Times Literary Supplement*, 11 April 1986) challenged the thesis, first put forward in the US *Strategic Bombing Survey* of 1945, that Britain succeeded in mobilising a higher proportion of its women than Germany did. But I am not convinced that like is being compared with like or that the last word on the subject has been said.

103 J. McIntyre, 'Women and the Professions in Germany 1930–1940' in A. J. Nicholls and E. Matthias (eds), *German Democracy and the Triumph of Hitler* (1971), p. 202.

104 Kater, as II 17, pp. 148–53.

105 McIntyre, as No. 103, pp. 206–8.

106 Schoenbaum, as II 1, p. 273.

107 Caplan, as II 16.

108 Winkler, as II 44.

109 G. J. Giles, 'The Rise of the National Socialist Students Association' in

P. Stachura (ed.), *The Shaping of the Nazi State* (1978). This and the next paragraph as a whole is based on this essay and also on Giles, as II 49.

110　Scholder, as II 28, vol. II, p. 34.

111　A. Klönne, *Gegen den Strom* (Hanover 1957), p. 109.

112　A. Klönne, 'Jugendprotest und Jugendopposition' in M. Broszat *et al.* (eds), *Bayern in der NS-Zeit* (Munich 1981), vol. IV, pp. 389–91: also as No. 111.

113　Klönne, as No. 112, p. 619; D. Peukert, 'Edelweiss Piraten, Meuten. Jugend Subkulturen im 3ten Reich' in G. Huck (ed.), *Sozialgeschichte der Freizeit* (Wuppertal 1980); H. Muth, 'Jugendopposition im 3ten Reich' in *VfZ* XXX (1982).

114　Klönne, as No. 112, pp. 589–93; Peukert, as No. 68, pp. 317–18.

115　Peukert, as No. 68, p. 327.

116　Peukert, as No. 68, p. 319; W. Klose, *Generation in Gleichschritt* (Hanover 1964), p. 222.

117　Peukert, as No. 68, p. 326.

118　I. Kershaw, 'Widerstand Ohne Volk? Dissens und Widerstand im 3ten Reich' in Schmädeke and Steinbach, as II 41, p. 790.

119　I was in Detmold soon afterwards and was told about the fight. It was not the only one of its kind.

120　See esp. Dicks, as I 9. Goebbels in his Diary entry for 4 April 1945 put the proportion of active Party Members at 10 per cent of the population. It should be emphasised that these figures are not based merely on personal impressions but on systematically obtained facts. Anyone who wishes to disagree with them must demonstrate the invalidity of their statistical base.

121　P. Grassmann, *Sozialdemokraten Gegen Hitler* (Munich 1976), p. 29.

122　M. Broszat, E. Fröhlich and F. Wiesemann, 'Der Bezirk Ebermannstadt 1929–1945' in *Bayern in der NS-Zeit*, as II 27, vol. I, p. 126.

123　E. Fröhlich, 'Gegenwärtige Forschungen zur Herrschaft- und Verwaltungsgeschichte in der NS-Zeit' in Klessmann and Pingel, as No. 49, p. 32.

124　U. von Hassell, *Vom Anderen Deutschland* (Zurich 1946), 24 June 1940.

125　Steinert, as No. 23, pp. 469–90; H. Boberach, 'Chancen eines Umsturzes im Spiegel der Berichte des Sicherheitsdienst' in Schmädeke and Steinbach, as II 41, pp. 813–21; discussion in Schmädeke and Steinbach, p. 1147.

126　Quoted by Boberach, as No. 125, p. 821.

127　I. Kershaw, 'Führer Image and Political Integration' in W. Mommsen and L. Kettenacker (eds), *The Fascist Challenge and the Policy of Appeasement* (1983), pp. 133–61.

Chapter IV　Modes of *Widerstand*

1　See especially Löwenthal, 'Widerstand im totalen Staat' in Löwenthal and von zur Mühlen, as III 75; Kershaw, as III 118.

2　M. Broszat, 'Resistenz und Widerstand' in M. Broszat *et al.* (eds), *Bayern in der NS-Zeit* (Munich 1981), vol. IV, pp. 697–9.

3　J. Klepper, *Unter dem Schatten deiner Flügel. Aus den Tagebüchern 1932–1942* (D.t.v. Munich 1976).

4　G. Beier, *Die Illegale Reichsleitung der Gewerkschaften* (Cologne 1981).

5　As for III 3.

6　1926–35: *Statistisches Jahrbuch;* 1942–3: P. Hoffmann, *The History of the German Resistance 1933–1945* (1977), p. 17, citing papers in the Bundesarchiv. It is possible that the two sets of figures rest on different bases.

7　Personal knowledge. As he was partly Jewish he would in due course have been forced to leave but his decision was taken long before this became clear.

8 W. Röder, *Die deutsche sozialistischen Exilgruppen in Gross-Britannien* (Bonn 1973), pp. 15–18; H. E. Tutas, *NS Propaganda und deutsches Exil* (Worms 1973).

9 L. Hill in *Central European History* (1981), p. 373; P. Grassmann, as III 121; W. Brandt, 'Aus dem Bewusstsein Verdrängt' in Bundeszentrale für Politische Bildung, *Widerstand und Exil* (Bonn 1985), pp. 48, 278.

10 A. Merson, *Communist Resistance* (1985), p. 197; Hill, as No. 9; Mammach, as III 25, p. 174.

11 Treue, as III 31, p. 928.

12 E. Calic, *Reinhard Heydrich* (NY 1985); Kater, as II 22, p. 157 (for Lessing); E. Howe, *The Black Game* (1982), p. 59; K. T. Grossmann, *Emigration* (Frankfurt 1969), pp. 83–97.

13 C. Zuckmayer, *Carlo Mierendorf, Porträt eines deutschen Sozialisten* (Berlin 1947).

14 Balfour and Frisby, as II 6, p. 80. Moltke did not in the end emigrate, although he might have done so if peace had lasted a month or two longer

15 A. Reichwein *et al.* (eds), *Adolf Reichwein. Ein Lebensbild aus Briefen und Dokumenten* (Munich 1974), p. 117.

16 K. Schönhoven, as III 16, p. 633.

17 E. Frhr von Weizsäcker, *Erinnerungen* (Munich 1950), p. 117.

18 C. F. Latour, 'Goebbels ausserordentliche Rundfunkmassnahmen' in *VfZ* XI (1963), p. 418.

19 P. Hüttenberger 'Heimtückefälle vor dem Sondergericht München 1933–39' in M. Broszat *et al.* (eds), *Bayern in der NS-Zeit*, (Munich 1981), vol IV, pp. 435–526.

20 G. Benn, *Das gezeichnete Ich. Briefe aus den Jahren 1910–1956* (Munich 1962), p. 105. Authorship of the phrase has also been attributed to General von Hammerstein, which may well be correct as Benn was writing in 1949.

21 Klotzbach, as III 35, p. 102.

22 H. Gottfurcht, 'Als Gewerkschaftler im Widerstand' in Löwenthal and von zur Mühlen, as III 75, p. 51.

23 H. Mehringer, 'Die bayerische Sozialdemokratie bis zum Ende des NS-Regimes' in M. Broszat *et al.* (eds), *Bayern in der NS-Zeit* (Munich 1983), vol. V, p. 432; Allen, as III 94, p. 851.

24 Mehrringer, as No. 23, p. 432.

25 Schabrod, as III 36, p. 67.

26 Kershaw, as II 58, p. 166.

27 Hüttenberger, as No. 19, p. 451. Goebbels used a woodcutter in Bad Aibling as a stock example of the audience to which his propaganda was addressed.

28 G. Weisenborn, *Der lautloser Aufstand* (Frankfurt 1974), pp. 278–95.

29 *Das Reich*, 22 February 1942.

30 Beier, as No. 4, p. 33.

31 Peukert, as III 68, p. 175.

32 Hoffmann, as No. 6, p. 16; Peukert, as III 68, p. 333; Kater, as II 17, p. 81.

33 Duhnke, as III 78, p. 457, citing Weisenborn (No.28).

34 M. Oppenheimer, *Der Fall Vorbote* (Frankfurt 1969).

35 C. Nitzsche, *Die Saefkow–Jacob–Bästlein Gruppe* (E. Berlin 1957), pp. 150–90.

36 Travelling exhibition organised by the Government of the Federal Republic of Germany, Catalogue of Exhibits, *The German Resistance Movement 1933–1945* (1986), pp. 258–61.

37 Grassmann, as III 121, p. 113.

38 R. Mann, as III 82.

39 As No. 36, p. 82.

40 Balfour, as III 57, p. 96.

41 U. Grünheid, 'Wir Wollten doch Ueberleben' in *Widerstand und Exil*, as No. 9, pp. 150, 152.

42 K. R. Grossmann, *Die unbesungenen Helden* (Berlin 1961).

43 Lill and Oberreuther, as III 3, pp. 393–409.

44 D. Childs, *Germany Since 1918* (1980), p. 99.

45 Mammach, as III 77, p. 85. A further book by the same author (*Widerstand 1939–1945*, E. Berlin 1986) came to hand after the final text of this book had been sent for typing. It contains details of many more strikes but making space for their inclusion would have been too complicated.

46 Beier, as No. 4, p. 82.

47 R. R. Count von Thun-Hohenstein, *Der Verschwörer: General Oster und die Militäropposition* (Berlin 1982), p. 146; G. van Roon, *German Resistance to Hitler. Count von Moltke and the Kreisau Circle* (1971), p. 170.

48 Ehlers, as I 3, p. 63, citing E. Henk writing in 1946 in Heidelberg.

49 *Bayern in der NS-Zeit*, as II 27, vol. I, p. 274, 284.

50 B. R. Kroener, 'Squaring the Circle: Blitzkrieg Strategy and Manpower Shortage 1939–1942' in W. Deist (ed.), as III 5, p. 294.

51 Peukert in Löwenthal and von zur Mühlen, as III 75, p. 181.

52 Nitzsche, as No. 35, p. 178.

53 D. Wassowitz, 'Erfahrungsbericht' in Klessmann and Pingel, as III 38, pp. 238–42.

54 Weisenborn, as No. 28, p. 164.

55 Balfour and Frisby, as II 6, p. 220.

56 W. von Oven, *Mit Goebbels bis zum Ende* (Buenos Aires 1949), vol. I, p. 212.

57 Scheurig, as III 15, pp. 100–4, 110–12.

58 L. Yahill, *The Defence of Danish Jewry. Test of a Democracy* (1969).

59 Giles, as II 49, p. 206.

60 M. Balfour, *The Kaiser and His Times* (1964), pp. 193–4, 199.

61 Zeller, as I 1, p. 86.

62 Ehlers, as I 3, p. 36.

63 Adolph, as III 46, p. 159.

64 E. Kordt, *Nicht aus den Akten* (Stuttgart 1950), p. 366.

65 Ehlers, as I 3, p. 178; Scholder, as II 28, vol. II, p. 157.

66 Müller, as II 9, p. 54.

67 Balfour, as No. 60, p. 150.

68 H. Gräfin von Schall-Riaucour, *Aufstand und Gehorsam* (Wiesbaden 1972), p. 46.

69 A. Dulles, *Germany's Underground* (NY 1957), p. 65.

70 Balfour and Frisby, as II 6, p. 170; H. Broszat, H. A. Jacobsen and H. Krausnick, *Anatomie des SS-Staats* (d.t.v. Munich 1969), vol. II, p. 208.

71 Scheurig, as II 4; see also *Documents on British Foreign Policy* (1947 etc.), Third Series, vol. III, pp. 683–96.

72 R. Graf von Thun-Hohenstein, 'Wilderstand und Landesverrat am Beispiel des Generalmajors Hans Oster' in Schmädeke and Steinbach, as II 41, p. 760.

73 Public Record Office, File FO 371/30912. Two official British 'Summaries of Principal Peace Feelers' between 1939 and 1942 will be found in L. Kettenacker (ed.), *Das 'Andere Deutschland' im Zweiten Weltkrieg* (Stuttgart 1977), pp. 164–200.

74 Balfour and Frisby, as II 6, p. 273.

75 Review in *Die Zeit*, 2 May 1986; M. Hyde, *The Quiet Canadian* (1962), p. 176.

76 F. W. Deakin and G. R. Storry, *The Case of Richard Sorge* (1966).

77 Europa Publications, *Die Vollmacht des Gewissens* (Frankfurt etc. 1960), vol. I, p. 473.

78 Hoffmann, as No. 6, p. 548.

79 L. Hill, *Die Weizsäcker Papiere 1933–1950* (Frankfurt 1974), p. 562, citing B. Whaley, *Codeword Barbarossa* (Cambridge Mass. 1973).
80 Gersdorff, as No. 5, p. 151.
81 Balfour and Frisby, as II 6, p. 185.
82 Among the most tragic stories in the Third Reich is that of Jehovah's Witnesses who, because of their refusal to co-operate with the state, and in particular to bear arms, were persecuted mercilessly but maintained their attitude until even their oppressors began to feel a reluctant respect for them. See F. Zipfel, *Der Kirchenkampf in Deutschland 1933–45* (Berlin 1965), pp. 175–203.

Chapter V The difficulties of the *Widerstand*

1 Balfour and Frisby, as II 6, pp. 217, 179.
2 K. Hildebrand, *The Third Reich* (1984), p. 62.
3 H. Rothfels, 'Zur Wiederkehr des 20 Juli 1944' in *VfZ* XVII (1969).
4 Fröhlich, as III 77, p. 593.
5 Mammach, as III 77, p. 167.
6 M. Foot, *An Outline History of the Special Operations Executive* (1984), p. 246.
7 Balfour and Frisby, as II 6, p. 220.
8 Weisenborn, as IV 28, p. 57.
9 Balfour and Frisby, as II 6, ch. XXVII; I. von der Lühe, *Elisabeth von Thadden. Ein Schicksal unserer Zeit* (Düsseldorf 1966); E. Boehm, *We Survived* (NY 1949).
10 H. Deutsch, 'Loyalty and Resistance' in *Central European History*, 1981.
11 P. Hoffmann on the same subject in *Central European History*, 1981, p. 344.
12 As No. 11.
13 Weisenborn, as IV 28, p. 57.
14 Oppenheimer, as IV 2.
15 H. Deutsch, *The Conspiracy Against Hitler in the Twilight War* (Minneapolis 1968), pp. 127–36.
16 Weizsäcker, as IV 17, p. 369.
17 Ehlers, as I 3, p. 100; Dulles, as IV 69, pp. 185–210.
18 Dulles, as IV 69, p. 147 ff.
19 Deutsch, as II 7, p. 196.
20 There is a considerable literature on this subject. See esp. *Vollmacht des Gewissens*, as IV 77, vol. I, pp. 532–5; Messerschmidt, as II 11, p. 35; Müller, as II 9, pp. 133–9; F. von Schlabrendorff, *The Secret War Against Hitler* (1966), p. 223.
21 Ehlers, as I 3, p. 60.
22 *Vollmacht des Gewissens*, as IV 77, p. 535.
23 Müller, as II 9, p. 552.
24 R. Cecil, *Hitler's Decision to Invade Russia* (1975), p. 158, citing R. M. Kempner, *Das dritte Reich im Kreuzverhör* (Munich 1969), p. 87.
25 See for example H. Troll, 'Atktionen zur Kriegsbeendigung im Frühjahr 1945' in M. Broszat *et al.* (eds), *Bayern in der NS-Zeit* (Munich 1985), vol. V, pp. 660–77.
26 H. Maier, 'Die SS und der 20 Juli 1944' in *VfZ* XIV (1966), pp. 299–316. No authority is given for this statement.
27 Messerschmidt, as II 11, p. ix.
28 Confirmed to the author by his son, Ludwig Frhr v. H.-E., May 1986.
29 Hassell, as III 124, entry for 4 October 1941.
30 Kaiser Diary, cited in Hoffmann, as IV 6, p. 298.
31 Schlabrendorff, as No. 21, pp. 126.
32 C. Müller, *Oberst i/G Stauffenberg* (Düsseldorf, no date), p. 290.

33 US State Department, *Foreign Relations of the United States 1944* (Washington 1966), p. 565.
34 Hoffmann, as IV 6, pp. 281–3; Scheurig, as III 15, pp. 138–41.
35 Balfour and Frisby, as II 6, p. 166.
36 H. B. Gisevius, *Wo Ist Nebe?* (Zurich 1966), p. 36.
37 D. Ose, *Erwin Rommel* in Lill and Oberreuter, as III 3, pp. 263–7.
38 Hoffmann, as IV 6, p. 251–3, lists attempts by Luther 1933; Hirsch 1936; Döpking and Kremin 1938; Barnaud 1938; Hoffmann, Schulz and Tosch 1940; Rust and Schmitt 1942; Römer and von Halem 1942, besides the three famous ones.
39 Hoffmann, as IV 6, p. 252.
40 See on Hitler's security in general P. Hoffmann, *Die Sicherheit des Diktators. Hitler's Leibwachen, Schutzmassnahmen and Hauptquartiere* (Munich 1975).
41 Kordt, as IV 64, p. 370.
42 H. Groscurth, *Tagebücher eines Abwehroffiziers 1938–1940* (Stuttgart 1970), p. 223.
43 Foot, as No. 6, p. 73.
44 Public Record Office File FO 371/16404.
45 P. Ludlow, 'Papst XII. Die britische Regierung und die deutsche Opposition im Winter 1939/40' in *VfZ* XXII (1974), p. 334, citing FO document 800/318.
46 G. C. Peden, 'Democracy, Dictatorship and Public Opinion: Some Economic Aspects of Foreign Policy' in *Opinion publique et politique extérieure*, vol. II, 1915–40, p. 361, Collection de l'École Française de Rome 54/2, Università di Milano and École Française de Rome, 1984; W.N. Medlicott, 'The Coming of War in 1939' in W. N. Medlicott (ed.), *From Metternich to Hitler* (1963), p. 241. I owe these references to Professor David Dilks.
47 T. Taylor, *Munich, the Price of Peace* (NY 1979), pp. 987–9.
48 Webster and Frankland, as III 69, vol. I, p. 78; Deist, as II 10, pp. 68–9; C. Andrew, *Secret Service* (1985), pp. 547–50.
49 K. A. Maier, 'Total War and German Air Doctrine Before the Second World War' in Deist (ed.), as III 5, p. 216.
50 Public Record Office File FO 371/22969. The French figure states the position after 18 days; after a month it would have risen to 96.
51 A. Adamthwaite, 'France and the Coming of War' in Mommsen and Kettenacker, as III 127, p. 252.
52 This is the only sensible way in which I can explain a statement by Chamberlain to a Labour Party delegation, 'The French have only 21 aeroplanes equal to the German and they have only 500 altogether,' cited in R. Douglas, 'Chamberlain and Appeasement' in Mommsen and Kettenacker, as III 127, p. 85.
53 R. Ovendale, *Appeasement and the English-speaking World* (Cardiff 1975); R. Ovendale, 'Britain, the Dominions and the Coming of the Second World War' in Mommsen and Kettenacker, as III 127, pp. 323–8; N. Mansergh, *Survey of British Commonwealth Affairs* (1952).
54 Public Record Office, Cabinet Minutes 46th meeting, 8 December 1937.
55 Dulles, as IV, p. 49.
56 K. J. Müller, 'Zur Struktur and Eigenart der nationalkonservativen Opposition bis 1938' in Schmädeke and Steinbach, as II 41, p. 344.
57 G. Ritter, *The Schlieffen Plan* (1958), p. 66.
58 P. Ludlow, 'Britain and the Third Reich' in H. Bull (ed.), *The Challenge of The Third Reich* (Oxford 1986), pp. 140–62.
59 P. Ludlow, 'The Unwinding of Appeasement' in Kettenacker (ed.), as IV 73.
60 H. Ben-Israel, 'Im Widerstreit der Ziele: Die Britische Reaktion auf dem deutschen Widerstand' in Schmädeke and Steinbach, as II 41, p. 738.

Chapter VI The aims of the *Widerstand*

1 W. Leonhard, *Child of the Revolution* (1957), p. 358.
2 B. Scheurig, *Verrat hinter Stacheldraht?* (Munich 1965); A. Fischer, 'Die Bewegung 'Freies Deutschland in der Sowjetunion: Widerstand hinter Stacheldraht?' in Schmädeke and Steinbach, as II 41, pp. 954–75; Balfour, as III 57, ch. XLVI.
3 *Foreign Relations of the United States 1943. Conferences of Moscow and Tehran* (Washington 1971), p. 154; *1944*, vol. IV, pp. 805, 872.
4 W. Ritter von Schramm, *Beck and Goerdeler. Gemeinschaftsdokumente für den Frieden 1941–1944* (Munich 1965); G. van Roon, as IV 47, pp. 310–86; W. Schmitthenner and H. Buchheim (eds), as III 38, essays by H. Graml, and H. Mommsen; B. Scheurig, *Deutscher Widerstand 1938–1944. Fortschritt oder Reaktion?* (Munich 1969); Balfour and Frisby, as II 6, ch. XXIV.
5 For Beck and Goerdeler, see Part II of this book and the references given there.
6 For Popitz, Jessen and Hassell, see J. W. Wheeler-Bennett, *The Nemesis of Power* (2nd edn 1967), pp. 705–15; also essays on P. and H. in Lill and Oberreuter as III 3.
7 For Kreisau, see Balfour and Frisby, as II 6, pp. 188, 193–4; van Roon, as IV 47, pp. 16–19; W. E. Winterhalter (ed.), *Der Kreisauer Kreis, Begleitband zu einer Ausstellung der Stiftung Preussischer Kulturbesitz* (Berlin 1985), pp. 16–83; R. Bleistein (ed.), *Dossier Kreisauer Kreis, Aus dem Nachlass von Lothar König S.J.* (Frankfurt a/M 1987). The papers contained in this volume seem mostly to have been submitted at early stages in the Kreisau discussions and are out of line with the *Grundsätze für die Neuordnung*, while closer to the solutions ultimately adopted in the Bonn *Grundgesetz*.
8 For Schulenburg, see A. Krebs, *Fritz Dietlof von der Schulenburg* (Hamburg 1964); U. Heinemann, 'Fritz Dietlof von der Schulenburg' in Schmädeke and Steinbach, as II 41, pp. 416–35.
9 G. Meyer, *Nacht über Hamburg* (Frankfurt 1971).
10 Scheurig, as No. 2, p. 80.
11 Von Hassell, as III 124, 19 August 1943.
12 G. Ritter, as II 63, pp. 570–6, conveniently in Scheurig, as No. 4, p. 209. A map included in the König *Nachlass* (see No. 7 above) and dating from August 1943 proposes similar frontiers. This is another respect in which the König evidence is out of line with that previously available and further discussion is needed before its implications can be evaluated.
13 Balfour and Frisby, as II 6, p. 178.
14 C. Dipper, 'Der Widerstand und die Juden' in Schmädeke and Steinbach, as II 41, pp. 598–616.
15 Von Hassell, as III 124, 22 January 1943; Balfour and Frisby, as II 6, pp. 206–7.
16 Text in van Roon, as No. 4, pp. 378–9. See also R. Albrecht, *Carl Mierendorff und das Konzept einer Demokratischer Volksbewegung* in Schmädeke and Steinbach, as II 41, pp. 838–48. Mierendorff gave a copy of his text to Moltke, who had become a close friend. Nothing is known of any other copy or of any discussion of its contents. Its date of composition prevented it from being discussed at the simultaneous (and last) Kreisau meeting. Mierendorff no doubt discussed it with his friends Haubach and Leber but Haubach did not come to Kreisau on this occasion and Leber not at all. The document reads like a gesture by someone who was worried that the revolution would not go far enough and wanted to enlist support for going further. It would not have survived at all if Moltke had not felt enough sympathy with it to put his copy among the other Kreisau papers.
17 Van Roon, as No. 4, p. 373. How far the document represents Moltke's views

is uncertain. It was written in German by two Germans resident in Istanbul on the basis of talks with him but after he had left. It was translated into English by another German resident and given to the local OSS office. The only surviving copy is in English.

18 Public Record Office, File No. FO 371/39059. Minute of 12 April 1944 by D. Allen.

19 As No. 17. On an earlier visit to Istanbul Moltke had argued against unconditional surrender but had been told by his interlocutors that it was hopeless to try to get this changed. In August 1945 his widow told Dorothy Thompson of his belief that only complete military defeat could root out the poison of Fascism (van Roon, as III 60, p. 317).

20 Zeller, as I 1, p. 265. The attribution to Stauffenberg is by no means certain.

21 Graml, as No. 4, p. 24.

22 Balfour and Frisby, as II 6, p. 157.

23 Scheurig, as II 4, p. 106.

24 Balfour and Frisby, as II 6, p. 220.

25 See for example K. J. Müller, *Zur Struktur und Eigenart der nationalkonservativen Opposition bis 1938* in Schmädeke and Steinbach, as II 41, p. 329 and in the same author's *Der deutsche Widerstand 1935–1945* (Paderborn etc. 1986).

Chapter VII The West and the *Widerstand*

1 See M. Balfour, 'The Origin of the Formula "Unconditional Surrender" in World War II' in *Armed Forces and Society*, vol. V, Winter 1979, pp. 281–301; A. E. Campbell, 'Franklin Roosevelt and Unconditional Surrender' in R. Langhorne (ed.), *Diplomacy and Intelligence during the Second World War* (Cambridge 1985), pp. 218–41.

2 R. E. Sherwood (ed.), *The White House Papers of Harry L. Hopkins* (1949), vol. II, p. 693; Public Record Office, *War Cabinet Memorandum* 1943, No. 3.

3 US State Department, *Post-war Foreign Policy Preparation 1939–45* (Washington 1950), p. 127; H. Feis, *Churchill, Roosevelt, Stalin. The War they Waged and the Peace they Sought* (Princeton 1957), p. 108; D. Dilks (ed.), *The Diaries of Sir Alexander Cadogan 1938–1945* (1971), p. 506.

4 Feis, as No. 3, p. 109.

5 W. S. Churchill, *The Second World War* (1948–54), vol. IV, p. 613.

6 *FRUS 1943, Conference at Casablanca* (Washington 1968), pp. 833, 840.

7 Campbell, as No. 1, suggests that Roosevelt may have wished to placate Churchill because he had refused to exclude Italy, as Churchill (but not the rest of the Cabinet) wished.

8 See for example *FRUS 1944*, pp. 501, 546; Dilks, as No. 3, p. 620.

9 See for example speech of 21 September 1943.

10 As No. 8, *Diplomatic Papers*, vol. I, p. 700.

11 Notably in the *Daily Telegraph* and on the BBC World Service on 25 and 30 June 1943.

12 Campbell, as No. 1, thinks that Roosevelt's chief motive in proposing unconditional surrender was to reassure US public opinion on this point. For evidence as to the attitudes of the British and US publics towards Germany, see Balfour, as III 57, p. 490 and A.J. Nicholls, 'American Views of Germany during World War II' in Kettenacker, as IV 73, p. 78.

13 Churchill, as No. 5, vol. IV, p. 617 and V, p. 621.

14 Sherwood, as No. 2, vol. I, p. 225.

15 *Encounter*, September 1969.

16 Ritter, as II 63, p. 260.

17 The first directive which the German media received about the Casablanca Conference was that 'there is no reason why the unsuccessful meeting between Roosevelt and Churchill should receive much prominence.' Neither that directive nor the text circulated by the German News Agency DNB for publication in the German press mentioned the formula. It did not figure in the big speech on Total War which Goebbels made at the Sportpalast three and a half weeks later. British analysts of German output only noticed three references to it in February and March 1943. The Foreign Broadcasting Intelligence Service of the US Federal Communications Division told the State Department in May 1944 that the term 'had been rarely used in German propaganda' (*FRUS 1944*, vol. I, p. 518). Goebbels certainly called the formula 'an asininity of the first order. I could never myself have thought of a more compelling slogan for my propaganda' (von Oven, as IV 56, vol. I, p. 204). But he only did so in private a year after Casablanca. See Balfour, as III 57, ch. XL.
18 Ehlers, as I 3, p. 50, citing Schmidt.
19 See for example Bundesarchiv Koblenz, R 83 Luxemburg 9, *Rundschreiben* of 29 November 1943; W. Boelcke, *Wollt Ihr den totalen Krieg? Die geheimen Goebbels-Konferenzen 1939–1943* (Stuttgart 1967) entry for 22 September 1942; Institut für Zeitgeschichte (and elsewhere) unpublished Goebbels diary entry for 23 September 1942; Public Record Office File FO 898/185 Weekly Survey *German Propaganda and the Germans* for 2 January 1944.
20 A.M. Winkler, *The Politics of Propaganda. The Office of War Information 1942–1945* (New Haven 1978), p. 14.
21 Churchill, as No. 5, vol. III, p. 539.
22 The same, speech on 10 November 1942.
23 Public Record Office, File FO 371/35261/U2011, 2 May 1943.
24 Public Record Office, paper of Ministry of Information – Political Warfare Executive – Special Issues Committee in FO 371/34457, 22 March 1943.
25 B. Martin, 'Das aussenpolitische Versagen des Widerstands 1943/44' in Schmädeke and Steinbach, as II 41, pp. 1037–60.
26 In House of Commons 20 May 1945.

Part TWO   A portrait gallery

1 Georg Elser

1 The main authority for Elser is now his own account, as given in L. Gruchmann (ed.), *Autobiographie eines Attentaters – Johann Georg Elser* (Stuttgart 1970). This has superseded A. Hoch, 'Das Attentat auf Hitler in Münchener Bürgerbräukeller 1939' in *VfZ* XVII (1969), and is not much added to by A. Hoch and L. Gruchmann, *Georg Elser, der Attentater aus dem Volke* (Frankfurt 1980). But see also Gisevius, as V 36, pp. 197–200, 208–14.
2 Elser's version of his own story has been challenged by E. Calic, *Reinhard Heydrich* (NY 1985), pp. 313–48, who has revived the theory that it was a put-up job by Heydrich and Schellenberg.
3 The chief objection to this explanation is the complete lack of hard evidence. It assumes either that Elser, and the five people who corroborated his relations with them, learnt up and repeated a fictitious story, without any of them ever saying so publicly afterwards, or that Elser was set by the SS to do what he did without any close control being exercised over him, which would have been a risky procedure. The curious part of his story is the amount of incriminating evidence which he took to the frontier with him. But perhaps he wished to have corroborative material on hand in case he should later want to claim the credit for Hitler's death.

2 Henning von Tresckow and Fabian von Schlabrendorff

1 The main sources are: F. von Schlabrendorff, *Revolt Against Hitler* (1948); the same, *The Secret War Against Hitler* (2nd revised edition of preceding 1966); B. Scheurig, *Henning von Tresckow* (Oldenburg etc 1973); R. C. von Gersdorff, *Soldat im Untergang* (Berlin etc. 1977); F. O. Frhr von Aretin, 'Henning von Tresckow' in Lill and Oberreuter, *20 Juli. Portraits des Widerstands*, as III 3.
2 Scheurig (p. 66) attributes this remark, on the authority of Schlabrendorff, to a Count von Eulenburg; E. Zeller, *Geist der Freiheit* (Munich 1952, 5th edn 1965) p. 174, refers to an unpublished paper held by Gräfin von der Schulenburg saying that her husband was the author.
3 H. Grosscurth, *Tagebücher eines Abwehroffiziers* (Stuttgart 1970), p. 427.
4 G. Engel (ed. Kotze), *Heeresadjutant bei Hitler* (Stuttgart 1974), p. 45.
5 The liqueur supposed to be in the bottle is often said to have been brandy but only Cointreau has bottles which compare in shape to the square bombs.
6 Our knowledge of this whole episode rests entirely on Schlabrendorff's account.

3 Claus Philipp Maria Schenck, Graf von Stauffenberg

1 The main sources are J. Kramarz, *The Life and Death of an Officer* (Eng. tr. 1967); C. Müller, *Oberst i.G. Stauffenberg* (Düsseldorf 1970); P. Hoffmann, *The History of the German Resistance 1933–1945* (1977); K. Finker, *Stauffenberg und der 20 Juli* (E. Berlin 1967).
2 Zeller, as I 1, p. 303; Hoffmann, as No. 1.
3 These views were expressed in the course of SS interrogations and represent what the speakers thought was the best defence, which may not have been the same as their genuine views and motives. H. A. Jacobsen (ed.), *Spiegelbild einer Verschwörung. Die Opposition gegen Hitler und der Staatsstreich vom 20–vii–1944 in der SS Berichterstattung* (Stuttgart 1984).
4 Zeller, as No. 2, citing A. Stauffenberg (twin brother of Berthold).
5 Balfour and Frisby, as II 6, pp. 290–1.
6 Goerdeler passed on his suspicions to Gisevius, whose only meeting with Stauffenberg, late at night on 11–12 July, consisted largely of misunderstandings. Gisevius took this view of Stauffenberg in his book *To the Bitter End*, which was one of the first about the *Widerstand* to come out after the war so that for some considerable time a misleading picture gained currency.
7 According to P. Hoffmann ('Warum mislang das Attentat vom 20 Juli 1944' in *VfZ* XXXII, 1984, pp. 441–62), the explosive was German made to the British pattern. There is said to be no evidence that the brief-case was moved after Stauffenberg put it in position.
8 The evidence on a number of points is inadequate and we probably shall never be able to apportion blame for the delay with certainty. Some accounts make Thiele report to Olbricht about an hour earlier than I have done. There is even some uncertainty as to the airfield at which Stauffenberg landed.
9 The main source for Goebbels's behaviour on 20 July is W. von Oven, *Mit Goebbels bis zum Ende* (Buenos Aires 1949), vol. II, p. 59; also A. Speer, *Inside the Third Reich* (1970), p. 38. The plotters failed to realise the importance of the News Agency's radio teleprinter (*Hellschreiber*) and arrange for it to be seized.
10 What gave rise to this belief is a minor mystery which has never been explained. Brauchitsch, who had been retired for three and a half years, was not in Berlin on 20 July.
11 According to another account (S. Krolak in Schmädeke and Steinbach as II 41,

p. 556, what Stauffenberg shouted was 'secret Germany' (*geheimes Deutschland*), the title of a poem by George describing his circle.

4 Ludwig Beck

1 The main sources are: W. Foerster, *Generaloberst Ludwig Beck. Sein Kampf gegen den Krieg* (Munich 1953); N. Reynolds, *Treason Was No Crime: Ludwig Beck, Chief of the General Staff* (1976); K. J. Müller, *General Ludwig Beck* (Boppard 1980); L. Beck (ed. H. Speidel), *Studien* (Stuttgart 1955), a collection of Beck's own writings; Hoffmann, as IV 6; Deutsch, as II 7. See also essays by Hoffmann, Müller and Deutsch in *Central European History* XIV (1981).
2 M. Balfour, *The Kaiser and His Times* (1964), pp. 405–12.
3 Schall-Riaucourt, as IV 68, p. 219.
4 Deist, as II 10, p. 94.
5 Deist, as III 5, p. 136.
6 Evidence of Gisevius at International Military Tribunal, Nuremburg, vol. XII, p. 266.
7 R. A. Blasius, *Für Grossdeutschland gegen den Grossen Krieg: Staatssekretär Ernst Freiherr von Weizsäcker in den Krisen um die Tschechoslowakei und Polen 1938/9* (Cologne 1981), p. 258.
8 Schall-Riaucour, as IV 68, p. 221.
9 Hoffmann, as IV 6, p. 69.
10 K. J. Müller, as No. 1 pp. 298–301; P. Hoffmann, 'Ludwig Beck. Loyalty and Resistance' in *Central European History* XIV (1981), pp. 340–9.
11 Schall-Riaucour, as IV 68, p. 214.
12 Thun-Hohenstein, as IV 47, p. 91.
13 Ehlers, as I 3, p. 35.
14 Deutsch, as V 15, p. 90.
15 Schall-Riaucour, as IV 68, p. 216.
16 Deutsch, as V 16, pp. 103–36.
17 For texts, see von Schramm, as VI 4.
18 Hassell, as III 124, 22 January 1943.
19 Hoffmann, as IV 6, p. 376, citing Nebgen, *Jakob Kaiser* (Stuttgart 1967).
20 H. B. Gisevius, *Bis zum bitteren Ende* (Hamburg 1964), p. 551.

5 Günther von Kluge

1 There is no monograph on Kluge and his story has been put together from such sources as Scheurig, as III 15; Gersdorff, as IV 5; Schlabrendorff, as IV 21; H. Speidel, *Invasion 1944* (Tübingen 1949).
2 Schlabrendorff, as IV 21, pp. 129–31.
3 There is no evidence of any meeting between Kluge and Stauffenberg.
4 W. von Schramm, *Aufstand der Generäle. Der 20 Juli in Paris* (Munich 1954), p. 64.
5 According to Speidel, as No. 1 (p. 138), the word 'consequences' was preceded by 'political'. But doubt has been expressed as to this and the original document has been lost.
6 W. Bargatzky, *Hotel Majestic. Ein Deutscher im besetzten Frankreich* (Freiburg 1987), p. 129.
7 M. Domarus, *Hitler, Reden und Proklamationen* (Neustadt am Aisch 1962), vol. IV, p. 2131.
8 Schramm, as No. 4, p. 280.
9 Kluge's son, a military doctor, is said to have told American Intelligence that the Marshal had talked about the possibility of surrendering the entire Western

Front. He had gone to the front but had been unable to get in touch with the Allied commanders. A secretary in Patton's 3rd Army also stated that its commander had vanished for a whole day in mid-August and on returning said he had been trying to make contact with a German emissary who had not shown up (D. Irving, *Hitler's Wars*, 1977, p. 696). On the other hand there is clear evidence that Kluge really was immobilised (see Schramm, as No. 4, pp. 354–8). This does not necessarily prove that he had not intended to make contact, although Gersdorff (p. 153) dismisses this as impossible.

10 Zeller, as I 3, p. 467.

6 Wilhelm Canaris

1 H. Höhne, *Canaris* (Munich 1976) is the authoritative book on the subject and has superseded K. H. Abshagen, *Canaris* (tr. 1956) as well as R. Manvel and H. Fraenkel, *The Canaris Conspiracy* (1969). But it is not always complete or accurate.
2 For fuller details of a complicated story, see P. Hoffmann, as V 40, pp. 29–43, and in even greater detail, M. Broszat, H. A. Jacobsen and H. Krausnick, *Anatomie des SS-Staates* (Olten etc. 1965), vol. I, ch. I.
3 Deutsch, as II 7, p. 233.
4 C. Andrew, *Secret Service* (1985), p. 580.
5 H. R. Trevor-Roper (Lord Dacre), Essay included in *The Philby Affair* (1968).
6 N. West, *M.I.6. British Security Service Operations 1909–1945* (1983), pp. 116–17; I. Colvin, *Chief of Intelligence* (1951); Gisevius, as Beck 20, pp. 452–3.
7 Andrew, as No. 4, p. 773.
8 Colvin, as No. 6, p. 92.
9 R. Cecil, 'C's War' in *Intelligence and National Security* I (1986), p. 182; Dacre, as No. 5.
10 Höhne, as No. 1, p. 460; Cecil, as No. 9.
11 H. Höhne, 'Canaris und die Abwehr zwischen Anpassung und Opposition' in Schmädeke and Steinbach, as II 41, p. 407.
12 J. Runzheimer, 'Die Grenzzwischenfälle am Abend vor dem deutschen Angriff auf Polen' in W. Benz and H. Graml (eds), *Sommer 1939, Die Grossmächte und der europäische Krieg* (Stuttgart 1979), pp. 107–47.
13 Weizsäcker used the phrase *Finis Germaniae* to Ribbentrop in 1938 (Blasius, as Beck 7, p. 45) which suggests that it was common currency at the time.
14 S. P. Best, *The Venlo Incident* (1950); W. Schellenberg, *Memoirs* (tr. 1956); Andrew, as No. 4, pp. 609–16.
15 Weizsäcker, as V 16, p. 175.

7 Hans Oster

1 For Oster the main authority is R. G. von Thun-Hohenstein, *Der Verschwörer. General Oster und die Militäropposition* (Berlin 1982), also the same author in Lill and Oberreuter, as III 3, pp. 223–35, and in Schmädeke and Steinbach, as II 41, pp. 751–61. See also H. Graml, 'Der Fall Oster' in *VfZ* XIV (1966); H. C. Deutsch, *Hitler and His Generals* and *The Conspiracy Against Hitler in the Twilight War* (as II 7 and V 15.)
2 *Spiegelbild einer Verschwörung*, as Stauffenberg, 3, p. 451.
3 The customary chronology makes Oster receive his orders from Halder on 4 November (Deutsch, *Conspiracy*, p. 220) and we know that Brauchitsch saw Hitler on 5 November. It hardly seems possible that the amount of planning which appears to have been done could have been accomplished in twenty-

four hours. Groscurth, as V 42, had a discussion with Halder on the internal political situation on 31 October and it may well have been at this meeting that he was asked to convey the commission to Oster.
4 The discovery was made as the result of a report volunteered by the driver who had originally helped to transfer the filing cabinets to Zossen, an interesting example of a working-class man siding with the Nazis against their opponents.
5 Cited by Deutsch, as V 15, p. 52
6 The same, p. 100.

8 Arthur Nebe

1 For information about Nebe we are almost entirely dependent on the two books by H. B. Gisevius, *To The Bitter End* (tr. 1948) and *Wo Ist Nebe?* (Zurich 1966).
2 Strasser was in fact shot on 30 June 1934, an affair in which Nebe does not seem to have been involved.
3 Himmler arrived at Hitler's headquarters from his own adjacent centre before 13.30 on 20 June, so that he cannot have been in Berlin until he arrived late in the evening. It is odd that Nebe should not have known this. For him to kill or arrest Goebbels would have been much more easily feasible.

9 Carl Goerdeler

1 The main source of information about Goerdeler is still G. Ritter, *Carl Goerdeler und die deutsche Widerstandsbewegung* (Stuttgart 1956, shortened translation 1958). Ritter had the advantages of having known Goerdeler and shared many of his views. But out of a desire to prove the existence of 'another Germany', he played down the extent to which Goerdeler had collaborated with the régime up to 1938. This has to some extent been corrected by E. Kosthorst, *Carl Friedrich Goerdeler* in Lill and Oberreuter, as III 3; M. Krüger-Charlé, 'Carl Goerdelers Versuch der Durchsetzung einer alternativen Politik 1933–1937' in Schmädeke and Steinbach, as II 41; the same author, 'Carl Goerdeler and Great Britain 1937–1939', paper presented to Leeds Conference 1986. For texts, see Schramm, as VI 4. See also essays by Graml and Mommsen in Schmitthenner and Buchheim, as III 38. Also K. Hildebrand, 'Die ostpolitischen Vorstellungen im deutschen Widerstand' in *Geschichte in Wissenschaft und Unterricht*, 1978.
2 J. Noakes, 'Oberbürgermeister and Gauleiter. City Government between Party and State' in Hirschfeld and Kettenacker, as II 37, p. 213.
3 Deutsch, as II 7, pp. 37–8, 378–9.
4 Public Record Office, File FO 371/21659.
5 The same.
6 The Crown Prince refused to become involved in the conspiracy and advised his son Louis Ferdinand to do the same. His other son William was killed in action in 1940.
7 Traces of this suspicion of the common man can be found in the Basic Law of the Federal Republic, e.g. the election of the President by a special college instead of a nation-wide plebiscite, the inability of the Bundestag to vote a Chancellor out of office without naming a successor.
8 Texts of the documents can be found in Ritter, pp. 569–95, 609.
9 The story goes that at the beginning of the war the Wallenberg brothers agreed that Jacob should handle their contacts with Germany and Marcus those with the British.
10 See selection edited by H. Boberach, *Meldungen aus dem Reich* (Neuwied etc. 1965). A complete edition is now being published.

11 Ritter says that a further sorrow during his last days was the execution of his brother Fritz for complicity. But Fritz was only condemned on 23 February and executed on 1 March, whereas Carl was executed on 2 February.

10 Ernst Freiherr von Weizsäcker

1 The main sources are E. Weizsäcker, *Erinnerungen* (Munich 1950); L. E. Hill, *Die Weizsäcker Papiere 1933–1950* (Berlin 1974); Trials of War Criminals Before the Nuremburg Military Court, Case XI, US v. Ernst v. Weizsäcker *et al.*; R. Blasius, *Für Grossdeutschland gegen den grossen Krieg. Ernst v. Weizsäcker in den Krisen um die Tschechoslowakei und Polen* (Cologne 1981); Hill and Blasius, essays in Schmädeke and Steinbach, as II 41; E. Kordt, *Nicht aus den Akten* (Stuttgart 1950).
2 W. Goerlitz (ed.), *The Kaiser and His Court, the Diaries, Note Books and Letters of Admiral Georg von Müller, Chief of the Naval Secretariat 1914–1918* (1961).
3 These rumours have usually been taken as the product of Czech nerves. But I find it hard to believe that nothing ulterior lay behind them, possibly (a) 'plants' by Canaris to provoke the British into action, or (b) movements by the General Staff to discover what the Czechs planned to do in a real crisis. See F. Moravec, *Master of Spies* (1975).
4 The Army Command and the AA were forbidden to communicate with one another directly!
5 Hassell Diary, as III 124, 10 October 1938 and 26 January 1939. See also Blasius, as No. 1, p. 75.
6 Public Record Office, File COS 872, 22969/174.
7 Schall-Riaucour, as IV 68, p. 259.
8 Hassell Diary, 31 August 1939.
9 The same, 17 October 1939.
10 S. Welles, *A Time For Decision* (NY 1944), p. 99.
11 Weizsäcker, *Erinnerungen*, p. 338.
12 In an article in *Die Zeit* for 5 June 1987, Weizsäcker's elder surviving son argued that there was no point in refusing to concur since deportation would have gone ahead regardless of the AA's attitude. It may well be that Weizsäcker had no power to influence events. But he had justified his continuance in office on the ground that he would be able to influence events. His apologists cannot have it both ways! He cannot be excused both for condoning mass murder and for hanging on to his job. Admittedly the consequence of abandoning either course might have been unpleasant and his reluctance to decide is easily understood. But it was because too many Germans evaded such decisions that Hitler stayed in power so long.
13 L. Hill, 'The Wilhelmstrasse in the Nazi Era' in *Journal of Modern History*, 1967.
14 Chadwick, III 53, pp. 310–12.
15 Deutsch, as V 15, citing C. J. Burckhardt, *Meine Danziger Mission* (Munich 1960).
16 P. C. M. Meehan, *The Foreign Office and the Opposition: an Investigation of Attitudes in the Aftermath of War*, Paper presented to Anglo-German Conference at Leeds, May 1986.
17 Verdict at Nuremburg Trial, as No. 1, p. 955.
18 Hassell Diary, 27 December 1943.
19 The same, 27 May 1942, 1 November 1942, 31 December 1942, 15 May 1943, 27 December 1943. For an example of Hassell's own garrulity, see Deutsch, as V 15, p. 307.

11 **Adam Freiherr von Trott zu Solz**

 1 The only complete biography of Trott is C. Sykes, *Troubled Loyalties* (1968). A personal memoir giving a vivid description of him is S. Grant-Duff, *The Parting of the Ways* (1982); another, slightly less illuminating, is D. Hopkinson, *The Incense Tree* (1968). H. Rothfels edited three important documentary articles; 'Zwei aussenpolitischen Memoranda der deutschen Opposition' in *VfZ* V (1957); 'Adam von Trott und der State Department' in *VfZ* VII (1959) and 'Trott und die Aussenpolitik des Widerstandes' in *VfZ* XII (1964). There was an extended correspondence about him in *Encounter* between December 1968 and September 1969. A rather hostile portrait is given by J. W. Wheeler-Bennett in *The Nemesis of Power* (2nd revised edition 1967). Three recent studies using some new material are H. O. Malone, *Adam von Trott zu Solz. Werdegang eines Verschwörers* (biography up to 1938, Berlin 1968); the same in Schmädeke and Steinbach, as II 41, pp. 252–663 and R. Blasius in Lill and Oberreuter, as III 3. The Adam von Trott Memorial Lectures, delivered in Oxford in 1983 and published in 1986 under the title *The Challenge of the Third Reich* (ed. H. Bull, Oxford), are mostly concerned with general aspects of the *Widerstand* but contain an eloquent plea on Trott's behalf by D. Astor.
 2 Isaiah Berlin, as quoted in Grant-Duff, as No. 1, p. 56.
 3 I left Balliol myself the term before Trott came up and, although I remained in Oxford, we never met.
 4 These quotations are from Grant-Duff and Hopkinson, as No. 1.
 5 See the Trott–Grant-Duff letters, *A Noble Combat* (ed. Klemperer 1988).
 6 Sykes, as No. 1, p. 159.
 7 Sykes, p. 178. The man to whom the remark was made was Fritz Schumacher, who later wrote the book *Small is Beautiful*.
 8 Malone, as No. 1, pp. 149, 207.
 9 Isaiah Berlin in *Balliol College Annual Record*, 1986, p. 61. The date given there is 1938 but this is mistaken, since Trott did not get back to Europe until the November of that year and then went straight to Germany. It was not until February 1939 that he returned to Oxford.
10 There is no mention of Trott in the Moltke letters until May 1940 but Trott, in a letter which he sent to Brüning from New York on 4 October 1939 said that he had seen Moltke in Germany a fortnight previously (Malone, as No. 1, p. 298). I cannot accept a suggestion by Blasius that it was Hans von Haeften who brought Trott and Moltke together in 1940 since Trott is recorded as having seen Moltke six times in that year whereas Haeften only returned from Bucharest towards the end of it. Haeften may however have helped Moltke and Trott to understand one another better.
11 Text in van Roon, as IV 47, pp. 358–61.
12 Public Record Office, File FO 371/34462.
13 *FRUS, 1944* vol. I, p. 523.
14 Dulles, as IV 69, p. 138. See also Balfour, as III 57, p. 97.
15 P. Kleist, *European Tragedy* (Isle of Man 1965), p. 142.
16 Malone, as No. 1, p. 225.
17 Sykes, as No. 1, p. 425.
18 Fritz Hesse, who was present when Stauffenberg called on Trott in the AA in the spring of 1943, got the impression that they had known one another for some time. Malone, as No. 1, pp. 215 and 298.
19 *Spiegelbild einer Verschwörung*, as VI 20, p. 101.
20 Sykes, as No. 1, p. 438.
21 Text in A. Leber (ed.), *Das Gewissen Steht Auf* (Berlin 1955), p. 222.

12 Helmut James Graf von Moltke

1 The two basic books for Moltke are M. Balfour and J. Frisby, *Helmuth von Moltke. A Leader Against Hitler* (1972) and G. van Roon, *The German Resistance to Hitler. Count von Moltke and the Kreisau Circle* (1971, a shortened translation of *Neuordnung im Widerstand*, Munich 1967). The latter covers the whole group and includes all the most important documents. The last letters were published in the *Round Table* for June 1946 and immediately afterwards as a separate book *A German of the Resistance* (Oxford 1946). A further collection of documents has been edited by G. van Roon, *Völkerrecht im Dienste der Menschen* (Berlin 1986) which incorporates most of the substance of the same author's article in *VfZ* XVIII (1970). K. Fincke, *Graf Moltke und der Kreisauer Kreis* (E. Berlin 1978) gives the Communist viewpoint. See also E. Gerstenmaier, 'Der Kreisauer Kreis' in *VfZ* XV (1967) and the same author's essay in Lill and Oberreuter, as III 3; G. van Roon in Schmädeke and Steinbach, as II 41, pp. 560–70 and W. E. Winterhager (ed.), *Der Kreisauer Kreis. Porträt einer Widerstandsgruppe. Begleitband zu einer Ausstellung* (Berlin 1985). A full German edition of Count von Moltke's letters, edited by Dr B. von Oppen, is due in 1988.

2 Sir James's forebears had migrated from Scotland to South Africa early in the nineteenth century, as had those of his wife.

3 Statement by Franz Speer at his trial on 10 January 1945 (*A German of the Resistance*, p. 49). He was executed on the same day as Moltke.

4 Balfour and Frisby, p. 71. The wording has been exactly reproduced so as to show that, good as his knowledge of English was, he sometimes slipped up. This has been attributed to the fact that the family did not speak English between 1914 and 1918.

5 He asked me at the beginning of March to visit him in Germany as he could not manage to come to England at that particular moment and had some information which he wished to convey. On my arrival he told me the whole story in virtually the form which has been confirmed by subsequent research (although naturally without all the details).

6 See G. van Roon, 'Graf Moltke als Völkerrechtler im OKW' in *VfZ* XVIII (1970), pp. 12–61.

7 *Begleitband*, as No. 1, pp. 232–4.

8 In conversation with me 1971.

9 But in his 1943 letter to Curtis he said that many of the most brutal men had been drawn from Austria or the Sudetenland, only a minority from Germany itself and only a minute minority from Prussia. It was therefore 'a need of German internal politics to bring these men to justice, possibly even to death without justice' but this would be made impossible if they could be represented as national heroes, suffering for Germany at the hands of an international body instead of being punished by Germans.

10 *Begleitband*, as No. 7, pp. 234–5.

11 G. Kennan, *Memoirs 1955–1950* (Boston 1967), pp. 120–1.

12 Van Roon 1971, p. 129. I cannot however accept the story, related by Fr Rösch to Professor van Roon in 1961, that Moltke (in 1941) specifically mentioned the early summer of 1945 as the date when the Russians would arrive in Berlin. Rösch did not mention this in his own account of the meeting (R. Bleistein, *Augustin Rösch kampft gegen den Nationalsozialismus*, Frankfurt 1985, p. 266). See also Balfour and Frisby, p. 165.

13 Texts in *A German of the Resistance*, pp. 30–52 and Balfour and Frisby (a new translation), pp. 317–30.

14 I am grateful to Countess von Moltke for letting me have the texts of these letters, written in October 1944, which have never been published in full.

13 Julius Leber

1 The main sources are J. Leber, *Ein Mann geht seinen Weg* (Writings, Speeches and Letters, Berlin 1952); D. Beck, *Julius Leber: Sozialdemokrat zwischen Reform und Widerstand* (Berlin 1983); D. Beck, essay in Lill and Oberreuter, as III 3.
2 The main source of information about the meetings in May and June is to be found in the reports of the SD Commission of Inquiry under Kielpinski (the so-called Kaltenbrunner Berichte, *Spiegelbild einer Verschwörung*. second improved edition edited by H. A. Jacobsen, Stuttgart 1984). But, as has been explained (Stauffenberg 3), both the Commission and the accused had (varying) purposes to serve in the way they presented their evidence and it cannot be assumed that what they claimed to have happened really did happen in the way and for the reasons they made out.

14 Wilhelm Leuschner

1 The main source is J. G. Leithauser, *Wilhelm Leuschner. Ein Leben für die Republik* (Cologne 1962); G. Beier, essay in Lill and Oberreuter as III 3; G. Beier, *Die illegale Reichsleitung der Gewerkschaften 1933–1945* (Cologne 1981).

15 Adolf Reichwein

1 The main sources are: James L. Henderson, *Adolf Reichwein* (Stuttgart 1958); R. Reichwein *et al.* (eds), *Adolf Reichwein. Ein Lebensbild aus Briefen und Dokumenten* (Munich 1974); H. E. Ruppert and H. E. Witting (eds), *Reichwein. Ausgewählte pädagogische Schriften* (Paderborn 1978); W. Huber and A. Krebs (eds), *Adolf Reichwein 1898–1944* (Paderborn 1982). Most of these are more concerned with his pedagogic than with his political activities.
2 As in IV 15.
3 Used by Reichwein in his *Hungermarsch durch Lappland* but apparently on a number of other occasions as well. See Huber and Krebs, as No. 1, pp. 17 and 43.
4 *Spiegelbild einer Verschwörung*, as Leber No. 2, p. 492.
5 W. Schuchardt in Huber and Krebs, as No. 1, p. 58.

16 Anton Saefkow

1 The principal source is G. Nitzsche, *Die Saefkow–Jacob–Bästlein Gruppe* (E. Berlin 1957). There is also information to be found in H. Duhnke, as III 26; E. Weisenborn, as IV 28 and K. Mammach, as IV 45. For a list of other Communist activists, see L. Kraushaar (ed.), *Deutscher Widerstandskämpfer 1933–1945* (2 vols, E. Berlin 1970).
2 Duhnke, as No. 1, p. 505, citing R. Pechel, *Deutscher Widerstand* (Zurich 1947). The remark was made to Frau Pechel.
3 Nitzsche, as No. 1, p. 149.
4 Nitzsche as No. 1, pp. 201–3.
5 A. Merson, *Communist Resistance* (1985). Duhnke, as III 26, p. 508.

17 Harro Schulze-Boysen

1 The principal source is H. Höhne, *Kennwort Direktor: Die Geschichte der Roten Kapelle* (Frankfurt 1970).
2 H. Rothfels 'Zur Wiederkehr des 20 Juli 1944' in *VfZ* XVII (1969) citing E. Schulze-Boysen, *Das Bild eines Freiheitskämpfers* (Dusseldorf 1957).

18 Martin Niemöller

1 The fullest account of Niemöller's position during the early years of the Third Reich is to be found in K. Scholder's *Die Kirchen und das Dritte Reich* (as II 28); however it only goes as far as October 1934. W. Niemöller, *Das Pfarrernotbund*, as III 32, carries the story further but all books concentrate on the early years of the struggle since the later ones were largely a story of failure. J. Bentley, *Martin Niemöller* (Oxford 1984); D. Schmidt (tr. L. Wilson). *Pastor Niemöller* (1959) and J. S. Conway, *The Nazi Persecution of the Churches 1933–45* (1968) are useful sources in English.
2 Scholder, as No. 1, vol. I, p. 476.
3 Scholder, vol. I, p. 576.
4 Scholder, vol. I, p. 613.
5 Scholder, vol. II, p. 59.
6 E. Robertson, *The Shame and the Sacrifice* (1987), p. 15.
7 A. Boyens, 'Das Stuttgarter Schuldbekenntnis' in *VfZ* XIX (1971).
8 Bentley, as No. 1, p. 79.

19 Dietrich Bonhoeffer

1 The principal source is E. Bethge's monumental biography (Munich 1967, tr. 1970) but English readers unfamiliar with German theology and Church organisation may find it easier to start with M. Bosanquet, *The Life and Death of Dietrich Bonhoeffer* (1968). E. Robertson, *The Shame and the Sacrifice* (1987) contains much information about Bonhoeffer's religious career and his writings but goes frequently astray on historical fact.
2 I am grateful to the Rt Revd Richard Harries, Canon R. Preston and Mr V. Sproxton for advice on this matter. In 1939 Niebuhr became chairman of the US society 'Friends of German Freedom'.
3 Scholder, as Niemöller 1.
4 For Bell, see not only R. C. D. Jasper, *George Bell, Bishop of Chichester* (Oxford 1967) but also K. Slack, *George Bell* (1971).
5 Slack, as No. 4, p. 60.
6 Bethge, as No. 1, p. 549.
7 The same.
8 *Gesammelte Schriften* (Munich 1958), vol. I, p. 400.
9 Bonhoeffer met Niebuhr both in Sussex (Bethge, as No. 1, p. 543) and also in Edinburgh where Niebuhr was giving his Gifford Lectures (information from Mr Sproxton who met Bonhoeffer there).
10 Bethge, as No. 1, p. 559.
11 Thun-Hohenstein, as IV 47, p. 249.
12 Bethge, as No. 1, p. 648.
13 Review in *Die Zeit*, 24 January 1986, of Eberhard Röhm, *Sterben für den Frieden. Spurensicherung: Hermann Stöhr und die ökumenische Friedensbewegung* (Stuttgart 1985).
14 Moltke's friendship with Gerstenmaier may later have been a bar between him and Bonhoeffer, since Gerstenmaier had been Heckel's assistant. But Moltke did not meet Gerstenmaier until just after the journey to Scandinavia.

15 Our knowledge of the Stockholm–Sigtuna conversations rests on four main sources: (a) a report by Bell on his conversations with Schönfeld and Bonhoeffer, written soon afterwards and submitted to Eden; (b) a written statement left by Schönfeld with Bell; (c) an article by Bell in the *Contemporary Review* for October 1945; (d) a lecture by Bell at Göttingen in 1957. The four are by no means identical, although there are no flagrant contradictions. All four are handily reprinted in Bonhoeffer, *Gesammelte Schriften*, vol. I, pp. 372–413. Some British official papers are in Public Record Office file FO 371/30912 (including Eden's minute when he first heard of Bell's proposed visit: 'This seems a strange choice. Is he not a pacifist?') There is a purely formal Embassy report on the visit but this does not even hint at any meeting with Germans. The really interesting file which must contain the original copy of Bell's letter to Eden and the ensuing Foreign Office discussion as to how it should be answered, is conspicuous by absence! Some of the papers on 30912 are closed until 2018!

16 Höhne, *Canaris*, as Canaris 1, p. 493; Gisevius, as Beck 20, p. 472.

20 Bishop Konrad Graf von Preysing

1 The main sources are three books by W. Adolph, *Hirtenamt und Hitlerdiktatur* (Berlin 1968); *Kardinal Preysing und zwei Diktaturen* (Berlin 1971); *Geheime Aufzeichnungen aus dem national-sozialistischen Kirchenkampf* (Mainz 1980). See also B. Schneider (ed.), *Die Briefe Pius XII an die deutschen Bischöfe 1939–1944* (Mainz 1966).
2 E. N. Petersen, *The Limits of Hitler's Power* (Princeton 1969), pp. 309–19; Kershaw, as II 34, pp. 17, 203–4.
3 Scholder, as II 28, vol. I, pp. 498–9.
4 Bonhoeffer, *Letters and Papers From Prison* (1953), Second paper. See also *Gesammelte Schriften*, vol I, p. 365.
5 H.J. Stehle in *Die Zeit*, 26 December 1980 and 25 November 1981 on the authority of Scholder.
6 *Briefe Pius XII*, as No. 1, no. 37.
7 H. J. Stehle in *Die Zeit*, 26 December 1980.
8 J. S. Conway, as Niemöller 1, pp. 267–72; E. Klee, as III 47.
9 Balfour and Frisby, as II 6, pp. 160, 202.
10 C. Müller, as V 33, p. 391, citing Kramarz, Stauffenberg 1, p. 160 but not in English translation.

21 Bernhard Lichtenberg

1 The principal source, in addition to the books by Adolph cited in Preysing, as No. 1, is A. Erb, *Bernhard Lichtenberg* (Berlin no date but pre-1971).
2 E. Klee, as III 46.

22 Franz Jägerstätter

1 The information about Jägerstätter is entirely drawn from G. C. Zahn, *In Solitary Witness: the Life and Death of Franz Jägerstätter* (NY 1964).

23 'The White Rose'

1 The principal source is the book by Inge Scholl, sister of Hans and Sophie, *Die weisse Rose* (Frankfurt 1953, Eng. tr. *Six Against Tyranny* 1955). Further

information in C. Petry, *Studenten aufs Schafott. Die weisse Rose und ihr Scheiten* (Munich 1968).
2 Giles, as II 49, p. 121.
3 These are the words attributed to her by her sister. But according to another account, she said, 'Our heads may roll today but yours will do so tomorrow' and 'You know as well as we do that this war is lost. Why are you too cowardly to admit it?' There is also a story that she was brought into court with a leg broken in prison but it is hard to think that, if this had been so, her sister would not have mentioned it.
4 Giles, as II 49, p. 300.

24 Kurt Gerstein

1 The chief sources are: H. Rothfels, 'Augenzeugebericht zu den Massenvergasungen' in *VfZ* I (1953); H. Franz, *Aussenseiter des Widerstandes der Kirche gegen Hitler* (Zurich 1964); S. Friedland, *Counterfeit Nazi. The Ambiguity of Good* (1969); P. Joffroy, *Spy For God* (1971).
2 Balfour, as III 57, ch. XXXVIII. The list is illustrative rather than exhaustive.

Part THREE   Six questions

1 E. Wolf, in Schmitthenner and Buchheim, as III 40, p. 223.
2 The *Independent* 20 July 1987, 29 February 1988.
3 Nitzsche, as IV 35, p. 158.
4 G. A. Bell, 'Die Oekumene und die innerdeutsche Opposition' in *VfZ* V (1957).
5 Balfour and Frisby, as II 6, p. 185.
6 '*Schuld*' is the 38th in the series '*Moabiter Sonette*' (Berlin 1948). A translation is to be found on p. 239 of Lord James Douglas-Hamilton, *Motive for a Mission* (1971).
7 P. von Yorck, 'Gedenkrede zur Einweihung der Stauffenbergkapelle', in *VfZ* XII (1964).
8 Cited in van Roon, as IV 47 but only in German edn, p. 122.
9 A. Boyens, 'Das Stuttgarter Schuldbekenntnis vom 19 Oktober 1945 – Entstehung und Bedeutung' in *VfZ* XIX (1971).
10 van Roon, as IV 47, pp. 367–75.
11 See Annex A below.
12 Zeller, as I 1, p. 143, citing Buchholz in *Die Neue Zeit*, October 1945.

Annex A   Numbers

1 M. Broszat, 'Nationalsozialistische Konzentrationslager 1933–1945' in *Anatomie des SS-Staates* (Dtv. edn, Munich 1967), vol. II, p. 24.
2 Cited in G. Weisenborn, *Der lautloser Aufstand* (Rororo edn, Hamburg 1962), p. 149.
3 Bundeszentrale für politische Bildung, *Widerstand und Exil* (Bonn 1985), p. 66.
4 Weisenborn, as No. 2, pp. 38–9.
5 The same citing Gestapo records.
6 H. Rothfels, 'Zur Wiederkehr des 20 Juli 1944', *VfZ* XVII (1969), citing Nuremburg records.
7 Broszat, as No. 1, p. 91. K. Mammach, *Widerstand 1939–1945* (E. Berlin 1987), pp. 28, 125. No source given.
8 Weisenborn, as No. 2, pp. 38–9.
9 Broszat, as No. 1, pp. 131–2.
10 As No. 9.

11 P. Hoffmann, as IV 6, p. 16.
12 Weisenborn, as No. 2, p. 39.
13 K. Finker, 'Probleme des militärischen Widerstandes und des Umsturzversuches von 20 Juli in Deutschland' in Klessmann and Pingel (eds), *Gegner des NS-ismus* (Frankfurt etc. 1980), p. 158; M. Messerschmidt, 'German Military Law in World War II' in W. Deist (ed.), *The German Military in the Age of Total War* (Leamington 1985).
14 Broszat, as No. 1, pp. 125–6.
15 Weisenborn, as No. 2, p. 240.
16 *Statistisches Jahrbuch* 1937.
17 W. Roder, *Die deutschen sozialistischen Exilgruppen in Gross-Britannien 1940–1945* (Bonn 1973), pp. 15–18, citing League of Nations High Commissioner for Refugees.
18 K. Hildebrand, *The Third Reich* (1984), p. 40.
19 As No. 17.
20 International Military Tribunal, vol. XXXI, p. 86, Doc. 2738.
21 *Freiheit und Recht*, August–September 1959, pp. 15–19.
22 *Rückblick zur Mauerwald* (Munich 1965), p. 167.
23 *Die Verschwörer, General Oster und die Militäropposition* (Berlin 1982), p. 260.
24 Hoffmann, as IV 6, p. 715.
25 Hoffmann, 3rd German edn, p. 864.
26 Balfour and Frisby, as II 6, p. 313.

Annex C   Did the British and Americans regard the Germans as 'collectively guilty'?

1 Public Record Office, File No. WO 220/214.
2 The same, Files Nos WO 220/220 and 233.
3 The same, File No. FO 1005/739.
4 Files of the *British Zone Review* will be found in the British Library and in the Bodleian Library, Oxford.
5 B. von Oppen (ed.), *Documents on Germany Under Occupation* (Royal Institute of International Affairs, London 1955), pp. 13–27.
6 H. Hurwitz, *Die Stunde Null der deutschen Presse* (Cologne 1972), pp. 68–76.

Index

Biographical details have been mainly confined to the period of the book. An asterisk after a date shows that the person concerned was still alive then and is not known to have died since.